Grzegorz Kosc, Clara Juncker, Sharon Monteith,
Britta Waldschmidt-Nelson (eds.)
The Transatlantic Sixties

America ··· Culture - History - Politics
Volume 4

The series **America: Culture – History – Politics** is edited by Christof Mauch, Michael Hochgeschwender, Anke Ortlepp, Ursula Prutsch, and Britta Waldschmidt-Nelson.

Grzegorz Kosc, Clara Juncker,
Sharon Monteith, Britta Waldschmidt-Nelson (eds.)

The Transatlantic Sixties

Europe and the United States in the Counterculture Decade

[transcript]

GERMAN HISTORICAL INSTITUTE
WASHINGTON DC

This book is published with the generous support of the German Historical Institute Washington, DC, the Lasky Center for Transatlantic Studies at the University of Munich, and the University of Southern Denmark.

Bibliographic information published by the Deutsche Nationalbibliothek
The Deutsche Nationalbibliothek lists this publication in the Deutsche Nationalbibliografie; detailed bibliographic data are available online at http://dnb.d-nb.de.

Cover layout: Kordula Röckenhaus, Bielefeld
Cover illustration: photograph of a mural in San Francisco's Haight-Ashbury district, 2006; courtesy of Sascha Pöhlmann.
Printed by Majuskel Medienproduktion GmbH, Wetzlar
ISBN 978-3-8376-2216-4

Contents

Introduction

The 1960s was a decade of pivotal importance that continues to fascinate historians and cultural critics. On the one hand, it was a period of sustained economic growth in the United States and most European countries; on the other, it presented fundamental challenges to the existing social and economic order. Students were often in the vanguard of protest movements against social injustice, and demonstrations against America's war with Vietnam turned into a global phenomenon both on the streets and in cultural terms more broadly. For example, European protests against the John Wayne-produced pro-war movie *The Green Berets* (1968), which Wayne hoped would "help our cause throughout the world," included a Stuttgart daily newspaper comparing the film to Nazi propaganda.[1] In the 1960s the African American civil rights movement reached the peak of its success, with its major goals translated into national legislation, and its rhetoric and strategies inspiring many other protest movements, such as civil rights campaigns by other "minority" groups, including women's and gay rights movements in the US and in Europe. While activists failed to achieve a fundamental restructuring of society, especially regarding class and income distribution, they paved the way for many social changes and for a new counterculture. Some social changes were deemed so radical that they sparked the backlash among conservatives that would lead to a hardening of conservative positions over the next ten years and to the rise of the neocons in the decades that followed; other supposedly countercultural shifts stemmed from a longer tradition and of American individualism, including

1 J. Hoberman, *The Dream Life: Movies, Media, and the Mythology of the Sixties* (New York: The New Press, 2003), 208.

the hippie movement's de-emphasizing of government controls and central leadership models, and communal living echoing mid-nineteenth-century utopian experiments such as Brook Farm in Massachusetts. The end of the 1960s also saw the rise of identity politics and the beginning of the so-called culture wars, which have since become a serious source of cultural and political division in the United States and affected European countries in many different ways.

This collection pays attention to such crosscurrents. It is transnational and transatlantic in scope and character, taking a close look at the global flows between Europe to the United States and back again. It explores something of the "global unbinding of energies" that Fredric Jameson once identified as central to the sensibility of the sixties. It builds on scholarship that asserts and tests the validity—historiographical and ideological—of "a world sixties" as advocated in the special issue of *boundary 2* entitled "The Sixties and the World Event," edited by Christopher Connery and Hortense J. Spillers in 2009, with essays ranging from Latin American studies to literary criticism. Working in interdisciplinary ways helps to shake up national models and to conceptualize larger shifts in historical consciousness. A US-European dialectic reveals new models and trends, like those identified in civil rights historiography, for example, in Brian Dooley's *Black and Green: The Fight for Civil Rights in Northern Ireland and Black America* (1998), in Martin Klimke's *The Other Alliance: Student Protest in West Germany and the United States in the Global Sixties* (2010), or in Stephen Tuck's work on Malcolm X's 1964 visit to Oxford University and its significance regarding race relations in the US and Britain (2013).[2] New essays in this volume also reveal the transatlantic scope of the African American freedom struggle and point to the ways in which racism, discrimination, and social protest may be understood as transnational phenomena in a global context.

The twenty-first century has seen a significant rise in academic interest in transatlantic literary studies and comparative studies of media and musical cultures, notably in edited collections including Günter H. Lenz and Peter J. Ling's *Transatlantic Encounters: Multiculturalism, National Identity*

2 Stephen Tuck, "Malcolm X's Visit to Oxford University: U.S. Civil Rights, Black Britain, and the Special Relationship on Race," *American Historical Review* 118, no. 1 (2013): 76–103.

and the Uses of the Past (2000); Joseph Patrick Ward's *Britain and the American South: From Colonialism to Rock and Roll* (2003); Richard Gray and Waldemar Zacharasiewicz's *Transatlantic Exchanges: The South in Europe—Europe in the American South* (2007); *Globalizing American Studies* (2010), edited by Brian T. Edwards and Dilip Parameshwar Gaonkar (2010); and *Re-Framing the Transnational Turn in American Studies*, edited by Winfried Fluck, Donald E. Pease, and John Carlos Rowe (2011). Eve Tavor Bannet and Susan Manning's *Transatlantic Literary Studies, 1660–1830* and Jill Terry and Neil A. Wynn's *Transatlantic Roots Music: Folk, Blues, and National Identities* were both published in 2012. Essays in this volume build on and extend this work.

The transnational turn in American Studies is not new insofar as the examination of patterns of travel and exploration, slavery and colonialism, and migration and acculturation characterizes a substantial body of work initiated on both sides of the Atlantic. Similarly, a transatlantic perspective has been crucial to the study of modernity, modernism, and, most particularly, to explorations/investigations of American expatriates in Paris, in studies ranging from Malcolm Cowley's *Exile's Return* (1933) and Michel and Geneviève Fabre's groundbreaking work, including Michel Fabre's epic survey *From Harlem to Paris: Black American Writers in France, 1840–1980* (1992) to Daniel Katz's *American Modernism's Expatriate Scene* (2007) and Anita Patterson's *Race, American Literature and Transnational Modernisms* (2008). However, newer conceptualizations of globalization have shortened the distance between continents and nations further, extending the comparative and transnational turn in scholarship beyond the ways in which migrants and exiles "break barriers of thought and experience," as Edward Said noted in "The Mind of Winter: Reflections on Thought and Exile" (1984). Attempts to forge a more "worlded" American Studies and to construe "the Sixties" as a worlded decade rather than as exceptional to cultural shifts in the US or Paris in May '68 have reinforced the need to understand local and regional inequalities, differences and commonalities, as well as the genealogies of the cultural forms that represent and express places and spaces. New media and digital cultures point the way to the "postnational" and to the de-localization and re-territorialization of communication, disturbing if not challenging notions of national distinctiveness.

The editors of this volume have been involved in constructing a transatlantic American Studies in various ways. For example, Clara Juncker and

Russell Duncan edited *Trading Cultures: Nationalism and Globalization in American Studies* in 2002 and *Transnational America: Contours of Modern U.S. Culture* in 2004. Sharon Monteith acts as an advisory editor of journals including *The Global South* and the *Irish Journal of American Studies*. She also examined transatlantic connections between the US South and Europe with her US co-editor Suzanne Jones in *South to a New Place: Region, Literature, Culture* (2002) and with another US co-editor in *The New Encyclopedia of Southern Culture: Media* (2011). Together with Markus Hünemörder and Meike Zwingenberger, Britta Waldschmidt-Nelson edited *Europe and America: Cultures in Translation* in 2006.

The essays in *The Transatlantic Sixties* explore the impact of the African American civil rights movement in Germany, paying attention to the influence of Black Power politics and to the reception of Angela Davis in East and West Germany; the lines of inspiration and influence between American and Scandinavian feminisms; and the truly global nature of the counterculture movement—no more vigorous in Haight Ashbury than in London's Soho or in Copenhagen. Contributors delve into the vicissitudes of Europe's status in American foreign policy relations; the impact of, and changes made to, the Vietnam War Memorial that reflect the ways in which the nation has commemorated other wars; and the role of avant-garde American and European documentary cinema in building opposition to the war in Vietnam. While the transatlantic trajectory of the Beatles is a key motif of the global phenomenon that was pop music in the 1960s, one essay considers how many European bands "re-packaged" American rock 'n' roll and exported it back to the US. Topics of other essays include the meaning of Robert Frost's diplomatic visit to the Soviet Union, Polish fiction in the 1960s as driven by the same sense of political futility as John Barth's "literature of exhaustion," and the influence of cybernetics on the arts in the US and Italy. The closing essay examines how three nonviolent civil rights demonstrations in Paris, France; Aberystwyth, Wales; and Selma, Alabama, have been assiduously remembered or strategically forgotten since the 1960s.

The same political, social, economic, and technological changes that sparked a transnational or globalized American Studies drove this publication. It brings together the work of European American Studies scholars who participated as faculty in an Erasmus-sponsored intensive summer academy entitled "Coming Together or Coming Apart: Europe and the

United States in the 1960s" in 2011. The program, which took place at the John F. Kennedy Institute in Berlin, was organized by Britta Waldschmidt-Nelson and Michael Hoenisch under the joint auspices of the University of Munich and the Free University of Berlin, with colleagues from ten universities across Poland, Denmark, Germany, Italy, France, and the UK. The volume thus brings together essays by contributors from the fields of history, politics, literature, culture, music, and the arts; their approach to this singular decade is also characterized by interdisciplinary expertise as well as by their individual national and cultural experiences.

The editors would like to thank the European Union, the Ludwig-Maximilians-Universität of Munich, and the Free University of Berlin for sponsoring the Erasmus Intensive Program (IP), which was the bedrock of this volume. Special credit should be given to Claudia Agne for her hard work behind the scenes and to other colleagues whose contributions may not be in this volume but who were essential to the success of the IP. Finally, we are most grateful to the German Historical Institute in Washington, DC, the Lasky Center for Transatlantic Studies at the University of Munich, and the University of Southern Denmark for their support of this publication. It is dedicated to the students who participated in the program.

Grzegorz Kosc
Clara Juncker
Sharon Monteith
Britta Waldschmidt-Nelson

New or Larger?

JFK's Diverging Visions of Europe

DUCCIO BASOSI

> We believe that a united Europe will be capable of playing a greater role. . . . We see in such a Europe a partner with whom we can deal on a basis of full equality.
> JOHN KENNEDY, 4 JULY 1962[1]

> Two thousand years ago the proudest boast was "civis Romanus sum." Today, in the world of freedom, the proudest boast is "Ich bin ein Berliner."
> JOHN KENNEDY, 26 JUNE 1963[2]

During his one thousand days in the White House, US President John F. Kennedy hardly spent a week without addressing publicly some "European" issue. It was during his time in office that Berlin saw the high drama of the construction of the Wall. It was during his time in office that discussions and negotiations took place across the Atlantic, about the Multilateral Force plan for nuclear weapons sharing (MLF), and the GATT's "Kennedy

1 John Kennedy, "Address at Independence Hall, Philadelphia," 4 July 1962. If not differently specified, the full texts of all the presidential public speeches cited in this essay are available in *American Presidency Project*.

2 John Kennedy, "Remarks in the Rudolph Wilde Platz, Berlin," 26 June 1963.

round" of tariff reductions. It was also during his time in office that the US government actively sponsored Britain's entry into the European Economic Community (EEC), only to suffer the shock of the application's rejection at the hand of French President Charles de Gaulle in January 1963.[3]

Understandably, an engaging body of work has addressed the US President's foreign policy with regard to areas and institutions conventionally connected to the notion of "Europe," with an emphasis on the origins and aftermath of Kennedy's "declaration of interdependence" speech of 4 July 1962, quoted in the epigraph to this essay.[4] The speech offered "Europe" a partnership with the United States, that is, a cooperative relationship between two roughly equal actors—the two weights of a dumbbell, with the Atlantic Ocean as the connecting bar.[5] This all came to be popularized as a *Grand Design* in the highly successful 1962 pamphlet bearing the same title and written by reporter Joseph Kraft.[6]

The special link between Kennedy and Europe has also been stressed by his biographers. In the very first lines of *JFK*, historian Robert Dallek describes Kennedy as "a European."[7] Indeed, in his youth Kennedy had traveled extensively in what was then generally considered Europe. After taking economics classes at the London School of Economics in 1935, the young Harvard student made his first "European grand tour" in 1937, at the age of twenty, with his friend Lem Billings. They visited France, Spain, Italy, Germany, and Britain. Following his father's appointment as ambassador to Britain by President Franklin D. Roosevelt, in December 1937, John Kennedy's contacts with Europe only became closer: often visiting Britain, France and Germany, between 1938 and 1939 he also went skiing in Switzerland, and visited Leningrad, Moscow, Kiev, Bucharest, Ankara, Warsaw, Prague, and Athens. During these sojourns, Kennedy gathered information for his graduation thesis on Britain's appeasement policy toward Nazi Germany, published in 1940 with the title *While England Slept*. In

3 For a general treatment of these relations, see Lundestad, *United States*, 111–42.
4 Costigliola, "Failed Design"; Winand, *Eisenhower*; Brinkley and Griffiths, *John Kennedy and Europe*; Bozo, *Two Strategies*.
5 For "dumbbellism," see Weisbrode, *Atlantic Century*, 159–77.
6 Kraft, *Grand Design*.
7 Dallek, *JFK*, 13.

1947, after serving in the Pacific during World War II, he finally visited his ancestral homeland in Ireland.[8]

The study of the way US administrations form and present to the public their visions of foreign lands helps addressing both the general theme of the relations between ideology and foreign policy, and the more specific themes of the relations between mental maps and foreign policy, and national identity and foreign policy.[9] Based on Kennedy's public speeches as well as on declassified documents from his administration, this essay will analyze Kennedy's image of Europe.

PRE-KENNEDY VISIONS OF "EUROPE" IN THE US

When Kennedy became President, "Europe" had just been recast in a fundamental way in US political discourse, through the notion of it being part of the "Atlantic Community." This was a brand new entity successfully "imagined" by the influential reporter and public intellectual Walter Lippmann in support of intervention in World War II. In a 1943 pamphlet, Lippmann explained that "the Atlantic Ocean is not the frontier between Europe and the Americas. It is the inland sea of a community of nations allied with one another by geography, history, and vital necessity."[10] Lippmann's Atlantic Community included a "Europe" made of Britain, the Netherlands, France, Spain, Portugal, Belgium, Denmark, and Norway.[11] In the immediate postwar years, the Truman administration managed to adjust the borders of this Europe to meet the necessities of its anti-Soviet Cold

8 Ibid., 60–77.

9 Harper, *American Visions*; Mariano, *Defining the Atlantic Community*; Balis and Serfaty, *Visions of America and Europe*; Preston, "John F. Kennedy and Lyndon B. Johnson." According to political scientist Alan Henrikson, a mental map can be understood as "an ordered but continually adapting structure of the mind by reference to which a person acquires, codes, stores, recalls, reorganizes, and applies, in thought or in action, information about his or her large-scale geographical environment, in part or in its entirety." See Henrikson, "Geographical 'Mental Maps,'" 498. Henrikson's definition is largely inspired by the work by Gould and White, *Mental Maps*.

10 Cited in Mariano, "US Discovers Europe," 161–85. Also see Steel, "How Europe Became Atlantic," and Mariano "Re-mapping America." On "imagined communities," see Anderson, *Imagined Communities*.

11 Mariano, "US Discovers Europe," 166.

War, including (West) Germany in the picture, as well as Italy, Greece, and Turkey.[12]

As noted by Marco Mariano, to present "Europe" as part of a wider Atlantic Community was an extremely subtle ideological operation: in fact, if the Atlantic was now seen as a bridge, for almost two centuries it had not been perceived in this way. On the contrary, there is wide agreement among historians that "Europe" had been rather the main "external other" in comparison to which the US defined its identity.[13] To be sure, US intellectuals in the early 1960s did not miss the point, even when they were inviting their fellow countrymen to look at Europe with new eyes. For example, in a pamphlet published in 1960, historian Daniel Boorstin arrayed references from Thomas Jefferson to Sinclair Lewis and beyond in order to stress the "tendency to discover ourselves as a kind of non-Europe."[14] Three years later, Cornell University historian Cushing Strout confirmed that, for much of their history, "whether they condemned Europe's vices or yearned for its virtues, Americans agreed that it was a polar opposite of the New World."[15]

Interestingly enough, both authors admitted that for "Americans" the concept of Europe reflected more a cultural construct than a clear geographical area. It goes without saying that conceiving of Europe in these terms was not a prerogative of US intellectuals and policymakers only. The definition of Europe's borders has been—and still is—an ancient ambition of mankind, practiced both by those who aspired to define themselves "Europeans" and by those who searched in "Europe" for something different from themselves.[16] As a consequence, ever since the word first appeared in classical Greece (in latent opposition to Persian "Asia"), "Europe" has had shifting borders. In imperial Rome, it appeared rarely to indicate some vague portion, north of the Mediterranean, of the much denser concept of *romanitas*. By the ninth century of the Christian era, the geographical content of the term had actually moved to the North and to the West, and was briefly used by Charlemagne to indicate his Holy Roman Empire (which, ironically, now meant excluding Greece). After virtually disappearing again from the maps, the term experienced an impressive comeback during the

12 Steel, "How Europe," 22–26.
13 Bonazzi, "Constructing and Reconstructing Europe," 11–26.
14 Boorstin, *Image of Europe*, 20.
15 Strout, *American Image*, ix.
16 For a general discussion, see Balestracci, *Ai confini dell'Europa medievale*.

fifteenth century, beginning with Pope Enea Silvio Piccolomini's use of it to encompass the entire Christian world (now in opposition to the Muslim Turks who were about to vanquish Constantinople). New adaptations came during the Enlightenment, Romanticism, and the Industrial Revolution, with two powers traditionally thought of as "Asian," as Russia and the Ottoman Empire, playing at various levels an important role in "European" politics and, to an extent, proclaiming themselves "Europeans."[17]

To be sure, most maps of Europe printed in the United States in the second half of the nineteenth and first half of the twentieth centuries stretched from the North Cape to the northern shores of the Mediterranean, nd from Iceland to the Urals and the Bosporus. These were most likely the maps with which John Kennedy grew up. However, some of the closest acquaintances of John's father saw the geography of the continent differently. For example, ardent anti-communist William Bullitt adamantly stated that "the eastern boundary of Europe is not the Ural Mountains but the swamps which extend from Finland, past Poland, to Romania."[18] In the late 1930s, Bullitt was the US ambassador to Paris, where he often hosted young John Kennedy.[19]

Besides the perennial complexity of the theme, during the nineteenth and early twentieth centuries there had perhaps been a further justification for the relative vagueness with which US culture thought about Europe's geographical content. Most of the key documents of US foreign policy—from George Washington's *Farewell Address* to the Monroe Doctrine—actually carried the message to beware of Europe. As Boorstin noted, it was only with the two world wars and the Great Depression in between that this attitude had slowly begun to change.[20]

In the late 1940s and in the 1950s, to present "Europe" as part of the wider Atlantic Community was thus a viable way to conceal the traditional negative image of the "Old World" and provide ideological support to the Marshall Plan and to the continuing US military permanence across the ocean. The Atlanticists' definition of "Europe" as a shortcut to indicate the non-American countries of NATO also had a rather precise content in political terms (with anti-communism as the common denominator). Obviously,

17 Chabod, *Storia dell'idea di Europa*.
18 Cited in Harper, *American Visions*, 52.
19 Dallek, *JFK*, 70.
20 In general: Del Pero, *Libertà e impero*.

the entire operation came with two implications: on the one hand, besides the conventionally accepted notion of "Europe" extending to Russia, there came to life a much smaller "Europe"—often also referred to as "Western Europe." As underlined by Ronald Steel, "with the Russians excluded [from the Marshall Plan] each side had 'its' Europe. . . . Rather than helping to unite Europe, the Marshall Plan served to divide it further."[21] On the other hand, the positive quality of this "Europe" in US eyes was not really its being European, but rather its being Atlantic.

Kennedy's "European Partner"

"Atlantic" was a crucial word also in Kennedy's design for transoceanic interdependence. However, instead of thinking of the Atlantic community as a "community of values" with few distinctions between its various members, Kennedy articulated it as a two-pillar structure. This vision of "Europe" had been largely inspired by the thinking of George Ball, then the Undersecretary of State for Economic Affairs, and other like-minded officials in the administration who strongly supported the notion that a "united Europe," of equal weight to the US, would be the optimal partner with which the US could hope to build a true Atlantic Community.[22] These officials, often referred to as "Europeanists," saw the EEC as the embryo of such a "Europe" and supported its strengthening both institutionally and in terms of membership. As Pascaline Winand has stressed, they did not differ much from the Atlanticists as to their final goal. However, while the latter aimed at merging the US and Canada with "Europe"—that is, NATO Europe—without intermediate passages, the former believed that only two senior equal partners could eventually delegate power to common institutions.[23]

Typically, the image of the transatlantic partnership among equals depicted by the President in his 1962 "declaration of interdependence" speech was the term of comparison against which historians evaluated the achievements and failures of US policies toward "Europe" for most of the

21 Steel, "How Europe," 25. Also see Winand, *Eisenhower*, 9.
22 Priest, "George W. Ball," 172–91.
23 Winand, *Eisenhower*, 144.

1960s, including the Johnson administration (1963–68).[24] Indeed, that speech was not a collection of improvised remarks; given on US Independence Day, in Philadelphia's Independence Hall, the speech had been carefully conceived as an exercise in symbolism and a major operation for the administration.

Idealism, however, was only one of the various driving forces behind Kennedy's design. According to Winand, the President himself was never committed to any particular notion of European integration. In fact, many of his closest and most influential advisers on European affairs perceived that, "although the President was not opposed to European integration, it was not a topic or an issue that preoccupied him greatly."[25] It was not Europeanist idealism, to be sure, that bought the Atlantic partnership the approval of pragmatists like National Security Adviser McGeorge Bundy, or even Atlanticists like Christian Herter, the former Secretary of State who served as Kennedy's Special Trade Representative. Rather, it was the careful observation of some general trends, in both the EEC and the United States, that suggested they search for a fresh approach. On the other shore of the Atlantic, de Gaulle was actively promoting the notion of a "European Europe," one with fewer Atlantic connections.[26] Even those who mistrusted de Gaulle, however, often cultivated the notion that "Europe" should develop into a bigger player in order to maintain the Atlantic link. Jean Monnet, the French businessman and diplomat whose name was most easily associated with the concept of supranationalism, was actually among the main supporters of the Europeanist idea, and George Ball had been Monnet's lawyer in the US.[27] In the US, by 1960 certain economic sectors were beginning to feel competition from the EEC, and the deteriorating balance of payments was judged by Kennedy to be a problem second only to a nuclear war.[28] Protectionist feelings were on the rise, with "the Europeans" accused of being free riders under the US nuclear umbrella.

It is a platitude that the Kennedy team saw a key to addressing these challenges in Britain's entry into the EEC. London had a tradition of free

24 Guderzo, *Interesse nazionale e responsabilità globale*; Schwartz, *Lyndon Johnson and Europe*; Colman, *'Special Relationship'?*
25 Winand, *Eisenhower*, 139.
26 Lundestad, *United States*, 111–13.
27 Weisbrode, *Atlantic Century*, 171.
28 See Barnet, *Allies*, 298.

trade and a tight, if not special, relationship with Washington.[29] When Britain's conservative government, adequately encouraged by Kennedy, finally applied for a full EEC membership in the summer of 1961, Kennedy felt 'gratified.'[30] However, it was unclear which other countries, if any, the US government had in mind for the building of its European partnership. Even though US officials made it known that they would possibly consider favorably a Danish or Norwegian application, Kennedy never clearly defined the issue in public.[31] Kraft's pamphlet on the *Grand Design* counted up to ten prospective new members in the EEC, the most important of which was recognizedly Britain, but it also included all the neutrals from Sweden to Switzerland and Austria.[32] In reality, most high officials in the administration, George Ball first among them, were clearly disturbed by the perspective of neutral countries joining the EEC, with only different shades of dislike to distinguish the abhorred cases of Sweden and Switzerland (neutrals by choice) from the tolerated case of Austria (neutral by an international treaty).[33] Rather, in broad intellectual terms, the map of Kennedy's "European partner" implicitly resembled that depicted by political scientist Ernst Haas in his 1958 volume on *The Uniting of Europe*, with the EEC and Britain clearly at the center of the scene.[34]

The same vagueness applied to the institutional form of "Europe," an issue on which, the US President declared, "the Europeans" had to decide themselves. Christian Herter possibly best expressed the philosophy behind such ambiguity in a 1962 speech to the Atlantic Convention of NATO nations, where he declared that:

> With very few exceptions, even among those who most enthusiastically support the idea of an Atlantic Community, no clear definition is given as to what nations are embraced within that Community. . . . As of this moment it is both natural and pru-

29 Bange, *EEC Crisis of 1963*, 40; Dobson, "Years of Transition," 239–58.
30 John Kennedy, "The President's News Conference," 10 August 1961.
31 Winand, *Eisenhower*, 281.
32 Kraft, *Grand Design*, 21.
33 Ball, *Past Has Another Pattern*, 208–22.
34 To be sure, in the preface to the 1958 edition of his work, Haas admitted that the concept of a "united Europe" was rather obscure even for those who most often made reference to it, being alternatively applied to "the Six of 'Schumania' or the Fifteen of the Council of Europe." See Haas, *Uniting of Europe*, xxxi.

dent to avoid a dogmatic approach, both as to the nations which should be included at the outset and as to the form of political institutions which should evolve.[35]

At the same time, while prudence counseled not to overplay the American hand, Kennedy's characterizations of the "European partner" were not less prescriptive for the fact of being vague. It might have been up to "the Europeans" to decide on the delicate "question of the federation versus confederation," as the President once declared.[36] But there was no question that Europe had to be supranational in institutions, liberal in international trade, and strongly connected to the US—"Atlantic"—in military affairs. As the President explained, he wanted "an outward-looking Europe with a strong connection to the United States."[37]

AN ACTIVE NEW "EUROPE" FOR THE PARTNERSHIP

While the ambiguity of the contours of the "European partner" largely served Kennedy's need not to irritate "the Europeans," the President also needed to address rising concerns about "Europe" at home. Thus, Kennedy's European partner had a paradoxical characteristic: it was ambiguously defined in many ways, but also had a very clear personality. From this standpoint, Kennedy introduced two major novelties into US discourse about "Europe."

First of all, Kennedy's rhetoric allowed "Europe" to come back as an international player for the first time since the end of World War II. In basic grammar, Kennedy began to use "Europe" as the subject of his sentences. This first happened during the recordings of a speech for French radio in May 1961, when he declared that "a strong Europe strengthens freedom."[38] Such a use of the term then became extremely common during 1962, in the run-up to the "interdependence declaration" speech and in its

35 Herter, *Toward an Atlantic Community*, 64.

36 John Kennedy, "The President's News Conference," 17 May 1962.

37 Cited in Lundestad, *United States*, 120. In his 23 July 1962 news conference, the President declared: "We're asking Europe to make the Common Market an increasingly open institution."

38 John Kennedy, "Transcript of Interview With the President Recorded for French TV and Radio," 30 May 1961.

aftermath: Europe was often depicted as "free, growing, and expanding."[39] In his 1963 State of the Union message, Kennedy credited Europe for "moving" toward interdependence.[40] Europe could even be conceptualized as having a will opposite to US proposals, as when the President declared that "Europe might decide that the MLF isn't what they want."[41]

The fact that in Kennedy's speeches Europe became a political actor should not be taken lightly. President Harry Truman had given a very limited number of speeches in which Europeans actively did something—including "saving their continent" and "desiring European unity"—but in most cases they were simply the recipients of choices made by others.[42] Throughout the entire Eisenhower administration, Europe was portrayed as a player of international affairs only on one occasion, in a June 1958 message about the signing of an agreement between the US and Euratom—with "Europe" then understood to be the Six members of the community that had just been created.[43] In all other instances, for Eisenhower "Europe" was always preceded by prepositions as "in," "from," or "to"; for all the administration's encouragement to the fledgling European Communities, and possibly to Bismarck's happiness, Europe largely remained a "mere geographical notion" in the golden years of Atlanticism.[44]

The second innovation was an even deeper one. It came when Kennedy began to associate this active European partner with the idea of newness. The phrase "new Europe" first appeared in the President's 1962 State of the Union message. This was a Europe that the US considered its main partner "in aid, trade, defense, diplomacy, and monetary affairs."[45] On another oc-

39 John Kennedy, "Toasts of the President and Chancellor Adenauer," 14 November 1962.

40 John Kennedy, "Annual Message to the Congress on the State of the Union," 14 January 1962.

41 John Kennedy, "The President's News Conference," 6 March 1963.

42 See, for one of these rare exceptions, Harry Truman, "Statement by the President on German Steps Toward Acceptance of the European Defense Community Agreements," 6 December 1952.

43 Dwight Eisenhower, "Special Message to the Congress Transmitting International Agreement Between the United States and Euratom," 23 June 1958.

44 In the late 1870s, in a letter to the Russian Foreign minister, Prince Gortchakov, the Prussian Chancellor Otto Von Bismarck famously scribbled "*Europe. Notion géographique*," adding a few lines lower down that "*Qui parle Europe a tort.*" Bismarck cited in Woodward, *Prelude to Modern Europe*, 57.

45 John Kennedy, "Annual Message to the Congress on the State of the Union," 11 January 1962.

casion, Kennedy described this "new Europe" as a "Europe of equals instead of rivals— . . . born of common ideals, instead of the old Europe, torn by national and personal animosities."[46] In short, this was "Europe" as a "vast new enterprise," a "great new edifice," a "new union now emerging," and a "new house," to which Kennedy offered his "declaration of interdependence" for the building of a stronger Atlantic partnership.[47] And, obviously, this was a "united Europe," as the President declared in a highly publicized speech given at the Paulskirche in Frankfurt during his "European" tour of June 1963 (although, as usual, the President cared to make it clear that "the choice of paths to the unity of Europe is a choice which Europe must make").[48]

Indeed, the references to the newness of Europe were always accompanied by reminders of the Atlantic connection. As the President explained in the 1962 State of the Union message, "the emergence of the new Europe is being matched by the emergence of new ties across the Atlantic."[49] When Kennedy began to make references to the newness of Europe, however, his language was almost revolutionary: for almost two centuries, Europe had been the "old world" by definition.[50]

It was the perspective of European unity that made the passage from old to new possible, against a tradition that stretched back to some of the most sacred texts of US foreign policy, that had traditionally associated "Europe" with "wars and quarrels" (as in Thomas Paine's *Common Sense*), or with "frequent controversies" (as in George Washington's *Farewell Address*).[51] Understandably, the association of the two terms "new" and "Europe" had been dared only twice before in the history of US presidential speeches, by Truman in the early 1950s.[52] When Truman spoke of "new Europe," how-

46 John Kennedy, "Address Before the Conference on Trade Policy," 17 May 1962.

47 John Kennedy, "Address at Independence Hall, Philadelphia," 4 July 1962.

48 John Kennedy, "Address in the Assembly Hall at the Paulskirche in Frankfurt," 25 June 1963.

49 John Kennedy, "Annual Message to the Congress on the State of the Union," 11 January 1962.

50 Strout, *American Image.*

51 Del Pero, *Libertà*, 10–24.

52 Harry Truman, "Special Message to the Congress on the Mutual Security Program," 6 March 1952; "Address in Springfield at the 32d Reunion of the 35th Division Association," 7 June 1952.

ever, he always spoke in the future tense. In Kennedy's public speeches, this new Europe was a present reality.

KENNEDY'S "LARGER EUROPE"

In 1965, Henry Kissinger, a well-known Harvard professor who had briefly served as an adviser to Kennedy and who would later become the national security adviser and the Secretary of State of the Nixon and Ford administrations, wrote a harsh critique of Kennedy's approach to "Europe."[53] The biggest problem with the policies of the Kennedy administration, according to Kissinger, was not in the negotiating tactics or the diplomatic postures with which "Europe" had been approached. Rather, it was in the very conception of Europe that the administration had embraced. In short, Kissinger wrote, there was nothing across the ocean that really resembled the kind of actor Kennedy represented: indeed, there were several institutions symbolizing some form of European unity. But NATO was intergovernmental in nature, the OECD was a very lose economic transatlantic organization, the EEC was supranational only to a limited extent and, despite all its political ambitions, for the time being, the EEC Commission in Brussels dealt only with trade issues. And, obviously, Britain's application to the EEC did not equal Britain's membership in it.[54] In short, Kennedy's "new Europe" was a chimera.

In the mid-1960s, the imaginary elements of Kennedy's European partner had already been exposed by de Gaulle's rejection of Britain's entry.[55] Thus, it could be said that Kissinger was writing from a comfortable van-

53 Kissinger, *Troubled Partnership*.

54 Ibid., 21.

55 It was also relatively easy for Kissinger to underline that de Gaulle's decisions hit Kennedy's European partner in two different but interconnected ways: institutionally, de Gaulle supported a Europe that was intergovernmental as opposed to supranational and moderately protectionist as opposed to liberal. Geographically, de Gaulle's Europe notoriously went from the "Atlantic to the Urals," as the French President had declared in 1960. Kissinger noted that de Gaulle's vision, though received in Washington with alarm, was of remote, unspecified future, especially in relation to the Eastern border; it it was not an invitation to the communist Soviet Union to join "Europe." As for the Western border, however, the "Atlantic" placed Britain objectively in a limbo—if not entirely outside. Kissinger, *Troubled Partnership*, 57.

tage point.[56] However, not everyone in the US foreign policy establishment shared his judgment. On the contrary, it is well known that, after a reflective pause, the Kennedy administration opted for confirming the objectives of the Atlantic partnership and that, with minor emphasis, the Johnson administration also worked towards the same perspective, when it took over in late 1963 (at least until Ball's resignation in 1966).[57] As discussed above, the active and positive new Europe hinting at the enlarged and reformed EEC did not disappear from Kennedy's speeches. On the contrary, it remained a powerful image until the abrupt end of his Presidency.

At the same time, however, the administration began to nurture greater doubts as to the existence of that "Europe." For example, in a February 1963 press conference on the cumbersome negotiations for the MLF, Kennedy did refer to "Europe" as a single and active entity. But while in form this resembled his 1962 enthusiasm for the European partner, in substance the President was rather coming to the opposite conclusion. In fact, he declared the following:

> It is a very difficult area because the weapons have to be fired in 5 minutes, and who is going to be delegated on behalf of Europe to make this judgment? . . . Somebody has to be delegated with that authority. If it isn't the President of the United States, in the case of the strategic force, it will have to be the President of France or the Prime Minister of Great Britain, or someone else. And that is an enormous responsibility.[58]

According to historian Thomas Gijswijt, in the preparation of his 1963 trip to "Europe," Kennedy candidly admitted to one of his aides that "there isn't any Europe."[59] Four months after the President's assassination, Secretary of State Dean Rusk, by then serving under Johnson, came to a similar conclusion in a harsh reply to his own collaborators in Washington:

56 To be sure, Kissinger's understanding that "Europe" was not actually a single actor did not help him much in framing and managing his ill-fated 1973 "Year of Europe" initiative, for which he famously ended crying, out of frustration, "who do I call when I need to speak to Europe"? For a more general overview of Kissinger and "Europe," see Lundestad, *United States*, 181–85.

57 Winand, *Eisenhower*, 337.

58 John Kennedy, "The President's News Conference," 14 February 1963.

59 Gijswijt, "Running for President," 152–71.

I find it difficult to be patient in face of whining from various quarters across the Atlantic. Reftel should have broken down words Europe and Europeans into their component parts because on these matters there is no such thing as Europe.[60]

In the aftermath of the Cuban missile crisis of October 1962, Kennedy also undertook a gradual rethinking of US-Soviet relations. As Federico Romero has noted, this was a very contradictory process, as is well exemplified by the two speeches Kennedy gave in Berlin on 26 June of 1963. The extreme Cold War overtones of the "*Ich bin ein Berliner*" speech delivered in the morning in the Rudolph Wilde Platz were smoothed out in the afternoon, when the President hinted at the possibility of a frank dialogue with the Soviets in his remarks at the Free University.[61]

However, if one thing connected the two speeches, this was the vision of a different "Europe" from the "European partner" Kennedy had focused on in the previous year—and on which he was still focused despite his growing doubts. This was in many ways the Europe of his 1937 "grand tour." This was the "great continent of Europe," as he called it in his inflammatory morning speech. This was a "larger Europe," that is "the commonly accepted geography of Europe—west of Asia," as he explained in his afternoon remarks.[62]

To be sure, in Kennedy's public speeches there had always been references to this broader notion of Europe, next to the one aimed at strengthening rhetorically the Atlantic partnership. In a 1961 toast for Italy's Prime Minister Fanfani, the President recognized that Italy had a "commanding position . . . in the Mediterranean, the southern part of Europe."[63] While Kennedy's 1962 remarks to Vice-President Johnson on his departure for "Southern Europe and the Near East" were not detailed enough to decipher whether Cyprus was in Europe or not, Turkey had its seat guaranteed in a 1961 speech where the President exalted the success of the "Truman doc-

60 "Telegram From Secretary of State Rusk to the Department of State Saigon, April 17, 1964," in *Foreign Relations of the United States, 1964–1968*, doc. 18. For similar judgments from the old guard of the Atlanticists, see Weisbrode, *Atlantic Century*, 161.

61 Romero, *Storia della Guerra Fredda*, 242.

62 John Kennedy, "Address at the Free University of Berlin," 26 June 1963.

63 John Kennedy, "Toasts of the President and Prime Minister Fanfani of Italy," 12 June 1961.

trine."[64] Whereas the President never mentioned Iceland in any of his public speeches, in June 1963 he assured the Irish Parliament that "Ireland is part of Europe."[65] Last but not least, the Soviet Union was explicitly mentioned as one of the "countries of Europe" in a May 1961 address to the National Association of Broadcasters.[66]

However, this broader image of "Europe" was used as a vague geographical notion before 1963, to refer to things or processes that took place "in Europe." With his speeches of 26 June, Kennedy began to indicate that "Europe" as a goal."[67] And yet, while broadening Europe in geographical terms, Kennedy also left Europe without any clearly defined personality: the equation between "*Ich bin ein Berliner*" and "*civis romanus sum,*" and Kennedy's claim to be a proud citizen of Berlin, left little autonomy to Europe, squeezed at it was in a new version of the ancient opposition between *romanitas* (the Atlantic community) and *barbaritas* (the communist world).

CONCLUSION

While so far historians of transatlantic relations have mainly identified Kennedy's Europe in that depicted for the purpose of pushing forward his design for a transatlantic partnership, by 1963 an alternative vision also began to emerge in the President's rhetoric. Both images of Europe elaborated by the Kennedy administration—the "new Europe" and the "larger Europe"—generally carried a positive connotation. This added to a trend which had begun in the early 1940s and which broke with a long and consolidated US tradition. Besides this, however, there was little in common between the two. One was conceived—at least in principle—as an active

64 Respectively: John Kennedy, "Remarks to Vice President Johnson on His Departure for Southern Europe and the Near East," 22 August 1962; and John Kennedy, "Remarks and Question and Answer Period at the Press Luncheon in Paris," 2 June 1961.

65 John Kennedy, "Address Before the Irish Parliament in Dublin," 28 June 1963.

66 John Kennedy, "Address at the 39th Annual Convention of the National Association of Broadcasters," 8 May 1961.

67 In one case, the reunification of the "great continent" seemed a very distant objective. In the other case, the President claimed that it was "not too early to think once again in terms of all of Europe, for the winds of change are blowing across the curtain as well as the rest of the world.

and autonomous player in international affairs. The other was a rather amorphous, albeit larger, entity. The former was supposed to serve ideologically the construction of a partnership between the two roughly equal members of the "Atlantic community." The latter was supposed to serve Kennedy's attempts at *détente* with the Soviet Union.

The President did try to show that there existed a potential link between these two alternative visions. In his words, it was the "new Europe of the West—dynamic, diverse, and democratic—[that] must exert an ever-increasing attraction to the people of the East."[68] However, in practice, when he began using the image of Europe as the larger continent, the administration was undergoing a phase of growing doubts about the existence of the previously cherished "new Europe." Kennedy's—and later Johnson's—failures in putting in practice the vision of an equal partnership between the United States and "Europe" have often been ascribed to the clash of his vision with the alternative vision supported by de Gaulle. Indeed, de Gaulle's vision of Europe did represent a major obstacle on Kennedy's road. However, the analysis carried out in this essay indicates that the Europe Kennedy conceived for the making of the Atlantic partnership was largely imaginary. The understanding of "Europe" was not unequivocal within the Kennedy administration, and old Atlanticist dreams tended to come back to the surface when the Europeanist approach suffered its first setbacks. However, the fact that both images were actually used by the administration during the year 1963, after de Gaulle's traumatic rejection of Britain's application to the EEC, seems more the symptom of a certain difficulty in dealing with the subject, than the astute ideological operation of someone who wants to play at multiple tables.

Bibliography

The American Presidency Project. Edited by John T. Woolley and Gerhard Peters. Santa Barbara, CA. http://www.presidency.ucsb.edu/.

Anderson, Benedict. *Imagined Communities: Reflections on the Origin and Spread of Nationalism*. London: Verso, 1991.

68 John Kennedy, "Address at the Free University of Berlin," 26 June 26 1963.

Aubourg, Valérie, and Giles Scott-Smith, eds. *Atlantic, Euratlantic or Europe-America?* Paris: Soleb, 2011.

Balestracci, Duccio. *Ai confini dell'Europa medievale.* Milano: Bruno Mondadori, 2008.

Balis, Christina V., and Simon Serfaty, eds. *Visions of America and Europe: September 11, Iraq, and Transatlantic Relations*. Washington, DC: CSIS Press, 2004.

Ball, George W. *The Past Has Another Pattern: Memoirs.* New York: Norton, 1982.

Bange, Oliver. *The EEC Crisis of 1963: Kennedy, Macmillan, de Gaulle, and Adenauer in Conflict.* New York: Palgrave, 1999.

Barnet, Richard J. *Allies: America, Europe, and Japan since the War.* New York: Simon and Schuster, 1984.

Bonazzi, Tiziano. "Constructing and Reconstructing Europe." In Vaudagna, *Place of Europe*, 11–26.

Boorstin, Daniel. *America and the Image of Europe: Reflections on American Thought.* Gloucester, MA: Peter Smith, 1976. First published 1960.

Bozo, Frédéric. *Two Strategies for Europe: De Gaulle, the United States, and the Atlantic Alliance.* Lanham, MD: Rowman and Littlefield, 2001.

Brinkley, Douglas, and Richard T. Griffiths, eds. *John F. Kennedy and Europe.* Foreword by Theodore Sorensen. Baton Rouge: LSU Press, 1999.

Chabod, Federico. *Storia dell'idea di Europa.* Bari: Laterza, 2005. First published 1961.

Colman, Jonathan. *A 'Special Relationship'? Harold Wilson, Lyndon B. Johnson, and Anglo-American Relations 'at the Summit', 1964–68.* Manchester: Manchester University Press, 2004.

Costigliola, Frank. "The Failed Design: Kennedy, de Gaulle, and the Struggle for Europe." *Diplomatic History* 8, no. 3 (1984): 227–52.

Dallek, Robert. *JFK: John Fitzgerald Kennedy, una vita incompiuta.* Translated by Nicoletta Lamberti. Milano: Mondadori, 2005.

Del Pero, Mario. *Libertà e impero: Gli Stati Uniti e il mondo 1776–2006.* Bari: Laterza, 2008.

Dobson, Alan. "The Years of Transition: Anglo-American Relations 1961–1967." *Review of International Studies* 16, no. 3 (1990): 239–58.

Foreign Relations of the United States, 1964–1968. Volume 13. *Western Europe Region*. Edited by Charles Sampson. Washington, DC: Government Printing Office, 1995.

Gijswijt, Thomas. "Running for President of the West: Kennedy's European Trip in June 1963." In Aubourg and Scott-Smith, *Atlantic*, 152–71.

Gould, Peter, and Rodney White. *Mental Maps*. New York: Penguin, 1974.

Guderzo, Massimiliano. *Interesse nazionale e responsabilità globale*. Firenze: Aida, 2002.

Haas, Ernst B. *The Uniting of Europe: Political, Social, and Economic Forces, 1950–1957*. Notre Dame, IN: University of Notre Dame Press, 2004. First published 1958.

Harper, John Lamberton. *American Visions of Europe: Franklin D. Roosevelt, George F. Kennan, and Dean G. Acheson*. Cambridge, UK: Cambridge University Press, 1994.

Henrikson, Alan. "The Geographical 'Mental Maps' of American Foreign Policy Makers." *International Political Science Review* 1, no. 4 (1980): 495–530.

Herter, Christian A. *Toward an Atlantic Community*. New York: Harper and Row, 1963.

Kissinger, Henry A. *The Troubled Partnership: A Re-Appraisal of the Atlantic Alliance*. New York: McGraw-Hill, 1965.

Kraft, Joseph. *The Grand Design: From Common Market to Atlantic Partnership*. New York: Harper, 1962.

Lundestad, Geir. *The United States and Western Europe since 1945: From "Empire" by Invitation to Transatlantic Drift*. Oxford: Oxford University Press, 2005.

Mariano, Marco, ed. *Defining the Atlantic Community: Culture, Intellectuals, and Policies in the Mid-Twentieth Century*. London: Routledge, 2010.

———. "Remapping America: Continentalism, Globalism, and the Rise of the Atlantic Community, 1939–1949." In Mariano, *Defining the Atlantic Community*, 71–86.

———. "The US Discovers Europe." In Vaudagna, *Place of Europe*, 161–85.

Preston, Andrew. "John F. Kennedy and Lyndon B. Johnson." In *Mental Maps in the Early Cold War Era, 1945–68*, edited by Steven Casey and Jonathan Wright, 261–80. New York: Palgrave Macmillan, 2011.

Priest, Andrew. "George W. Ball, the Multilateral Force and the Transatlantic Alliance." In Aubourg and Scott-Smith, *Atlantic*, 172–91.

Romero, Federico. *Storia della Guerra Fredda: l'ultimo conflitto per l'Europa*. Torino: Einaudi, 2009.

Schwartz, Thomas Alan. *Lyndon Johnson and Europe: In the Shadow of Vietnam.* Cambridge, MA: Harvard University Press, 2003.

Steel, Ronald. "How Europe Became Atlantic: Walter Lippmann and the New Geography of the Atlantic Community." In Mariano, *Defining the Atlantic Community*, 13–25.

Strout, Cushing. *The American Image of the Old World.* New York: Harper and Row, 1963.

Vaudagna, Maurizio, ed. *The Place of Europe in American History: Twentieth-Century Perspectives*. Turin: Otto, 2007.

Weisbrode, Kenneth. *The Atlantic Century: Four Generations of Extraordinary Diplomats Who Forged America's Vital Alliance with Europe.* Cambridge, MA: Da Capo Press, 2009.

Winand, Pascaline. *Eisenhower, Kennedy, and the United States of Europe.* New York: Palgrave Macmillan, 1996.

Woodward, Llewellyn. *Prelude to Modern Europe, 1815–1914.* London: Methuen, 1972.

Body Counts and Memorials

The Unexpected Effect of the Vietnam Veterans Memorial as a Model of Memory

MARK MEIGS

Strangely, the commemorative model established by the Vietnam Veterans Memorial has displaced the meaning of war away from military victory and the establishment of political goals into an emotion-filled realm, where what counts is an attempted quantification of sacrifice for the nation by specific, named persons. And though the model was invented implying, or at least permitting, a critique of that war and wars in general, it has become a model that can be applied to other wars, even a war without end and without victory as a goal, like the "War on Terrorism" in which the United States is now involved. The lessons of Vietnam were briefly embodied in the elements of the Powell Doctrine. This included "overwhelming force" applied to a winnable conflict measurable by well-defined military and political goals. It required the support of the American people, exhausting diplomatic and other solutions before going to war, and creating international consensus about the war. But these lessons can now be seen in the light of memory lessons, too, even as the Powell Doctrine fades along with Colin Powell's reputation.[1]

1 The list of elements in the Powell Doctrine is often cited. See, for example, Prados, "Wise Guys," 107. Prados cites Colin Powell with Joseph E. Persico, *My American Journey* (New York: Random House, 1995), 434.

Making memorials to sacrifice with no reference to the political aims of that sacrifice has become acceptable in a national context. Perhaps memorializing sacrifice always had a special potential in a society like that of the United States, where personal fulfillment is so admired. Certainly American families with the means to do so have built plenty of monuments expressing grief or loss with little or no political reference. What is new, since Vietnam, though, is the national setting for a list of the names of people who died violently or young elaborated only by categorization and quantification to become a national shrine. The role of the United States as a political force in this kind of memorial can vanish as sacrifice overbalances victory or lack of victory or any political goal.

This is an unexpected destiny for the Vietnam memorial, but it was perhaps inevitable as the lure of force in international relations proves itself to be more resilient to historical change than Carl von Clausewitz's famous dictum that "war is politics by other means." It turns out that "war is politics by other means" only if the war must some day come to an end and the warring parties must eventually come to the negotiating table. In a world of asymmetric economic means and asymmetric access to technology, the possibility of perpetual war, perpetual violent force being exerted on enemies, seems to exist.

THE BACKWARDS TIMELINE OF WAR MEMORIALS ON THE NATIONAL MALL

A chronological sketch of the memorials on the National Mall can serve as shorthand evidence for the relative importance and different qualities of the memory of different wars of the twentieth century. These memorials have evolved considerably over a century of almost continual military conflicts. Concentrating on the Vietnam Veterans Memorial as the first of these memorials to be built, this article will deploy other major conflicts as supporting evidence of the shift in meaning of American military dead brought about by Vietnam. The Gulf War and the opening acts of commemoration for the present "War on Terror" will form an epilogue, but this essay argues that the way that casualties were quantified and recorded in the Vietnam War is revealing of the way in which meaning has been attached to American war dead ever since.

The first national monument to twentieth-century American wars that was constructed on the Mall was the Vietnam Veterans Memorial. It was predated by another project authorized by Congress as early as 1924 but this older monument was dedicated only to the residents of the District of Columbia. With the names of only Washingtonians, it was hardly a national memorial. Since 2008 a foundation has existed to transform that local monument into a national one, but that has not happened yet. The World War II National Memorial on the Mall was not approved until 1993 and not dedicated until 2004. The Korean War Veterans Memorial was authorized by Congress in 1986, designed by 1989, but dedicated only in 1993, over forty years after that war ended. The oldest was therefore the Vietnam Veterans Memorial initiated when veteran Jan Scruggs founded the Vietnam Veterans Memorial Foundation (VVMF) in 1979. It became the subject of an important and controversial design competition and was dedicated twice, in 1982 and then, with modifications to allay certain controversies, in 1984.

The explanation for this reversed timeline on the Mall—first Vietnam, then Korea, then World War II, and maybe someday, World War I—follows a trajectory away from the celebration of political purpose and victory towards sorrow, memory, and loss. Expressing these emotions on the National Mall places them at the center of American culture and motivations. The first model for American war memorials in the twentieth century did not include the Mall at all. When Americans in large numbers died in wars across the world, the model was set by World War I and reaffirmed in World War II. It is in evidence across Europe, especially in France, but also in North Africa, Latin America, and the Philippines near Manila. In ten countries there are twenty-four cemeteries meticulously maintained by the American Battlefield Monuments Commission (ABMC) brought into being by Congress in 1923. Memorialization preceding this date is scattered and diverse—e.g., a monument in Mexico City commissioned in 1851 for 750 unknown soldiers from the Mexican American War. It is simply an obelisk inscribed to those "known but to God." A cemetery near Panama City contains some of the Spanish American war dead but was mostly intended for the approximately 5,000 Americans who died building the Panama Canal. The repatriated dead of the Spanish American War are scattered in different cemeteries, mostly along the Pacific coast, with no particular designation. It was World War I that brought the ABMC into being and also the typical design for an American war cemetery and monument until Vietnam.

THE WORLD WAR I AND II AMERICAN MEMORIAL MODEL ABROAD: A DEPARTURE FROM PREVIOUS PRACTICE

The American war memorials for the World Wars, in France and elsewhere, exemplifying a national model, have crosses or stars of David bearing names and marking graves with bodies in them. Unidentified bodies and names without bodies have markers and space, too. Each memorial has a statue representing some aspect of the American martial spirit. The memorials include a chapel dedicated to no particular religion and a visitor center that is informative but familiar and unthreatening, like the mayor's office of a small town. There is a monumental structure, modernist but suggesting classical models. Somewhere, carved in stone, a battle map explains the military reasons for sacrifice and graves both in local terms and in war theater terms. The Stars and Stripes flies at all times. The structures, with the possible exception of the visitors' center, are of white marble or creamy limestone. Lawns are trimmed; shrubs and sometimes trees are clipped (fig. 1).

These elaborate cemetery memorials were built abroad as signs of the desire of the United States to involve itself permanently in the affairs of other nations, especially in Europe, after World War I. They can be seen as an extension or an extra guarantee of President Woodrow Wilson's Fourteen Points. The United States would join in the collective security and the self-determination of peoples and there would be *de facto* American territory, fertilized with American blood and bones, left on the fields of battle: territory to be defended along with principles. With explanatory maps and visitor centers, American History was inscribed in foreign places.

The decision to leave American soldiers in foreign fields was not without controversy. The most visible military cemeteries in the United States were those of the Civil War at Gettysburg in Pennsylvania, at Shiloh in Tennessee, at Antietam in Maryland and other battlefields and, of course, at Arlington, Virginia, just across the Potomac from Washington, DC. All were within the territory of the United States. In the fifty years between the Civil War and World War I, those cemeteries had become important sites of national mourning where people from both the victorious North and the defeated South could participate in what one Civil War historian has called a republic of suffering. The pain of the Civil War, shared by the white population of North and South, was an important element in rebuilding the nation in its aftermath.[2] During that war, it had seemed natural that families with the means would repatriate their own dead to family and parish burial plots across the United States and that municipalities would build monuments to the Civil War dead on town squares while the states, according to their abilities, built monuments to their dead on the various battlefields. There was thus a communication of suffering between families, the states in which they lived, and the federal government that undertook to memorialize the great battlefields.[3]

The dead of World War I were too far away for this *ad hoc* and mixed practice. The war effort had been undertaken by the United States, not by the individual states. The cemeteries and monuments built in France were to be emphatically national cemeteries and monuments. Missouri and Pennsylvania built monuments to their dead in France in the early 1920s, but Congress made a law prohibiting the practice. The majority of those in favor of large monuments abroad saw them as part of international relations, a realm reserved for Washington, DC, not the states.[4]

Some citizens objected to their soldier sons being subsumed to the national purpose. In the isolationist spirit that rejected the League of Nations and rejected Woodrow Wilson's handling of the Versailles treaty, they insisted that it was the duty of the War Department to bring the bodies home. In the end, about half the bodies of those who died in battle were repatriated. Some were put in national cemeteries such as Arlington, but most found their way to grave plots near their families. The emotional claim that parents should be able to visit soldier graves was strong enough that Congress eventually appropriated money to send a family member, usually the mother, to visit all the graves left in France. Thus a Civil War model in which

2 Faust, *This Republic of Suffering* and *A Riddle of Death*. Faust makes a study of this shared pain and its representations, but the phenomenon is readily discernible in memorial works produced much closer to the war and intended for consumption in both North and South. See, for example, Miller, *The Photographic History of the Civil War*. The editors were careful to include a great many photographs of the dead of both sides and to write about loss on both sides. D. W. Griffith's *The Birth of a Nation* (1915) mirrors death in a family from the North with one from the South for the same purpose. *The Birth of a Nation* also emphasizes a shared racism and growing consensus on the subject of segregation, another legacy of the Civil War.

3 See Fahs and Waugh, *Memory of the Civil War*, especially Stuart McConnell, "Epilogue: The Geography of Memory," 258–65.

4 Becker, "Les Deux rives de l'Atlantique."

Figure 1: Normandy American Cemetery and Memorial at Omaha Beach

The "classical" structure, the statue, the park-like setting, the white grave markers and the flags are all visible. The statue is hardly military, but it might be interpreted as an expression of a free youthful spirit entirely in harmony with an ideal of American GIs. US National Archives, ARC Identifier 6003593.

memorial responsibility was shared by citizens, the states, and the United States was adapted to an overseas war in a way that moved the meaning of the dead, with some resistance, towards the purposes of national and international policy. If half the war dead were returned home, half stayed in the magnificent American memorials in France.[5]

The memorials of World War II expanded and confirmed this model of American military memory. Cemeteries at Omaha Beach in France, near Anzio in Italy, in Tunisia and near Manila commemorate the sacrifice of American soldiers during the Normandy landings, Monte Casino, the North African campaign and the Pacific, during World War II. The World War I cemeteries, left partly empty by the repatriation of soldier bodies, were

5 Meigs, *Optimism at Armageddon*, 143–87; Piehler, "War Dead"; see also *History of the American Graves Registration Service*.

filled later by World War II dead. The model of white crosses and Stars of David, each one spaced from the others so that every marker is part of a large grid pattern, but also so that each grave maker is the center of a star pattern when a mourner stands by it, became fixed in the minds of Americans and attached, after World War II, to a victory in an unambiguously successful war that implied an ongoing commitment to international systems of collective security. Even the Punchbowl, now inside Hawaii, the 50th state, was outside the United States at the time of its creation, and given the nature of the Pearl Harbor attack, the memorial could be seen as a token of commitment to threatened territory.

Monuments to the war in the Pacific innovated in ways that foreshadowed the Vietnam Veterans Memorial. "Walls of the missing," at the cemetery near Manila and at the Punchbowl, near Honolulu, complete a process of naming at those cemeteries. Each cross and Star of David usually bears the name attached to a body buried beneath it. But the body can be missing under the cross or there can be a body marked by a Star of David but no name. Thus the World War I and II memorials took care of these eventualities. Furthermore, for both World Wars I and II, there is an "Unknown Soldier" monument at Arlington to acknowledge when names were severed from bodies and to turn that sense of loss into a national message about the political war aims that prevailed.[6]

Innovative Memorialization of the Korean War without a Memorial Model

The dead from the Korean conflict might have been treated according to this existing model. After all, if American cemeteries existed around the world to advertise an American willingness to intervene on behalf of international order even when a conflict did not threaten American soil, Korean War dead could fit in that model. Some of the Korean War dead are in the 146 cemeteries around the United States that bear the designation "United States National Cemetery." These do not include the twenty-four cemeteries abroad maintained by the ABMC that include Manila where some Ko-

6 Hawley, *Remains of War*, 199. For his description of the Puchbowl, Hawley quotes Mayo, *War Memorials*, 105.

rean War dead are buried. Some of the dead from the Korean War fill out the pattern established in these places set after World War II. But most went to family graveyards. Of all those National Cemeteries and Monuments not one was specifically designated for Korean War dead. A small number of unidentified American dead were buried in the United Nations cemetery at Tanggok within the Pusan perimeter, the southeast corner of Korea that the United Nations and the United States never lost control of during the war. That United Nations cemetery has soldier dead from all United Nations forces participating in the defense of the Republic of Korea. The existence of the cemetery, and its dedication by General Matthew Ridgway during the war, can be seen as a high water mark of American memorial participation in international war efforts. Even before the end of 1950, before Ridgway gave his dedication speech at that UN cemetery, the decision had been made to remove all American dead from Korea, even during hostilities, something that had not been done before. *The Quartermaster Review* of March and April 1953, recounted with understandable pride, the accomplishments of the American Graves Registration Service during this war of sweeping movements in harsh conditions.[7]

Initially, as they must, commanders had taken care of the United Nations dead at the divisional level and lower, by quick burial. During the initial advances of the North Korean army when the UN forces were forced well south of Seoul into the Pusan district of the southeast, several of these divisional cemeteries had been lost. They were recovered at the time of the Inchon Beachhead and the breakout from the Pusan perimeter. Upon recovery, graves registration personnel took over the job of looking after those cemeteries and of locating burial sites scattered across the hills and rice paddies of Korea's rugged terrain. The fighting swept north almost to the Chinese border at the Yalu River leaving new hastily dug graves. Those graves and some older ones again fell into communist hands when North Koreans and Chinese forces, advanced south, and pushed United Nations forces below the 38th parallel at the end of 1950. The Americans and UN forces eventually moved north of the 38th parallel again before the armi-

7 Cook, "Graves Registration."

stice, signed by the United States but not by South Korea, reestablished that line of latitude as the border between North and South Korea.[8]

The decision to disinter American dead from their graves in the path of an advancing army in foreign territory was an innovation in Korea and contrary to previous practices. In other wars, the resources to dig up bodies and move them from temporary battlefield graves to well-arranged permanent cemeteries were only available when hostilities had stopped. Graves Registration personnel did it because they realized that in the advance beyond the 38th parallel, they had taken territory and buried men in ground that the United States and its allies would not continue to hold. Given the back and forth sweep of the war, the idea of permanent memorials must have seemed remote indeed. In addition to the shifting battlefield, the perceived implacable nature of the communist enemy must have played a role in the decision. According to George Kennan's famous analysis of 1946, no real reconciliation would ever be possible with communists.[9] And, in fact, after the armistice, the war continued by other means including negotiations over prisoners and bodies.

Though the United States did not lose the war in Korea, it did not win control over territory, and in the Cold War manner described first by George Kennan, the implacable enemy was not interested in making concessions. Perhaps communist North Koreans understood or guessed the self-torture Americans were capable of in the face of ambiguity over the fate of individual soldiers in an ideological war. As POWs American soldiers made 250 broadcasts from North Korea praising communism. Prisoners wrote letters home asking their families to work for peace. They wrote letters to newspapers accusing the United States and capitalism of being at fault in the war. When soldier prisoners were returned from North Korea in operation Big Switch after the armistice, only about half the expected num-

8 I have consulted a number of internet sources for this information and make no claims for having done definitive research on the Korean War dead. See the report of quartermaster Cook, "Graves Registration." Good photographs of the Kanggok United Nations Memorial are posted as part of "United Nations Memorial Cemetery in Korea (Busan)," Wikimapia, last modified ca. 2010. http://wikimapia.org/3997112/United-Nations-Memorial-Cemetery-in-Korea. The Australian Department of Veteran Affairs lists cemeteries and other sites with Australian Korean War dead.

9 George Kennan's "Long Telegram" of 1946 was published as "The Sources of Soviet Conduct" in *Foreign Affairs* in 1947. Originally, it was signed "X."

ber was still alive. Twenty-three of the 3,958 American soldiers returned opted to go to China rather than the United States. Meanwhile of the 98,427 Chinese and North Koreans returned from South Korean camps, 22,604 went to Taiwan.[10] The options had been insisted upon by American military and State Department officials to permit Nationalist Chinese among Chinese prisoners to choose to go to Taiwan rather than to communist China. The huge numbers choosing Taiwan should have been a propaganda success for the United States, but in the poisoned atmosphere of the McCarthy era, the 23 Americans who chose China weighed heavily on American consciousness. When two of those 23 went to the United States after all, they were convicted by well-publicized tribunals in the US as collaborators with the enemy. All other returned American prisoners were treated as suspects.

Obvious defenses for having shown signs of collaboration were strangely denied these men. Coercion and miserable treatment, visible in the statistics, had taken a toll too. The category "Missing in Action – Declared Dead – No Remains" on the Congressional casualty lists now numbers 4,549. Some of these might have been presumed captured. The category "Captured – Declared Dead – No Remains numbers 1,891."[11] What happened to these men in communist control is unknown. Obviously, some sort of bargaining may have taken place even if it was a matter of exchanging a letter or radio broadcast against food or medical treatment. In the popular imagination brain washing was a strong possibility. But army authorities preferred to deny the possibility of brainwashing, fearing the psychological damage for the whole United States should they admit the possibility of sleeper "Manchurian Candidates."[12] The press actually accused a whole post-World War II generation of being too soft to resist. As a result, other returned prisoners and other veterans did not wish to make demands on the United States government for any sort of memorial or recognition. In the shadow of World War II that left images of liberating GIs, veterans of the Korean War preferred silence. They had not won; after all, some of them seemed to have collaborated. The ambiguous categories—"Captured – Declared Dead – No Remains 1,891; Missing in Action – Declared Dead – No

10 Keene, "Lost to Public Commemoration," 1101.

11 Leland and Oboroceanu, "American War," 10.

12 Keene, "Lost to Public Commemoration," 1103. *The Manchurian Candidate* is a 1963 film in which a returned POW from Korea is "programmed" to assassinate a presidential candidate.

Remains 4,549"—meant shame in mid-1950s.[13] These were forgotten soldiers in a forgotten war.[14] Many fewer soldiers in these ambiguous categories would have an entirely different effect on Vietnam commemoration.

During the McCarthy era when ambiguity translated into shame, it is hardly surprising that American authorities went to such lengths to keep even the bodies of American soldiers out of the hands of North Koreans. The possibility of American war dead remaining beyond the reach of American authorities building and maintaining suitable memorials, and beyond the reach of ordinary Americans to mourn their dead, would play an important role in memorial practices in Vietnam.

Fighting in Vietnam as It Affected Memorial Practices

The Vietnam War bore some important similarities to the Korean War. It was fought in a country divided between a communist regime and one connected to free markets that the United States hoped would become democratic and that, in any case, the United States could support against the advance of communism. The ongoing Cold War context made victory in "proxy" wars of this kind ambiguous. When the Soviet Union and the United States did battle in some other country's territory and with that country's population at stake, the Cold War could not be won or lost, but a United States victory in such a war could at least be read as a sign that the United States was not falling behind. By the same token, the damage to the United States due to defeat in such a conflict could be negligible in terms of economic consequences, but if prestige and anti-communist momentum were the yardsticks used, the prospect of defeat took on a disproportionate importance.

Though it lacked the sweeping offensives and counter offensives that characterized the war in Korea, continual taking and retaking of territory in Vietnam on a smaller, village-by-village scale gave the impression that no place was secure. On a couple of occasions, communist forces overran the fortress-like American Embassy in Saigon, the South Vietnamese capital.

13 Leland and Oboroceanu, "American War," 10.

14 Keene, "Lost to Public Commemoration," 2011–12.

Where, then, could any final resting place be built? In the end, the war was a defeat for the United States and it withdrew its forces in 1973. In 1975, the South Vietnamese regime ceased to exist. The next ten years in Vietnam were a chaos of communist recriminations and reeducation and economic reforms for the South that left hundreds of thousands dead and provoked an exodus of boat people that took the lives of hundreds of thousands more. There were wars with China and Cambodia, and a famine in 1988. The United States did not reestablish diplomatic relations until 1995. Any American authority interested in preserving the memory of American soldiers killed in Vietnam was correct in the decision that memorialization should take place in the United States where most of the bodies arrived, first in body bags from the battlefields, later in metal coffins. Authorities had already made a similar decision in Korea and for similar reasons.

In the absence of territory controlled and of a political regime with measurably gathering prestige and power to support, counting other things, especially bodies, became important in the Vietnam War. Winning the war could never be achieved by taking territory, because the communist Viet Cong enemy was inside the country among the population. Winning the war could not be achieved by propping up a popular democratic government or aiding it to take better control of the country, because both the Kennedy and Johnson administrations understood that the regimes they supported in South Vietnam were neither democratic nor popular. The United States had three strategic possibilities left to keep a domino nation from falling to communism and weakening the ties to the West of the potential domino countries around it. First was the hope, often dashed, that some better political regime would emerge in South Vietnam. Second was the dream of total control of South Vietnam's rural society in "Strategic Hamlets." Last came the dream of eliminating the communist threat one communist at a time, while cutting them off from resupply and reinforcement from the North. Cutting off supplies meant coercing North Vietnam by either bombing or threatening to bomb the North. At one period cutting off supplies included planting a mine field, enhanced by sound censors as well as other hi-tech devices, and hedging it with barbed wire across Vietnam at a narrow point just south of the Demilitarized Zone (DMZ) that divided North from South. This "barrier," a cleared area 600 to 1000 yards wide, was to stretch from the coast to the Laotian border 30 kilometers inland.[15] The censors would permit American air and artillery strikes against anything moving in the area and thus prevent infiltration into the South. This McNamara Line, as it came to be called, shared with the idea of "Strategic Hamlets" the hope of territorial control in a situation in which there was no territorial control.

There was no means of measuring when some better political regime would emerge. The success of the other options, however, offered opportunities for measurement that were often illusory. How much of the population was protected in the strategic hamlets? Was the number growing? How many communists had been killed? Was that number growing? How many communists came down from the North? Was this number growing or diminishing? The possibility of measuring success by measuring the number of communists dead and alive in a military and political situation that resisted the measures of other sorts of success had proved attractive as early as September 1963, when secretary of defense Robert McNamara, after a trip to Vietnam, reported that "if enough of the enemy can be identified and killed by methods his department has been so successful in developing, there will be a time to concentrate on the political and social welfare of the people in those countries where insurgency exists."[16] Counting dead communists, in other words, had already begun to take precedence in Kennedy's cabinet, over the intransigent problem of finding a political solution in South Vietnam. Later, under President Johnson, the idea would become formalized and other notions of how to win the war would fall away. The Vietnam Veterans Memorial Wall, with the illusion it has provided of one hundred percent accuracy in the matter of who died and who went missing, is a fitting tribute to a war that has struck a chord with many Americans, and even provided a model of memorial for wars without end and without clear objectives.

Whether or not Kennedy could have resisted reduction of strategy to body counts is not certain. His assassination, soon after the coup that ended the undemocratic and repressive Diem regime in South Vietnam, will forever obscure our knowledge of what he might have done. Kennedy's participation in the plotting of the Diem coup as well as his distress at the news

15 Tucker, *Encyclopedia of the Vietnam War*, 415–16.

16 Michael V. Forrestal's report of a White House meeting, 23 September 1963, quoted by Freedman, *Kennedy's Wars*, 386.

of Diem's death are at least indications of a preoccupation with a political solution in South Vietnam and frustration when it did not cohere.[17] Lyndon Johnson's own political skill at manipulating the American Congress, unmatched by all accounts in the history of American presidents, perhaps blinded him to the fatal results of the weak position of his political partners in South Vietnam. He was famously dismayed when he was unable to affect such a breakthrough by cutting a Great Society type deal with Ho Chi Minh in 1965, promising a billion dollars in development money to Vietnam if the North Vietnamese would stop supporting the Viet Cong in the South.[18] Cutting deals advantageous to their constituencies is what politicians did, especially weak politicians faced with strong ones like Johnson. "Old Ho can't turn me down," he said in disbelief at Ho's refusal, as if Ho were a stubborn congressman.[19] He must have expected a political breakthrough to occur at any moment. Until a solution became apparent, the United States had to appear to be winning.[20]

Lacking a winning political regime to back, Johnson's managers searched for some non-political quantitative measure. The answer lay in statistics. "No conflict in history was studied in such detail as it was being waged," wrote Stanley Karnow in his 1983 study:

> Military and civilian officials from nearly every Washington agency would sooner or later conduct surveys in Vietnam, along with specialists from dozens of private think tanks, like the RAND Corporation and the Stanford Research Institute. They included weapons technicians, economists, sociologists, political scientists, anthropologists, agronomists, biologists, chemists, and public opinion pollsters. They investigated the effects of defoliants, the impact of bombs, the efficiency of cannon. They scoured villages and interviewed peasants. They interrogated the enemy defectors and prisoners. They pored over captured Communist documents and scrutinized Ha-

17 John Kennedy's reaction to the news of Diem's death is described by McNamara, *In Retrospect*, 84.

18 McNamara, *In Retrospect*, 181. Lyndon Johnson's address at Johns Hopkins University, "Peace Without Conquest," April 7, 1965.

19 Quoted in Karnow, *Vietnam*, 337.

20 Recent scholarship has underlined the understanding of American administrations of the inadequacies of South Vietnamese political leadership. See Nguyen, *Hanoi's War*.

noi statements—and they produced voluminous graphs, charts, pamphlets, brochures, and books.[21]

Robert McNamara (1916–2009), Secretary of Defense under Presidents Kennedy and Johnson from 1961 to 1968, usually gets the credit and blame for this quantification of Vietnam. He had been an effective executive for the Ford Motor Company, where he and others of his "Whiz Kid" generation had streamlined management and applied sociological studies to automobiles to design lighter and safer vehicles at the close of the 1950s. He helped bring an end to the era of huge and ostentatious cars, thought till then to be a given on the American market. He is sometimes said to have applied business principles of productivity to the production of enemy dead in war. But well before he worked for the Ford Motor Company, McNamara had put his Harvard Business School degree of 1939 to use for the US military and been impressed with the power of numbers when used in a military context. In the valedictory interviews he gave to Errol Morris for the documentary *The Fog of War* (2003), McNamara recounted his military training under General Curtis LeMay during World War II, the good war, the war that provided the model of remembrance for American war dead in the twentieth century:

> MCNAMARA. LeMay was focused on only one thing: target destruction. Most Air Force Generals can tell you how many planes they had, how many tons of bombs they dropped, or whatever the hell it was.
>
> But, he was the only person that I knew in the senior command of the Air Force who focused solely on the loss of his crews per unit of target destruction. I was on the island of Guam in his command in March of 1945. In that single night, we burned to death 100,000 Japanese civilians in Tokyo: men, women, and children.
>
> ERROL MORRIS. Were you aware this was going to happen?
>
> MCNAMARA. Well, I was part of a mechanism that in a sense recommended it. I analyzed bombing operations, and how to make them more efficient.[22]

General LeMay had had the task of directing strategic bombing against Japan at the end of World War II, including the missions that dropped atomic

21 Karnow, *Vietnam*, 271.
22 See *Fog of War*.

bombs. He had adopted a plan of incendiary bombing that destroyed 64 Japanese cities, including Tokyo, reduced to ashes by the most violent bombing attack of the war that may have killed 500,000 civilians and left 5 million Japanese without homes. The question LeMay asked McNamara and that McNamara answered was whether the rate of destruction could be continued, given the losses to American forces. The destruction itself, in LeMay's analysis, was bound to be effective eventually. In the interviews of 2003, McNamara repeated LeMay's conviction that what they did to Japan would have been cause for their trials as war criminals had the war been lost, even while admiring LeMay for his single-minded determination to turn the abstract numbers of destruction into some analytical measure towards victory. McNamara's lesson of World War II, then, was how to measure the advance towards the end of a war using sheer force. McNamara's contribution to the strategy in Vietnam can be seen as essentially LeMay's thinking applied to the later war: measuring the destruction of the enemy's resources against the cost to American forces. Could the Johnson administration sustain the effort until victory?

Initially, this form of counting involved strategic hamlets. If American and South Vietnamese forces could protect the South Vietnamese peasants in large enclosures that included fields, they could essentially starve the Viet Cong who relied on the peasants for food and other kinds of support. In 1961 the project was launched. In rich agricultural districts in the South the hamlets were set up. By September 1962, the Diem regime was able to announce with improbable precision that more than 4,322,034 South Vietnamese, or 33.39 percent of the country's population, were living behind barbed wire in these huge protected compounds. This was the kind of performance that lent itself to charts and positive press conferences. A trend showing such rapid defensive organization of such a large population would have the countryside sequestered from communists in a short time. But the numbers soon proved misleading. Peasants resented being forced into strategic hamlets away from their traditional lands and the burial places of their ancestors. Some hamlets were Potemkin villages designed to impress visitors and maintain financing. It is now generally agreed that the corruption and coercion of the program actually played into the hands of the Viet Cong and helped in their recruiting efforts. When a peasant had been torn from his home and subjected to coercive prices for farm supplies from government suppliers, he had less to lose by opposing the regime in

Saigon and new motives for siding with the communist opposition. Later it was discovered that Colonel Pham Dgoc Thao, the man the Saigon regime put in charge of strategic hamlets, was a communist who carried out the plans in a brutal way with the purpose of forcing a wedge between peasants and Saigon.[23]

By the time of McNamara's information-gathering trip to Vietnam after the Diem and Kennedy assassinations in late 1963, he was only able to give very gloomy reports to the new President, Lyndon Johnson.[24] The political situation in Saigon had become chaotic. The strategic hamlets were an illusion. A change of strategy was necessary. General LeMay, now as Air Force Chief of Staff, was true to his established role as an advocate for strategic bombing and advised massive destruction in the North. The joint chiefs of staff were ready to direct the war themselves rather than play a supporting role to the Vietnamese army. They advocated "Americanizing" the war by sending in tens of thousands, then hundreds of thousands of troops. By 1965 Johnson had done all these things. But could the success of any of this be measured? Robert McNamara with his background in statistics from World War II, and his businessman's sense, offered a consistent answer to this difficult question. Management techniques could supply answers to questions of progress in the war while leaving basic questions about the sustainability of the South Vietnamese regime unanswered. A war could be won even when taking visible territory could not be a measure of success and where the political aim of the war was in doubt.

General William Westmoreland, who in his early days in Military Assistance Command, in mid-1964, had advised withdrawal from Vietnam if the South Vietnamese could not undertake the fighting themselves, soon had a growing army at his disposal in search of a winning tactic and strategy. The tactic became Search and Destroy. The words referred to locating Viet Cong and North Vietnamese soldiers and destroying them. This could only achieve strategic importance when connected to the idea that there was a finite number of communists in South Vietnam and that one could destroy them all. The iconic image of GIs or Marines moving across a grassy forest clearing or through the jungle or across rice paddies, from their helicopter drop-off spot to the location where another helicopter would come to col-

23 Karnow, *Vietnam*, 273–74.

24 Ibid., 341–42; McNamara, *In Retrospect*, 105.

lect them, was the image of this mopping-up exercise. The body counts of destroyed communists were the product. The body counts and desertions of communists matched to the casualty rates of the GIs and Marines were the measure of efficiency which would eventually lead to victory. The body counts and desertions subtracted from the North Vietnamese Order of Battle, an estimate of communist forces in the South, would be a measure of how close the United States was to victory.

This Vietnam logic was criticized at the time and afterwards. If American officers received the approbation of their superiors for greater destruction, they inevitably would become creative in their counting. Old people and children might count as enemies killed rather than as collateral damage. Wrecking bicycles could become destruction of important equipment. The very efficiency of helicopter deployments and redeployments meant that American soldiers in Vietnam saw more combat time than soldiers in any other American war, contributing to the stresses, psychological and otherwise, that they suffered. Increased combat time suggests the possibility that, soldier for soldier, Americans caused more death and damage in the Vietnam War than in other wars even while their officers were emphasizing the statistics of that destruction for their own promotion. Combat stress could be mitigated by time limits on service, which meant that units were always evolving as men moved in and then out when they fulfilled their time obligation. Unit instability added another level of stress just as numbering the days until departure added another count to the memory the war. The newcomer killed before his unit could learn his name, and the friend killed within days of his scheduled departure from Vietnam became standard motifs in Vietnam memoirs. In a compounding of the body count logic, emphasis on killing and destruction could lead to the infamous phrase about a village that "in order to be saved, it had to be destroyed." And that of course led to the mentality that produced the My Lai Massacre and other similar massacres. These atrocities have left a well-documented trail in the annals of US Army investigations into war crimes, as carefully compiled by investigative reporter Deborah Nelson in *The War Behind Me*.[25]

25 Nelson, *War Behind Me*, especially chapter 3, "A My Lai a Month," 73–106, and chapter 4, "Body Count," 107–38. Appendix A, 209–24, includes 77 "Case Summaries of U.S. War-Crime Investigations Compiled by Army Staff," and 180 "Cases Closed by Army Investigators as Unsubstantiated, Unfounded, or closed "Due to Insufficient Evidence." Of the 77 "Case Summaries of U.S. War-

In his memoir, Robert McNamara referred to "Westy's attrition strategy" and distanced himself from it by listing a host of ills suffered by the South Vietnamese as a consequence of that strategy:

> It often proved difficult to distinguish combatants from noncombatants. Between 1965 and 1967, U.S. and South Vietnamese air forces dropped over a million tons of bombs on the South, more than twice the tonnage dropped on the North. Fighting produced more and more civilian casualties and squalid refugee camps. The increasing destruction and misery brought on the country we were supposed to be helping troubled me greatly . . . And it hurt any effort at building popular support for the Saigon government, which was crucial to defeating the Vietcong.[26]

But what he did not emphasize was his own contribution to this strategy, though perhaps he considered that to be understood background to anything he might write. According to General Robert G. Gard, Jr., a military assistant to McNamara from 1966 to 1968, when the Secretary of Defence was, in Nelson's words, "grasping for a more reliable system of measuring enemy losses than the inflated estimates pouring into his office from military leaders in Vietnam" who also wished to enhance their reputation for efficiency, he said, "If these reports were accurate we would have killed the North Vietnamese army twice. . . . I don't think we should be reporting enemy killed unless we have concrete evidence."[27] That, according to Gard, was how, "we got into the body counting business."[28] Search and Destroy became search and destroy and count and sometimes provide or invent proof of the count. The principle of eliminating a limited number of communists in South Vietnam had become a formalized policy.

Controversy over counting was inevitable. McNamara concentrated on improving the validity of the numbers of the killed, but the ability of the Viet Cong and the North Vietnamese to recruit was strangely underestimated. This was a hobbyhorse of Sam Adams, a CIA analyst who reported a growing rather than a diminishing strength among the communists. His as-

---

Crime Investigations," 36 ended in General Courts Martial and of those, 19 ended in convictions of 29 individuals. The period covered is 1966–1971, the period of highest concentration of U.S. military presence in Vietnam.

26 McNamara, *In Retrospect*, 243.

27 Nelson, *War Behind Me*, 165.

28 Ibid.

sertions on television in 1982, along with those by reporters from CBS who he had assisted, resulted in one of the great post-Vietnam-era controversies. They accused General Westmoreland of deliberately misleading President Johnson into believing that by 1967 the communist threat was on its last legs, when in fact the North Vietnamese and the Viet Cong were planning the Têt Offensive. In a meeting with Johnson in July of 1967, after a trip to Vietnam and after briefings with Westmoreland, McNamara himself seemed to have succumbed to the general's reading of the numbers, or maybe they were McNamara's own. Either way, the Secretary of Defense reported that sticking to the strategy they were following would win.[29] The numbers involved, described by Sam Adams in his posthumously published book, were achieved by counting neither certain parts of the Viet Cong militia nor their political arm, nor, at later meetings, "new" formations in the communist Order of Battle. Military intelligence was so intent on showing progress using the tools they had available—namely, body counts—that they subtracted bodies from the units they knew and refused to imagine new units.[30]

General Westmoreland sued CBS and Sam Adams for $120 million in a libel suit that was settled out of court in 1985 with both sides claiming victory. In his memoir, Robert McNamara deplored both the suit and the aggression against the honor and integrity of the soldier William Westmoreland, while also saying that Westmoreland exaggerated the progress made against the "enemy" while he minimized the number of enemy forces. That had not mattered, argued McNamara, perhaps disingenuously, because he, the President, and everyone else had other sources upon which to draw.[31] In any case, the enemy was "a highly technical, ambiguous, and even elusive issue." But of course the strategy in this war depended on numbers in order to measure progress, and, as McNamara pointed out, measuring progress was what an executive of a motor company or of a war was supposed to do.[32] The guilt of this or that cabinet official is not so important here as the extreme forms that counting communists took. These in-

29 Tucker, *Encyclopedia*, 414; McNamara, *In Retrospect*, 283. McNamara's memoir makes the contingency that the South Vietnamese government would have to perform well too.

30 Adams, *War of Numbers*, 115–218.

31 McNamara, *In Retrospect*, 239–40.

32 Ibid., 238.

cluded extreme measures to control the environment in which the counting took place. Later in the autumn of 1967, McNamara offered his resignation to Johnson. He left the Department of Defense at the end of February, 1968, after the Têt Offensive had proved just how wrong the numbers were, and just how little control he had over the Vietnamese environment.

Protecting the population became more important to American strategy after Têt, when General Creighton Abrams took over command from Westmoreland. By then, however, the presidential campaigns in the United States were debating Vietnam in terms of American withdrawal. Withdrawal would be the political goal behind any future Vietnam policy regardless of what Abrams or anyone else might do in the next five years. "Progress" in the war under these circumstances was difficult to measure or even define. Communists in South Vietnam remained under counted. And atrocities requiring court martial investigations continued. At the time of the Easter Offensive of 1971, when the North Vietnamese staged a second Têt, Sam Adams made the same criticism of American CIA and Army intelligence reporting he had made three years earlier.[33] The statistics on atrocities such as My Lai compiled in War Department documents do not demonstrate a departure from the emphasis on producing vast numbers of dead Vietnamese for the period up to 1971.[34]

BUILDING THE VIETNAM VETERANS MEMORIAL

The delay between American withdrawal from Vietnam in 1973, the defeat of the South Vietnamese Republic in 1975, and the creation of the Vietnam Veterans Memorial Foundation by veteran Jan Scruggs in 1979 does not seem long when compared to the duration of the war, or the time taken over withdrawal after Johnson's resignation to 1973. The time lapses between other wars and the memorials built for them on the Mall are much longer. But delay is a standard element of the Vietnam memorial narrative. Secretary of Defense Caspar Weinberger acknowledged the delay on the day of the first dedication, Veterans Day, November 11, 1982, when he admitted, "We have finally come to appreciate your sacrifice." Ronald Reagan em-

33 Adams, *War of Numbers*, 203–206.
34 Nelson, *War Behind Me*, Appendix A, 209–24.

phasized the delay at the same ceremony. In a few words, Reagan managed to claim the building of the wall as a justification of his own brand of anti-communism and for his own interpretation of the war while he ignored the non-political ambition of the monument. Everyone is now "beginning to appreciate that they were fighting for a just cause."[35] he said wiping out years of controversy.

A major reinvention of American national war memorials took place between the end of the Vietnam War and the dedication of the Vietnam Veterans Memorial. The World War I model followed for most of a century had become obsolete. First, this new memorial would be inside the United States, not far away on the field of some battle where it inevitably became an extension of American prestige and power. Second, there would be no bodies present and yet it should be a place where visitors could mourn their loss. Third, it would be on the Mall where the Washington, Lincoln, Jefferson, and Grant memorials dominated. Three of the four presidents had careers connected with important wars, but only Grant's monument emphasized war over all else. Until the Vietnam Veterans Memorial, the Mall had not been *about war*. When the Vietnam Veterans Memorial was erected, that changed.

Jan Scruggs, a wounded Vietnam infantryman who began the Vietnam Veterans Memorial Fund that collected money for a monument, had been inspired by Michael Cimino's movie *The Deer Hunter* (1978) that emphasized the personal, physical, and psychological damage wrought by the war, and the difficulties of honoring what soldiers sacrificed and of conveying the details of that sacrifice back in the United States. The competition for the design of the Vietnam Veterans Memorial was announced in October of 1980. President Jimmy Carter had signed the act allotting land on the Mall to the project in July of that year. The requirements were four: that the structure be reflective and contemplative in character; that it harmonize with its surroundings; that it contain the names of those who had died in the conflict or who were still missing; and that it make no political statement about the war. None of these requirements would necessarily disqualify any of the memorial elements evident in American military cemeteries, with the

35 Quoted in Wagner-Pacifici and Schwartz, "Vietnam Veterans Memorial," 378. Originally in the *Washington Post*, November 14, 1982, sec. A, p. 1, 18, 20, and *New York Times*, November 11, 1982, sec. A, p. 1.

possible exception of the explanatory military maps which would have been difficult to conceive for the Vietnam War. But the dignified individual grave markers, the classic seeming architecture, the white stone eagles, and the flags spoke of an American commitment to an international order. Repeating that architectural vocabulary on the Mall would have been profoundly political.

The memorial wall was built according to the winning design of Yale architecture student Maya Ying Lin. She included the names of the dead, as she had been instructed to do, and her minimalist design harmonizes well with the landscaping of the Mall but the traditional elements of war memorials were missing. The design called for black granite, not white marble. There was to be no flag, no statue, no chapel, no visitor center, no map—and no bodies. Maya Ying Lin's design included only the names of the dead and the missing on two wedges of black polished wall emerging from and then swallowed back into the earth.

The innovative design drew criticism. Early supporters, including H. Ross Perot who had financed the competition and based his political legitimacy partly on the support of veteran causes, withdrew aid. James Watt, President Reagan's Secretary of the Interior, refused a building permit. The winning design had been chosen during the spring of 1981. By July 1982 the Vietnam Veterans Memorial Fund had decided that the leading sculptural entry in the competition by respected realist military sculptor Frederick Hart should be added to the memorial and by October 13, 1982, the U.S. Commission of Fine Arts had approved the addition of a flagpole for what had become a memorial group. The three elements were dedicated together on November 11, 1984. On one side, people said that the integrity and elegance of the wall had been damaged by the addition of the "Three Service Men," or "Three Fighting Men," and the flag (fig. 2). There were others who pointed out that the three soldiers who were sculpted as burdened by their equipment, as if they were emerging from a forest and combat, looked confused and a little sad, like the visitors reflected in the wall, and that the modernist abstract design of the wall was strong enough to absorb this figurative addition. In any case, the VVMF had managed to add elements to the Vietnam memorial that made it more like other American war memorials while also building something strikingly different that announced a different memorial purpose from that of the World War I and II memorials that had become the norm.

Figure 2: The "Three Soldiers" sculpture by Frederick Hart seen from behind with the Vietnam Veterans Memorial Wall designed by Maya Ying Lin beyond

The addition of the sculpture, with all its specific military and human detail from the Vietnam period, resolved the controversy caused by the abstract wall. Photograph courtesy of Professor Michael O'Malley of George Mason University, October 2012.

By any measure, the memorial has been a success. It attracts large numbers of people. It invites contemplation and elicits strong emotions. The addition of "The Three Soldiers" statue can be seen as exemplary of the Culture Wars of the 1980s and 1990s. Another statue, the Vietnam Women's Memorial to American women who had served in Vietnam was added in 1993. In 2004 a memorial plaque was also added with the names of soldiers who had died some time after the war but of wartime injuries that fell outside of Department of Defense guidelines for the status of war dead. The result is a complex memorial informed by the all-inclusive representational spirit of the notion of the "politically correct," forced onto an open-ended symbolic memorial plan that continues to draw the attention of and solicit emotional responses from many Americans.

In a sense, the Vietnam Veterans Memorial is an ongoing exercise rather than a monument to an event. Attaching memory and meaning to exact numbers and exact names placed in exact categories in an attempt to adhere to a chronological order has concentrated attention on accuracy rather than any message, even one of mourning. Names are required to have their status changed if a soldier who was MIA (missing in action) becomes a KIA (killed in action) or KIA/BNR (killed in action body not recovered). The addition of the memorial plaque with the names of dead soldiers who fall outside Department of Defense categories is a symptom of the changing status accorded to claims made on behalf of specific dead soldiers, not acts of national mourning. Removing the Unknown Soldier for the Vietnam War from Arlington National Cemetery, identifying him through DNA testing and returning him to his family, is another symptom of change that affects a national message.[36] The unknown soldiers symbolized the loss of identity into service for the state. The Vietnam Veterans Memorial, with its precisely carved names of all the American military dead of that war, refuses to make the transformation from individual loss to national purpose. Its specifically apolitical commission requirements demanded that this be the case and Maya Ying Lin's pristine design ensured an apolitical message—a message that purports to acknowledge the exact cost of war in American dead and does not obscure that cost behind the national purpose.

In the absence of a political message, the message of sorrow for the suffering of specific soldiers has ballooned to fill the emotional space once filled by patriotism. A considerable literature has amassed on the subject of the MIAs of Vietnam, in which the search for the dead in Laos, Cambodia and Vietnam, decades after the end of the war, continues as a kind of shadow story to the Vietnam Veterans Memorial on the National Mall. Since the imponderables of sorrow for the suffering of vanished soldiers cannot be transformed into a symbol of the national purpose, their location, wounds, and missing parts have to be made available in as much detail as possible to fill a memorial need. Earl Swift's book of 2003, *Where They Lay*, describes the expenditure, ongoing at the time of publication, of $100 million a year by the United States Army Central Identification Laboratory to recover in-

36 Sheehan, in "Missing Plane," explains the process by which the Unknown Soldier for Vietnam was first chosen, his identity obscured, and then, through advances in forensic science, inevitably revealed.

formation about 60 unrecovered bodies in Cambodia, some 1,400 in Vietnam and 400 in Laos. He asks rhetorically why this is done for these soldiers when there were 78,000 missing in World War II and 8,000 in Korea. His answer, albeit insufficient, is that Vietnam "proved to be a slow-healing wound . . . All yearned for answers."[37] A better answer would have been that in all wars the families of dead soldiers have desired news of their loved ones' death, but that the special circumstances of Vietnam—the loss of the war, the lack of access to the ground where the dead lay, the lack of a national consensus about the political meaning of the war, coupled with forensic advances that make it possible to identify a body when very little of that body is preserved, and the obsessive counting of bodies and calculation of resources as the only means of determining progress towards victory—have turned this emotional personal need into an expression of national culture.[38]

People critical of the United States' role in a foreign civil war where their country had no viable government to support, and critical of the way the United States undertook to use sheer force and body counts when other measures of success failed, greeted Maya Ying Lin's design with enthusiasm as a fitting memorial to American loss without attempting to turn that loss into a sign of national purpose. But as the memorial projects have succeeded each other on the National Mall, that point of view may seem naïve. Counting dead bodies, and bodies that are unaccounted for, can be a way of continuing the hostilities of the war. Thomas Hawley, in *The Remains of War* (2005), tried to explain the American obsession with soldiers missing in action in Vietnam. He hoped that a critique of this kind of numerical memory might call into question the choice of violence as a policy and enumerating the dead as a memorial practice.[39] He mentioned the huge disproportion in the numbers between Americans missing—varying but by no

37 Swift, *Where They Lay*, 6–7.

38 For the importance of specific news of the death of a soldier, see Meigs, *Optimism at Armageddon*, 143–87. For another example of the positive, journalistic, celebratory version of the MIA searches, see Robinson and Dunn, *Search for Canasta 404*. See also Stern, *Imprisoned or Missing*. For a critical view of the MIA controversy and the ways in which administrations, especially Nixon's, manipulated the possibility of prisoners held without record by communists in Vietnam to prolong negotiations and avoid ending the war before 1973, see Franklin, *M.I.A.*; Hawley, *Remains of War*.

39 Hawley, *Remains of War*, 36–7.

count reaching beyond 2,000—and the estimated 300,000 Vietnamese missing from the same war. But Hawley did not specifically make the connection between body counts during the war and the obsession with the numbers of MIAs after. The Vietnamese dead had been counted and recounted and overcounted as a matter of measuring the war's progress to answer McNamara's question: could the effort be sustained until every communist was dead. To answer that question in a satisfactory way during the war, American suffering had to be undercounted or minimized. American mourning practice and building memorials with names but no political explanation has turned this situation around. Jerry and Sandra Strait in a book of 1988 were able to locate and describe over 300 Vietnam memorials around the United States. Most featured the names of dead soldiers and little in the way of political statement. Since that book, some elaborate urban memorials—ones that presumably took more time and political will to build—have been dedicated, all attempting to name and categorize those who served and suffered as if by exact categorization.[40]

The authorization of the Korean War Veterans Memorial in 1986, the design competition in 1989, the ground breaking in 1992 and dedication in 1995, 42 years after the armistice that ended the war, suggests that the pain and ambiguities of the Korean war could not be expressed until the Vietnam Veterans Memorial allowed for the expression memory that is neither resolute nor triumphant (fig. 3). The memorial includes nineteen poncho-clad and heavily burdened American military men moving awkwardly over a rough terrain of granite slabs and juniper bushes. The sculptures, bigger than life size and in stainless steel, were designed by Frank Gaylord. The memorial is bounded on one side by a black granite wall with photographs sand-basted into its otherwise mirror-smooth surface. This wall of photographs, designed by Louis Nelson, showcases wartime personalities, soldiers, equipment of the times, the reflected image of anyone visiting and the reflected images of the 19 sculptures, thus doubling their number to 38. The reference to the Vietnam Memorial must have been among the intentions of the designers—Cooper-Lecky Architects. The mourning black of the granite, the faces and identities of visitors' reflections, mixed with the identities and faces of people from the war, were similarly present already on the Mall in the form of the Vietnam Veterans Memorial. The strong if

40 Strait and Strait, *Vietnam War Memorials.*

Figure 3: The Korean War Veterans Memorial

The photograph shows statues of American service men in their ponchos and their reflections in the black granite wall. Photograph courtesy of Professor Michael O'Malley of George Mason University, October 2012.

bewildered figures with no immediately understandable goal are a reminder of the "Three Soldiers" of the Vietnam Veterans Memorial, strong but bewildered too.

A major difference from the Vietnam memorial that is designed into the Korean War Veterans Memorial is an obscure reference to the final goal of the war. The number 38, the number of sculptures increased by the number of their reflections, refers to the 38th degree of latitude which divides North and South Korea: the border between the two sections of Korea when the war started that formed the border when the war ended. The purpose of the Korean War for Americans and U.N. forces at the beginning and at its conclusion, if not always during its aggressive middle period, was to reestablish the 38th parallel as the boundary between communist North Korea and South Korea. The Korean War Veteran Memorial, built in the back-

Figure 4: National World War II Memorial

The inside of one of the triumphal arches. The Eagles seem restrained from their international purposes. Outside, several pillars representing individual states can be seen. Photograph courtesy of Professor Michael O'Malley of George Mason University, October 2012.

ward questioning shadow of Vietnam, can only draw attention to that obscure triumph in this obscure way.

The latest, and in some ways the strangest war memorial built in the Mall in Washington is the National World War II Monument (fig. 4). It is strange because, dedicated in 2004, it is the latest in the backwards chronology of wars represented on the Mall. It is also strange because it exists at all on the Mall when the great memorials to World War II include the idea of American commitment abroad. Those war memorials have been regularly used by American military men and politicians as staging areas for diplomacy and foreign policy. Every recent president has stood at Omaha Beach amid the American war dead to renew and modify American foreign commitments. This latest monument in so prominent a place on the National Mall, however, turns inward, away from foreign engagements. Like the Vietnam Veterans Memorial or the Korean War Veterans Memorial, it counts the dead, even when it is made of light colored granite instead of funereal black, and even when it must do the counting 100 at a time to account for the 404,800 American dead in the war. It uses 4,048 large gold stars reminiscent of the gold stars American families were encouraged to display in their windows during the war when a family member had been killed. In half a century, this counting has moved from the realm of personal choice in a dead soldier's home to the discrete, if public, contemplative landscaping at the sides of the Mall where the Vietnam and Korean War Memorials were built; to the central axis of the Mall where it must balance the dignified Lincoln Memorial at the other end of the Reflecting Pool and the Washington Monument on a little rise behind it. Counting the war dead has changed from being an unfortunate necessity of war with an unfortunately, even catastrophically, important position in the Vietnam War when no other means of measuring progress presented itself, to the central axis of American history that includes George Washington, the nation's founder, and Abraham Lincoln, its defender. The Vietnam model of memory had this unexpected backwards effect on American history.

The National World War II Memorial consists of a large fountain surrounded by 56 menhir-like pillars decorated with metal funeral wreaths, whose rhythm is punctuated by two triumphal arches in a monumental, if unornamented, style. Each of the pillars is named for one of the 48 states in the union at the time of World War II along with eight others standing for possessions including the giant Alaska and the smaller Samoa. The two triumphal arches were named Atlantic and Pacific to indicate the European and Pacific theaters of the war. The arches contain dynamic, tense, bronze Eagles on high perches, holding funeral wreaths, sculpted by Raymond Kaskey. Crowded under these arches, they seem to be caught beating their wings in large masonry birdcages.

The monument has transformed the pedagogical explanations of the World Wars I and II memorial model into the names of oceans on the arches and 24 bas relief panels depicting scenes from an imagined soldier's journey from induction through training, battle, burying the dead and homecoming. Architect Raymond Kaskey has transformed that pedagogy from a lesson in military and political history into the imagined narrative of the service of an individual for the country. The most political of the bronzes shows American and Russian soldiers shaking hands when the armies of the eastern front met the armies of the western front in Europe. If there is a political message, it is either heavily ironic sort unannounced by the rest of the monument, or a cynical act of forgetting the Cold War, for which monuments like the one at Omaha Beach were important symbols of American involvement for fifty years.

The monument was heavily criticized. The Supreme Court refused to hear a case against it and Congress passed legislation outlawing legal challenges to its design to allow its construction.[41] The critics objected to a number of design elements. First, the emphasis on individual states and territories of the country, when those states and territories were certainly subordinate to the purposes of the United States during the war, seemed misplaced at best. At worst, that emphasis seemed like a projection of the conservative Republican agenda from Ronald Reagan through the Newt Gingrich period, when the monument was proposed and the George W. Bush administration when it was dedicated, to revive states' rights and dismantle the New Deal. Second, the heavy classicism of the design by an Austrian-born American architect Friedrich St. Florian, suggesting Roman and Greek models but without specific reference to classical orders was called Nazi. The most serious critics have defended this look, pointing out that much of Washington shares a 1930s New Deal style with what remains of 1930s Rome or Berlin. It also has the look of the World War I and II monuments built around the world in the 1920s and 1940s.[42]

More important than either of those criticisms is the Vietnamization of World War II in a monument that twists the memory of loss into the conservative interpretation Ronald Reagan promulgated in his dedication

41 Michael Janofsky, "An Academic Touches the Masses with War Memorial," *New York Times*, May 26, 2004, http://www.nytimes.com/2004/05/26/arts /an-academic-touches-the-masses-with-war-emorial.html?pagewanted=2&src=pm.

42 Herbert Muschamp, "An Appraisal; New War Memorial Is Shrine to Sentiment," *New York Times*, June 7, 2001, http://www.nytimes.com/2001/06/07 /arts/an-appraisal-new-war-memorial-is-shrine-to-sentiment.html?src=pm.

speech of the Vietnam Veterans Memorial, rather than permitting the wider interpretations of loss that the minimalist design permitted. Everyone is now "beginning to appreciate that they were fighting for a just cause," Reagan said of American dead in Vietnam. Did he mean that death in the armed services of the United States, under any circumstances, even in the benighted, mismanaged, strategically flawed Vietnam War, was death in a just cause? Can this monument to World War II, a war with a clear national and international purpose for Americans, function without reference to that international purpose while illustrating a message about personal service? "Can't we take the war for granted anymore? Do we need reminding about what it means?" Friedrich St. Florian asked during an interview in 2001 after Congress had put a stop to controversy over his design. Florian asserted that:

> The most important obligation for the memorial is to remind future generations of what the world war generation did: namely, to go to war and save the world. So that future generations feel compelled to do likewise. And that's easy to say but very difficult to do.[43]

World War II, according to Florian, was about service with young people in the United States heading out to save the world without being specific about what that meant; remembering them is designed to encourage other Americans to do the same without reflection. Memory, in other words, is to encourage, even to compel future sacrifice. Counting the dead, made grotesque by the strategy and tactics of the Vietnam War, and made infinitely sorrowful by the Vietnam Veterans Memorial, has been made a sufficient reason for American involvement in any war in the future.

BIBLIOGRAPHY

Adams, Sam. *War of Numbers: An Intelligence Memoir.* South Royalton, VT: Steerforth Press, 1994.

43 Thomas Keenan, "The Way We Live Now: Questions for Friedrich St. Florian; The Greatest Veneration," *New York Times*, July 1, 2001, http://www.nytimes.com/2001/07/01/magazine/the-way-we-live-now-questions-for-friedrich-stflorian-the-greatest-veneration.html?ref=friedrichstflorian.

Australian Department of Veteran Affairs. "Korean War." Last updated August, 30, 2012. http://www.dva.gov.au/commems_oawg/OAWG/remembering_war_dead/Pages/korean%20war.aspx.

Becker, Annette. "Les Deux rives de l'Atlantique. Memoire américaine de la Grande Guerre." *Annales de l'Université de Savoie* 18 (January 1995): 16–23.

Cook, John C. "Graves Registration in the Korean Conflict." *Quartermaster Review* 32, no. 5 (1953): 18, 131, 133, 135–44. http://www.qmmuseum.lee.army.mil/korea/gr_korea.htm.

Fahs, Alice, and Joan Waugh, eds. *The Memory of the Civil War in American Culture*. Chapel Hill: University of North Carolina Press, 2004.

Faust, Drew Gilpin. *A Riddle of Death: Mortality and Meaning in the American Civil War*. Gettysburg, PA: Gettysburg College, 1995.

———. *This Republic of Suffering: Death and the American Civil War*. New York: Alfred A. Knopf, 2008.

The Fog of War: Eleven Lessons from the Life of Robert S. McNamara. Directed and produced by Erroll Morris. Sony Pictures Home Entertainment, 2003. DVD, 95 min.

Franklin, H. Bruce. *M.I.A., or, Mythmaking in America*. Brooklyn: Lawrence Hill Books, 1992.

Freedman, Lawrence. *Kennedy's Wars: Berlin, Cuba, Laos, and Vietnam*. New York: Oxford, 2000.

Hawley, Thomas M. *The Remains of War: Bodies, Politics, and the Search for American Soldiers Unaccounted For in Southeast Asia*. Durham, NC: Duke University Press, 2005.

History of the American Graves Registration Service: QMC in Europe. Washington: Library Office of the Quartermaster General, n.d., ca. 1922.

Karnow, Stanley. *Vietnam: A History*. New York: Penguin Books, 1997.

Keene, Judith. "Lost to Public Commemoration: American Veterans of the 'Forgotten' Korean War." *Journal of Social History* 44, no. 4 (Summer 2011): 1095–113.

Kennan, George F. "The Sources of Soviet Conduct." *Foreign Affairs* 25 (July 1947): 566–82.

Leland, Anne, and Mari-Jana "M-J" Oboroceanu. "American War and Military Operations Casualties: Lists and Statistics." Congressional Research Service, Washington, DC, 2010. Site: Congressional Research Service, 7–5700, www.crs.gov RL32492.

Mayo, James M. *War Memorials as Political Landscape: The American Experience and Beyond*. New York: Praeger, 1988.

McNamara, Robert S. *In Retrospect: The Tragedy and Lessons of Vietnam*. New York: Vintage, 1996.

Meigs, Mark. *Optimism at Armageddon: Voices of American Participants in the First World War*. New York: New York University Press, 1997.

Miller, Francis Trevelyan, ed. *The Photographic History of the Civil War in Ten Volumes*. New York: Review of Reviews, 1912.

Nelson, Deborah. *The War Behind Me: Vietnam Veterans Confront the Truth About U.S. War Crimes*. New York: Basic Books, 2008.

Nguyen, Lien-Hang T. *Hanoi's War: An International History of the War for Peace in Vietnam*. Chapel Hill: University of North Carolina Press, 2012.

Piehler, G. Kurt. "The War Dead and the Gold Star: American Commemoration of the First World War." In *Commemorations: The Politics of National Identity*, edited by John R. Gillis, 168–85. Princeton, NJ: Princeton University Press, 1994.

Prados, John. "Wise Guys, Rough Business: Iraq and the Tonkin Gulf." In *Iraq and the Lessons of Vietnam; or, How Not to Learn from the Past*, edited by Lloyd C. Gardner and Marilyn B. Young, 106–23. New York: New Press, 2007.

Robinson, Melissa B., and Maureen Dunn. *The Search for Canasta 404: Love, Loss, and the POW/MIA Movement*. Boston: Northeastern University Press, 2006.

Sheehan, Susan. "A Missing Plane, Identification." *New Yorker* May 19, 1986: 76–81.

Stern, Lewis M. *Imprisoned or Missing in Vietnam: Policies of the Vietnamese Government Concerning Captured and Unaccounted for United States Soldiers, 1969–1994*. Jefferson, NC: McFarland, 1995.

Strait, Jerry L., and Sandra Strait. *Vietnam War Memorials: An Illustrated Reference to Veterans Tributes Throughout the United States*. Jefferson, NC: McFarland, 1988.

Swift, Earl. *Where They Lay: Searching for America's Lost Soldiers*. Boston: Houghton Mifflin, 2003.

Tucker, Spencer C., ed. *Encyclopedia of the Vietnam War: A Political, Social, and Military History.* Santa Barbara, CA: ABC-CLIO, 1998.

Wagner-Pacifici, Robin, and Barry Schwartz. "The Vietnam Veterans Memorial: Commemorating a Difficult Past." *American Journal of Sociology* 97, no. 2 (September 1991): 376–420.

"We Shall Overcome"

The Impact of the African American Freedom Struggle on Race Relations and Social Protest in Germany after World War II

BRITTA WALDSCHMIDT-NELSON

When Barack Obama gave a speech in Berlin during his 2008 presidential campaign, more than 200,000 Germans enthusiastically applauded him, and millions more watched on TV. When he won the election that made him the first African American President of the United States, there were celebratory parties all over the Federal Republic of Germany (FRG). Moreover, the level of Obama's popularity since he took office has been consistently higher among Germans than among Americans.[1] The roots of this remarkable phenomenon can be traced back to the civil rights movement of the 1950s and 1960s, which was crucial not only for political rise of Barack Obama in the United States, but also to changes in race relations and understandings of social justice in Germany. In his 2006 political memoir *The Audacity of Hope,* Obama writes, "I've always felt a curious relationship to the sixties. In a sense I'm a pure product of that era."[2] He stresses that his mother viewed the civil rights movement as central to what was good about the 1960s. She deeply admired Martin Luther King, Jr., and encouraged her son to follow King's lead in standing up for social justice, equality, and tol-

1 See, for example, Marschall, *Obama*, and Remnick and Griese, *Obama.*
2 Obama, *Audacity of Hope*, 29.

erance.[3] It was no coincidence that Obama, who describes his own success as deriving directly from the accomplishments of the civil rights movement, timed his acceptance speech for the Democratic Party's nomination exactly on the forty-fifth anniversary of King's "I Have a Dream" speech. Obama and King became entwined in popular consciousness, and many Americans—and people all over the world—saw Obama's election as the fulfillment of King's Dream.

While this essay cannot discuss the accuracy of such a claim[4], it will focus on an interesting international dimension of the civil rights movement that has received comparatively little scholarly and public attention. German high school books, for example, often provide detailed descriptions of the well-known milestones of the movement (such as the Montgomery Bus Boycott and the March on Washington) [5], but are silent on this movement's relevance for German postwar society.[6] This essay seeks to fill this lacuna by focusing on the interconnectedness of the black freedom struggle in America with race relations and the struggle for social justice in Germany during "the long 1960s," that is, from the aftermath of World War II until the early 1970s.

GERMANY AND BLACK PEOPLE BEFORE WORLD WAR II

To understand the remarkable change in black and white race relations in Germany during the postwar era, it is essential to outline the history of the relationship and attitudes that Germans had toward people of African descent. Up to the 1920s, most of the contact between Germans and black people was a byproduct of Germany's missionary and colonial activities in

3 Ibid.

4 For a discussion of this topic, see, for example, King, *Obama and Race*; Iffill, *Breakthrough*; Touré, *Post-Blackness*.

5 The well-known German schoolbook publishers Klett, Schöningh, and Cornelsen offer materials for high school students' English lessons that include the history of the civil rights movement and racial problems in the United States today. Klett even offers a whole book on Rosa Parks and the Montgomery Bus Boycott; see http://www.klett.de/produkt/isbn/3-12-580606-2.

6 The number of historians who focus on this topic still remains rather limited. Most noteworthy are Belinda Davis, Maria Höhn, and Martin Klimke.

Africa.[7] Germany was never a colonial power on the scale of Great Britain, France, or Spain, but in 1884 the German empire acquired (by purchase and protective treaties) four regions in Southwest and East Africa as colonies (today's Tanzania, Namibia, Togo, and Cameroon) and kept them until World War I. During this period, German colonial officers, who ruled over the territories supposedly with the "noble goal" of civilizing and Christianizing their African subjects, often ruthlessly exploited their labor and land resources.[8] Following the British lead, Germans quickly picked up on negative prejudices against black Africans and then actively contributed to the dominant racial discourse of the time that defined white Europeans—and in this case, Germans in particular—as a civilized "people of culture" (*Kulturvolk*) while stigmatizing black Africans as primitive "people of nature" (*Naturvolk*).[9] Beyond a belief in the general cultural superiority of the white "master race" (*Herrenvolk*), more specific negative racial stereotypes also became increasingly popular within Germany during that time. Blacks were supposedly primitive, ugly, lazy, unreliable, unintelligent, potentially violent, and, on top of that, morally depraved. Young black females were seen as seductive temptresses and black males were suspected of constantly lusting after white women.[10] Even though some whites—most notably a number of missionaries in Africa—did not fully share these stereotypes,

7 There were some very well respected blacks individuals living in Germany during earlier centuries, for example Anton Wilhelm Amo, the first African to obtain a doctoral degree in Germany (at the university of Halle in 1729), who went on to became a professor of philosophy in Germany and published several scholarly works in Latin. In the nineteenth century, a number of African Americans visited Germany as well. W. E. B. DuBois, for example, studied at Berlin's Humboldt University in 1893–94. But the number of these black people was too small to attract broader public attention.

8 See Perraudin and Zimmerer, *German Colonialism*; Friedrichsmeyer and Zantop, *Imperialist Imagination*; and Förster et al., *Bismarck, Europe and Africa.*

9 For the construction of Africa as the "Dark Continent," and the establishment of anti-black racial stereotypes in the colonial discourse, see, for example, Brantlinger, *Rule of Darkness*; Keim, *Mistaking Africa*; Pallua, *Eurocentrism.* For a postcolonial critique of the above-mentioned phenomenon, see, for example, Bhabha, *Location of Culture*; Said, *Orientalism;* and Dirks, *Colonialism and Culture.*

10 Ibid.; Schubert, *Der Schwarze Fremde*; Lorbeer and Wild, *Menschenfresser.* For information on how these negative stereotypes were used to justify slavery in the United States, see Frederickson, *Black Image in the White Mind*; Faust, *Ideology of Slavery*; Finkelman, *Defending Slavery*; and Waldschmidt-Nelson, "Are All Men Created Equal?"

they could not prevent their consequence. As a result of most Germans' complete lack of respect for the culture and humanity of black people, many Africans were not treated much better than slaves during the colonial period. Besides everyday beatings and other physical abuse, attempts to resist the colonial rulers were punished mercilessly. Among the most infamous crimes committed by Germans during that time was the killing of over three quarters of the rebellious Herero tribe in 1904—a planned military extermination campaign that many scholars refer to as the first genocide of the twentieth century.[11]

World War I effectively ended Germany's colonial rule and, in accordance with the Treaty of Versailles, most of its former African territory was distributed among Britain, France, and Belgium in 1919. But the loss of these colonies did not cause a decline in most Germans' belief in white superiority. On the contrary, the pseudoscience of eugenics became increasingly popular in the early twentieth century. Indeed, the fear of miscegenation grew into an obsession, especially after a number of children fathered by black French colonial troops occupying the Rhineland were born to German mothers. These children were referred to negatively as the Rhineland Bastards, and the interracial relationships that they sprang from were publicly condemned as shameful acts of "racial treason" (*Rassenschande*). German nationalists also regarded the offspring of such unions as a dangerous threat to German "racial purity." During the Nazi era, these Afro-Germans suffered constant harassment and many were sterilized against their will.[12]

But not all black people encountered hostile attitudes in Germany. During the 1920s, jazz played by African American musicians started to become very popular in Germany and other European countries. A number of black American artists, such as Josephine Baker, Louis Armstrong, Duke Ellington, and Tiger Ray, achieved remarkable fame and admiration. Despite hostility from conservative and nationalist circles who despised "Negro culture" and opposed anything they saw as contributing to the supposed Americanization of Germany (fig. 1), there was a sizable part of the

---

11 See Sarkin, *Genocide of the Herero*, and Lemarchand, *Forgotten Genocides*.

12 See Adams, *Wellborn Science*; Ehrenreich, *Nazi Ancestral Proof*; and Campt, *Other Germans*.

Figure 1: Nazi propaganda against black musicians

"Entartete Musik" ("Degenerate Music"). Nazi propaganda on the front page of a brochure published by the Weimar National Theater in 1938. Courtesy of Bildarchiv Preussischer Kulturbesitz, Berlin.

German population, especially younger people, who loved this music. Many of them also became interested in other forms of black art, and some developed close friendships with African American artists who were living and performing in Germany.[13] To counter this popularity and as part of their general campaign to instill hatred against Jews, blacks, and other sup-

13 See Kater, *Different Drummers*, and Lotz, *Black People.*

posedly inferior racial and ethnic groups, the Nazis publicly discredited and harassed black artists. After gaining control in 1933, they used their power to drive these "undesirables" out of the country. One way to achieve this goal was to propagate their belief in the fundamental racial inferiority of all blacks, declaring any friendship with people of African descent a form of moral treason for Germans. Then there were the Nuremberg Laws of 1935, which deprived Jewish and nonwhite Germans of most of their citizenship rights, established legal discrimination, and prohibited any form of interracial marriage. After almost a decade of racist policies and intense propaganda, the attitude of most Germans towards people of African descent had reached a low point by the mid-1940s, when black US soldiers fought against Germans and helped to defeat the Third Reich.[14]

The Significance of World War II for the Civil Rights Movement and German Attitudes on Race

World War II was doubtlessly one of the most important factors in the fundamental transformation of race relations in both the United States and Germany. Over one million African American soldiers served in Europe between 1941 and 1945. For many of them, especially those from the US South, it was their first time in an environment without racial segregation and where white people, including women, treated them with respect.[15] These black GIs returned to the United States with a much heightened sense of self-esteem, and many joined the civil rights movement. The war also exposed the hypocrisy of a democratic American government that fought a war against Nazi Germany and denounced Hitler's racism, while condoning

14 During the Nazi era many black artists were arrested and beaten up, and at least one was murdered. (The dancer Hilarius Gilges, who had married a white German woman, was brutally killed by the Gestapo in 1933). Black people who lived in countries occupied by Germany were often put into internment camps. See Friedman, *The Other Victims*; Lusane, *The Historical Experiences of Afro-Germans*; and Pützstück, "AfrikanerInnen in Deutschland."

15 Lieutenant Colin Powell, the first black US Secretary of State, said about his time as a military officer in the FRG: "For black GIs, especially those of the South, Germany was a breath of freedom." Powell, *American Journey*, 53. See also Höhn and Klimke, *Breath of Freedom*, 21–88.

racism in large parts of the United States. Consequently, more and more people supported the Double V campaign, victory over racism in Europe and the United States. Civil rights organizations such as the National Association for the Advancement of Colored People (NAACP) experienced huge membership increases, intensifying pressure on the US government to take a stand against segregation. In this way, World War II helped to prepare the ground for the American civil rights revolution of the following decades. Together with the Cold War, it also internationalized the issue of civil rights and black equality.[16]

In Germany, black-white race relations quickly gained importance during the American occupation.[17] Given the previously widespread German belief in black inferiority, the presence of large numbers of African American soldiers in positions of military authority presented quite a challenge to many Germans. This issue was further highlighted by the significant number of relationships between white German women and black American soldiers that developed during the postwar years. For black soldiers, especially those coming from the American South, having a white girlfriend was in many cases a kind of a "dream-come-true," since touching or openly desiring a white woman was still the ultimate taboo for black men in the South (a taboo that, if broken, could easily get a black man killed).[18] Moreover, there were very few "marriageable" German men available at the time because so many had been killed during the war, were in jail for war crimes, or still in Soviet prisoner-of-war camps. Many others were physically and psychologically damaged. In this context, young, healthy American soldiers with food and money made an attractive choice for unmarried German women. And black soldiers had a reputation for being particularly polite and generous to the "Fräuleins." Germany was certainly not free from racism, and the hostility towards the so-called *Ami-Liebchen* (women

16 See ibid. and Klimke, "Civil Rights Struggle," 93–98. For a more detailed description of the roles of World War II and the Cold War in the history of the civil rights struggle, see also Borstelman, *Cold War and Color Line*, and Plummer, *Window on Freedom.*

17 Unless differently noted, the term "Germany" stands for "West Germany" here, since most of the examination refers to the FRG.

18 Alleged sexual advances of black men toward white women were a frequent cause of lynching in the South. One of the most infamous cases was the brutal killing of fourteen-year old Emmett Till in Mississippi in August of 1955. See Metress, *Lynching*; Berg, *Lynching*; and Waldrep, *Lynching*.

Figure 2: Interracial wedding

Wedding photograph of a black GI and his German bride, 1945.
H. Kremer; courtesy of the Library of Congress.

who fraternized with American soldiers) may have been even more pronounced if the American partner was black. Nevertheless, the willingness of so many German women to engage in friendships, intimate relationships, and even marriages with African American males clearly revealed a noticeable shift in German racial attitudes (fig. 2).[19] The presence of interracial children that came out of these relationships began to create a small but growing Afro-German presence, which further challenged traditional views on the significance of race and what it meant to be German. The fate of these *Besatzungskinder* (occupation children) was often difficult though, especially if the father did not marry the mother but moved (or was ordered) back to the United States alone. While many of the children were loved and well cared for by their mothers and other family members, many others were given up for adoption (mostly to African American families in

19 For more details on interracial relationships in postwar Germany, see Höhn, *GIs and Fräuleins*; Höhn and Klimke, *A Breath of Freedom*; Goedde, *GIs and Germans*; and Schroer, *Recasting Race.*

the United States), and those growing up in Germany often felt unaccepted as full and equal members of German society.[20]

GERMAN SUPPORT OF THE US CIVIL RIGHTS MOVEMENT AND KING'S VISIT TO BERLIN

The presence of so many black GIs in Germany, the extraordinarily close relationship between Germany and the United States during the Cold War, and the extensive news coverage of the civil rights movement led to a growing interest among many Germans in the African American liberation struggle during the 1950s and 1960s. German newspapers and magazines published detailed articles about the Montgomery bus boycott, the sit-in movement, the March on Washington, the Selma campaign and other major civil rights events. By 1964, Martin Luther King had become a popular figure in both West and East Germany. Most of his books had been translated into German, and many who read these texts and witnessed the unfolding of the civil rights movement in the news became deeply sympathetic to the cause of black equality. Among them were, for example, the Protestant ministers Heinrich Grosse and Heinrich Grübner. Grosse, who had become interested in the black protest movement as a theology student in Hamburg, moved to the United States in 1967 to study at Boston University and soon became involved in the movement. He met and marched with King, who inspired him not only to support the civil rights cause but also the movement against the Vietnam War. After King's assassination, Grosse moved back to Germany, where he translated many of King's sermons and other writings. In 1971, he also published the first German historical study of the black civil rights movement. An ordained minister and later also a professor of theology in Hannover, Grosse continues to work for racial and social justice in Germany. He also numbers among the main supporters of the Martin-Luther-King-Zentrum für Gewaltfreiheit und Zivilcourage (MLK Center

20 Robert Stemmle's 1952 movie *Toxi* is a romanticized example of such a difficult Afro-German childhood. See Fehrenbach, *Race after Hitler*; Lemke Muniz de Faria, *Fürsorge und Ausgrenzung*; and Pützstück, "AfrikanerInnen in Deutschland."

for Nonviolence and Civil Courage), which was founded in Werdau in 1998 by peace activists from the former East and West Germany.[21]

Heinrich Grübner was already an established minister and church leader when he first heard of King and the black civil rights movement. As an outspoken opponent of the Nazis who had helped Jews hide from persecution, Grübner was arrested and spent three years in a concentration camp. Almost two decades later, during a 1962 speaking tour through the United States, he witnessed the black civil rights struggle directly for the first time. Deeply moved, Grübner began corresponding with King, comparing his struggle against racism and discrimination with his own fight against fascism and Nazi terror: "I write in the bond of the same faith and hope, knowing your experiences are the same as ours were." He also stressed, "During the time of Hitler, I was often ashamed of being a German, as today I am ashamed of being white. I am grateful to you, dear brother, and to all who stand with you in this fight for justice, which you are conducting in the spirit of Jesus Christ."[22] Grübner also invited King to come to Berlin, which he did in September 1964 (fig. 3). This visit did not garner much attention from the media at the time or from historians later, but it marked a new high point in alerting Germans on both sides of the Berlin Wall to the inequality that black Americans still suffered in the United States. First, King was enthusiastically received by the people of West Berlin, including Mayor Willy Brandt, who praised him as a hero of the black freedom struggle and as a role model for all people fighting for liberty—whether from racial, colonial, or communist oppression. King visited several areas of West Berlin and preached before more than 20,000 people at the Waldbühne on September 13. He compared racial segregation in the United States with the ideological oppositions that separated his host city and explained that Berlin for him was "a symbol of the divisions of men on the face of the earth." While sharing details of the African American freedom struggle with his audience and asking for their support, he also stressed that the oppressive barriers of race, creed, and ideology could ultimately only be overcome

21 See Grosse, *Die Macht der Armen*. Grosse also published a number of other works on King and on Dietrich Bonhoeffer. For more information on the King Center in Werdau, see their website at http://www.king-zentrum.de.

22 Heinrich Grübner to Dr. Martin Luther King, July 15, 1963 and December 16, 1963, cited in Höhn and Klimke, *Breath of Freedom*, 92.

Figure 3: King at the Berlin Wall

Martin Luther King, Jr., together with Ralph Abernathy at the Berlin Wall (Bernauer Straße/Schwedter Straße), September 13, 1964. J. Jung; courtesy of the Landesarchiv Berlin.

by faith in God and his love and by belief in the common humanity of all people.[23]

On the same evening, King travelled to East Berlin to preach at St. Mary's Church, which was so full that some 2,000 people were left outside waiting to hear him. King later gave another sermon in nearby Sophia Church. The reaction of his audience was even more enthusiastic than in West Berlin. Reports of the event described the listeners as "spellbound" by King, deeply moved by his words and by the mere fact that he had come to them, to East Berlin, with a message of freedom and hope.[24] Significantly, though, no German Democratic Republic (GDR) government officials participated in the event or met with King. Although he was a representative of the "other America," King was also a devout Christian and not yet an outspoken critic of US capitalism. So the communist government may have

23 "Martin Luther King in der Waldbühne," *Welt am Sonntag*, September 6, 1964, 29; also cited in Höhn and Klimke, *Breath of Freedom*, 95. For a detailed description of King's visit to East and West Berlin, see ibid., 89–105.

24 Ibid., 100–102.

wanted to avoid affording him official recognition. Moreover, GDR officials could have been worried that King's visit might inspire East Germans to articulate their own dissent. In any case, they kept their distance. The people in East Berlin, however, who met King, exulted in his visit. They besieged him after his speech, trying to touch him or shake his hand and asking him to return.[25] The event may not have had any immediate visible effect in 1964, but it certainly had a long-term impact. King's visit and message gave the Christian minority in the GDR new hope. His theology and the method of nonviolent resistance doubtlessly inspired the GDR opposition in the following decades and thus—at least to some degree—contributed to the eventual downfall of the communist regime there. In the late 1980s, "We Shall Overcome," the anthem of the civil rights movement, became the marching song of the GDR opposition movement. Moreover, the Martin Luther King Center was established in Saxony, that is, in the former East Germany, and the center also houses the archive of the Saxon civil rights movement.[26]

TRANSNATIONAL PROTEST NETWORKS AND THE RADICALIZATION OF THE STUDENT MOVEMENT

German university students also engaged in the cause of black equality during the 1960s. In September 1963, for example, some 100 students organized a protest march against racial discrimination in Frankfurt. They delivered a petition signed by 450 people to the US consul general calling upon President Kennedy to give more support to African Americans.[27] Questions about civil rights, democratic participation, and nonviolent direct action were debated on university campuses, in churches, and in political institutions throughout Germany in the 1960s. Representatives of the African American freedom struggle became quite influential in Germany, not only in terms of politics but also with regard to popular culture. Besides King, more radical figures, such as Malcolm X, Amiri Baraka, Stokely Carmi-

25 Ibid., 102–3.
26 See ibid., 104; and http://www.king-zentrum.de.
27 See Klimke, "Civil Rights Struggle," 99.

chael, Huey Newton, Bobby Seale, and Angela Davis, were seen as role models by members of the German student movement.[28]

Quite a few German students travelled to the United States (many as participants of government-sponsored exchange programs) and became supporters of the black freedom struggle there. Most felt especially attracted to the Student Nonviolent Coordinating Committee (SNCC), founded by participants of the sit-in movement in North Carolina in 1961, which had become a major force in the organization of direct action campaigns and voter registration drives. More radical and confrontational than the established civil rights organizations (such as the NAACP or King's Southern Christian Leadership Conference), members of SNCC also became important figures in the free speech movement, the anti-Vietnam War movement, and the women's rights movement.[29]

German students visiting the United States soon realized that the involvement of young white students in SNCC's Freedom Summer campaign of 1964 had been an important factor in promoting the rise of the American student protest movement and the formation of Students for a Democratic Society (SDS). Some Germans, like Michael Vester, for example, became active members of the American SDS and contributed significantly to its internal political debates.[30] He and other young Germans involved with the American civil rights and student movements eagerly shared their insights with friends back home. They not only discussed the relevance of the black freedom struggle for social protest in Germany but copied and adapted strategies and techniques developed by the civil right movement for strategic use in Germany. Vester also served as vice chairman of the German Socialist Student League (Sozialistischer Deutscher Studentenbund), called SDS too. Thus many of the student protest marches, teach-ins and sit-ins

28 See ibid For an analysis of this cultural exchange, including black music, literature, and art, and the emergence of African American Studies in Germany, see Dietrich and Heinrich, *Cultural Crossovers*.

29 See Carson, *In Struggle*; Forman, *Black Revolutionaries*; and Hogan, *SNCC's Dream*.

30 Vester, for example, worked closely with Tom Hayden and was directly involved in formulating the final draft of the SDS manifesto in 1962, the Port Huron Statement. See Klimke, *Other Alliance*, 18–26.

organized in the FRG in the 1960s mirrored the methods and actions of the SNCC.[31]

Based on the experiences of German SDS members such as Michael Vester, Karl-Dietrich ("KD") Wolff, Günter Amendt, and others who had spent significant amounts of time in the United States and witnessed racial discrimination and violence against African Americans, there was also a strong sense of solidarity with the emerging black nationalist movement, especially the Black Panther Party (BPP), which was founded in Oakland, California, in 1966. Although the passage of the Civil Rights Act and the Voting Rights Act in 1964 and 1965 ostensibly ended legal discrimination against African Americans, economic inequality and institutionalized racism continued to be major problems, especially in urban ghettos. Aware of these inequities, the German SDS denounced US racial policies, and following the race riots in Newark, Detroit, and other American cities in the summer of 1967, its leadership issued an official statement supporting Black Power during their twenty-second national convention:

> The violent struggle of the blacks who conceive of themselves as 'Afro-Americans' in the US makes the solidarity with the national liberation movements of the Third World concrete. As they create a second Vietnam in the USA itself, their struggle against American capitalism is tied, in practice to the international class struggle against imperialism.[32]

Of course, the radicalization of the German student movement after 1965—including the SDS's solidarity with Black Power and with the American SDS—was also spurred by political and cultural developments in the FRG. Although the country's close alliance with the United States during the Cold War brought growth, stability, and affluence (as well as an influx of American popular culture) to Germany, there were still quite a few Germans, especially of the younger generation, who opposed Chancellor

31 See Klimke, "Civil Rights Struggle," 99. For an excellent analysis of the connection between the German and the US student protest movements throughout the 1960s, see Klimke, *Other Alliance*.

32 "Die XXII. Ordentliche Delegiertenkonferenz des SDS (Resolutionen und Beschlüsse)," 26, in *Papers of Ronny Loewy*, vol. 1 (SDS 1966–1970), Hamburger Institut für Sozialforschung. Cited in Höhn and Klimke, *Breath of Freedom*, 112.

Adenauer's policies of Western alignment and West German rearmament. Moreover, as further information about the Nazi regime became more readily available, many young Germans were appalled by what they perceived as their government's lenient policies towards some former high-ranking Nazis. Their outrage over how many political decision-makers had been allowed to stay in power despite their tainted pasts served as a primary catalyst of the 1960s student movement. Awareness of the Holocaust and other horrible crimes that had resulted from Nazi racism caused a sense of "collective guilt" or "special responsibility" in many Germans. Racism had to be fought wherever in the world it occurred, which was also a reason to support the African American freedom struggle.[33] Moreover, as the Spiegel Affair of 1962 demonstrated, most German students disapproved of their government's rigid anti-communism and harsh suppression of internal dissent.[34] Following that incident, concern about the FRG's new emergency laws grew even stronger. These laws, first debated in 1958 and finally passed in May 1968, expanded the government's executive powers in case of an internal or external emergency. Their critics saw them as a severe threat to German civil liberties and to the democratic founding principles of the FRG.[35] Some student protesters even compared them to the Nazi seizure of power in 1933. A smaller group also pointed to the lack of democracy in the country's university system as a major problem. Many SDS members felt that the German government's internal policies and its support for the United States, including what the students perceived as an imperialist war in Vietnam, were undermining the country's democracy and depriving them of their rights as free citizens. These sentiments added to their identification with the radical wing of the African American freedom struggle, especially with SNCC and the Black Panther Party. In the view of these young Germans, black nationalism was an integral part of the larger

33 A number of German students openly compared the situation of blacks in the South to the one of Jews in Nazi Germany. See, for example, Schultz, "Seltsam schönes Land." Some older Germans shared this feeling, as the letters of Heinrich Grübner to King cited above show.

34 In this infamous affair, German Defense Minister Franz-Josef Strauss had ordered the arrest of some politically opposed journalists on charges of treason. As it turned out, the state possessed no evidence of the alleged crime, Strauss had violated due process and blatantly overstepped his constitutional powers.

35 For a detailed discussion of the political tensions and generational conflict during this time, see Gassert and Steinweis, *Coping with the Nazi Past.*

international class struggle against American imperialism and capitalism. Therefore, they felt that they should not only support it, but help to coordinate it with liberation movements all over the world.[36]

In February 1968, SDS organized an international Vietnam Congress at the Technical University of West Berlin, which was attended by over 5,000 activists. Speakers such as SNCC's Dale Smith argued that the Vietnam War was also "a war against us and against the bit of humanity that remains to us," and SDS leader Rudi Dutschke added that the Vietnam War threatened to impose "a long period of authoritarian world domination from Washington to Vladivostok" (fig. 4). Both activists stressed that it was essential for people to come together to create a "second front" in the fight against "global imperialism."[37] This Vietnam Congress can be seen as the first public evidence of a new, revolutionary alliance between the German student movement and the radical black civil rights activists that went beyond demanding black legal equality to advocate a global agenda of fighting for racial justice and freedom from imperialist oppression. In this way, they advanced an agenda already pursued by W.E.B. Du Bois in the early twentieth century and by Malcolm X and Martin Luther King during the final months of their lives.[38]

Only six weeks after the Vietnam Congress, the assassination of Dr. King on April 4, 1968 shocked the world. Many activists interpreted his murder as evidence that the policy of nonviolence had failed and that Black Power was the only available option. In Germany, SDS members proclaimed King's murder a "clarion call for revolutionary action." As Ekkehart Krippendorff put it, "We are the ones who must satisfy his demand for a truly revolutionary change of our society . . . [T]he legacy of Martin Luther King is, for us, the continuation of this social-revolutionary struggle with his—but also with our—methods, here in our own country."[39] Accordingly, the German student movement intensified its protests, especially in Frankfurt and Berlin. It also stepped up its sup-

36 See Höhn und Klimke, *Breath of Freedom*, 107–18.

37 Smith and Dutschke, cited in ibid., 107.

38 See Lewis, *Du Bois*; Davis, *Changing the World*, 255–73; and Waldschmidt-Nelson, *Dreams and Nightmares*, 99–152.

39 Krippendorff, "Über King"; also cited in Höhn and Klimke, *Breath of Freedom*, 113.

Figure 4: Dale Smith together with Rudi Dutschke

German SDS leader Rudi Dutschke together with SNCC delegate Dale Smith during the Vietnam Congress at West Berlin's Technical University, February 17, 1968. Mehner; courtesy of ullstein bild.

port for Black Power in various ways. One organization, the Berlin Committee for Black Power, openly tried to collect money to arm black people. German activists translated publications by the Black Panthers and other texts by radical black nationalists. SDS also supported black GIs in their efforts to fight racism and discrimination at US military installations in Germany, for example, by collaborating in the publication of the radical black

GI newspaper *Voice of the Lumpen* and through their Free the Ramstein 2 campaign.[40]

Two other events reflecting the German student movement's further radicalization and embrace of Black Power were the founding of the Black Panther Solidarity Committee (BPSC) in 1969 and the Angela Davis Campaign in the early 1970s. The Frankfurt-based BPSC was established by KD Wolff after his return from the United States in November 1969. It had three official goals: "1. Education about the party's struggles and about the fascist terror of the ruling class in the USA; 2. Agitation and propaganda among GIs stationed in Germany, and 3. Material support of the Black Panthers."[41] The committee published translations of key texts from the Black Panther Party and it organized fundraisers and demonstrations, reading groups, lectures, film screenings, and solidarity rallies for prominent BPP leaders including Eldridge Cleaver, Bobby Seale, and Ericka Huggins. Embracing Black Power and socialist ideas while harshly denouncing German support for what they saw as American racist and imperialist policies, BPSC members clearly viewed the FRG as part of the arena for worldwide liberation and thus called on students to join their radical revolutionary movement. A key player in the transatlantic support network linking black and white students, the BPSC existed until the BPP splintered in 1971–72.

The BPSC was also heavily involved in the campaign to support Angela Davis in the early 1970s. Born in 1944 in Birmingham, Alabama, where she also grew up, Davis studied German philosophy at Brandeis University with Herbert Marcuse and was awarded a scholarship to study at the University of Frankfurt from 1965 to 1967. There she became involved with the German SDS. After returning to the United States, she joined the Black Power movement and the American Communist Party (CPUSA), completed her PhD, and became an assistant professor of philosophy at the Univer-

40 Ibid., 143–70. The *Voice of the Lumpen* was edited by black GIs and veterans in cooperation with SDS; it was printed by a press owned by KD Wolff and supported by German subscribers, so GIs could obtain copies for free. The so-called Ramstein 2 were Edgar Jackson and William Burrel, two black editors of the *Voice of the Lumpen* who were arrested in November of 1970 after a shootout with a German guard at Ramstein Air Base. Their arrest led to massive protests and solidarity demonstrations in Germany. In July 1971 Burrell was acquitted and Lawrence was sentenced to six years in prison.

41 BPSC, "Solidaritätskomitee für die Black-Panther-Partei"; Höhn and Klimke, *Breath of Freedom*, 114–15 and Klimke, *Other Alliance*, 116–26.

sity of California, Los Angeles. She also became a well-known advocate for the rights of black prisoners in that state. On August 7, 1970, Jonathan Jackson, the brother of inmate George Jackson, whom Davis knew well, tried to free three black prisoners in a Marin Country courtroom by armed force. During the ensuing shootout, Jackson and five other people, including the prisoners and the presiding judge, were killed. The police ascertained soon afterwards that the guns used by Jackson had been registered in Angela Davis's name. Davis fled California, was put on the FBI's Ten Most Wanted Fugitives list and was arrested in New York City on October 13.[42]

Her arrest caused an unprecedented international outcry. Davis's friends in Germany and the United States, including many faculty members in California and Frankfurt, denounced the incident as a blatant case of injustice and a brutal attempt to silence political protest. Marcuse warned that, if Davis was found guilty, she could face capital punishment. He stressed that she could only be saved by "a powerful protest, a protest that is present everywhere and cannot be stifled."[43] Following this call, German students were the main contributors to what became a huge, international protest movement in support of Davis (fig. 5). The BPSC disseminated information materials about her cause and held demonstrations for her acquittal. Moreover, an official Angela Davis Solidarity Committee (ADSC) was founded in May 1971. Its members proclaimed that "[t]he German people, especially, have a right to be educated about the ongoing racism in the world. And precisely those who have made their inner peace with the Jews should consider that their credibility depends on their willingness to fight without compromise against the social causes of racial discrimination wherever it appears."[44] Solidarity with Angela Davis was thus seen as an indicator of a true antifascist and antiracist mindset. In June 1972, the ADSC organized a congress in Frankfurt entitled "The Example of Angela Davis," which was attended by over 10,000 people.[45]

42 For more details, see Aptheker, *Morning Breaks*; James, *Angela Y. Davis Reader*; and Davis, *Autobiography*.

43 Marcuse, cited in Höhn and Klimke, *Breath of Freedom*, 119.

44 ADSC, "Freiheit für Angela Davis!" paper cited ibid., 120–21.

45 Ibid., 121–22, and Klimke, *Other Alliance*, 134–42.

Figure 5: German Free Angela Davis demonstration

A demonstration organized by women's groups in Frankfurt in support Angela Davis on March 13, 1971. M. Tripp; courtesy of Hamburger Institut für Sozialforschung.

In Davis's remarkable case, the solidarity campaigns were not only transatlantic but also reached behind the Iron Curtain. For the regime in the German Democratic Republic, Davis was the perfect representative of "the other America." The authorities there regarded her as an innocent African American communist who was persecuted by evil capitalist forces and who was therefore deserving of East German support. Thus, GDR media reported the case in detail. East German citizens signed petitions in Davis's behalf, raised money for her defense, and sent protest letters to President Richard Nixon. School children painted "sunflowers for Angela Davis" and wrote letters to her. When she was finally acquitted on June 4, 1972, Erich Honecker congratulated her with a personal telegram. Three months later, Davis visited the GDR. There she was enthusiastically celebrated by the East German people. She received an honorary degree from the University of Leipzig, was awarded the Great Star of Friendship among the Peoples by Walter Ulbricht, and became the heroine of an official documentary movie. The regime turned Davis into a kind of "communist superstar," and she apparently gladly accepted this role.[46]

FROM BLACK POWER TO THE RED ARMY FACTION

The Angela Davis campaign was without doubt one of the major successes of the international alliance of German students and African American freedom activists, but it also marked a turning point in the movement. There was a growing sense of frustration and disgust among many young Germans with what they perceived as the decay of democratic values in the United States and Germany. The killing of student activist Benno Ohnesorg during a demonstration in Berlin on June 2, 1967, and the assassination attempt on Rudi Dutschke on April 11, 1968 (who survived with severe brain damage that caused his death a few years later) significantly added to the anger and fear of radical German students, who felt they were threatened by the same type of violent opposition as their African American friends in the southern United States.[47] Their trust in the democratic legitimacy of their own and the US government deteriorated. When interrogated by the US Senate Subcommittee on Internal Security in March 1969, KD Wolff, for example, harshly denounced what he saw as the illegitimate repression of liberal protest movements. He asserted that there was a dangerous "emergence of a new institutional fascism both in West Germany and the United States" and called the senators "a bunch of criminal bandits."[48] Many young Germans agreed with his analysis and thus, at the end of the 1960s,

46 In her speech, "Not Only My Victory," delivered in German in East Berlin on September 11, 1972, Davis lauded communism and the social order of the Soviet Union and the GDR, and denounced American racism and imperialism. She concluded by saying: "Long live the GDR! Long live proletarian internationalism!" See Davis, "Nicht nur mein Sieg," 63. For a discussion of the GDR's support of Davis and other socialist black visitors, such as Du Bois and Paul Robeson, also see Höhn and Klimke, *Breath of Freedom*, 123–41. Sophie Lorenz at the University of Heidelberg is working on a manuscript entitled "Peace, Friendship, Solidarity? East Germany and Angela Davis, 1965–1989," which will be completed in 2013.

47 For a firsthand account of this process, see Aly, *Unser Kampf.* I would like to thank Robert Winkler for referring me to this book and for other valuable insights regarding the "dark side" of the German student movement.

48 Wolff, cited in Höhn and Klimke, *Breath of Freedom*, 195.

voices grew louder among the more radical activists calling for "armed resistance" against what they saw as a fascist government. As activist Gudrun Ensslin put it after the assassination of Benno Ohnesorg, "This fascist state wants to kill all of us. We have to organize the resistance. Violence can only be answered by violence. This is the generation of Auschwitz—you cannot argue with them."[49]

Ensslin, who had spent a year in the United States as a high school student, worked with the SDS and BPSC during the 1960s and supported a desertion campaign for black GIs in West Germany (many of whom found refuge in the GDR). She eagerly embraced the ideas of Black Power early on and saw the BPP not only as a welcome ally in the international struggle against American imperialism but also as an inspiration for standing up to government power. Together with Andreas Baader and two other friends, Ensslin set two shopping malls on fire in April 1968. Her aim was "to protest the ignorance of the people watching the genocide in Vietnam."[50] Two years later, in June 1970, Ensslin, Baader, and Ulrike Meinhoff founded the Red Army Faction (RAF). Named after Lenin's revolutionary army of 1917, the RAF was a terrorist organization with the explicit aim of organizing armed revolution to overthrow the German capitalist—and in their view, fascist—government. Their founding document, "Build up the Red Army!" (published on June 5, 1970) and other texts such as "The Concept of the Urban Guerilla" (written in 1971) revealed that the philosophy of the RAF was based on a mix of various revolutionary doctrines, including Marxism-Leninism, Maoism, Frantz Fanon's concept of the liberating force of revolutionary violence, and Che Guevara's ideal of revolution by way of guerilla warfare .[51]

Seeing themselves as part of an international revolutionary struggle against capitalism and imperialism, members of the RAF were willing to cooperate with all kinds of other liberation movements (including the Palestinian Liberation Organization), but early on it showed a special affinity for radical black nationalism. The RAF's leaders admired the militancy of the Black Panther Party, especially the open display of weapons, which to them signified determination and strength. RAF members therefore made it a

49 Ensslin, cited in Aust, *Der Baader-Meinhof-Komplex*, 60.

50 Ensslin, cited in Sontheimer, "Wie Alles anfing."

51 See Klimke, *Other Alliance*, 127–32. For a detailed history of the RAF, see Aust, *Der Baader-Meinhof-Komplex*, and Proll, *Hans und Grete*.

priority to arm themselves, and there is some evidence that they might have received some guns from Black Panther groups in Germany.[52] More remarkable than ideological similarities and practical cooperation between the RAF and BPP, however, was the process of cultural appropriation that occurred. RAF leaders not only copied the style of the BPP by carrying weapons or using militant rhetoric (they called policemen "pigs" [*Schweine*], for example), but they emphatically stressed their solidarity with the black freedom struggle, frequently quoting Black Panther statements in their publications, "The Concept of the Urban Guerilla" concluding with a statement from Eldridge Cleaver.[53] Black culture, music, and literature were very popular among RAF members, and many of them identified with the situation of African Americans because they perceived themselves as similarly oppressed outcasts under deadly attack by a fascist government. As Meinhoff and Ensslin declared on May 22, 1970, "Did the pigs, who shot first, really believe we would let ourselves be killed nonviolently like slaughterhouse animals? Gandhi and Martin Luther King are dead. The bullets of their murderers, the bullets fired at Rudi . . . have ended the dream of nonviolence. The one who does not resist dies. . . . Berlin is an outpost of American Imperialism . . . the enemy of all blacks in the US, the enemy of the workers in Berlin—the enemy is American Imperialism."[54] There was also much admiration for the courage and defiance of black prisoners such as George Jackson. While in prison in the 1970s, Ensslin and other RAF leaders quoted from his published work in their prison letters in order to encourage each other to follow Jackson's example of self-sacrificing dedication to the cause of liberation.[55] The most obvious sign of the RAF's admiration for the BPP was the fact that they appropriated the Party's logo (a black panther jumping forward) and combined it with the image of a Russian Kalashnikov in their founding manifesto (fig. 6).[56]

52 See ibid., 10, and Klimke, *Other Alliance*, 127.

53 See RAF, "Das Konzept Stadtguerilla."

54 Meinhoff and Ensslin, "Die Rote Armee aufbauen" (translation by author).

55 Ensslin, for example, wrote in a 1974 letter, "[L]et Jackson teach you the whole thing—his joy in doing this job, for example here: 'If you ask me generally how this struggle will end, I answer: With a victory. If you ask me specifically, I answer: With death.' Or do you perhaps have anything to lose anymore?" Cited in Klimke, *Other Alliance*, 133.

56 See image of the manifesto in ibid., 128.

Figure 6: The founding manifesto of the RAF

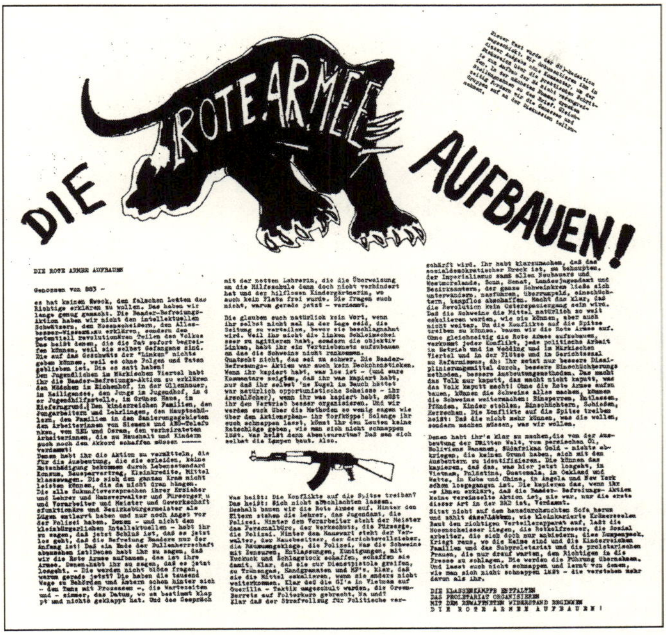

"Die Rote Armee aufbauen!" ("Building up the Red Army"), founding manifesto of the RAF, originally published in *Agit 883*, no. 62, June 5, 1970, 6.

Despite affinities and proclamations of a common agenda, however, there were also significant differences between the RAF and BPP. In contrast to the Panthers, who also engaged in community programs, the RAF despised reformist efforts to improve the existing system. The only strategy acceptable to them was violent revolution. Consequently, the RAF grew increasingly ruthless during the 1970s and 1980s, engaging in a campaign of brutal terrorism that ultimately killed more than thirty people. Although there were some Panthers, especially Cleaver, who also favored revolutionary militancy (and there can be no doubt, that the FBI, especially J. Edgar Hoover, perceived the BPP as an actual threat to US security, and so waged a brutal campaign against them), BPP founder Huey Newton always stressed that their arms were solely for self-defense. Newton and cofounder Bobby Seale took a much more reformist stance than Cleaver, and eventually—

after heated internal debates—they prevailed. The BPP never fully embraced, and finally distanced themselves from, the agenda of violent revolutionary action followed by the RAF.[57] This may explain why after 1972 the official RAF logo no longer contained the image of a black panther, whereas that of the Kalashnikov remained.

Historical connections between the Black Panthers, the radical German student movement, and the RAF clearly show that young German radicals drew inspiration from the black nationalist movement in the United States, appropriated many of its ideas and cultural iconography, and actively cooperated with the BPP during the late 1960s and early 1970s. As the RAF began its terrorist campaign, however, its agenda proved incompatible with the Black Panthers'. The BPP's main focus was the survival of their community. Finding the most effective way towards improvement of the social, cultural, economic, and political situation of African Americans was ultimately more important to them than fighting for world communism or engaging in what would have been a suicidal attempt to overthrow the US government. So although the BPP played a certain role in the emergence of the West German terrorist movement, this alliance was short-lived and had remarkably little influence on the perception of African Americans by the German public at large. In fact, most German people never noticed the connection between the BPP and the RAF.[58] Throughout the 1970s, the German media focused much more on Angela Davis as the icon of black radicalism. Despite her communist affiliation and her stinging critique of Western capitalism and racism, Davis never openly advocated violence and was therefore not perceived as a threat. Eventually this brilliant, beautiful activist, who spoke fluent German and advocated social justice, racial equality, and women's rights, became very popular in both German states, perhaps helping to further improve the general attitude of white Germans towards African Americans.

---

57 Cleaver was ousted from the party in 1972, but internal differences had significantly weakened the BPP and contributed to its demise. One of the splinter groups, the Black Liberation Army (BLA) endorsed revolutionary violence. THE BLA apparently planned some terrorist attacks, but never succeeded and remained politically insignificant. For more, see Austin, *Up Against the Wall.*

58 Klimke, in *The Other Alliance*, was one of the first historians to explore this phenomenon, 126–42.

CONCLUSION

One can certainly observe much improvement in many areas of black-white race relations in Germany since World War II. Nevertheless, as ongoing incidents of discrimination against Afro-Germans and other people of color show, racism continues to exist in Germany. In contrast to the 1960s, most of the about 500 000 black people living in Germany today do not come from the United States but from sub-Saharan Africa, many having entered Germany as refugees from war-torn countries with the intention of returning home some day. But there is also an increasing number of descendants of African Americans and Africans who were born in Germany, are German citizens and want to be treated as such. Perhaps inspired by the civil rights movement of the 1960s, they began organizing a new black movement and founded the Initiative Schwarze Deutsche (Initiative of Black Germans) as well as ADEFRA e.V.—Schwarze Frauen in Deutschland (Black Women in Germany, the acronym ADEFRA standing for Afrodeutsche Frauen) in 1986. Through local and national meetings, workshops, demonstrations, online networks, and publications,[59] both of these organizations promote the social, cultural, and political inclusion of Afro-Germans. They fight against discrimination and racism and help to build a supportive community and positive sense of identity for black people in Germany.[60] Having grown up in a nation that does not have the historic multiethnic and multicultural background of the United States, many white Germans still struggle with the concept that someone who is not white or Christian can be is just as German as they are. As current political debates indicate, however, the number of Germans willing to work for a more inclusive society appears to be on the rise. Organizations such as Gesicht

59 See, for example, *Farbe bekennen: Afro-deutsche Frauen auf den Spuren ihrer Geschichte* by Katharina Oguntoye, May Opitz, and Dagmar Schultz. This book, first published in 1986, is viewed by many as the "founding document" of modern Afro-German identity.

60 Just as ADEFRA changed its name from "Afro-German Women" to "Black Women in Germany," ISD has also been renamed *Initiative Schwarze Menschen in Deutschland* (Initiative of Black People in Germany) in order to include non-German blacks who live in the FRG. See the organizations' websites http://neu.isdonline.de/verein/ and http://www.adefra.de/. See Oguntoye, Opitz, and Schultz, *Showing Our Colors*; Pützstück, "AfrikanerInnen in Deutschland"; and Mazón and Steingröver, *Not So Plain as Black and White.*

Zeigen!, Verein gegen Ausländerfeindlichkeit und Rassismus, the Amadeu Antonio Foundation, and the Martin Luther King Center for Nonviolence and Moral Courage are firmly committed to fighting against racism and intolerance and to promoting social justice in Germany.[61] The popularity of Afro-German sport or media stars (such as Gerald Asamoch, Steffi Jones, Cherno Jobatey or Arabella Kiesbauer) may also be seen as a sign of progress. There is still a long way to go, but one should remember that in the wake of the African American freedom struggle after World War II, the first significant steps to overcoming racial prejudices among Germans were already taken during the long 1960s. Certainly there are still many problems, and too many white Germans (as well as other white Europeans and Americans for that matter) continue to hold on to some anti-black, racist stereotypes. But the hope remains that "we [all] shall overcome some day."

BIBLIOGRAPHY

Adams, Mark B. *The Wellborn Science: Eugenics in Germany, France, Brazil, and Russia.* New York: Oxford University Press, 1990.

Aly, Götz. *Unser Kampf: 1968—ein irritierter Blick zurück.* Frankfurt am Main: Fischer Taschenbuch Verlag, 2008.

Aptheker, Bettina. *The Morning Breaks: The Trial of Angela Davis.* Ithaca, NY: Cornell University Press, 1999.

Aust, Stefan. *Der Bader-Meinhof-Komplex.* Munich: Wilhelm Goldmann Verlag, 1998.

Austin, Curtis. *Up Against the Wall: Violence in the Making and the Unmaking of the Black Panther Party.* Fayetteville: University of Arkansas Press, 2006.

Bauer, Karin. "From Protest to Resistance: Ulrike Meinhof and the Transatlantic Movement of Ideas." In Davis, *Changing the World*, 172–88.

Berg, Manfred. *Popular Justice: A History of Lynching in America.* Chicago: Ivan R. Dee, 2011.

61 See ibid. and the website of the King Center at Werdau as well as http://www.gesichtzeigen.de/, http://migration-online.de/biblio._aWQ9OTYz_.html, and http://www.amadeu-antonio-stiftung.de/.

Black Panther Solidarity Committee. "Solidaritätskomitee für die Black-Panther-Partei." In *Sozialistische Correspondenz-Info* 24, December 6, 1969, 11.

Borstelmann, Thomas. *The Cold War and the Color Line: American Race Relations in the Global Arena.* Cambridge, MA: Harvard University Press, 2001.

Brantlinger, Patrick. *Rule of Darkness: British Literature and Imperialism, 1830–1914.* Ithaca, NY: Cornell University Press, 1988.

Campt, Tina. *Other Germans: Black Germans and the Politics of Race, Gender and Memory in the Third Reich.* Ann Arbor: University of Michigan Press, 2004.

Carson, Clayborne. *In Struggle: SNCC and the Black Awakening of the 1960s.* Cambridge, MA: Harvard University Press, 1981.

Davis, Angela Y. *An Autobiography.* New York: International Press, 1988. First published 1974 by Random House.

———. "Nicht nur mein Sieg." In *Angela Davis*, edited by Willi Baer, Carmen Bitsch, and Karl-Heinz Dellwo, 59–63. Hamburg: LAIKA Verlag, 2010.

Davis, Belinda, Wilfried Mausbach, Martin Klimke, and Carla MacDougall, eds. *Changing the World, Changing Oneself: Political Protest and Collective Identities in West Germany and the U.S. in the 1960s and 1970s.* New York: Oxford University Press, 2010.

Dietrich, Maria, and Jürgern Heinrich, eds. *From Black to Schwarz: Cultural Crossovers between African America and Germany.* Berlin: LIT, 2010.

Dirks, Nicholas B. *Colonialism and Culture.* Ann Arbor: University of Michigan Press, 1992.

Ehrenreich, Eric. *The Nazi Ancestral Proof: Genealogy, Racial Science, and the Final Solution.* Bloomington: Indiana University Press, 2007.

Faust, Drew G., ed. *The Ideology of Slavery: Proslavery Thought in the Antebellum South, 1830–1860.* Baton Rouge: Louisiana State University Press, 1981.

Fehrenbach, Heide. *Race after Hitler: Black Occupation Children in Postwar Germany and America.* Princeton, NJ: Princeton University Press, 2005.

Finkelman, Paul, ed. *Defending Slavery: Proslavery Thought in the Old South: A Brief History with Documents.* New York: Bedford/St. Martin's Press, 2003.

Forman, James. *The Making of Black Revolutionaries.* Seattle: University of Washington Press, 1997.

Förster, Stig, Wolfgan Mommsen, and Roland Robinson, eds. *Bismarck, Europe and Africa.* London: Oxford University Press, 1988.

Frederickson, George M. *The Black Image in the White Mind: The Debate on Afro-American Character and Destiny, 1817–1914.* New York: Harper and Row, 1971.

Friedman, Ina R. *The Other Victims: First-Person Stories of Non-Jews Persecuted by the Nazis.* Boston: Houghton Mifflin, 1990.

Friedrichsmeyer, Sara Lennox, and Susanne Zantop, eds. *The Imperialist Imagination: German Colonialism and Its Legacy.* Ann Arbor: University of Michigan Press, 1998.

Gassert, Philipp, and Alan E. Steinweis, eds. *Coping with the Nazi Past: The West German Debates on Nazism and Generational Conflict, 1955–1975.* New York: Berghahn Books, 2006.

Grosse, Heinrich. *Die Macht der Armen: Martin Luther King und der Kampf für soziale Gerechtigkeit.* Hamburg: Furche Verlag, 1971.

Hogan, Wesley C. *Many Minds, One Heart: SNCC's Dream for a New America.* Chapel Hill: University of North Carolina Press, 2007.

Höhn, Maria. *GIs and Fräuleins: The German-American Encounter in 1950s West Germany.* Chapel Hill: University of North Carolina Press, 2002.

Höhn, Maria, and Martin Klimke. *A Breath of Freedom: The Civil Rights Struggle, African American GIs, and Germany.* New York: Palgrave Macmillan, 2010.

Ifill, Gwen. *The Breakthrough: Politics and Race in the Age of Obama.* New York: Anchor Books, 2009.

James, Joy, ed. *The Angela Y. Davis Reader.* Malden, MA: Blackwell, 1998.

Kater, Michael H. *Different Dummers: Jazz in the Culture of Nazi Germany.* New York: Oxford University Press, 1992.

Keim, Curtis A. *Mistaking Africa: Curiosities and Inventions of the American Mind.* Boulder: Westview Press, 1999.

King, Richard H., ed. *Obama and Race: History, Culture Politics*. Special issue, *Patterns of Prejudice* 45, nos. 1–2 (February–May 2011): 1–197.

Klimke, Martin. "The African American Civil Rights Struggle and Germany, 1945–1989." *German Historical Institute Bulletin* 43 (2008): 91–106.

———. "Black Power, die Black-Panther-Solidaritätskomitees und der bewaffnete Kampf." In *Die RAF und der linke Terrorismus*, edited by Wolfgang Kraushaar, 562–82. Hamburg: Hamburger Edition, 2006.

———. *The Other Alliance: Student Protest in West Germany and the United States in the Global 1960s*. Princeton, NJ: Princeton University Press, 2010.

Klimke, Martin, and Joachim Scharloth, eds. *1968 in Europe: A History of Protest and Activism 1956–77*. New York: Palgrave Macmillan, 2008.

Krippendorff, Ekkehart. "Über Martin Luther King." *Berliner Extra-Dienst*, April 10, 1968, 10.

Lemarchand, René, ed. *Forgotten Genocides: Oblivion, Denial, and Memory*. Philadelphia: University of Pennsylvania Press, 2011.

Lemke Muniz de Faria, Yara-Colette. *Zwischen Fürsorge und Ausgrenzung: Afrodeutsche 'Besatzungskinder' im Nachkriegs Deutschland*. Berlin: Metropol Verlag, 2002.

Lewis, David L., ed. *W. E. B. Du Bois: A Reader*. New York: Henry Holt, 1995.

Lorbeer, Marie, and Beate Wild, eds. *Menschenfresser—Negerküsse...: Das Bild vom Fremden im deutschen Alltag*. Berlin: Elefanten Verlag, 1991.

Lotz, Rainer E. *Black People: Entertainers of African Descent in Germany and Europe*. Bonn: Lotz Verlag, 1997.

Lusane, Clarence. *The Historical Experiences of Afro-Germans, European Blacks, Africans, and African Americans in the Nazi Era*. London: Routledge, 2002.

Marschall, Christoph von. *Barack Obama: Der schwarze Kennedy*. Zürich: Orell Füssli, 2009.

Meinhoff, Ulrike, and Gurdrun Ensslin. "Die Rote Armee aufbauen." *Agit 883*, May 22, 1970. Accessed July 14, 2012. http://labourhistory.net/raf/read.php?id=0019700 522.

Metress, Christopher, ed. *The Lynching of Emmett Till: A Documentary Narrative*. Charlottesville: University of Virginia Press, 2002.

Obama, Barack. *The Audacity of Hope: Thoughts on Reclaiming the American Dream*. New York: Crown Publishers, 2006.

Opitz, May, Katharina Oguntoye, and Dagmar Schultz, eds. *Showing Our Colors: Afro-German Women Speak Out*. Translated by Anne V. Adams. Foreword by Audre Lorde. Amherst: University of Massachusetts Press, 1992. Originally published as *Farbe bekennen: Afro-deutsche Frauen auf den Stpuren ihrer Geschichte* (Berlin: Orlanda, 1986 / Frankfurt: Fischer, 1992).

Pallua, Ulrich. *Eurocentrism, Racism, Colonialism in the Victorian and Edwardian Age: Changing Images of Africa(s) in Scientific and Literary Texts*. Heidelberg: Universitätsverlag Winter, 2006.

Perraudin, Michael, and Jürgen Zimmerer, eds. *German Colonialism and National Identity*. New York: Routledge, 2011.

Plummer, Brenda Gayle, ed. *Window on Freedom: Race, Civil Rights and Foreign Affairs, 1945–1988*. Chapel Hill: University of North Carolina Press, 2003.

Poiger, Uta G. *Jazz, Rock, and Rebels: Cold War Politics and American Culture in a Divided Germany*. Berkeley: University of California Press, 2000.

Powell, Colin. *My American Journey*. New York: Random House, 1995.

Proll, Astrid. *Hans und Grete: Die RAF, 1967–1977*. Göttingen: Steidl, 1998.

Pützstück, Lothar. "AfrikanerInnen in Deutschland und schwarze Deutsche—Geschichte und Gegenwart." In *Begegnungen: Geschichte und Gegenwart der afrikanisch-europäischen Begegnung*, edited by Marianne Bechhhaus-Gerst and Reinhard Klein-Arendt. Münster: LIT Verlag, 2004.

Remnick, David, and Friedrich Griese. *Barack Obama: Leben und Aufstieg*. Berlin: Berlin Verlag, 2010.

Rote Armee Fraktion (RAF). "Das Konzept Stadtguerilla." April 1971. http://www.rafinfo.de/archiv/raf/konzept_stadtguerilla.php.

Said, Edward W. *Orientalism: Western Conceptions of the Orient*. Harmondsworth, UK: Penguin Books, 1991.

Sarkin, Jeremy. *Germany's Genocide of the Herero: Kaiser Wilhelm II, His General, His Settlers, His Soldiers*. Rochester, NY: James Currey, 2011.

Schroer, Timothy L. *Recasting Race after World War II: Germans and African Americans in American-Occupied Germany*. Boulder: University Press of Colorado, 2007.

Schubert, Michael. *Der schwarze Fremde: Das Bild des Schwarzafrikaners in der parlamentarischen und publizistischen Kolonialdiskussion in Deutschland von den 1870er bis in die 1930er Jahre.* Stuttgart: Steiner, 2003.

Schultz, Dagmar. "Seltsam schönes Land—Land der Ungerechtigkeit." *Frankfurter Hefte* 21, no. 9 (1966): 627–34.

Siegfried, Detlef. "White Negroes: The Fascination of the Authentic in West German Counterculture of the 1960s." In Davis, *Changing the World*, 191–213.

Sontheimer, Michael. "RAF-Serie (3): Wie Alles Anfing." *Der Spiegel,* September 24, 2007. Accessed July 14, 2012. http://www.spiegel.de/spiegel/print/d-53060246.html.

Touré. *Who's Afraid of Post-Blackness? What It Means to Be Black Now.* New York: Free Press, 2011.

Waldrep, Christopher. *Lynching in America: A History in Documents.* New York: New York University Press, 2006.

Waldschmidt-Nelson, Britta. "Are All Men Created Equal? Zur Kontroverse über die Legitimität der Sklaverei in den USA." *Mitteilungen der Charles Sealsfield Gesellschaft* 12, München: CSG, 2003, 9–31.

———. *Dreams and Nightmares: Martin Luther King, Jr., Malcolm X, and the Struggle for Black Equality in America.* Gainesville: University Press of Florida, 2012.

The Transatlantic Women's Movement

Literary and Cultural Perspectives

CLARA JUNCKER

In 1968, Tammy Wynette co-authored and recorded "Stand by Your Man," which forty-plus years later would be added to the Library of Congress National Recording Registry, an annual selection of recordings considered "culturally, historically, or aesthetically significant."[1] She appeared on the *Johnny Cash Show* (February 11, 1970) dressed in a sequined red cowboy shirt, her platinum blonde hair sprayed into a helmet framing her white-powdered face. Introducing her, Cash towers above her, while Wynette shyly compliments him on his recent awards. His famous deep voice goes soft and protective as he assures her that she deserves an award herself for the hit that remains controversial for its promotion of women's subservience.[2] The Library of Congress calls it "an ode to the weakness of men, the strength of their women, love, loyalty and support," but the description also notes that in the emerging Women's Movement, "Stand by Your Man" created "dissent."[3] While Wynette's woman stands by her man and forgives him everything, because "after all, he's just a man," many other American

1 "The National Recording Registry 2010," *The National Preservation Board of the Library of Congress*, http://www.loc.gov/rr/record/nrpb/registry/nrpb-2010 reg.html.

2 "Stand by Your Man."

3 "The National Recording Registry 2010," *The National Preservation Board of the Library of Congress*, http://www.loc.gov/rr/record/nrpb/registry/nrpb-2010 reg.html.

women wanted to leave him behind and to change their own roles, visions and hopes.

When a rising number of women in North America and Europe joined the labor force in the 1950s and early 1960s, they could look forward to earning approximately 63% of what their husbands, boyfriends, brothers or fathers made.[4] Still-at-home suburban wives and mothers felt a strange and inexplicable discontent, which Betty Friedan first diagnosed in *The Feminine Mystique* (1963), the exposé of (white) middle-class feminine lives that helped to ignite the Women's Liberation Movement in the US. Friedan argued that even white and middle-class educated women had to resort to marriage and children to locate an identity and a life, and she encouraged her large readership to "find themselves," to seek their own private and public paths to freedom and success rather than being defined exclusively by patriarchal norms and traditions. At the same time, grassroots inventions such as local women's houses, women's fairs, women's communes, and consciousness-raising groups barring male participation helped women to become aware of their limited opportunities. Feminists enacted a series of countermoves against gender oppression, including mass demonstrations, protests at beauty pageants, the symbolic burning of bras in the streets, and revisions of academic canons. The birth control pill, approved for contraceptive use in 1960, helped young women imagine identities not exclusively defined by wife- and motherhood and became a contributing factor to both the feminist movement and the sexual revolution of the 1960s. The drastic changes in women's roles and perspectives surfaced in literary and cultural texts on both sides of the Atlantic, where feminist writers and activists protested existing gender arrangements.

American writers such as Gwendolyn Brooks, Adrienne Rich, and Anne Sexton explored the problem that had no name, the frustrated women's lives in postwar America, though feminists of color would develop their own branch of "womanism."[5] Brooks, Rich, and Sexton scrutinized in their prose and poetry a masked femininity, since the gender relations in the 1950s and early 1960s did not allow for the open resistance towards patriarchal power that exploded later, with feminist bestsellers such as *Our Bod-*

4 Source: U.S. Women's Bureau and the National Committee on Pay Equity. "Women's Earnings as a Percentage of Men's, 1951–2010," *Infoplease.com*, http://www.infoplease.com/ipa/A0193820.html#ixzz1srLl7GLP.

5 Walker coins and defines the term in *Our Mothers' Gardens*.

ies, Ourselves (1971) by the Boston Women's Health Book Collective and *Fear of Flying* (1973) by Erica Jong. Both feminist manifestos of sorts, they helped export the celebration of women's bodies and freedom to Europe. Across the Atlantic, the Women's Liberation Movement and the cultural works it inspired took on both similar and different forms. In Scandinavia, Alice Walker's emphasis on race and class found a special audience, as Nordic feminists combined their awareness of white middle-class women's oppression with an interest in African American women, defined as the ultimate victims of US patriarchal structures. In France, psychoanalytically trained feminists such as Julia Kristeva, Luce Irigaray, and Hélène Cixous theorized a new language intended to articulate feminine bodies and experiences outside of "phallogocentric" linguistic orders. The cross-fertilization of American and European feminist ideologies made a lasting imprint on women's lives and futures on both sides of the Atlantic.

HOUSEWIVES AND TIGERS

In 1951 Adrienne Rich published "Aunt Jennifer's Tigers," which in the 1960s became a favorite among the American and European feminist daughters who had witnessed first-hand their mothers' or aunts' frustrations. Rich's feminist classic takes up as little space as the title figure herself, who sits modestly on her sofa with her embroidery. Within this narrow textual and domestic space, Aunt Jennifer feels the burden of gender and role requirements as her nervous fingers try to pull the thread: "the massive weight of Uncle's wedding band / Sits heavily upon Aunt Jennifer's hand."[6] Defined by her familial role and her husband's patriarchal inscription, she imagines alternative scenarios, represented by the needlework tigers of Rich's title: "Aunt Jennifer's tigers prance across a screen / Bright topaz denizens of a world of green." These formidable predators embody the emotions Aunt Jennifer herself can express only through art: anger, strength, daring, freedom. Rich herself admitted to wearing "asbestos gloves" when handling explosive artistic material she "couldn't pick up barehanded." She veiled her dissatisfaction behind the third-person narration and generational displacement of her "Aunt Jennifer" poem, in which

6 Rich, "Aunt Jennifer's Tigers."

the aunt struggles with the needle, her "fingers fluttering through the wool." Despite the resistance she imagines with fearless tigers, Jennifer cannot yet envision a female or feminist agent of revolt. The tigers "pace in sleek chivalric certainty" and thus subscribe to patriarchal traditions of chivalry. Though they embody Jennifer's embryonic feminism, the masculine tigers frame her efforts by usurping both the first and the last lines of Rich's poem. They will go on prancing after Jennifer's demise: "When Aunt is dead, her terrified hands will lie / Still ringed with ordeals she was mastered by." As Thomas B. Byars argues, the tigers represent the individual artist's effort to overcome women's suppression, but they participate in masculine myths of honor and chivalry and also serve as colonialist icons. The ivory needle enabling them may cause Aunt Jennifer trouble, but the ivory implicates her with imperialism and capitalism.[7] In Rich's controlling symbols—the wedding band and the tapestry tigers—the personal meets the political in ways that cannot be resolved in 1951, but will dominate feminist fictions in subsequent decades. In its investigation and articulation of power, "Aunt Jennifer's Tigers" suggests a relation between repression and rebellion, between the individual and the social, and between the personal and the political.[8]

Though rarely accorded feminist credentials, Gwendolyn Brooks called attention to the plight of housewives that the Women's Movement would protest. In 1953, Brooks published the semiautobiographical novel *Maud Martha*, which contemporary reviewers saw as a ladylike celebration of marriage and domesticity in the face of adversity. In reality, this pioneering work deals with bitterness and rage, concealed with silence for self-protection. Mary Helen Washington notes that "what the reviewers saw as exquisite lyricism was actually the truncated stutterings of a woman whose rage makes her literally unable to speak."[9] Brooks's protagonist rarely talks and never voices her opinion. She hides behind a mask of politeness and servility and consistently checks her own activities and desires. Instead of openly rejecting her husband, Paul, who is reading a book called *Sex in the Married Life* in bed and tries to interest Maud Martha in its possibilities, she gets up and asks "pleasantly": "Shall I make some cocoa? . . . And toast

7 See "On 'Aunt Jennifer's Tigers,'" *Modern American Poetry*.

8 See Meg Boerema Gillette's section in "On 'Aunt Jennifer's Tigers,'" *Modern American Poetry*.

9 Washington, "'Taming all that anger.'"

some sandwiches?"[10] This young housewife recognizes her own habit of manipulative reaction and resistance, and her desire to change becomes a plot incentive.[11] Maud Martha's silences echo as well in the short, tight-lipped vignettes that often fill up only one page and a half, with blank sheets of paper articulating things unsaid or barely thought. Since no connections between vignettes exist, Maud Martha's life appears frozen and fragmented, its flow as checked as her own emotions and reactions. Short main clauses, with only occasional frills, further testify to Maud Martha's stiff upper lip and locked-up thoughts. She hides her disappointment with marriage and settles into pleasing and obeying her husband, though she feels imprisoned, cramped and "unexpressed" as a wife. She suffers and is still.[12]

Maud Martha implicitly communicates her romantic expectations, as well as her marital disillusion, through the tone of her internal monologs. In the vignette titled "if you're light and have long hair," she attends the Annual Foxy Cats Dawn Ball with her handsome husband, joining the twenty good-looking members of the Foxy Cats Club and their wives or girlfriends. Maud Martha enters the main room of Club 99, where the Ball takes place, and immediately responds to the romantic, even erotic, possibilities of this festive space: "the drowsy lights, the smells of food and flowers, the smell of Murray's pomade, the body perfumes, natural and superimposed; the music, now steamy and slow, now as clear and fragile as glass, now raging, passionate, now moaning and thickly grey."[13] The lush style with which Brooks suggests her heroine's romantic desires competes in this vignette with a more sober, even ironic, voice that expresses Maud Martha's thwarted expectations. She notes that the Foxy Cats do little work except trying to be "hep" and that "each year they spent hundreds of dollars on their wonderful Dawn Ball, which did not begin at dawn, but was scheduled to end at dawn."[14] The event appears rich with romantic potential, but Maud Martha's mockery suggests her disappointment. She recognizes her husband's ambition, which involves neither social ascent nor loving his pregnant wife: "on the strength of his appearance and sophisticated

10 Brooks, "Maud Martha," 193.
11 Washington, "'Taming all that anger,'" 250.
12 See Chapter 16 of Brooks, "Maud Martha" and Washington, "'Taming all that anger,'" 250–51.
13 Brooks, *World*, 210.
14 Ibid., 206.

behavior at this Ball might depend his future admission (for why not dream?) to *membership*, actually, in the Foxy Cats Club!"[15] Maud Martha conceals her cold and silent hate, which results in scorn and manipulation.[16] Behind her feminine face, obedient and pleasant, hides a monster whose rage intensifies in the encounter with intra-racial discrimination at Club 99.

Contemporary critics saw the title figure as "a spunky Negro girl" whose life includes "disturbances" as well as "the delicate pressure of the color line," but they focused on the optimism and the lyricism of Brooks's fictional autobiography.[17] Like her author, however, Maud Martha is dark-skinned, and in "if you're light and have long hair," her husband prefers the high-yellow Maella. Accordingly, Maud Martha finds herself up against several forms of discrimination: as a wife, as an African American woman, and as one failing the brown bag test that earlier in the century had kept dark members of her race from admittance or acceptance. Faced with double, or triple, discrimination, the cynical and hostile Maud Martha gives way to a kinder, braver, and more compassionate figure. She quietly articulates her own racial and gendered position, as Paul leaves the dance floor with the curvaceous, white-looking Maella:

> "Not," thought Maud Martha, "that they love each other. It oughta be that simple. Then I could lick it. It oughta be that easy. But it's my color that makes him mad. I try to shut my eyes to that, but it's no good. What I am inside, what is really me, he likes okay. But he keeps looking at my color, which is like a wall. He has to jump over it in order to meet and touch what I got for him. He has to jump away up high in order to see it. He gets awful tired of all that jumping."[18]

Maud Martha gets tired herself. As the other to Paul's self, she sees herself through his eyes and determines to achieve the housewifely excellence that constituted the feminine mystique in the postwar era. She struggles with gender issues relating to ideals of American beauty, to race, work, marriage, sexuality and reproduction, housework, media, consumption, and economy. Despite her artistic sensibilities and talents, she surrenders to domesticity and femininity by giving birth to a female child, not to a poem.

15 Ibid., 208.
16 Washington, "'Taming all that anger,'" [249].
17 Ibid., [249].
18 Brooks, *World*, 213–14.

She cannot voice the feminism that her author conveys in prose and poetry and instead produces a baby, though this conclusion to the novel is subject to interpretation.[19] Childbirth might, in feminist terms, become a creative process, or an independent act of rebellion, the screams that accompany a new beginning or perhaps a powerful protest. But in the early 1950s, the African American world of Gwendolyn Brooks was ignored by mainstream white feminist protest groups, though she anticipates the themes of silence, the search for identity and creativity, and the personal and political resistance that feminists of all colors voiced later.

A decade after Aunt Jennifer and Maud Martha's domestic despair, Anne Sexton published "Housewife" (1962), which proposes that women marry houses rather than men. As Friedan would argue in *The Feminine Mystique* the following year, suburban housewives get hysterically attached to or consumed by these life partners. Sexton took up even less space than Rich and Brooks in describing their narrow existences:

> Some women marry houses.
> It's another kind of skin; it has a heart,
> A mouth, a liver and bowel movements.
> The walls are permanent and pink.
> See how she sits on her knees all day,
> Faithfully washing herself down.
> Men enter by force, drawn back like Jonah
> into their fleshy mothers.
> A woman is her mother.
> That's the main thing.[20]

Sexton's woman merges with her house, which becomes not just a life partner, but her own body: skin, heart, body waste, pink walls. The woman kneels and washes her house, while men thrust into the pink walls of her vagina, to enter their mothers through another birth canal. In Sexton's poem, the housewife nurtures, satisfies and mothers her husband. Indeed, she becomes her own mother in fulfilling traditional female obligations, domes-

19 For a series of interpretations, including more victorious readings, see Washington, "'Taming all that anger,'" 259–61.

20 Sexton, "Housewife," 1911.

tic and sexual. Through writing confessional poetry, Sexton explored her own struggles with motherhood, guilt, loss, suicidal depression, and death, and the ways in which women collaborated with their oppressors, or danced with their jailers.

Before the Women's Liberation Movement, Rich, Brooks, Sexton and others represented femininity (and feminism) as veiled, since their protagonists' hidden frustrations and desires could not be articulated openly. In "Womanliness as Masquerade" (1929), Joan Riviere theorized "womanliness" as a mask intended to hide a female masculinity offensive to the surrounding culture, such as ambition, success, or intellectual achievements. In a radical move, she equates womanliness with masquerade: "My suggestion is not, however, that there is any such difference; whether radical or superficial, they are the same thing."[21] Stephen Heath explains this equation, or identification, between femininity and carnival: "In the masquerade the woman mimics an authentic—genuine—womanliness but then authentic womanliness is such mimicry, *is* the masquerade ('they are the same thing'); to be a woman is to dissimilate a fundamental masculinity, femininity is that dissimulation."[22] Aunt Jennifer's demure face and fluttering fingers constitute, in short, her gender identity, just as Maud Martha's silences constitute hers. The mask *is* the femininity, and the covert feminism as well. Behind the mask is nothing; to be a woman is to wear a mask with which to meet masculine egos or desires. Taking off this mask reveals not an authentic face, but a non-entity or an abyss.

BODIES, DADDIES, AND FLIGHTS

By the end of the 1960s, the Boston Women's Health Collective began to construct a new identity for women by designing a female body. Immediately upon publication in 1971, *Our Bodies Ourselves* became a primer for the Women's Liberation Movement; by 1976, it had sold 850,000 copies. *Our Bodies Ourselves* openly, and insistently, bridged personal and political spheres by claiming the female body they had just discovered. Biology was no longer considered destiny, and the Women's Health group set out to

21 Riviere, "Womanliness as Masquerade," 38.
22 Heath, "Joan Riviere," 49.

reclaim their bodies and literally delve into their hidden power. In Boston and elsewhere, feminists converted physical and emotional weaknesses to strengths and tried to use themselves productively and actively. The introduction to *Our Bodies Ourselves* claims that new "task-oriented" activities have inspired in the authors a need for recognition and success, which an accompanying photograph illustrates. It depicts a young woman in sturdy work-clothes drilling a floor, surrounded by various phallic paraphernalia. Her body posture is masculine: legs crossed for drill access, right elbow raised dramatically, facial expression concentrated. Since her bare midriff and tumbled curls signal femininity, she signifies the androgynous, or cross-gendered, behavior the Boston Women's Health Collective advocates: "Our new confidence has led us to rediscover physical activity, climbing, canoeing, karate and car maintenance, and to take care of ourselves." Images of female bodies engaged in traditionally male activities prompted women never to be "weak, dependent and helpless again."[23] A new generation of women sought strength in each other, in the plural "we" that writes and empowers its communal body. The authors of this feminist manifesto confess in "Learning to Value Ourselves" that their previously perceived inferiority was "merely a reflection of the way power is distributed in society."[24]

For women's groups in the 1960s and 1970s, the feminist body represented a new frontier, an unexplored terrain wide open to investigation. The Boston Women's Health Collective explains that "some of us have taken a while to get over our inhibitions about seeing or touching our genitals," and an anonymous feminist testifies to similar embarrassment: "When someone first said to me two years ago, 'You can feel the end of your cervix with your finger,' I was interested but flustered." Her story ends with success and the proud acquisition of a speculum. The detailed illustrations that accompany her narrative stress the close connection between female body parts and words. In these close-ups of female genitalia, the authors teach their readers the vocabulary of the medical profession: "Mons," "perineum," "pubic symphysis," and more. By speaking their master's language, feminist pioneers felt able to take control of uncharted terrain. They wrestled their bodies and themselves from the medical and patriarchal estab-

23 Boston Women's Health Collective, *Our Bodies Ourselves*, 16.
24 Ibid., 14.

lishment by surprising their doctors with a professional vocabulary and by challenging those who "appear outwardly pleased while continuing to 'manage' us with new tactics."[25]

Tensions between femininity and feminism remain. Throughout *Our Bodies Ourselves*, the authors try to escape traditional roles while struggling with hidden anxieties. Their uncertainty results in a series of confessions that modifies the dominant liberation narrative. The communal voice lets us know that "we still have many bad feelings about ourselves that are hard to admit" and that it is difficult "to erase decades of social influence in a few years." Members of the Boston Women's Health Collective protest adamantly that "we *can* take care of ourselves" and even tell readers that "we are forever fighting a constant inner struggle to give up and become weak, dependent and helpless again."[26] The illustration called "Vulva," a head-on view of female genitals, suggests this tension. Is the vaginal opening a gun firing directly at resisting readers, or a bullet hole hiding internal wounds or vulnerabilities? Like the text itself, "Vulva" represents simultaneously power and lack.

Feminists sought phallic power through rebutting Sigmund Freud, whose theories on psycho-sexual development they considered misogynist. In "On the Sexual Theories of Children" (1908), Freud first discussed the penis envy that he presented more fully in *On Narcissism* (1914).[27] He famously theorized children's mental and sexual processes from the oral and phallic stages through the latency period. Critics of Freud zoomed in on the phallic stage, when the child is age three and a half to six years old and the penis becomes central to both boys and girls. In Freud's analysis, the male organ triggers important, gendered discoveries, the Oedipus complex for boys and the Electra complex for girls. Anatomical differences between boys and girls had far-reaching consequences in the Freudian psychoanalytical project, which feminists in the 1960s labeled patriarchal and antifeminist. By first contesting Freud, a whole generation of women defied other Daddy figures blocking their way. Frank Sinatra's daughter, Nancy, sang that her boots were made for walking and announced to her famous father, his cohorts, and men in general, that "one of these days these boots are

25 Ibid., 19.
26 Ibid., 19, 16.
27 Freud, "On the Sexual Theories."

going to walk all over you." In her bestselling *Fear of Flying* (1973), Erica Jong mocked the psychoanalytical community of men, grabbed phallic sexual power, and inspired young women on both sides of the Atlantic with her flight from home.

Jong takes on Daddy Freud in the opening lines of her feminist classic: "There were 117 psychoanalysts on the Pam Am flight to Vienna and I'd been treated by at least six of them. And married a seventh."[28] Jong mocks the 117 members of Freud's profession, who in their "flatfooted literal-mindedness" have used penis envy to explain hers to herself: "You dream about breaking your leg on the ski slope. You have, in fact, just broken your leg on the ski slope. . . But the broken leg in the dream represents your own 'mutilated genital.' You always wanted to have a penis and now you feel guilty that you have *deliberately* broken your leg so that you can have the pleasure of the cast, no? No!"[29] In having the psychoanalysts fly to Vienna, Jong highlights their alliance with Freud, who is part of her own intellectual and emotional luggage. She is Jewish and has residual sympathy for the father of modern psychoanalysis, who in 1938 fled from his office in Berggasse because of threats against his family. To purge herself, she links the psychoanalytical community to the Nazis and repeatedly quotes Sylvia Plath, her precursor in despair and revolt, as in the epigraph to Chapter 2: "Every woman adores a Fascist / The boot in the face, the brute / Brute heart of a brute like you."[30] She links her flying psychoanalysts with Freud, with Fascism, and with marriage, thus taking on a full package of patriarchal fathers as she heads towards their terrain.

In Vienna, Jong's heroine Isadora, possibly named after the corset-free, barefoot dancer Isadora Duncan, meets the sixties masculine ideal: long-haired, unambitious, empathetic, mobile, and, as it turns out, sexually irresponsible. Aptly named Adrian Goodlove, he represents to Isadora what Jong (in)famously labeled "the zipless fuck." This incidental sex, with no guilt, no past and no future, supposedly gave women the same freedom as men and lustily dissolved the gender hierarchy that located women below men in terms of sexual and social power. "Sex is zipless," Isadora explains,

28 Jong, *Fear of Flying*, 3.
29 Ibid., 7.
30 Ibid., 15.

"because the incident has all the swift compression of a dream and is seemingly free of all remorse and guilt. . . ." She continues:

> Because there is no rationalizing, because there is no talk at *all.* The zipless fuck is absolutely pure. It is free of ulterior motives. There is no power game. The man is not "taking" and the woman is not "giving." No one is attempting to cuckhold a husband or humiliate a wife. No one is trying to prove anything or get anything out of anyone. The zipless fuck is the purest thing there is.[31]

What follows is a feminist road novel, with Isadora and Adrian crisscrossing European sites heavy with history and eventually unable to let go of their own. Only in motion will past, present and future merge into a Utopian bliss; at the end of the road wait husbands, wives, role expectations, and financial considerations. Nonetheless, *Fear of Flying* created a breathing space in which second-wave feminists might glimpse a more egalitarian future, which began with sexuality, the female body, and Daddy's words. Like the Boston Women's Health Collective and the readers of *Our Bodies Ourselves*, Isadora learns her master's language.

Central to her feminist voice is Isadora's own body, introduced in loving detail on the opening page of *Fear of Flying*, as the heroine describes her take-off terror:

> My fingers (and toes) turn to ice, my stomach leaps upward into my rib cage, the temperature in the tip of my nose drops to the same level as the temperature in my fingers, my nipples stand up and salute the inside of my bra (or in this case, dress—since I'm not wearing a bra) . . . .[32]

As in *Our Bodies Ourselves*, fear competes with bravery, icy toes with erect nipples. As the novel progresses, Isadora lets go of her husband's hand and takes over his language. She often tells Bennett to marry "someone more phallic, castrating, and narcissistic" than herself and shares with her readers this secret weapon: "First technique of being a shrink's wife is knowing how to hurl all their jargon back at them, at carefully chosen moments."[33]

31 Ibid., 14.
32 Ibid., 3.
33 Ibid., 8.

In the war between the sexes, mastering the master's language is mastering the master, or, as in *Fear of Flying*, becoming the master. Jong and Isadora are as wedded to obscenity as any Norman Mailer. Four-letter words fly across the pages, the airplane, European roads and into the motel bedrooms where Isadora engages in all varieties of the activity that Country Joe cheered at Woodstock. With linguistic promiscuity, Jong invites multiple registers of masculine expression into her text. But her declarative statements, foreign languages, satirical comments, all sprinkled with Yiddish, situate her among victims as well as oppressors. Like *Our Bodies Ourselves*, *Fear of Flying* remains suspended between erotic and linguistic assertion and its meek counterparts: insecurity and dependency. Isadora delivers italicized exclamations, an emotional overconsumption barely hiding the anxiety that ultimately ends her flight. On the last page of the novel, Isadora is taking a bubble bath in a London hotel bathroom. She is immersed in the luxurious fluids that French feminists associated with creative processes, but though she implies an open ending to her journey, and possibly her marriage, she is less than convincing. With her Tampax string, she fishes the water like a wounded Hemingway hero trying to overcome trauma and disillusion, and in the last sentence of Jong's novel, husband Bennet walks (back) in. Implicitly, the ending stresses the financial dependency that white middle-class feminists ignored, for a while. Isadora is sick of primitive lodging and broke, and the "fear" in Jong's title wins.

LITERARY COMMUNITIES

European women consumed Adrienne Rich, Anne Sexton, Erica Jong, Marilyn French, Germaine Greer, and other feminist writers and activists, but their path to liberation took other directions as well. In Scandinavia, young feminists discovered African Americans and found in their oppression a counterpart to their own. Anthologies such as *Black-Eyed Susans* (1975) and *Midnight Birds* (1980), both edited by Mary Helen Washington, collected the texts Danish women had xeroxed and distributed in women's houses and other feminist sites. African American women writers opened a window to Black America, and to the supposed Other in American life and culture, and in so doing also revealed to Scandinavian women their own oppression. Joyce Ladner's *Tomorrow's Tomorrow: The Black Woman*

(1971) helped to further the mixture of voyeurism, pity and admiration that sent Scandinavian feminists to the early works of Gwendolyn Brooks, Toni Cade Bambara, Toni Morrison, Ntozake Shange, and especially Alice Walker. In her sociological study, Ladner concluded that black women had successfully adjusted to and then overcome the social and psychological conditions that had failed to promote their health, recognition or success. Her tone was self-assured in describing black girls in urban settings:

> These young women talked about themselves as Black people in a very positive manner, but yet in a manner which strongly reflected the fact that was most important in their lives. Too much literature on identity has dealt with Black people as impotent, weak individuals who lack the power to shape their lives. These conceptionalizations negate the fact that they are *creators* who act, instead of being acted upon. Their environment is not so overwhelming that they have relinquished all control over it.[34]

Ladner's criticism of white America resonated with Northern European feminists, who saw themselves in homogenous societies beyond racial discourses and wished for the courage, the strength and the sass of African American sisterhood (fig. 1).

Mary Helen Washington identified in *Black-Eyed Susans* what African American women were *not* and thus exploded many stereotypes associated with women of her race. She is not Faulkner's Dilsey, the indestructible black superwoman. She is not the "super sex object," or "the domineering matriarch," or the "evil black bitch." But she might be the woman Zora Neale Hurston identified in *Their Eyes Were Watching God* (1937): "De nigger woman is de mule uh de world so far as Ah can see."[35] In Washington's words, the African American woman was "not a woman with power, not a liberated woman (if liberation means the freedom to make choices about one's life), but a mule, picking up the burdens that everyone has thrown down and refused to carry."[36] But then she might be a crazed woman artist like those "driven to a numb and bleeding madness by the springs of creativity in them for which there was no release," as Alice Walker

34 Ladner, *Tomorrow's Tomorrow*, 106.
35 Washington, *Black-Eyed Susans*, x–xi.
36 Ibid., xi.

Figure 1: Danish feminist artwork, produced at the women's festival on the island of Femoe, Denmark.

Photo by Miriam Dalsgaard/POLFOTO.

would claim in the 1970s.[37] Scandinavian feminists loved writings about African American women, who had been doubly oppressed and struggled with burdens white feminists could only imagine. Too young to have lived through the civil rights movement, they now sought out African American writers and activists who presented them both with the stereotypes at the bottom of American hierarchies and with the hidden potentials that Northern feminists now claimed for themselves. Obviously, middle-class feminists in Scandinavia were not the mules of the world, but they fought against the ideals of beauty that celebrated only the Barbie-dolls in their midst. They threw away their bras. They rejected the domestic work that bogged down women like Gwendolyn Brooks's Maud Martha, since field work in Hurston's Florida did not enter their vision and experience. They stopped picking up socks, found knitting creative or gave it up entirely, and flocked to university courses about women's oppression, at least in the Western hemisphere (fig. 2). In the process, they found their own foremothers, among them Isak Dinesen, in Denmark known as Karen Blixen.

37 Walker, *Our Mothers' Gardens*, 233.

Figure 2: Women's festival in Faelledparken, Copenhagen, 1974.

Photo by Morten Langkilde/POLFOTO.

Blixen had iconic status on the Danish literary and cultural scene, her skeleton-like frame, kohl-rimmed eyes and signature turban etched into the minds, if not the hearts, of all her fellow Danes. She suffered from syphilis, transmitted by her aristocratic Swedish husband, Baron Bror von Blixen-Finecke, whom she had married in 1913 to escape the boredom of her class and her native country. The marriage had been a practical arrangement, her money in exchange for his title and exotic possibilities. Their joint venture in Africa, the coffee plantation near Ngong Hills outside of Nairobi, had ended in disaster, as readers of *Out of Africa* (1937) will know. At the end of her life, Baroness Blixen had little feminist glamor. She was too sick, too old, too aristocratic, and too eccentric for most Danish feminists in the

1960s and 1970s, but her adventures, including her tragic affair with Denys Finch-Hatton, were powerful draws. She had traveled to America in 1959 and died in 1962 from malnutrition, but after her death, Danish women recognized that many of her stories, especially "The Blank Page" from 1957, had unmistakable feminist potential.

Dinesen, the pen name designed for American readers, sets this famous story in ancient times, in an all-female convent in Portugal, where the Carmelite nuns produce the finest flax of all. From this circumstance originates the privilege of procuring bridal linen for all royal Portuguese princesses through generations. Before a young bride receives her morning-after gift, high-positioned male officials, a Chamberlain or High Steward, inspect the sheet from her wedding bed and declare the princess to have been a virgin. The sheet is never again washed and its central piece is returned to the convent, where it is framed and exhibited in the secluded convent gallery. Adorned with a coroneted plate of exquisite gold, the long rows of gilt frames are, as the centuries pass, studied by queens, archduchesses and other high pilgrims, who find in the faded patterns the zodiac signs or the pictures their own imaginations and situations demand. Only one frame exhibits a snow-white piece of linen, without a name inscribed on its golden plate. And, Dinesen writes:

> . . . it is in front of this piece of pure white linen that the old princesses of Portugal—worldly, wise, dutiful, long-suffering queens, wives and mothers—and their noble old playmates, bridesmaids and maids-of-honor have most often stood still.[38]

"The Blank Page" became a feminist favorite for many reasons, its all-female textual universe among them. Dinesen focuses on women, whether trapped inside the convent or in marriage and motherhood, and her story unites generations of nuns, ladies and ladies' maids across centuries, their life conditions the same despite the passing of time. The male gatekeepers—the inspectors of the bridal sheets—appear in the text only to fulfill their scrutinizing role. The story trusts the female point of view, and the women who pass through the convent gallery act as interpreters of the signs on the linen. They read what they need to read, and in deciphering the codes in front of them, they unravel their own lives. The many pieces of

38 Dinesen, "Blank Page," 1394.

unwashed linen establish, like the story itself, an alternative history, or her-story. This story of female lives and texts exists, like Dinesen's story, in an indeterminate temporal setting, so as to subvert the linearity and the logic of traditional historical narratives. The nuns hang the artwork, the visiting ladies live it, their daughters and granddaughters learn from it, and they all collaborate as producers, writers, and readers.

This community of women transcends race, class, age, religion, and marital status. In the opening frame of "The Blank Page," an old "coffee-brown, black-veiled" storyteller begins her tale.[39] Towards its end, she encourages her audience to learn from it and recognize its wisdom. With the bridal centerpieces, generations of women have produced the linen with sweat or written their story with blood, their experiences inscribed with body fluids. But silence is also central to the story and women's mode of expression. The snow-white sheet speaks most eloquently of all the pictures in the gallery. Its silence communicates a hidden but articulate meaning, shared by the princess who lived it, the nuns who show it, and the ladies who study it. And Dinesen and her readers keep their tongues as well. At the core of "The Blank Page" is blankness, the spot where words give way to silence and to experiences that language cannot hold.

FEMININE LANGUAGES

French feminists would later theorize a feminine language (or *l'écriture féminine*) with which to write themselves. While American feminists were burning bras and writing escape novels, and Scandinavian feminists discovered Black America and hidden her-stories, French feminists embraced theory and poststructuralist fathers like Jacques Derrida and Jacques Lacan. These daughters of prominent deconstructionists rejected Anglo-American activism and pragmatism and invented something new. This "newly-born woman" emerged in French feminist discourse not as a biological creation, but as a linguistic position available to all.[40] In her wo/manifesto "The Laugh of the Medusa" (1975), Cixous redefined the snake-haired Medusa,

39 Ibid., 1391.
40 See Cixous and Clément, *Newly Born Woman*.

who turned men to stone, from demon or witch into a feminist icon.[41] Freud had associated the sight of Medusa's decapitated head with the terror of castration, but Cixous's laughing Medusa exploded traditional logic structures, celebrated chaos, and in the process subverted phallic power.[42] Cixous herself laughs off both Freud and Lacan, both rooted in "the sanctuary of the phallus":

> Too bad for them if they fall apart upon discovering that women aren't men, or that their mother doesn't have one. But isn't this fear convenient for them? Wouldn't the worst be, isn't the worst, in truth, that women aren't castrated, that they have only to stop listening to the Sirens (for the Sirens were men) for history to change its meaning? You only have to look at the Medusa straight on to see her. And she's not deadly. She's beautiful and she's laughing.[43]

In writing against "phallogocentrism," she and others formulated a theory of the unconscious, which Cixous called the "Imaginary" and Julia Kristeva "the Semiotic." In this pre-linguistic space, where gender identification has not yet occurred, French feminists located the language of the silenced Other, pregnant with meaning and body, which they encouraged women to explore: "And why don't you write? Write! Writing is for you, you are for you; your body is yours, take it."[44] To articulate themselves in unconscious linguistic realms, outside of the phallogocentric order, French feminists wrote in circles and repetitions, in digressions and details floating in the sea of babble from which an author would be born. Let us lick her shoulder in the introduction to *Le Livre de Promethea* by Cixous, the H of this extract, long enough to suggest the flavor:

> For a week H has struggled in vain. In all sincerity. As for Promethea, she is really the one who made the whole text already, the text from which I emerged just half an hour ago (my hair still clinging from the Atlantic and crystal flecks all over my body. Anyone who wants to know how this almost-finished work tastes would only have to lick my shoulder).

41 This text, originally written in French as "Le Rire de la Méduse" in 1975, was translated into English by Keith and Paula Cohen in 1976.
42 Freud, "Medusa's Head."
43 Cixous, "Laugh of the Medusa," 255.
44 Ibid., 246.

> I was saying: Promethea has already put in much that is hers and more, she drew unstintingly on her organs, her desires, her memory; the text can be said to be made, physically morally, nervously, and above all virtuously, mostly of her.
>
> This is not a preface. It is just half a chance to tell the truth about the origin of the text that I am in the process of leaving this very instant—refreshed, tossed about, inundated.[45]

This sample of *l'écriture féminine* gives to Cixous's readers the recipe that "The Laugh of the Medusa" also shared with women eager to be heard. In Cixous's Imaginary chaos, subject positions dissolve; H becomes Promethea, while "I" and "we" flow in and out of the site from which the text and its author(s) are born. Writing already exists, without the properties and ownership of phallic orders. It is a writing of the body, overflowing with feminine fluids: menstrual blood, milk, sweat, pleasure. As Cixous sings out in "Medusa," "She writes in white ink."[46] Cixous, H, and Promethea associate artistic activity with sexuality, with wetness and motion. In her pleasurable or libidinal economy, myths change, as when Prometheus turns into Promethea, and Medusa laughs at the "inevitable man-with-rock, standing erect in his old Freudian realm."[47] Laughter and silence, parentheses and omissions swim together into a new language, which allies itself with marginality, with bisexuality, which Cixous defines anew, as "the *other bisexuality* on which every subject not enclosed in the false theater of phallogocentric representation has founded his/her erotic universe." Her other bisexuality is "—of both sexes, nonexclusive either of the difference of one sex, and, from this 'self-permission,' multiplication and the effects of the inscription of desire, over all parts of my body and the other body."[48] Feminist theorists associated a writing of the body with confession, with autobiography, with pleasure or *joissance*. In the orgasmic realm of feminine writing, French feminists exploded linguistic orders associated with Logos and Phallos.

Cixous linked feminine sexuality and marginality with Africa as a "dark continent." Her intention was to deconstruct the "old Apartheid routine" that taught women wishing to speak that they ventured into terror and

45 Cixous, *Book of Promethea*, 5.
46 Cixous, "Laugh of the Medusa," 251.
47 Ibid., 255.
48 Ibid., 254.

blackness: "because you are Africa, you are black. Your continent is dark. Dark is dangerous. You can't see anything in the dark, you're afraid. Don't move, you might fall. Most of all, don't go into the forest. And so we have internalized this horror of the dark." In taking back contested terrain, Cixous allies herself with blackness: "We the repressed of culture, our lovely mouths gagged with pollen, or wind knocked out of us, we the labyrinths, the ladders, the trampled spaces, the bevies—we are black and we are beautiful." [49] As "I-woman, escapee," Cixous flees to Africa, where non-Western practices and sexualities might fare better, though this destination implicitly suggests her alliance with Western traditions. Cixous proceeds to construct a feminine writing in this dark utopia:

> If a woman has always functioned "within" the discourse of man . . . it is time for her to dislocate this "within," to explode it, turn it around, and seize it; to make it hers, containing it, taking it in her own mouth, biting that tongue with her very own teeth to invent for herself a language to get inside of. And you'll see with what ease she will spring forth from that "within"—the "within" where once she so drowsily crouched—to overflow at the lips she will cover the foam. [50]

Cixous, Kristeva and other French feminist theorists sought in their search for feminine expression to redefine genres, including the High Theory that signified authority and prestige to contemporary audiences. Unlike the tracts of Karl Marx or Jacques Derrida, their own theorizing aimed, like the woman overflowing at the lips, to participate in a libidinal economy, in which laws of profit, exchange, and grammar gave way for poetry and gift-giving. The textual bodies of French feminist writings celebrated excess, erotics, *jouissance*.

This joyfulness did not last. Ultimately, feminists in Western Europe and the United States faced a series of divisions within their own ranks and attacks from outside. Not only did womanists of color part from white sisters in the Women's Liberation Movement, but Marxists split from Essentialists, working-class activists from middle-class academics, pragmatists from post-structuralists, eco-feminists from the rest, and on and on. Unlike other 1960s movements, however, the Women's Movement radically

49 Ibid., 248.
50 Ibid., 246.

changed private as well as public life well into the twenty-first century, with its transatlantic revisions and re-imaginings of gender structures. As Heidi Slettedahl Macpherson writes in *Women's Movement* (2000), "there is no turning back to a pre-feminism world; but the way forward . . . does not necessarily point in one direction."[51] Feminists walked away from the Women's Liberation Movement along many paths, and their footsteps may be traced in political, cultural, economic and literary terrain. In the twenty-first century, many influential women—Hillary Clinton, Angela Merkel, Christine Lagarde among them—remain feminist icons, while a young author such as Yiyun Li calls attention to women's global struggles in China and Chinese America. In the end, Tammy Wynette's "Stand By Your Man" gave way to Helen Reddy's "I Am Woman," released in 1971, which became a feminist anthem, with lyrics empowering the women who sought change: "I am strong, I am invincible, I am woman."[52]

BIBLIOGRAPHY

Boston Women's Health Collective. *Our Bodies Ourselves*. 1971. Reprint, London: Penguin, 1978.

Brooks, Gwendolyn. "Maud Martha." 1953. In *The World of Gwendolyn Brooks*. [125]–306. New York: Harper and Row, 1971.

Cixous, Hélène. *The Book of Promethea* [*Le Livre de Promethea*]. 1983. Translated by Betsy Wing. Reprint, Lincoln: University of Nebraska Press, 1991.

———. "The Laugh of the Medusa." In *New French Feminisms*, edited by Elaine Marks and Isabelle de Courtivron, 245–61. New York: Schocken, 1981.

Cixous, Hélène, and Catherine Clément. *The Newly Born Woman [La Jeune Née]*. 1975. Translated by Betsy Wing. Reprint, Minneapolis: University of Minnesota Press, 1986.

Dinesen, Isak. "The Blank Page." In Gilbert and Gubar, *Norton Anthology of Literature by Women*, 1391–94.

51 Macpherson, *Women's Movement*, 224.

52 "Helen Reddy: I Am Woman."

Freud, Sigmund. "Medusa's Head." 1922. In *The Complete Works of Sigmund Freud*, edited by James Strachey, et al. 18: 273–74. 24 vols. London: Hogarth Press and the Institute of Psychoanalysis, 1953–74.

———. "On the Sexual Theories of Children." 1908. In *The Complete Works of Sigmund Freud*, edited by James Strachey, et al. 9: 207–26. 24 vols. London: Hogarth Press and the Institute of Psychoanalysis, 1953–74.

Gilbert, Sandra M., and Susan Gubar, eds. *The Norton Anthology of Literature by Women: The Traditions in English*. 2nd ed. New York: Norton, 1996.

Heath, Stephen. "Joan Riviere and the Masquerade." In *Formations of Fantasy*, edited by Victor Burgin, James Donald, and Cora Caplan, [45]–61. New York: Methuen, 1986.

"Helen Reddy: I Am Woman." *YouTube*. http://www.youtube.com/watch?v=MGMESM8JKOg.

Jong, Erica. *Fear of Flying*. 1973. Reprint, New York: Signet, 1974.

Ladner, Joyce A. *Tomorrow's Tomorrow: The Black Woman*. New York: Doubleday Anchor, 1971.

Macpherson, Heidi Slettedahl. *Women's Movement: Escape as Transgression in North American Feminist Fiction.* Amsterdam: Rodopi, 2000.

"The National Recording Registry 2010." *The National Preservation Board of the Library of Congress*. http://www.loc.gov/rr/record/nrpb/registry/nrpb-2010reg.html.

"On 'Aunt Jennifer's Tigers.'" *Modern American Poetry*. http://www.english.illinois.edu/maps/poets/m_r/rich/tigers.htm.

Rich, Adrienne. "Aunt Jennifer's Tigers." In Gilbert and Gubar, *Norton Anthology of Literature by Women*, 1955.

Riviere, Joan. "Womanliness as Masquerade." 1929. In *Formations of Fantasy*, edited by Victor Burgin, James Donald, and Cora Caplan, 35–44. New York: Methuen, 1986.

Sexton, Anne. "Housewife." In Gilbert and Gubar, *Norton Anthology of Literature by Women*, 1911.

"Stand by Your Man by Tammy Wynette on Johnny Cash TV Show." *YouTube*. http://www.youtube.com/watch?v=7Db3-2iaFhs.

Walker, Alice. *In Search of Our Mothers' Gardens: Womanist Prose*. New York: Harcourt Brace Jovanovitch, 1983.

Washington, Mary Helen, ed. *Black-Eyed Susans: Classic Stories By and About Black Women.* New York: Anchor, 1975.

———, ed. *Midnight Birds: Stories of Contemporary Black Women Writers*. New York: Anchor, 1980.

———. "'Taming all that anger down': Rage and Silence in Gwendolyn Brooks's *Maud Martha*." *Massachusetts Review* 24, no. 2 (Summer, 1983): 453–66.

"Women's Earnings as a Percentage of Men's, 1951–2010." *Infoplease.com*. http://www.infoplease.com/ipa/A0193820.html#ixzz1srLl7GLP.

The Paradox of Re-Colonization

The British Invasion of American Music and the Birth of Modern Rock

ANDREA CAROSSO

> Zoot suit, white jacket with side vents
> Five inches long,
> I'm out on the street again
> And I'm leaping along,
> I'm dressed right for a beach fight,
> But I just can't explain
> Why that uncertain feeling is still
> Here in my brain.
> THE WHO, "CUT MY HAIR" (FROM *QUADROPHENIA*, 1973)

QUADROPHENIA, OR REMINISCENCE ON THE BRITISH INVASION

The plot of the Who's seminal 1973 rock opera *Quadrophenia* centers on Jimmy, a young man "born in the war" and living in a mining town who is torn between the drudgery of his "dirty job" working-class condition ("I am man who drives a local bus / I take miners to work") and fantasies of individual and class redemption in the hope of impending change:

I'm getting put down,
I'm getting pushed round,
I'm being beaten every day,
My life's fading,
But things are changing,
I'm not gonna sit and weep again.[1]

His jacket "cut and slim and checked / Maybe a touch of seersucker, with an open neck," Jimmy rides "a GS scooter with [his] hair cut neat,"[2] perfectly fitting the profile of the Mod, the late 1950s sharp-dressing, amphetamine-pushing British rebel youngster, instrumental in introducing jazz, blues and R&B to the British (and European) taste. In *Quadrophenia*'s version, Jimmy the Mod is less the turn-of-decade existentialist extension of the coffee shop beatnik and more the precursor of 1970s disenfranchised punk. Jimmy rides to Brighton hoping to recapture the excitement of his teenage rebellion, but finds himself on a rock in the sea, where he contemplates whether to jump in and drown himself, or return to working-class oblivion.

Loosely referring to the real-life events of Easter 1964 in Brighton, when battles between rival youth gangs—the notorious Mods and Rockers—made national and international headlines, *Quadrophenia* could be read as Pete Townshend's artistic autobiography, in which Pete/Jimmy the Mod revisits that pivotal moment in his career, circa 1964, when together with a legion of other British musicians, he was instrumental in taking the rock 'n' roll revolution of the 1950s (personified by the Rockers) to new levels (personified by the Mods) which would shape the course of British and American popular music in the latter part of the century. Music scholar James Perone has described the Mods vs. Rockers dichotomy in early 1960s British culture as "a metaphor for the development of British Invasion rock,"[3] a proxy for the cultural tensions out of which, in the five years spanning 1959 to 1964, a revolution in musical and cultural styles emerged on the British music scene and was then exported to America, where it lay the foundation of rock music as it is known today. This essay will explore

1 The Who, "I've Had Enough," in *Quadrophenia*.
2 *Ibid.*
3 Perone, *Mods, Rockers, and the Music*, 2.

the ways in which American popular music was transplanted to Europe, especially Great Britain, "indigenized" as a consequence and then returned to sender through a phenomenon known as the "British Invasion," in ways that radically transformed popular music for decades to come.

THE INDIGENIZATION OF ROCK 'N' ROLL IN BRITAIN

Mods and Rockers were youth subgroups in postwar Britain emerging as the offspring of the Teddy Boys (and Teddy Girls), Britain's first self-styled teenage group. Early in the 1950s, the "Teds" had rejected the austerity of the postwar years by resorting to the fashions of Edwardian-era dandies and established teenagers as a self-identified subculture. In the Teddy Boys' wake at the end of that decade, and amid a backdrop of exploding juvenile rebellion across the country, Mods and Rockers "represented two very different approaches taken by disenfranchised British youth."[4] The Rockers were associated with heavy and powerful motorcycles, favored black leather and their musical tastes ran in the direction of white first-wave American rock 'n' rollers such as Elvis Presley, Bill Haley, Buddy Holly, and especially Eddie Cochran and Gene Vincent, who played the UK in a fateful 1960s tour during which the former was killed and the latter badly injured following an automobile accident. By contrast, the Mods were influenced by the Teddy Boys in dress and made a conscious attempt to appear more in touch with the times, or "modern" (hence their denomination), by favoring Italian scooters, modern jazz, ska-influenced sounds and R&B.

Musically speaking, the differences metaphorically staged by the Mods vs. Rockers confrontation revolved around the development of distinct youth musical styles that had their roots in American popular music, rock 'n' roll and blues in particular, but also radically departed from them through a process which Dave Laing has defined as "indigenization." American popular music arrived in Britain in the 1950s through the records that American servicemen and merchant seamen traveling to England brought with them (this being one of the reasons why Liverpool, a major port, became such hotbed of musical activity), and through the live performances of American rock 'n' rollers and bluesmen on tour this side of the

4 Ibid.

Atlantic. This led to the development of a fervent, albeit rudimentary, scene of young British musicians who adopted and appropriated American popular music, "indigenized" it, in fact, by reworking American rhythms in the direction of a style closer to Buddy Holly's, Eddie Cochran's and Gene Vincent's rockabilly than the harder-driving R&B-influenced rock 'n' roll of Little Richard and other African American artists such as Fats Domino or Bo Diddley, to better suit the playing skills of the British musicians as well as the preferences of their audiences. In a similar fashion, the adoption of the blues in Britain led to the birth of a local blues scene in the late 1950s which would push the style to new levels of innovation, emphasizing technical skill as well as a quasi-elitist, anti-commercial stance.

The first generation of homemade rock 'n' rollers was driven by local artists who often became popular in Britain before the American originals they closely imitated. Leading the pack were acts such as Lonnie Donegan and His Skiffle Group, Cliff Richard and Tommy Steele (the last two contending over the label of "the Elvis of Great Britain" and, like Elvis, soon moving from music to the movies). But just as important was a phalanx of other rockers such as Marty Wilde, Adam Faith, Bill Fury, and Johnny Kidd and the Pirates, whose "Shakin' All Over" topped the British charts during 1960.[5]

Lonnie Donegan, the acclaimed "King of Skiffle," was also the first British artist to break the US pop charts in 1956. A genre originating in America and typical of urban rent parties in the 1930s, skiffle was extremely popular in the UK after World War II, where it became, in Robyn Sitwell's words, "essentially an acoustic, low-tech version of rock 'n' roll."[6] It was a hybrid of American jazz, folk, blues, and country music, which could be performed with the makeshift instrumentation available in the penury of the war's aftermath. It only required a guitar, a bass and a washboard to fully equip a band. Skiffle lay at the root of the Beat revolution of the early 1960s and because it was home-made music, relying on cheap instrumentation and based on simple chords and rhythms, it had a huge appeal on working-class teens with limited financial resources and

5 Johnny Kidd's single eventually also made the US Top 40 in 1965, at the height of the British Invasion, in a distinctly Beat-sounding cover version by the Guess Who, a Canadian band.

6 Stilwell, "Music of the Youth Revolution," 435.

limited musical skills, who found it the ideal formula for "instant music"[7] and instant musicianship. Estimates place the number of skiffle bands in Britain in the late 1950s at anywhere between five and forty thousand.[8] Most British rock bands (including the Beatles) started out as skiffle bands and evolved more sophisticated styles whenever budgets and technical ability allowed.

Cliff Richard was, in the words of British Invasion historian Michael Bryan Kelly, "the rock 'n' roller in England, their Elvis [...] credited with getting rock 'n' roll off the ground."[9] His 1958 hit single "Move It," credited to Cliff Richard and the Drifters (later to be renamed the Shadows, to avoid clashes in the US with the much more popular R&B outfit by the same name) is often described as Britain's first rock and roll song. "Move It" proclaimed the ethos of rock 'n' roll as youth music ("it's rhythm that gets into your heart and soul / Well let me tell you baby it's called rock 'n' roll"). It defied those, on both sides of the Atlantic, who were proclaiming its incumbent demise ("They say it's gonna die but honey please lets face it / Well we just don't know what's a going to replace it"), and challenged the shallowness of styles that the music industry was pushing in its wake ("Well ballet and calypso's have got nothing on / Real country music that just drives along"). John Lennon is reported to have claimed that "before Cliff and the Shadows, there had been nothing worth listening to in British music."

By the late 1950s, as the thrust of the early rock 'n' roll revolution was waning on both sides of the Atlantic, a live dance music style which became known as "the big beat," and later simply "Beat," developed in Britain, taking the process of "indigenization" even further away from the original US rock 'n' roll. Combining rhythmic elements of rock 'n' roll, the vocal textures of doo-wop, the jazz-derived cadences of skiffle, and the African American traditions of R&B and soul, British Beat not only further incorporated American rock 'n' roll into the British popular music tradition, but paradoxically turned it into a commodity for re-exportation to the American market. Developing across several music scenes across the country, and with distinct outcomes in each of them, British Beat was

7 Millard, *Beatlemania*, 81.
8 Ibid., 98.
9 Kelly, *The Beatle Myth*, 15.

shaped mostly in Birmingham (with bands such as the Spencer Davis Group and the Moody Blues), London (most notably with the Dave Clark Five, the Rolling Stones, the Kinks and the Yardbirds) and, most prominently, Liverpool, where it took on the distinguishing denomination "Mersey Beat" and showcased some of the most prolific acts of the genre, including Gerry & the Pacemakers, the Searchers, Cilla Black, and, obviously, the Beatles.

Central to the development of British Beat was a preference for an 8/8 rather than 12/8 beat, which represented a departure from the syncopation of African American rock 'n' roll rhythmic patterns, less familiar to British musicians and audiences, in favor of "a changeless four-four offbeat" drumming style which "was thoroughly flexible [and] could be used to give a rhythmic propulsion, and therefore a simple dance beat to anything,"[10] including songs originating in traditions far removed from rock 'n' roll, as in the case of the Music Hall tradition (the British equivalent of vaudeville). Ironically, the development of this new drumming style took place not in England, but in Hamburg, Germany, where several of the Mersey Beat bands (including the Beatles) played lengthy sessions night after night in the city's red light district during the late 1950s and early 1960s. Comparing the British Beat style to that of Little Richard and Buddy Holly, Dave Laing has noted that

> in the Liverpool beat style, the chord-playing of the rhythm guitar was broken up into a series of separate strokes, often one to the bar, with the regular plodding of the bass guitar and crisp drumming behind it. This gave a very different effect from the monolithic character of rock, in that the beat was given not by the duplication of one instrument in the rhythm section by another, but by an interplay between all three. This flexibility also meant that beat music could cope with a greater range of time-signatures and song shapes than rock&roll had been able to.[11]

The wider musical range of British Beat included not only rock 'n' roll, black and white, but also the larger tradition of the blues (including R&B), which had undergone a major revival in Britain since 1957, after the Musicians' Union rescinded its ban against American jazz artists performing in

10 Laing, "Music Hall," 44.
11 Ibid.

the country. At a time when, in the words of Joe Boyd, "black music of most kinds was a minority taste in white America,"[12] American bluesmen came to regard Europe, and Britain in particular, as a kind of "Promised Land," where they performed before highly appreciative (mainly white) audiences. As bluesmen such as Bill Big Broonzy, Sonny Terry, Brownie McGhee, and Muddy Waters toured extensively in Britain in the late 1950s, a youth following for the blues developed, especially among working-class young Britons who "appropriated [it] as a signifier to define and reflect their sense of otherness,"[13] and creating an ardent circle of aficionado practitioners. The British blues revival climaxed with the formation in 1961 of Alexis Korner's Blues Incorporated, Britain's first amplified urban blues and R&B band and an incubator of a whole generation of white British bluesmen which included Jack Bruce and Eric Clapton (who would later form Cream), John Mayall (founder of the Bluesbreakers in 1963), Jimmy Page and Jeff Beck (forming, with Clapton, the trinity of Yardbirds guitarists; Page would form Led Zeppelin later in the decade), Alvin Lee (founding Ten Years After in 1966), Keith Richards, Mick Jagger, and Charlie Watts (of impending Rolling Stones fame). A significant part in the British blues revival was also played by British music scholar Paul Oliver, whose *Blues Fell This Morning* (1960) remained for decades the definitive book on the subject.

As with rock 'n' roll, British musicians indigenized the blues, especially in the fact that in Britain the division between folk-blues (purportedly the original, authentic form of blues) and R&B (its urban African American pop variation) was never as clear cut as the purists wanted it to be. And ironically, as with rock 'n' roll, the British adoption of the blues prepared for its popularization in later years among white, middle-class Americans: like the rock 'n' roll revival, the blues revival stormed America in the early 1960s not from its birthplace in the US South but as a product of transatlantic dialog. The nature and ways of this transatlantic dialog will be the focus of the remaining part of this essay.

12 Boyd, *White Bicycles*, 67.

13 Schwartz, *How Britain Got the Blues*, 74.

THE BRITISH INVASION OF AMERICAN MUSIC

British artists had tried to penetrate the American music market, by far the largest and most profitable of all, since the mid 1950s, when Lonnie Donegan peaked at number eight in the Billboard pop charts with his first US release, a skiffle rendering of Leadbelly's "Rock Island Line." Donegan broke into the US Top 10 again in 1961. Cliff Richard made headway in 1959 with "Living Doll," peaking at number 30 for one week, and again in 1963 with "Lucky Lips," which did not make it past the number 62 spot, to return in the Billboard Top 40 in 1964 (the magic year for Brit rock) with "It's all in the game."

Besides Lonnie Donegan and Cliff Richard, very few British acts appeared in the US charts before 1964. Those who did were mostly irrelevant to the Beat and rock revolution to come. As Michael Kelly has pointed out in his meticulous chronicle of the British Invasion, "most of the British records which hit the US charts [prior to 1964] had been . . . either jazz-oriented, instrumentals, skiffle, or a combination";[14] in other words, they were almost indistinguishable from the musical blandness that dominated the US charts in the late 1950s and early 1960s. English imports were one of many reservoirs (which also included Latin, mild jazz, and instrumentals) to which the American music industry was resorting in the attempt to clamber out of the swamp which had followed the demise of early rock 'n' roll.

Such demise had occurred towards the end of the 1950s, as original rock 'n' roll had fallen out of favor in the US due to a number of concurring factors, mostly concurrent with the demise of several of the key players.[15] Little Richard retired from music to become a born-again Christian in 1957; Elvis enlisted in the army in 1958, and then took off to Hollywood for a full decade; Jerry Lee Lewis was blacklisted from American radio following the staunch moral backlash of his third marriage to a thirteen-year-old cousin in the same year; Buddy Holly died in a plane crash on February 3, 1959 (a date remembered as "the day the music died"); Alan Freed, rock 'n' roll's legendary DJ and promoter, was fired from radio and TV in 1959 after being indicted for payola payments, a well established practice in the

---

14 Kelly, *The Beatle Myth*, 18.

15 See Altschuler, *All Shook Up*; Stilwell, "Music of the Youth Revolution"; Zak, *I Don't Sound Like Nobody*; Arnold Shaw, *The Rockin' '50s*.

music industry (also known as "pay for play"); and Chuck Berry was imprisoned a couple of years later under the Mann Act for supposedly transporting an underaged girl across state lines for immoral purposes.

Music scholars have offered diverging interpretations on what followed the eclipsing of rock 'n' roll in America in the late 1950s. Those looking at the dynamics of the music market have argued that, beginning in 1959, popular music in the US became bland and formulaic, driven by large doses of "teen" sounds put out by a growing number of independent labels. Rock historian Reebee Garofalo, for example, has argued that, as a "rather limited science," rock 'n' roll had—by the end of the 1950s—been absorbed into "the collective unconscious" of singers, songwriters, and producers, who used its fairly elementary formulas to endlessly mass-produce derivative artifacts, known in the industry as "schlock rock."[16] This brought about "a new generation of white, middle-class teen idols"—Fabian, Frankie Avalon, Bobby Rydell, and others—whose musical backgrounds barely scratched the surface of rock 'n' roll. A more sophisticated, and ultimately more compelling, interpretation has come from scholars interested not so much in what was happening in the sales charts, but rather in what was brewing beneath them. These scholars have argued that the 1959–1993 period is better described as a moment of transition in which "a genuine fusion of black and white music" took place, "on a level of intimacy not encountered since the early 1950s or, arguably, the mid-1920s."[17] Among African American artists, Solomon Burke, Sam Cooke, Ray Charles, and others demonstrated, as Hatch and Millward have argued, that an R&B artist "could still retain a vital relationship with the black audience while surviving in the teenage pop market and in a Las Vegas night-club context."[18] Among white artists, the mainstreaming of the folk revival brought renewed interest in the African American roots of American popular music and a quest to merge these with rock 'n' roll. Bob Dylan, an early rock 'n' roller who had embraced the blues through folk music in the late 1950s, did

16 Garofalo, *Rockin' Out*, 143.

17 See Friedlander and Miller, *Rock and Roll*; Hatch and Millward, *From Blues to Rock*.

18 Hatch and Millward, *From Blues to Rock*, 91.

just that, with his quest for a style which became epitomized by his 1965 defining single "Like a Rolling Stone."[19]

It is in the five-year hiatus between the demise of early rock 'n' roll and the Beatles' historic landing at JFK airport on February 7, 1964 that the roots of this new style were laid, as the British Invasion of American music took shape. According to music historian Charlie Gillett, "Britain served the useful function of re-establishing popular music as a medium for personal expression rather than as the raw material for mass-produced entertainment."[20] The Beat movement, which had been developing since the turn of the decade in Liverpool, Birmingham and London (but also as far away as Newcastle, Glasgow and Dublin), provided those sounds of self-expression and, despite some initial hesitation, America embraced them with sudden and unprecedented enthusiasm. The first British Beat single to appear in the Billboard charts was Del Shannon's 1963 cover of an early Beatles number, "From me to you," which Shannon (an American artist) had heard during the rehearsals of an all-star concert in London in which both he and the Beatles were featured. Faithfully replicating the Fab Four's original arrangement, Shannon's version can be legitimately be viewed as the spearhead in a trend reversal, in which British popular music no longer imitated American formulas, but in fact set novelty trends for the US market. That same year, the Beatles, who had already had three successful releases in Britain (in late 1962 and early and mid 1963), made repeated attempts at breaking the American market, all of them aborted.

Only on the strength of their next two singles, "She Loves You," released in the summer of 1963, and "I Want to Hold Your Hand," released in the fall of the same year, was EMI, the Beatles' British label, able to persuade Capitol Records, its US counterpart, to put their commercial muscle behind a major promotional campaign for the band, to include the US release of their latest singles and major television and live appearances. "I Want To Hold Your Hand" was released in America on January 2, 1964 and within three weeks shot to the top of the pop charts, where it remained for seven straight weeks. In the second week of January, Capitol put out "She Loves You," which replaced the previous hit at the top of the charts in

19 *Ibid.*, 110. For an in-depth discussion of the making and implications of Dylan's "Like a Rolling Stone", see Greil Marcus, *Like a Rolling Stone: Bob Dylan at the Crossroads*.

20 Gillett, *Sound of the City*, 230.

late March. "Please Please Me" (an earlier Beatles hit in the British charts) followed one week later, rapidly climbing to number three. These singles invariably championed the driving "Beat" rhythm which British rock 'n' rollers had "indigenized" from American sources. Before the year was out, the Beatles had charted 34 singles in the Billboard Top 100 pop (a historic high), six of which had climbed to number one, two to number two, and one to number three. Nineteen Beatles singles made it to the Top 40 in 1964 alone, including all of the four songs which had been unsuccessfully launched on the American market the previous year. Beatlemania had swept the US and the band had become, in Lennon's infamous words, "more popular than Jesus."

No account of the Beatles' sudden storming of the US pop charts in 1964 is complete without reference to their first US tour in February of that year. Lengthily discussed in print and film, the Beatles performed to screaming sold-out audiences in Washington, DC and New York City's Carnegie Hall, as well as making three appearances on the most powerful vehicle of youth culture promotion in America at the time: the Ed Sullivan Show. The television appearances drew audiences in excess of 70 million viewers each, with the first one of Sunday, February 9 reaching a record crowd of 73 million viewers—about two-fifths of the total American population and the largest number of viewers recorded on American television until that day. The documentary *What's Happening! The Beatles in the USA* (1964), by celebrated direct cinema auteurs Albert and David Maysles,[21] brilliantly captures the spirit of that first US tour, including the band's quick wit during press conferences (Q: "What do you think of Beethoven?" / RINGO: "Great. Especially his poems"),[22] crowd hysteria, and evidence of the Beatles' disbelief of their own success, best captured in the director's repeated filming of Paul McCartney obsessively glued to a transistor radio, contemplating his own stardom on the American airwaves.

---

21 An edited version of the documentary was re-released in DVD as *The Beatles: Their First US Visit* (and credited to Kathy Dougherty, Susan Frömke and Albert Maysles) in 1999.

22 For a full script of this press conference, see, for instance, *The Beatles Ultimate Experience*, Beatles press conference, American arrival, February 7, 1964, accessed June 26, 2012, http://www.beatlesinterviews.org/db1964.0207.beatles.html.

McCartney's amazement is our own, and a way of addressing it lies in what I call "the paradox of re-colonization," the conundrum by which a whole generation of young UK musicians, raised in the penury of postwar Britain and exposed to American rock 'n' roll and blues mostly through imported records, were able to master these style's key formal elements, absorbing instrumental techniques and singing styles (and accents) which were musically and culturally foreign to them, then take that newly-learned lingo to new stylistic heights and re-export it to the US, "re-colonizing" American music with American's own sounds. This is the paradox to which I will return momentarily.

THE MUSICAL ROOTS OF THE BRITISH BEAT

Although it was singles that determined an artist's success during the rock 'n' roll and Beat years (rock albums began to outsell singles precisely in the wake of the British Invasion), it is the early albums of the British Invasion bands that tell the full story of their music and reveal the full range of their sound matrix. The Beatles' first, second, fourth and fifth albums, as well as their fifth EP, "Long Tall Sally," all released between 1962 and 1965, included a large number of cover songs, spanning the wide range of musical influences which had shaped their sound. Such influences were no less than a comprehensive synthesis of American popular music.[23] Although no traditional rock 'n' roll number appears on their first album, *Please Please Me*, the pioneers of the early rock 'n' roll revolution are very well represented in all of the Beatles' subsequent releases which include cover songs. Chuck Berry ("Roll Over Beethoven," "Rock and Roll Music"), Carl Perkins ("Everybody's Trying to Be My Baby," "Honey Don't," "Match Box"), Little Richard ("Long Tall Sally," "Hey, Hey, Hey, Hey!") and Larry Williams ("Dizzy Miss Lizzy," "Slow Down") all figure prominently in the band's early albums. In that genre, the Beatles also cover Buddy Holly's "Words of Love" and "Kansas City," a song written by Jerry Leiber and Mike Stoller, the Jewish Tin Pan alley songwriting duo responsible for Elvis' defining "Hound Dog" of 1956. R&B, in its various sub-forms, is

23 It is interesting to notice that the Beatles stopped including covers in their albums roughly at the same time they stopped performing live.

another central node of attention in the Beatles' early albums. Their first and second LPs include four "girl group" covers: The Shirelles' "Boys" and "Baby It's You," The Cookies' "Chains," and The Marvellettes' "Please Mr. Postman." This last number is also one of three Motown covers, also including Smokey Robinson's "You Really Got a Hold on Me" and "Money (That's What I Want)," the Detroit label's first all-time release, co-written by the label's founder Berry Gordy and recorded by Barrett Strong in 1959. The Motown sound had captivated the Beatles for its unique combination of vocal harmony and powerful rhythm, characterized by its intense use of the back-beat, which once prompted Lennon to ask the Four Tops: "When you cats go into the studio, what does the drummer beat on to get that back-beat? You use a bloody tree or something?"[24] Among the R&B classics, the Beatles's early albums included covers of Phil Medley and Bert Russell's "Twist and Shout," which had previously been recorded by The Top Notes and by The Isley Brothers, as well as the lesser known "Mr. Moonlight," a song written by Roy Lee Johnson and quite popular in Britain at the time among R&B cognoscenti. Beatles covers also included one Tin Pan Alley standard ("A Taste of Honey"), two soul ballads (Arthur Alexander's "Anna" and Richard Drapkin's "Devil in His Heart"), the Broadway tune "Till There Was You," and a country & western number ("Act Naturally"), to demonstrate how well-versed the Mersey musicians were in the gamut of American popular music and to testify to the range of influences that textured their Beat sounds.

Although the choice of songs for the early Beatles albums was obviously dictated by factors that went beyond the band's individual preferences and were determined by production and marketing decisions, these selections nevertheless emphasize to what extent the Beatles were "imaginary Americans," as Leslie Fiedler once remarked.[25] And if classic rock 'n' roll was the central pillar of their sound, R&B and Soul were just as crucial in the making of their musical style. In fact rock 'n' roll covers in their first two albums were outnumbered by R&B and Soul classics, a genre in which the Beatles found the natural evolution of rockabilly, especially in the way

24 John Lennon, as quoted in Oscar Bettison, *"I Wanna Take You Higher:" The Stylistic Development and Cultural Dissemination of Post-Psychedelic Funk Music*. ProQuest, UMI Dissertation Publishing (September 3, 2011), 6.

25 For a discussion of Fiedler's contention and of the Beatles' international trajectory, see Monteith, *American Culture in the 1960s*, 60–61.

that it emphasized groups over solo artists, sophisticated arrangements over the more elementary formulae of early rock 'n' roll, and doo-wop-derived vocal harmonies over individual vocal performance.

Blues, R&B, and Soul proved to be crucial ingredients for the music of other British bands which also ranked high in the US pop charts in 1964 following the Beatles' breakthrough. In February, a London Beat (typically known as "Tottenham sound") outfit called The Dave Clark Five shot to number six with "Glad All Over," a driving R&B single written by two of the band members, Dave Clark and Mike Smith, and featuring some of the key ingredients of the Stax sound—a persistent saxophone line and percussion drumming—molded into a production closely reminiscent of Phil Spector's wall-of-sound experiments at Gold Star Studios in Los Angeles. As the Dave Clark Five stormed the US charts again a few months later with "Can't You See That She's Mine" (peaking at number four), another London band, The Rolling Stones, named after a Muddy Waters blues classic, appeared for the first time in the Billboard charts with "Not Fade Away," their third UK release. Credited to Buddy Holly and Norman Petty, "Not Fade Away" had been originally recorded by Holly's band The Crickets in 1957 and was based on the characteristic Bo Diddley beat, a beat drawn straight out of West African rhythms.

Two British Invasion bands joined the Beatles at the top of the US charts in 1964: an outfit from Newcastle upon Tyne called The Animals, which went to number one in September with an electric rendering of a blues traditional, "The House of the Rising Sun," also covered by Bob Dylan on his first album a couple of years earlier; and Manfred Mann, a jazz and R&B-influenced London band, whose "Do Wah Diddy" had originally been recorded by the predominantly-female black group The Exciters and was rooted in gospel-style call-and-response vocals. Manfred Mann's version of the song typified the British Beats' adoption of African American music: while preserving the call-and-response vocals, the group simplified the more sophisticated snare drum work of the original, replacing its heavy syncopation with a double pair of maracas that Mann played himself (a style Mick Jagger was very quick to pick up) and flavoring it with the distinctive wheedling tone of the Vox Continental organ.

To sum up, all British Beat bands had a deep commitment to many aspects of African American music. While for the Beatles it was mostly R&B, especially Motown, for the Stones, the Animals and Manfred Mann it was mostly the blues, together with Memphis R&B, as their early albums bear witness. The Animals drew on both country and city bluesmen, John Lee Hooker and Jimmy Reed in particular, and on R&B (Ray Charles, Sam Cooke, and Joe Tex especially); city blues was the foundation of Manfred Mann's sound (the band's first album included songs written or performed by Howlin' Wolf, Willie Dixon and Muddy Waters); the Stones' early albums were, in the words of bassist Bill Wyman, "totally obsessed by the blues,"[26] from early master Robert Johnson to the city sounds of Muddy Waters to Irma Thomas' R&B classic "Time is on My Side," which became a standard in the Stones' repertoire, although "black" rock 'n' roll (Chuck Berry, Bo Diddley) was also an important influence.

THE PARADOX OF RE-COLONIZATION

More British Invasion bands broke into the US Top 10 in 1964, including The Zombies, a band from St. Albans, Hertfordshire, whose "She's Not There," penned by Rod Argent, offered an unusual combination of cool jazz-tinged atmosphere, vocal harmonics, and double-time drumming (an explicit quotation of funk-oriented R&B rhythms)—a formula which many described as "ahead of its time."[27] Other significant chart-toppers were Gerry and the Pacemakers and Billy Kramer and the Dakotas, two Mersey Beat bands who, like the Beatles, were part of Brian Epstein's stable of artists; and the Kinks, a London outfit which proved highly influential during the British Invasion for their merging of a wide range of influences, from music hall to R&B to folk.

Before 1964 was out, 25 British Invasion bands had entered the Billboard charts, with a total of 93 hits, 60 of which ranked in the Top Forty for at least a week.[28] The following year, the number climbed to 108, setting an all-time record, and remained significantly high until 1968, showcasing, alongside already established names, new arrivals which included the Spencer Davis Group, from Birmingham (Steve Winwood, the band's leader, is author of a long string of R&B derived rock classics, including

26 Wynn, *Cross the Water Blues*, 6.

27 Kelly, *Beatle Myth*, 42.

28 All references to the Billboard charts are from Joel Whitburn's standard compilation, *Billboard Hot 100 Charts: The Sixties*.

"Gimme Some Lovin'"), the Them, from Dublin (fronted by R&B-influenced lead singer Van Morrison), the Yardbirds (a blues-inflected outfit from London, famous for enlisting, in close succession, Eric Clapton, Jimmy Page and Jeff Beck as lead guitarists), Herman's Hermits, the Troggs, the Hollies, and the Who, whose engrossing appearance at the Monterey Pop Festival of 1967 made them an overnight sensation in the US.

Beginning in 1968, the British Beat in the US began to wane due to factors in one way or another connected with a dramatic transformation of the American popular music scene in the wake of the British Invasion. The first of these factors was the development of an American native Beat movement, closely replicating the sounds of the British Beat bands, just as the British bands had been hard at work earlier in the decade imitating American sounds. The Monkees, assembled in Hollywood in 1966 for the launch of a television sit-com centering on four aspiring rock 'n' rollers, became the American response to the Beatles; likewise, The Turtles, another LA-based Beat band, and the Beau Brummels, from San Francisco, closely replicated not only the sounds but also the looks (and at times the British-inflected accents) of their transatlantic counterparts. Another factor in the decline of the British Invasion was the growing attention that African American music, and especially Motown, was receiving in the US pop charts (from 1965 through 1971 Motown had at least ten Top 10 hits per year) and the more funk-oriented soul records coming out the southern studios in Memphis and Muscle Shoals. Moreover, the concurrent development of a blue-eyed soul scene, with bands such as The Righteous Brothers and The Rascals, pointed to the fact that more white American acts were turning to African American music for new directions.

The driving force behind the decline of the British Invasion in America after 1968 was primarily, in Elija Wald's words, "a major change in orientation *[from] rock 'n' roll* (the earlier, teen-oriented music) *to rock* (its myriad post-Beatles offshoots)."[29] Beginning at mid decade (a good starting point might be the historic recording of Bob Dylan's "Like a Rolling Stone" in August 1965 and his infamous "electric" appearance at the Newport Folk Festival the previous month), American rock extended the adoption of African American musical language to a wider cultural territory and

29 Wald, *How the Beatles Destroyed Rock 'n' Roll*, 237, italics mine.

presiding over the inception of a plethora of subgenres, including folk rock (which stressed poetic or socially conscious lyrics with acts such as Dylan and The Byrds), blues rock (Steppenwolf, The Butterfield Blues Band, and the genre's British originators which had become a staple on the American charts), country rock (Creedence Clearwater Revival, Band, Poco), southern rock (The Allman Brothers Band, Lynyrd Skynyrd), psychedelia (The Shondelles, Vanilla Fudge, The Doors), west-coast sounds (Jefferson Airplane, The Grateful Dead, CSN&Y), funk rock (The Jimi Hendrix Experience, Sly & the Family Stone), and jazz-fusion rock (Blood, Sweat & Tears, Chicago).

And although it would be improper to locate the British Invasion as the sole factor for the emergence of rock, it was arguably its main enabling factor: specialists and aficionados might disagree with the finer subgenre distinctions, but the fact remains that the British Invasion was instrumental in the emergence of a rock scene in the mid to late 1960s, which took American popular music in so many new and transatlantic directions. This takes us back to the question of the "paradox."

In his study of the British Invasion, Michael Kelly has argued that the British Invasion bands' "penchant for redoing US hit songs of the recent and not so recent past" was a "paradoxical situation," the paradox, according to Kelly, lying in the fact that although the British bands had become popular in America because they presented themselves as an alternative to American rock 'n' roll, "nearly all of them redid old American material."[30] Although I share Kelly's idea of the paradox, I rather see it operating in another, much more decisive direction. The paradox of the British Invasion was, in my view, not in the music, but rather in the fact that it took precisely these British musicians—teenagers in the late 1950s who had grown up absorbing and replicating American blues, R&B and rock 'n' roll—to persuade white American audiences (driving record sales in the US) that African American music was the language of the postwar generation. In *The Crying of Lot 49* (1966), which is set in 1964, Thomas Pynchon satirizes the British Invasion through the collective character of The Paranoids, a fictional band composed of American teenagers who speak with an ordinary American accent but are instructed to watch British TV so that they can

30 Kelly, *Beatle Myth*, 28.

sound genuinely British.[31] Possibly an explicit reference to the Beatles (who called themselves Los Paranoias),[32] The Paranoids also function as a reminder of the uncanny nature of the British Invasion, whose bands spoke in strong (often working-class) British accents but sang with a distinct American twang. Moreover, those white working class Britons swept white America by drawing from a cultural reservoir that white America had always resisted coming to terms with.

It took the re-colonization of American music by a swarming British Invasion in the mid-1960s to enable the rise of a full-fledged rock movement in America and to endow Americans with a powerful cultural reservoir capable of granting a whole generation "a sound of their own."[33] Discussing the birth of southern rock, Mark Kemp articulates this very paradox:

> It's ironic that the genesis of southern rock goes back to the British Invasion of the mid-1960s, when acts such as the Beatles, the Rolling Stones, the Yardbirds, the Animals, Cream, and Led Zeppelin took southern American musical traditions such as the blues, country, and early rock & roll, and transformed them into a new sound. It was an exciting new style of rock & roll that reintroduced southern musical traditions to a new generation of Americans, including young southerners, who were hungry for a sound of their own, a sound that was distinct from the music of their parents yet culturally familiar.[34]

It took a sort of cultural triangulation, from Memphis and Chicago to the poverty-ridden urban centers of postwar Britain and back to the golden gates of the Billboard charts, to empower mainstream American popular music with the sounds of its own African American roots. The British Invasion musicians had adopted American blues (and its offshoots) for its musical merit, largely unaware of the cultural suspicion which had until that point segregated it from white audiences in America and which had in the process rendered the racial (and racist) critique inherent in American blues irrelevant. In fact, the early British invasion coincided with an albeit short-lived moment in the American music industry when the separation of white and black charts vanished, as the two consumer markets appeared to con-

31 See Monteith, *American Culture in the 1960s*, 60–61.
32 See Craig Cross, *Beatles-discography.com*, 393.
33 Kemp, *Dixie Lullaby*, xx.
34 Ibid.

verge into one largely shared template of popular music tastes.[35] To the British youngsters absorbing records imported from the US in the mid to late 1950s, American blues did not equal, as singer Cassandra Wilson effectively summarized, "low class, low income, sadness," but rather, in Keith Richards' words, "the most important thing America has ever given to the world."[36] And when British music had a chance to break through the US pop market, it had the paradoxical effect of suddenly neutralizing that cultural uneasiness and pushing it to the side of the equation. "One obvious effect of this European glamour," emphasizes Elijah Wald, "was to separate rock 'n' roll from its associations with juvenile delinquency and, more enduringly, with black Americans. Another was to smooth the path to its acceptance as art."[37]

By the mid-1960s, the British Invasion had become instrumental in enabling the emergence of an American rock scene, at first as an extension of that invasion, then as an autonomous cultural movement. Although raising issues of whether, in the words of Brian Ward, "whites should even try to express themselves using the music of a community of which they are not members, grounded in historical experiences they never share,"[38] the British Invasion helped erode long-held American myths of cultural identity. It would obviously be naïve to claim that the emergence of rock obliterated race issues in American music (let alone racial segregation in America): in spite of its roots in the blues, American rock became a largely white affair, with its own racist (or at best noncommittal) undertones. As Brian Ward has extensively documented, white consumption and adoption of black music did not eradicate racial prejudice; in fact, it was "deeply inscribed with many of the social, sexual, moral and economic and even racial values of the dominant culture" and ended up reinforcing racial stereotypes.[39] But it remains a fact that, beginning in the 1960s and into the following decades, the blues gained unconditional acceptance in white America. When in the summer of 1967 the Monterey Pop Festival catapulted Otis Redding to instant stardom among a white crowd that "complete[ly understood] the mu-

35 Billboard discontinued its R&B charts between November 1963 and January 1965.

36 Richards and Pallington West, *What Would Keith Richards Do?* 99.

37 Wald, *How the Beatles Destroyed Rock 'n' Roll*, 233.

38 Ward, "That White Man, Burdon," 3–5.

39 Ward, *Just My Soul Responding*, 4.

sical ley lines being drawn that night between rock and deep soul"[40] and prepared Jimi Hendrix (who had made his first US appearance precisely at Monterey) to become, within a couple of years, the highest-paid rock musician in the world,[41] it was clear that the American popular music scene had become less focused on the race of musicians, and more on the stuff of their music.[42] And although white artists remained for many years more marketable than the African American acts they admired,[43] the British Invasion also marked a defining watershed in the development of late twentieth-century popular music in the US, its shift away from early rock 'n' roll to a more cosmopolitan and sophisticated Mod aesthetics mixing African American styles and defining rock for the decades to come.

BIBLIOGRAPHY

Altschuler, Glenn C. *All Shook Up: How Rock 'n' Roll Changed America. Pivotal Moments in American History*. Oxford: Oxford University Press, 2003.

Bennett, Andy, and Jon Stratton. *Britpop and the English Music Tradition*. Farnham, Surrey, UK: Ashgate, 2010.

Boyd, Joe. *White Bicycles: Making Music in the 1960s*. London: Serpent's Tail, 2006.

Clayson, Alan. *Call Up the Groups! The Golden Age of British Beat, 1962–1967*. Poole, Dorset, UK: Blandford Press, 1985.

Cross, Craig. *Beatles-discography.com. Day-by-Day Song-by-Song Record-by-Record*, Lincoln, NE: iUniverse, 393.

Curtis, James M. *Rock Eras: Interpretations of Music and Society; 1954–1984*. Bowling Green, OH: Bowling Green State University Popular Press, 1987.

Ennis, Philip H. *The Seventh Stream: The Emergence of Rocknroll in American Popular Music*. Hanover, NH: Wesleyan University Press, 1992.

Fox, Jon Hartley. *King of the Queen City: The Story of King Records*. Music in American Life. Urbana: University of Illinois Press, 2009.

40 Inglis, *Performance and Popular Music*, 35.
41 Lang, *Road to Woodstock*, 84.
42 See also Werner, *A Change is Gonna Come*, 89.
43 Garofalo, *Rockin' Out*, 167.

Friedlander, Paul, and Peter Miller. *Rock and Roll: A Social History*. 1996. Reprint, Boulder, CO: Westview Press, 2006.

Garofalo, Reebee. *Rockin' Out: Popular Music in the USA*. 4th ed. Upper Saddle River, NJ: Pearson Prentice Hall, 2008.

Gillett, Charlie. *The Sound of the City: The Rise of Rock and Roll*. London: Souvenir Press, 1971.

Hatch, David, and Stephen Millward. *From Blues to Rock: An Analytical History of Pop Music*. Manchester, UK: Manchester University Press, 1987.

Inglis, Ian. *Performance and Popular Music: History, Place and Time*. Aldershot, Hampshire, UK: Ashgate, 2006.

Kelly, Michael Bryan. *The Beatle Myth: The British Invasion of American Popular Music; 1956–1969*. Jefferson, NC: McFarland, 1991.

Kemp, Mark. *Dixie Lullaby: A Story of Music, Race, and New Beginnings in a New South*. New York: Free Press, 2004.

Laing, Dave. "Music Hall and the Commercialization of English Popular Music." In Bennett and Stratton, *Britpop and the English Music Tradition*, 11–26.

Lang, Michael. *The Road to Woodstock*. New York: Ecco, 2009.

London, Herbert Ira. *Closing the Circle: A Cultural History of the Rock Revolution*. Chicago: Nelson-Hall, 1984.

Marcus, Greil. *Like a Rolling Stone: Bob Dylan at the Crossroads*. New York: PublicAffairs, 2006.

Millard, Andre J. *Beatlemania: Technology, Business, and Teen Culture in Cold War America.* Baltimore: Johns Hopkins University Press, 2012.

Monteith, Sharon. *American Culture in the 1960s*. Edinburgh: Edinburgh University Press, 2008.

Perone, James E. *Mods, Rockers, and the Music of the British Invasion.* Westport, CT: Praeger Publishers, 2009.

Richards, Keith, and Jessica Pallington West. *What Would Keith Richards Do? Daily Affirmations from a Rock 'n' Roll Survivor*. London: Bloomsbury, 2009.

Schwartz, Roberta Freund. *How Britain Got the Blues: The Transmission and Reception of American Blues Style in the United Kingdom.* Aldershot, Hampshire, UK: Ashgate, 2007.

Shaw, Arnold. *The Rockin' '50s: The Decade That Transformed the Pop Music Scene*. New York: Hawthorn Books, 1974.

Stilwell, Robynn. "Music of the Youth Revolution: Rock through the 1960s." In *The Cambridge History of Twentieth-Century Music*, edited by Nicholas Cook and Anthony Pople, 418–52. Cambridge: Cambridge University Press, 2004.

Terry, Jill, and Neil A. Wynn, eds. *Transatlantic Roots Music: Folk, Blues, and National Identities*. Jackson: University Press of Mississippi, 2012

Wadhams, Wayne, David Nathan, and Susan Gedutis Lindsay. *Inside the Hits: Seduction of a Rock and Roll Generation*. Pop Culture. Boston: Berklee Press, 2001.

Wald, Elijah. *How the Beatles Destroyed Rock 'n' Roll: An Alternative History of American Popular Music*. Oxford: Oxford University Press, 2009.

Ward, Brian. *Just My Soul Responding: Rhythm and Blues, Black Consciousness, and Race Relations*. Berkeley, CA: University of California Press, 1998.

———. "That White Man, Burdon: The Animals, Race and the American South." In *Transatlantic Roots Music: Folk, Blues, and National Identities*, edited by Jill Terry and Neil A. Wynn, 153–78. Jackson: University of Mississippi Press, 2012.

Werner, Craig. *A Change Is Gonna Come: Music, Race & the Soul of America.* New York: Plume, 2009.

The Who. *Quadrophenia.* MCA Records, MCAD2–11463, 1996, 2 sound discs. Originally released in 1973.

Whitburn, Joel. *Billboard Hot 100 Charts: The Sixties*. Milwaukee, WI: Hal Leonard, 1995.

Wynn, Neil A. *Cross the Water Blues: African American Music in Europe.* Jackson: University Press of Mississippi, 2007.

Zak, Albin J., III. *I Don't Sound Like Nobody: Remaking Music in 1950s America*. Ann Arbor: University of Michigan Press, 2010.

The Summer of Love and Protest

Transatlantic Counterculture in the 1960s

RUSSELL DUNCAN

IMAGINE

By 1971, with the American war in Vietnam in its seventeenth year, John Lennon created the single most admired anthem of the era. In many ways the song was a retrospective siren call to continue the counterculture. As balladeer for the love generation, Lennon asked for everything: "Imagine there's no countries. It isn't hard to do. Nothing to live or die for. And no religion too. Imagine all the people living life in peace." Lennon knew that that the defenders of the status quo "may say I'm a dreamer, but I'm not the only one. I hope some day you'll join us. And the world will live as one." During the 1960s, young people in the Western world were a political and cultural force, whether they took to the streets, stormed university offices, smoked dope, burned their military draft cards or their bras, ran away from home or dropped out. Youth culture and the counterculture intersected and coexisted and widened the generation gap.

The counterculture arose during a time of plenty and a time of protest.[1] The West was richer than it had ever been—that setting is important. Demanding more progress toward the promises of prosperity, those hoping for integration and equality included African Americans, Red Power advocates,

1 For the best overview of new social movements and the culture of the 1960s, see Monteith, *American Culture in the 1960s*.

the Gay Liberation Front, Chicano migrants, workers, feminists, and anti-war protestors. These groups did not forge the counterculture; but they did enable its creation or continuance by keeping society off balance. The American government responded to the pressure when President Lyndon Johnson signed voting rights legislation, declared a "war on poverty," and initiated the Great Society programs. For the majority of white teenagers, the simple facts of growing up privileged in this setting spawned a transatlantic youth culture that begat a counterculture.

A Cold War, arms buildups, and the space race fed anxieties that a nuclear exchange between the Soviet Union and the United States was absolutely possible. This threat forced many people towards the conclusion that something was terribly wrong with "the system" even though they lived in the "post-scarcity" economies of Western nations. There was an abundance of everything, but redistribution to all parts of society had failed. For example, property rights were protected over civil rights, male violence had more power than liberated sexuality, and ideals of competition ruled over cooperation. Moreover, the comfort of modern industrial society was a real "downer" in its insistence on conformity, environmental destruction, de-spiritualization from Nature, and an impersonal ethos. Wasn't there a better way to live? Many located the problem in too much wealth and a focus on consumer products and too little support for people's lives. The hallowed Western concepts of rationalism, work, wealth, and civilization had misfired when they mixed with advanced capitalism and its technology to produce mind-numbing work. Simplicity might result in a better lifestyle. And, of course, the opposite of work is play.

"The Times They Are A'Changin'"

"Don't trust anyone over thirty!" cautioned graduate student Jack Weinberg during the Free Speech Movement protests on the campus of the University of California at Berkeley in 1964. Weinberg called for the younger generation to believe in itself.[2] The Beatles had toured the US in 1964, linking American youth to British and European youth in romantic ballads which they sang in an American accent, including *I Want to Hold Your Hand*. A

2 Charters, *Portable Sixties Reader*, 192.

"rabid Beatlemania"—something British playwright Noel Coward called a "mass masturbation orgy"—swept through the media, the teenagers, and some of their parents too.[3] Songwriter Bob Dylan influenced youth culture everywhere with his powerful philosophical protests *Masters of War* (1963), *The Times They Are A'Changin* (1964), *Subterranean Homesick Blues* (1965), and others.[4] In Germany, not trusting those over 30 was linked to criticism of the Nazi past.[5] Elsewhere and everywhere the media picked up on the slogan, even though, in reality, most young people continued to trust their parents and teachers. Trusting parents was different from trusting the political and business establishments.

As the upheaval gained momentum, music bad boy Jim Morrison kicked in and opened the "doors of perception," as Aldous Huxley had termed it in his 1954 book by the same name, after a phrase taken from William Blake.[6] Mick Jagger led a whole band of bad boys and helped solidify the idea of a generational split with the obscure sexualized lyrics of Howling Wolf's *Little Red Rooster* (1965). Then Morrison covered the Stones's incendiary *Light My Fire* (1966/1967) and the transatlantic crossbreeding heightened a generational identification, a shared discourse of youth. More bands followed as the music revolution crisscrossed the Atlantic, accelerating from the early days of rock 'n' roll when the likes of Chuck Berry, Bill Haley, Jerry Lee Lewis and Little Richard became models for other innovators, including Tommy Steele, Cliff Richard, Eric Burden, the Yardbirds, and the Kinks. A thousand bands blossomed to supply the words that spread the romantic social movement that became the counterculture.

As it took a central role in the development of consciousness, the music led adherents away from the old ways. Some people even believe that if rock 'n' roll had not happened, nothing would have happened.[7] Importantly, the portable transistor radio, which was invented in 1954, became wide-

3 Braunstein, "Forever Young," 245; Noel Coward quoted in DeGroot, *Sixties Unplugged*, 224.

4 O'Neill, *Coming Apart*, 236.

5 Siegfried, "Don't Trust Anyone," 739.

6 Huxley, *Doors of Perception;* William Blake, *The Marriage of Heaven and Hell* (n.p. 1793) is a book of poems. In "A Memorable Fancy," Blake wrote: "If the doors of perception were cleansed, everything would appear to man as it is, infinite."

7 McKay, "Social and (Counter-) Cultural 1960s," 45.

ly owned by almost every teenager in Britain and America and provided non-stop access to the revolution when added to the car and home radio and a record player too.[8] Clearly, music became central to a youthful rebellion and a counterculture that widened the generation gap in American society. And yet, it is good to remember that the most popular single song in America in 1966 was Sergeant Barry Sadler's *Ballad of the Green Berets*, a paean to the virtues of god, family, country, military service, manhood, and violence. The culture wars hit full stride.

Rock 'n' roll sprang from the sexual cravings of a generation of kids who had secretly read the best parts of their parents' copies of the *Kinsey Reports* (1948 and 1953) on American sexual habits and looked at the centerfolds of *Playboy* magazine (since December 1953). Then they passed around Helen Gurley Brown's *Sex and the Single Girl* (1962) before graduating to *Human Sexual Response* (1966) and its research findings on clitoral arousal, vaginal lubrication, and multiple female orgasms.[9] It is clearly impossible to understand the sixties and the counterculture without becoming immersed in the pulsating, erotic, hopeful, danceable and life-altering protest music that commandeered the television and radio airways.

With all the excitement surrounding the generation's coming of age and with the War in Vietnam always there to end or influence their lives, there was a mood of tremendous angst as the baby boomers tried to decipher the perennial questions of "Who am I?" and "What does it all mean?" Hollywood tried to answer with films that quickly went transatlantic, including *The Graduate* (1967), *Bonnie and Clyde* (1967), *Easy Rider* (1969), and *Midnight Cowboy* (1969). Mostly, the parental generation resisted this tidal wave of youthful searching and, predictably, stayed away from these movies, scolded change, told the kids to be moral and to do their duty to god and country. But those rising into adulthood would not turn back. So, as the sixties gained strength, the older generations took up the music, fashion, and some of the ideas too. It is useful to note the difference in the early and later 1960s, as Peter Braunstein reminds us: "No longer simply an age cate-

8 Stuart Laing, "Economy, Society and Culture," 25; DeGroot, *Sixties Unplugged*, 19–24.

9 *The Kinsey Reports* is the popular name for two books on sexual behavior, *Sexual Behavior in the Human Male* (1948), and *Sexual Behavior in the Human Female* (1953). *Human Sexual Response* (1966) was authored by William H. Masters and Virginia E. Johnson.

gory, youth became a metaphor, an attitude toward life, a state of mind that even adults could access. . . . [a] persuasive rejuvenation mentality went on to imbue the ideology of the late-'60s counterculture."[10]

THE AGE OF AFFLUENCE AND THE GREAT REFUSAL

Identity questions needed resolution and many university students sought answers in the intellectual explorations of sociologists and philosophers. Together, these critics promoted a complete reevaluation of western capitalist societies. Reinhold Niebuhr's *The Children of Light and the Children of Darkness* (1944), David Riesman's *The Lonely Crowd* (1950), William Whyte's *The Organization Man* (1956), C. Wright Mills's *The Power Elite* (1956), Herbert Marcuse's *Eros and Civilization* (1955) and *One Dimensional Man* (1964), and Guy Debord's *The Society of the Spectacle* (1967) led the way. Their ideas encouraged young people and liberal leaders to understand and frame their own strategies of dissent. These books came of age as the baby boom generation came of age, and the ideas and the young people were born and grew up together.

Respectively, some of the lessons learned, even if only superficially enough to confirm the youth movement, included those from Niebuhr: the Children of Light, who believe in a harmony of the whole world, need to be aware that greedy forces of self-interest, the Children of Darkness, will use the former's optimistic, secular idealism against them; from Riesman: we are lonely and "other-directed" because our "inner-directed" individualism is fading before the onslaught of the media and business establishment that tell us what is important; from Whyte: we have become organization men because our personal desires and goals have been subsumed to the values of, loyalty to and security of corporate capitalism; from Mills: a power elite of bankers, businessmen, and government officials—a military, industrial, government complex—limits choices for those outside their ranks; from Marcuse: the history of capitalist work causes class stratification—"alienated labor"—which sublimates eros, our sex drive; also from Marcuse: we have lost a multi-dimensional character by a process of repression that has been driven into us by an advanced industrial society that has cre-

10 Braunstein, "Forever Young," 243.

ated "false needs"; and from Debord: we have been impoverished and alienated from our true selves by a society that makes a fetish of commodities and so we live in a superficial spectacle of consumerism that makes us unable to recognize what is really happening.

In the end, students mixed and matched these ideas as promulgated by philosophers and theorists from both sides of the Atlantic and took up Marcuse's subversive call to begin a "Great Refusal" based upon oppositional thought and behavior—a sort of finger in the face of the establishment. Historian Timothy Miller called the counterculture "the Disloyal Opposition" where "the culture of peace and love was also a culture of confrontation and conflict."[11] The Great Refusal became a dropping out and a misty-minded, yet determined, search for a utopian society. As cultural values were reappraised, everything was questioned and new avenues opened. Later on, Hippie-turned-Yippie Jerry Rubin would explain: "Fuck work—we want to know ourselves. . . . The goal is to free one's self from American society's sick notions of work, success, reward, and status. . . ."[12] I can see John Winthrop and his Puritan neighbors spinning in their graves as the Protestant work ethic is flushed down the toilet.

Rising out of what historians call the Age of Affluence (1942–1975), the baby boomers were among the richest, most pampered generation the world had ever seen.[13] Now, in defiance of the system and the Age, they held up middle fingers and made the slogan "Marx, Mao, Marcuse" commonplace. They tied proletarian, state, and popular communism together into a clever, if simplistically conceived, alliance.[14] In Europe, young rebels added Fidel Castro and Che Guevara to their list of heroes. Students also heard stories of their alienation in Paul Goodman's *gestalt* classic *Growing Up Absurd* (1960). Goodman wrote that youth had "grown up in a world too meaningless to learn anything" and would be better off being spontaneous, existential, and communitarian, while separating themselves from the

---

11 Miller, *Hippies and American Values*, 103.

12 Rubin quoted in DeGroot, *Sixties Unplugged*, 209–10.

13 The branding, "Age of Affluence," is credited to Roszak, *Making of a Counter Culture*, xxii–xxiii. See also Galbraith, *Affluent Society*.

14 The main theses of these thinkers are well-known and easily available. For a more in-depth discussion of the context of these ideas, see Watson, *Modern Mind*, esp. 421–70, 502–3, 536–8, 590–601; Hollinger and Capper, *American Intellectual Tradition*, vol. 2, esp. 286–91, 435–43, 490–9.

older generation.[15] Life was for living, not just enduring. Norman O. Brown taught that eroticism was debased by civilization as man lost touch with natural consciousness.[16] And, in 1967, thousands brandished Mao Zedong's *Quotations* ("the little red book")—the world's best-selling words of the year. The ideas of British psychiatrist R. D. Laing splitting theory from experience and holding that "truth must have a biographical, not merely an ideological, context" were widely adopted.[17]

The generation gap rose out of the booming economy, affluence, and demographic changes that came from a surge in births—the "youthquake"—after World War II. Then, in 1960, the birth control pill was a great enabler that made the sixties possible.[18] In 1964, the front edge of the 20 million baby boomers in America turned eighteen years old. These numbers created a vast potential for change. The leading age cohort for the next seven years was the seventeen-year-old age group. By 1968 the median age in the United States had fallen to 27.7 years old.[19] Combined with affluence, these demographics created an explosion of university-bound young people, all clustered together in colleges nationwide and becoming more and more politically sensitive.

Never had so many had it so good. Students enjoyed an affluence that no generation had ever seen before. They had disposable income and made up a consumer market of new proportions. By 1965 teenage Americans were collectively spending $25 billion a year. The parental generation had suffered through Depression and World War II and they were ready to enjoy the good life that a post-scarcity society offered. Suburbs expanded. The number of children expanded. Wealth expanded. Then discontent expanded. As historian Jay Stevens so aptly states, "It was an almost obscene ony, but the kids who had enjoyed the richest, most pampered adolescence in the history of the world had now decided that it was all crap."[20] Stevens was quick to add: "Of course . . . for each one who wanted to seize power, dismantle the Establishment, and redistribute the wealth, there were

15 Goodman quoted in O'Neill, *Coming Apart*, 258.

16 For the best discussion of Brown's books *Life Against Death* (1959) and *Love's Body* (1966), see Roszak, *Making of a Counter Culture*, 84–120.

17 Roszak, *Making of a Counter Culture*, 49–57; see also R. D. Laing, *Politics of Experience*.

18 Braunstein, "Forever Young,"248.

19 Stevens, "Counterculture," 310; O'Neill, *Coming Apart*, 266.

20 Ibid., 311.

at least ten others who just wanted to get through school, get laid, get a job, and get out of going to Vietnam."[21] These sentiments hold true in Europe, but without the factor of Vietnam. The German newspaper *Die Welt* expressed what many experienced: "Without a doubt, this generational conflict is the greatest surprise of the postwar era, probably the greatest surprise of all unexpected happenings."[22]

HIPPIES, THE NEW LEFT, AND YOUTH CULTURE

Historian Theodore Roszak put a name to those who "decided that it was all crap." He called them the "Counter Culture" and praised their brave opposition to the technocrats who were ruling the world for profits.[23] For Roszak, the hippies who made up the opposition were arrayed against the hegemonic class of elite managers (a "technocracy") that depended on the myths of "objective consciousness"—meaning rationality, reason, science. These myths justified and led to racial discrimination, endless warfare, unequal wealth, environmental destruction, and set up a convincing and coercive argument that made citizens want to follow the rules. On the other hand, said Roszak, the counterculture offered a "subjective consciousness" of poetry, songs, dance, magic, natural cures, simple living, communal sharing, and love.[24]

The counterculture of hippies and near-hippies stemmed from the youth culture. So did the New Left. But the New Leftists fought from within the system, taking political stances in opposition to what they saw as a common peril in the face of The Bomb and the human degradation of racism. In the United States, Berlin, and Paris, respectively, the Students for a Democratic Society, "Red Rudi" Dutschke, and the Sorbonne Occupation Committee led the political charge. These were young people, mostly white university students and recent graduates who wanted to expand democracy.[25] They were not cultural radicals, as sociologist and former SDS president

21 Ibid., 312.
22 Siegfried, "Don't Trust Anyone," 731; for many excellent essays on the 1960s in Europe, see Shildt and Siegfried, *Between Marx and Coca-Cola.*
23 Roszak, *Making of a Counter Culture*, 42.
24 Ibid., 2–8, 22, 97, 208.
25 Rossinow, "'Revolution Is About Our Lives,'" 99.

Todd Gitlin made clear: "[We] had to confront the counterculture that was in many ways more attractive than radical politics." Gitlin knew well that hard-core activism was needed to confront the West's Cold War policies, but that SDS could not stand up to the counterculture's focus on sex, drugs and rock music. The call to drop out was romantic and very American—a movement to a frontier, to a New Eden, where passion and intuition would free humans from the failures of rationalism and order.[26] In the final analysis then, as Timothy Miller pointed out, the New Left was "not a fundamental threat to society" but the counterculture was a huge threat.[27]

Historian Terry Anderson pointed out that what the hippies—as escapists, rejectionists, and oppositionists—were able to do was remarkably political: "they significantly altered cold war culture. . . . The result is more personal freedom than at any time in the history of the Republic."[28] The counterculture provided at least a moment of heroic mobilization against Vietnam, racism, repressive sexual codes, and conformity. "Make Love, Not War" seemed the best way to fix the society—and Roszak asked us to remember how brave a statement this was to make in the militaristic 1960s.[29] So, while the SDS and the hippies were from the same white middle-class demographic group with the same music, sexual freedom, and affluence, they differed considerably. Hippies thought the New Left was stuck in the same old arguments that had existed since the 1920s—arguments that put them inside the system instead of outside of it. Besides, the SDS appeal to rationalism was in opposition to the spiritual direction the hippies sought. Moreover, the SDS did not seem to have much fun; for the hippies, the goal was pleasure. This difference also rotated around the dividing line of hippies wanting to improve the communal self and the New Left focus on improving society.[30]

In the 1960s, the counterculture was composed mainly of teenagers and people in their twenties who believed the Establishment was rotten to the core. This disaffection went to the level of teenage consciousness and into the deepest reservoirs of the self. The long-standing mantra of exceptionalism and the national character myths of experimentation, freedom, individ-

26 Miller, "Sixties-Era Communes," 329.
27 Miller, *Hippies and American Values*, 15.
28 Anderson, *Movement and the Sixties*, ix.
29 Roszak, *Making of a Counter Culture*, xxv.
30 Michals, "From 'Consciousness Expansion,'" 50.

ualism, frontier, youth, change, and novelty provided psychological support. The counterculture may not have been able to list its "goals" or set out a "roadmap," but that was the point—to get away from the "rational" line the conservative establishment worshipped.

TRANSATLANTIC INTERCOURSE

By winter 1967, with the killings of President John F. Kennedy and black nationalist leader Malcolm X in the recent past—and a year before the murders of Democratic presidential candidate Robert Kennedy and civil rights leader Martin Luther King, Jr.—and the escalating troop presence and deaths in Vietnam, novelist and political essayist Susan Sontag weighed in on the side of the new counterculture.[31] In the *Partisan Review*, Sontag wrote that the nation's anxiety came from "The unquenchable American moralism and the American faith in violence. . . . They constitute a full-grown, firmly-installed national psychosis."[32] Furthermore, she said, "American power is indecent in its scale."[33] Sontag had lost faith in the American government, called the nation's leaders "genuine yahoos," and suggested:

> About the only promise one can find anywhere in this country today is in the way some young people are carrying on, making a fuss. I include both their renewed interest in politics. . . and the way they dance, dress, wear their hair, riot, make love. I also include the homage they pay to Oriental thought and rituals. And I include, not least of all, their interest in taking drugs—despite the unspeakable vulgarization of this project by [Dr. Timothy] Leary and others. . . .[34]

---

31 The murders of liberal and relatively youthful icons included John F. Kennedy on 22 November 1963, Malcolm X on 21 February 1965, Martin Luther King, Jr., on 4 April 1968, and Robert F. Kennedy on 5 June 1968. These high profile deaths were on top of the killings of student activists in Mississippi during Freedom Summer in 1964, the killings of 4 students at Kent State University in 1969, and the more than 58,000 young American soldiers who died in the Vietnam War.

32 Sontag, "What's Happening in America," 121, 122.

33 Ibid., 120.

34 Ibid., 124.

Sontag believed that youthful expression might actually save the country in the end.

Now, as then, it is difficult to delineate exactly what youth culture imagined for itself and for the nation. In fact, is there any simple way to explain what went on in the sixties youth culture? Political scientist Mark Lilla remarked that we know what came before and what came after, but "we are still groping for the meaning of what happened in between."[35] What is clear is that while there was a transatlantic intercourse, the leading edge of what was happening, the hegemonic avant-garde was in the United States.[36]

The claim to the meaning of the counterculture was fought over during the1960s, and has been fought over ever since. In Britain, modern criticism of the era is an appeal to a quiet "middle England."[37] In the US the Republican Right blames the 1960s—particularly rock 'n' roll and hippies—for undermining American values and for America's decline. Conservatives like to quote Ronald Reagan, who was governor of California during this time: "A hippie is someone who dresses like Tarzan, has hair like Jane, and smells like Cheetah."[38] Reagan called the hippies, "the hotbed of evil." Even the term culture wars is derivative of the counter culture. Right Wing Jurist Robert Bork stated: "We are two cultural nations. One embodies the counterculture of the 1960s, which is today the dominant culture. . . . The other nation, of those who adhere to traditional norms and morality, is now the dissident culture."[39]

THE SPIRIT OF THE TIMES

The partisan divisions revolve around those who accept the changes of the 1960s in women's rights, students' rights, African American civil rights, gay rights, alternate lifestyles, and the expansion of social programs, and those who claim a "silent majority" and want to return to 1950s "family values" more or less based on patriarchal and biblical understandings. It is easy to see how an African American in the White House (Barack Obama),

35 Mark Lilla quoted in Young, Foreword, 4.
36 Meades quoted in McKay, "Social and (Counter-) Cultural 1960s," 56.
37 Harris, "Abstraction and Empathy," 15.
38 Reagan quoted in Braunstein and Doyle, *Imagine Nation*, 6.
39 Bork, "Conservatism and the Culture," 21.

a feminist as Secretary of State (Hillary Clinton), a movement to Occupy Wall Street ("We are the 99%"), an international "facebooked" youth culture, a decline in US economic power in relation to China, and an expansive social program (US health care) are reviving the culture wars

In trying to explain the counterculture, historians often point to the canonical items associated with psychedelia: visual arts, sex, drugs, new music, and hippie fashion.[40] In all of these forms, promiscuity was heroic when it aimed to overturn the repressive morality of the older generation. Sociologist Beth Bailey reminds us that "sex & drugs & rock 'n' roll" became a trinity of experiences to be worshiped and to use as a weapon to bludgeon parents. Many elders feared the "obscene" ways their daughters argued for a "sex = freedom equation" where their bodies were concerned.[41] Dope altered the mind and led to a sort of public orgasm of open expression at rock concerts. There were the essentialist elements, or rather a reduction to essentialism, in smoking dope to increase the excitement involved in fucking.[42] A back-to-the-land nativism or naturalism existed, as did a vegetarian, ecological and environmental dimension.

But there is more. Of central importance to our understanding is to remember how many people, at the same time, began to distrust their countries, their leaders, their parents, and their governments. There were too many lies, too many failures, and too much uproar over what seemed to be genocidal and racial wars prosecuted to procure oversized profits for greedy capitalists. Who could see the possibility of trusting those institutions in the same old ways ever again?

And who could understand the speed of change? Everything was moving faster and faster. Novelist Alvin Toffler wrote *Future Shock* (1970) to explain the amplified demands of modern life. New technologies of "everyone-knows-this-at-the-same-moment" communication and travel were leading to globalization and its discontents, although Toffler did not use those words. He defined future shock as "the shattering stress and disorientation that we induce in individuals by subjecting them to too much change in too short a time."[43] It is just this future shock that helped open the generation gap. For Toffler, the only way forward was to change, to find "totally

40 Harris, "Abstraction and Empathy," 9.
41 Bailey, "Sex as a Weapon," 305–7.
42 Harris, "Abstraction and Empathy," 10.
43 Toffler, *Future Shock*, 12.

new ways to anchor ourselves, for all the old roots—religion, nation, community, family, or profession—are now shaking under the hurricane impact of the accelerative thrust."[44]

For Jay Stevens, the spirit of the times seemed to be "a will to change" not unlike Frederick Nietzsche's "will to power"—an ambitious and creative determination to achieve a better way of life outside the "rat race" structure of daily lives—but not just for supermen, for everyone.[45] There was a general rebellion against conformity. Todd Gitlin said that there were two impulses in the youthful counterculture: libertarianism with its need "to overturn repression in the name of id"; and spiritualism in its longings for a communitarian public love experience.[46] Even with such a spot-on analysis, Gitlin cited the lyrics from the Buffalo Springfield's song *For What It's Worth*: "There's something happening here. What it is ain't exactly clear."[47]

In the 1960s there was a moment when many people believed, without being cynical, that it was still possible to make an all-out assault on the global capitalist system, on patriotic nationalisms everywhere. This patriotism was the possessive nationalistic kind that drew lines on the earth, built a wall in Berlin, set up an Iron Curtain between East and West, and made cold and hot wars over natural resources and ideology. Many people began to question the ugly sides of nationalism, began to protest imperialism, and sought to eradicate the entrenched ways of thinking that had brought World War I and World War II and the Cold War and Vietnam and, coming soon to your neighborhoods, World War III. Invoking the will to change, the counterculture insisted that Western leaders, governments and societies were deeply flawed. People needed to stop saluting flags and take time to paint peace signs.

Protest was of two general types, political and cultural, even though, as Clara Juncker reminds us in her essay in this volume, the personal is political and it was made political in literary texts that proved influential on both sides of the Atlantic in this period. Among young people in the United States, the most powerful instrument of political action was in the formation of Students for a Democratic Society (SDS). This was new politics

44 Ibid., 35.
45 Stevens, "Counterculture," 310.
46 Gitlin, *Sixties*, xviii–xix.
47 Ibid., 214–18.

for Americans. European youth had a long-existing tradition of left-wing socialism from Marx to powerful unions and sophisticated welfare states. Political protest is aimed at institutions, laws and policies. Cultural protest is critical of goes at values, consciousness, and the way people think.[48] In the 1960s there was an open sore between the violent realism of established structures and the utopian ideals of a peaceful global community—a sore that reached deep into international relations theory as set out by Thomas Hobbes's *Leviathan* (1651) and Immanuel Kant's hopes for "perpetual peace" (1795).[49] The self-interest of realism was at the center of the culture war when it clashed with the cosmopolitanism of global cooperation.

THE AGE OF AQUARIUS

By 1964, mainstream magazines in New York, and swiftly across the world, described a "New Bohemia" in the Lower East Side of Manhattan where "hipsters" were gathering. Cultural critic Norman Mailer had first used this word in his book *The White Negro* (1957).[50] By 1965, hipsters had been shortened to "hippies." Hippies were notably different from the bohemianism of the "Beats" in nearby Greenwich Village who were considered a non-threatening curiosity of brooders. The hippies had much larger numbers and were thought to be far more dangerous a threat to the Establishment, even in their optimistic playfulness.[51] Hippies soon placed the center of the hippie nation in the Haight-Ashbury section of San Francisco, described by historian Gretchen Lemke-Santangelo as "hippie central, a swirling, colorful, all-hours hub of youthful yearning."[52]

Visually, fashion and longer hair set hippies apart and became signifiers of the counterculture. Hippies seemed rougher, dirtier, hairier, more childlike, and clearly more androgenous than the Beats. Hippies were almost cartoonish, had kinkier sex (an unproven, if popular, assertion), different musical tastes, an expanded taste for drugs, and wore brighter clothes. The

48 Stevens, "Counterculture," 309.

49 For Thomas Hobbes, see Lloyd and Sreedhar, "Hobbes's Moral and Political Philosophy"; for Kant, see Rauscher, "Kant's Social and Political Philosophy."

50 O'Neill, *Coming Apart*, 234.

51 Tomlinson, "Psychedelic Rock Posters," 294.

52 Lemke-Santangelo, *Daughters of Aquarius*, 1.

Beats preferred the serious intellectualism, and drabness, of black. Hippies loved charade and posing in dance, theater and fashion—a celebration in tune with nature and instinct. Hippies evoked the myth of the American frontier in its cowboy leather, pieced together scraps of fabric, American Indian beadwork, woven, crocheted, and knitted handmades, Vietnam US Army shirts, and long hair. All of this was done in a unisex way. The posturing and sophistication of jazz clubs was replaced by individualist body street performances aligned with rock 'n' roll.[53] The military uniforms might seem at odds with the hippie ethos, but the idea was to use whatever was available, over-manufactured and abundant—a leveling of everyone from soldiers to hippies, all together now. By the late 1960s, wearing army shirts was also a way to reach out to those eighteen-year-olds drafted into the war by saying clearly: we aren't against the soldiers; we are against the war. All of this fashion was a move toward naturalism, primitivism, and recyclable anti-materialism.[54] Women wore see-through fabrics, feathers and silks, beads, no bras and, sometimes, no panties. Instead of "conspicuous consumption" there was "conspicuous thrift."[55]

It is impossible to exaggerate how much hair was on display. There was so much hair! The "Age of Aquarius" rolled along on an ocean of hair and beards, "long beautiful hair, shining, gleaming, streaming, flaxen, waxen; give me down to there, shoulder length or longer, here baby, there mama everywhere daddy daddy hair. Flow it, show it, long as God can grow it, my hair."[56] Conservatives and the older generation of "perms," "flat tops," "buzz cuts," oil-saturated and combed slickness disliked the implications of long, out-of-order, stringy hair. They wanted males to "look like a man!" and females to "brush your hair!" The gender bending of long hair on both sexes was a clear sign of disorder, anti-capitalist, military draft-dodging, and sexually-liberated leanings. When the musical "Hair" played in Memphis, Tennessee, in 1970, conservatives picketed the theater with signs reading "God Hates Hair" and "God Loves Clothes."[57]

---

53 Blackman, "Clothing the Cosmic Counterculture," 201, 211.

54 O'Neill, *Coming Apart*, 247–9.

55 Blackman, "Clothing the Cosmic Counterculture," 212; Lemke-Santangelo, *Daughters of Aquarius*, 72.

56 Lyrics from song *Hair*, by Galt Macdermot in *Hair: The American Tribal Love-Rock Musical*, ed. James Rado and Gerome Ragni (1967; opened on Broadway, 1968).

57 Monteith, *American Culture in the 1960s*, 51–54.

When the youth culture turned to hippie fashion, it was to the paisley patterns, miniskirts, micro-minis, or maxi skirts, boots, long hair, beads, and brightness. The fashion was both ultra modern and nostalgic/romantic. When Jacqueline Kennedy pulled on a miniskirt in 1966, women over 30 years old quickly joined in.[58] Males had only worn brighter garb in the eighteenth century.

TUNE IN, TURN ON, DROP OUT

Some Beats, notably Allen Ginsberg, acted as sort of a father to hippiedom, but it was Professor Timothy Leary and novelist Ken Kesey who pushed this part of the counterculture into mind-expanding drugs, so-called "Happenings," and different forms of creativity and spectacle. Even so, Leary described Ginsberg as "the secretary-general of the world's poets, beatniks, anarchists, socialists, free-sex/love cultists."[59] Leary preached a gospel of LSD (lysergic acid diethylamide), urging everyone to "drop acid," and "tune in, turn on, drop out."[60] LSD use made colors brilliant and stationary objects seemed to flow about in a spiritual "lava lamp" way. And sex was the best it could get—or so Leary claimed.[61]

Ken Kesey, who found fame in his first novel, *One Flew Over the Cuckoo's Nest* (1962), used his income to buy a school bus, paint it psychedelic colors, fill it with "Merry Pranksters," and set out for the open road, driving across the country and back prosletyzing for LSD and providing "acid tests" for the willing. "Freak freely" was his motto.[62] The object was to "Blow your mind!" The novelist Tom Wolfe made Kesey famous with the bestseller: *The Electric Kool-Aid Acid Test* (1967).[63] That same year, 1967, gave witness to one of the greatest drug songs of the psychedelic era, Jimi Hendrix's pulsating *Purple Haze*, released within months of the Beatles *Sgt. Pepper's Lonely Hearts Club Band*, with its LSD explicit track

58 Braunstein, "Forever Young," 246.
59 Leary, "Turning on the World," 333.
60 Ibid., 339–41.
61 O'Neill, *Coming Apart*, 239–40.
62 Medeiros, "Mapping San Francisco," 306–8; O'Neill, *Coming Apart*, 240–43.
63 Wolfe, *Electric Kool-Aid Acid Test*.

Lucy in the Sky with Diamonds. As John Lennon had so boldly announced in 1966, the Beatles were "more popular than Jesus now."[64]

By the fall of 1966, when an estimated 15,000 hippies lived in the Haight-Ashbury section of San Francisco, the state of California passed a law making LSD-use illegal.[65] Kesey, Ginsberg, Leary and others called for a "Human Be-In" to take place in January. This word play on "human being" is also related obviously to the "Sit-In" and "Love-In" gatherings of the era. Advertised as "The First Human Be-In," the gathering was not to be a protest or a political act, but was pitched as a "gathering of the tribes" to show identity and to be held "in the spirit of love."[66] The organizers were insistent that they should not organize any overtly political act—for to do so only legitimized the system. What was imagined was a cultural revolt, a subversive action by human bodies coming together to celebrate "Be-ing Human." An underground newspaper, *The Oracle*, announced: "Now in the evolving generation of America's young the humanization of the American man and woman can begin in joy and embrace without fear, dogma, suspicion, or dialectical righteousness."[67]

THE SUMMER OF LOVE, 1967

Approximately 25,000 people gathered in Golden Gate Park on January 14, 1967.[68] The atmosphere was electric with incantations for a better world, and hopeful optimism that we can change the world, man. We can really do it. People believed that in some unknown way, somehow, this show of communal love would triumph over the repressed, discriminatory, racist, unjust society. According to one participant, "the two most popular words that day were dope and revolution. Our secret formula was grass, LSD, meditation, hot music, consolidation, and a joyous sexuality."[69] No violence erupted. The police restrained themselves and mostly ignored the drugs. The officers basically saw the hippies as benign—especially in con-

64 DeGroot, *Sixties Unplugged*, 227.
65 Stevens, "Counterculture," 317.
66 Braunstein, "Forever Young," 250.
67 *The San Francisco Oracle*, January 1967, quoted in ibid.
68 Anthony, *Summer of Love*.
69 Ibid., 152.

trast to the political troublemakers in the SDS across the bridge in Berkeley.[70]

Members of a street theatre group, the San Francisco Mime Troupe, renamed themselves The Diggers, and used spectacle, pageantry and happenings to move the counterculture into public spaces and expand the audience.[71] They did things "just for the fuck of it," without thought of being paid and without political reward.[72] Claiming that "money lust is sickness," Diggers offered free services to those who came to the Be-In or to the Haight.[73] "Free" meant no charge; it also meant no restraint.[74] The Diggers opened a store where people could find and take used clothes and domestic items. Diggers helped people live beyond the cash economy by offering free recycling and making a new culture outside the culture industry. They distributed free food and set up food kitchens. They used a thirteen-foot-tall wooden frame, painted yellow to have people enter a new "frame of reference." Digger women often were seen at the vegetable and meat markets collecting the leftover food. There were daily scavenger hunts for anything that could be useful.[75] Diggers organized kindergartens, childcare and free medical clinics to help those who had been on bad trips or had a sexually-transmitted disease or two.[76]

The Summer of Love in 1967 was a global event for hippies and youth culture generally and was set to begin on the summer solstice. But young people were impatient and the celebration started around Easter time, when Spring break freed them from high schools and universities. People gathered in the big cities in America, all across Europe and Canada. Toronto, London, Prague, Warsaw, West Berlin, Copenhagen, Rome, Amsterdam, and Paris held huge gatherings. But the "will to change" *zeitgeist* epicenter of the youthquake was located in the 100,000 young people who made their way to San Francisco, many in hand-decorated VW vans.[77]

Music Festivals began and served as temporary communes for the faithful. In 1967, the first major Rock festival of the counterculture was the

70 Medeiros, "Mapping San Francisco," 344–7.
71 Doyle, "Staging the Revolution," 72.
72 DeGroot, *Sixties Unplugged*, 258–9.
73 Stevens, "Counterculture," 318.
74 DeGroot, *Sixties Unplugged*, 254.
75 Lemke-Santangelo, *Daughters of Aquarius*, 89.
76 DeGroot, *Sixties Unplugges*, 318–9; Doyle, "Staging the Revolution," 79–82.
77 Braunstein, "Forever Young," 250.

Monterey Pop Festival which brought in approximately 75,000 fans. As Terry Anderson recalled it, the people "came in peasant dresses, in bell bottoms, leather vests, in colors: mellow yellow, panama red, moby grape, deacon blue, Acapulco gold. [LSD chemist Stanley] Owsley supplied a new batch of LSD called Monterey Purple, dubbed Purple Haze, and the bands merged the San Francisco sounds with American pop rock, blues, soul, folk-rock, and the British Invasion."[78] The bands included Mamas and Papas, Buffalo Springfield, The Byrds, Grateful Dead, Janis Joplin, Country Joe and the Fish, Otis Redding, and Jimi Hendrix.[79]

Another fifteen thousand young people met in Central Park in New York City to celebrate their belief that "All You Need is Love." They dressed up in flamboyant costumes, tossed frisbees, joined hands in huge love circles, painted their faces, passed out marijuana joints, chanted about bananas, and told each other never to trust anyone over 30 years old. In what was widely rumored to be true, but later turned out to be a hoax, dried banana peels were believed to have hallucinogenic properties. All you had to do was scrape them and light them up. In June 1967 a new song, *San Francisco*, called to the faithful: "all across the nation, there's a new generation, people in motion . . ." who should make their way west and "be sure to wear some flowers in your hair. . . ."[80]

The media tried to keep up. Many writers were both empathetic and critical. The young people were to be admired for efforts to build an ideal community but others were taking advantage of them to make money on the music festivals and on mind-expanding drugs. Timothy Leary was often decried as a parasite. In 1967, journalist Joan Didion wrote "Slouching Towards Bethlehem" to decry the lack of a center among the hippies in San Francisco.[81] Didion felt the city was populated by masses of adolescent runaways being preyed on by drug dealers, scam artists, and rapists. Her conclusion was supported by Grateful Dead lead singer Jerry Garcia, who related what he saw:

78 Anderson quoted in McKay, "Social and (Counter-) Cultural 1960s," 44.

79 Onkey, "Voodoo Child," 198–9; Tomlinson, "Psychedelic Rock Posters," 300–1.

80 John Phillips of The Mamas and The Papas wrote *San Francisco* in 1967. The most popular version was sung by Scott McKenzie at the Monterey Pop Festival.

81 First published in the *Saturday Evening Post* magazine, see Didion, *Slouching Towards Bethlehem*, 96–7.

Pretty little 16-year-old-middle-class chick comes to the Haight to see what it's all about & gets picked up by a 17-year-old street dealer who spends all day shooting her full of speed again & again, then feeds her 3000 mikes & raffles her temporarily unemployed body for the biggest Haight Street gang bang since the night before last.[82]

Historian Gerard DeGroot wanted the Summer of Love to be renamed the Summer of Rape.[83] Didion noted that young mothers were feeding their children LSD. The streets were paranoid and the talk was banal. Didion blamed US society: "This was not a typical generational rebellion. At some point between 1945 and 1967 we had somehow neglected to tell these children the rules of the game we happened to be playing; maybe we had stopped believing in the rules ourselves."[84]

THE PEOPLE OF ZERO AND WOODSTOCK

As the Summer of Love moved into autumn, organizers planned a March on the Pentagon. In October, hippies joined the SDS and others to demonstrate against US military power. Some hippies formed a love circle, and tried to levitate the Pentagon building by using the magic word "Ommmmm. . ." as Ginsberg had taught them at the Human Be-In.[85] This effort seems to have failed. Other demonstrators placed flowers into the muzzles of the rifles held by the soldiers who blocked their paths. This seems to have worked when the photograph, "Flower Power," was distributed and celebrated worldwide.[86]

In 1967, when nearly 500,000 US soldiers were in Vietnam fighting for continuity, in San Francisco, London, Toronto, Copenhagen, Berlin, New York, and elsewhere, the Summer of Love represented change. People imagined a very different society. In London, an all night international Love-

82 Garcia quoted in Stevens, "Counterculture," 322.
83 DeGroot, *Sixties Unplugged*, 304.
84 Didion, *Slouching Towards Bethlehem*, 91, 97,127.
85 Anthony, *Summer of Love*, 154–55.
86 Jocelyn Stewart, "Bernie Boston, 74, Took 'Flower Power' Photo," *New York Sun*, January 24, 2008.

In gathered at Alexandra Palace.[87] The sweetish smell of marijuana lingered everywhere. Pink Floyd rocked the audience. In Liverpool an ongoing special psychedelic experience was offered.[88] Many accepted. The counterculture, in speaking for what might be possible, for peace and love and human community, provided a usable past, a legacy, attesting to our own humanity and to a better world.

The hippies called themselves "the people of Zero" to mean without history, having new beginnings, being less rational and more mystical and emotional, and consisting of a blank slate on which to write a new world.[89] A major theme was the absolute hopelessness of an "uptight" parental generation (ironically, it is just this parental generation that has redefined itself as "the greatest generation"—an extraordinary act of hubris given the groups complicity in WWII and the Cold War).[90] The best single book on the hippies is by Timothy Miller, *The Hippies and American Values* (1991) in which the author delves into the countercultural ethics of dope, sex, and rock music. Dope was not drugs—hippies were clear about this distinction. Dope was marijuana, peyote, mescaline, and LSD. Drugs were cocaine, heroin, and STP. Hippies understood the difference: dope was great but drugs were dangerous. Dope should be used sanely and under controlled circumstances—never to hurt others.[91] Timothy Leary liked to say, "Your only hope is dope."[92] Many hippies agreed that dope helped them cope with the evils of the society; was akin to a religious experience; put them in tune with nature; made for better sex; and was mostly harmless and maybe even medicinal. By 1974, studies of California hippie drug use showed 97% smoked marijuana and hashish, 91% tried LSD, and 80% dabbled in peyote and mescaline.[93] A side benefit of all this was that the older generation denounced it—thus proving to the counterculture that dope use must be ethical.

As promoted in the *Berkeley Barb* on 5 June 1970: "We announce the true spirit of the high holy act of fucking. People must be free to fuck with-

87 Braunstein, "Forever Young," 244.
88 See Murden, "Psychedelic Liverpool?"
89 Miller, *Hippies and American Values*, 3.
90 Brokaw, *Greatest Generation*.
91 Miller, *Hippies and American Values*, 25–26.
92 Leary quoted in Ibid., 30.
93 1974 survey cited in Lemke-Santangelo, *Daughters of Aquarius*, 116–7.

out molestation, without fear, without guilt."[94] Miller explained that whereby dope opened psychic pleasure, sex opened physical pleasure. Sex was fucking more than it was love making even though the distinction was lost on many. Sex was healthy, fun, and revolutionary. While no one should ever be forced to have sex, no person should ever be restrained from having sex—a freedom of speech right. The marital contract should be "open marriage," because possession was bourgeois. Open nudity was also encouraged as a communication device to let the body speak to others in nonverbal and fun way. And truly, many argued, as in fucking, if it feels good, do it. Nudity stood for freedom from corporate America's dictates. Genitals were to be seen because they were common and normal, not bad or ugly.[95] If all of this disgusted the older generation, so much the better.

Completing the ethics of the trinity, Miller wrote that rock 'n' roll upheld a way of life and was far more than just pleasurable sound. Rock formulated the cultural rebellion and counterculture in communal form. The transistor radio and the great rock festivals pulled the counterculture together time and again—as pilgrimages, camp meetings, and revivals of the faithful. Miller described dope as psychic pleasure, sex as physical pleasure and music as communal.[96] What could be more frightening to the older folks than thousands of hippies letting it all hang out?

The single biggest symbol of the youth and counterculture era was the Woodstock Festival in Bethel, New York, in 1969. Of course, and notwithstanding all the myths surrounding Woodstock, some things fell apart. It was, as Pete Townshend of the Who said, "a disgusting, despicable, hypocritical event. The most incredible duplicity everywhere. . . . A commercial event." [97] There was a lack of clean water, bathrooms, food, highway access, bathing, and sleeping facilities. And yet, Woodstock was the high water mark of free love, drugs, freedom from repression, nudity, all to the beat of the best rock music on the planet and, despite Townshend's lament, it was mostly free. After Woodstock, rock festivals were held all over Europe and at Altamont Speedway in California—where violence by Hells Angels

94 *Barb* quoted in Miller, *Hippies and American Values*, 51.
95 Ibid., 53–6.
96 Ibid., 74.
97 DeGroot, *Sixties Unplugged*, 237–40.

thugs put an end to these gatherings in the United States.[98] In Europe, the rock festivals would continue, still continue. In England, organizers based the 1970 concerts at Bath and Glastonbury on communal and hippie ethics of free admission and youthful exuberance. At Roskilde in Denmark, where hippies still roam, there has been a general celebration of youth, with sex, beer, hash, and rock 'n' roll since 1971. Belgium's Rock Werchter dates to 1974.

THE DEATH OF THE HIPPIE

On the street level, there were many confrontations between the hippies and lower middle class ethnic and racial groups in the neighborhoods the hippies entered.[99] There were only a few black hippies even though films focusing on the 1960s always made the group seem more multicultural than it was. Working-class families and their children were struggling desperately to grasp the American dream of being middle class.[100] While hippies were dropping out, minority and lower-class youth struggled to get in. Hippies were scorning just the material advances and successes for which these groups were fighting.

African Americans especially disliked the privileges: "the hippies really bug us because we know they can come down here and play their game for a while and then escape. And we can't."[101] Hippies were amoral, atheistic and played at poverty while being white and privileged. The flower children had been uninvited and violence became common. Joan Didion described the girls she met as naïve, superficial and drug obsessed hippie chicks who were far from feminism and women's liberation.[102] Sociologist Winifred Breines wrote that many girls were playing and pandering to boys they could or would never marry. These girls came from affluent families; they were white (97%) children of prosperity and many threw away their

98 O'Neill, *Coming Apart*, 261; see also Lydon, "Rolling Stones"; Miller, *Hippies and American Values*, 82–4.
99 Matusow, "Rise and Fall," 344.
100 O'Neill, *Coming Apart*, 271.
101 Quoted in Lemke-Santangelo, *Daughters of Aquarius*, 35.
102 Didion, *Slouching Towards Bethlehem*, 89–97, 127.

reputations with black boys or gang boys.[103] All hippies were basically defenseless against the gang violence of the ghettoes or the Hells Angels attacks on them. Thousands were raped, robbed, and beaten. It was safe to rape a hippie runaway girl—they usually reacted passively and could not go to the police for help.[104]

But the hippies had their defenders. Even the ultra-establishment *Time* magazine, praised the hippies for living "considerably more virtuous lives than the great majority of their fellow citizens."[105] In France, youth radical Jean-Jacques Lebel likened the seduction of the children of the bourgeoisie into the system was "the liberal version of Hitler's final solution of the youth problem. . . . It is time for us to create our own culture, our own lives."[106]

In San Francisco, the Diggers had performed one more street theatre, "the Death of Hippie." Diggers led a funeral march into Golden Gate Park where they set fire to a coffin labeled "Summer of Love." The original hippies said that crass materialism, violence and nihilism brought down the noble experiment. The original hippies and the later hippies were of different breeds. The crowd shouted "hippies are dead" and life in the Haight dissolved. The hippie era of flower power and hope was brief, usually marked as 1965–1972.[107]

COMMUNES FULL OF FLOWER CHILDREN

Many flower children built communes and developed a more feminist style. This was progress. The early counterculture was not a model for the equality of the sexes and did little to overturn the dominant gender roles or notions of sexuality. Dominated by men, the counterculture was openly sexist. The hippies challenged the Establishment, but gender constructs remained hierarchical and essentialist. Sexual liberation did not immediately mean women's rights, as one woman made clear: "If the sexual revolution is fucking a lot, then I did. If it incorporates things like the rights of women,

103 Breines, *Young, White, and Miserable*, 150.
104 O'Neill, *Coming Apart*, 253.
105 "Youth: The Hippies," *Time*, 7 July 1967, 20–22.
106 Lebel quoted in Miller, *Hippies and American Values*, 8.
107 DeGroot, *Sixties Unplugged*, 305.

I'm not sure my involvement meant a damn thing."[108] Beth Bailey reminds us that the sexual revolution was, "evolutionary, not revolutionary." The evolution was from fucking to making love—the new preferred word in the communes.[109]

If females refused sex, they were accused of being repressed, racist, or worse. Still, as the 1960s progressed and the urban hippie era ended, some women in communes embracing the essentialism and reclaiming the agrarian ideal, moved into feminism. The counterculture always emphasized cooperation, nature, anti-materialism, and nonaggression; women could use all these themes to gain power. Historian Gretchen Lemke-Santangelo notes the "thrill and excitement of breaking cultural taboos and the sensual pleasures of sex, drugs, and rock and roll. Nor were commitment [to countercultural feminism] and pleasure mutually exclusive."[110] Sociologist Barbara Ehrenreich noted that hippie women were far more dangerous to the prevailing culture than were those in SDS whose familiar kinds of protest were at least "comprehensible."[111] Counterculture women exhibited a liberating cultural feminism in the rebellion of running away, refusal to conform to rules of protest, fashion, hair, sex, and more.

Lemke-Santangelo has shown how the essentialism of hippie women became feminism. By dropping out and having the courage to do so, hippie women broke from suburban domesticity, threw off the sexual double standard, opened up female self-expression and autonomy. The counterculture allowed the freedom to break with the past and to forge new relationships. There were still domestic roles to fill, but when these were placed in the heart of what the counterculture valued, women gained agency from the essentialism. This was a cultural feminism based on what Allen Ginsberg termed "the affectionate feminine."[112] The communes consisted of "sisterhoods" where the ideals were, as Lemke Santangelo says: "very very female. The hippie women's experience was novel and liberating.[113] Ehrenreich agreed that this was true liberation, something male commentators and feminists missed or failed to acknowledge. As they learned to love

108 Lemke-Santangelo, *Daughters of Aquarius*, 22–7.
109 Bailey, "Sex as a Weapon," 307–23.
110 Ibid., 36.
111 Ehrenreich, *Fear of Falling*, 60–3.
112 Lemke-Santangelo, *Daughters of Aquarius*, 160, 181.
113 Ibid., 38, 57, 158.

themselves as women in a women-centered order, feminism gained many soldiers. This is perhaps more cultural feminism than political—if we can separate the two.

Hippies found hope in voluntary communities, collectives and communes. Hog Farm commune in California and Findhorn Commune in Scotland established agrarian communities that stressed back-to-the-land living patterns.[114] These arrangements represented an incredible diversity of lifestyles. There were rule-bound places and anarchic ones. The land was sometimes owned jointly and other times clearly subdivided. There were tens of thousands of different communes in the US alone, with foundations and examples reaching into American history, mostly in the nineteenth century. Most of the 1960s communes were romantic. Among the most successful were Morning Star Ranch and Wheeler's Ranch near San Francisco, The Farm in Summertown, Tennessee, and The Hog Farm in Tujunga, California. Citizens contributed what they could, worked together and shared food and bodies, with well-understood rules. The communes were overwhelming white and thoroughly middle-to-upper class social haves where highly-educated people came together.[115]

In the early years after the Summer of Love died, many survivors went to Morning Star or Wheelers. But because these communes were freewheeling and accepting of all newcomers, they both failed by 1973. The problem with open admission was eccentrics, misfits, and criminals easily took advantage of the others.[116] The Farm still exists, even if it is down from its 1,500 original inhabitants. The Farm is populated by vegans, supports and trains women to be midwives, and is anti-abortion because that breaks with the energy of the cosmos: "Hey Ladies! Don't have an abortion, come to the Farm and we'll deliver your baby and take care of it, and if you ever decide you want it back, you can have it."[117] About 200 citizens live at the Farm, now paying dues. Its existence provides a living legacy to the counterculture. As do the widespread culture wars with their partisan divides.

114 Miller, "Sixties-Era Communes," 343–4.
115 Ibid., 332–4, 336–7.
116 Ibid., 343; Miller, *Hippies and American Values*, 92.
117 Miller, "Sixties-Era Communes," 337.

BIBLIOGRAPHY

Anderson, Terry H. *The Movement and the Sixties: Protest in America from Greensboro to Wounded Knee.* New York: Oxford University Press, 1995.

Anthony, Gene. *The Summer of Love: A Photo-Documentary.* Berkeley, CA: Celestial Arts, 1980.

Bailey, Beth. "Sex as a Weapon: Underground Comix and the Paradox of Liberation." In Braunstein and Doyle, *Imagine Nation*, 305–24.

Blackman, Cally. "Clothing the Cosmic Counterculture: Fashion and Psychedelia." In Grunenberg and Harris, *Summer of Love*, 201–22.

Bork, Robert H. "Conservatism and the Culture." *The Canon* (Spring 2009): 18–22.

Braunstein, Peter. "Forever Young: Insurgent Youth and the Sixties Culture of Rejuvenation." In Braunstein and Doyle, *Imagine Nation*, 243–74.

Braunstein, Peter, and Michael William Doyle, eds. *Imagine Nation: The American Counterculture of the 1960s and '70s*. New York: Routledge, 2002.

Breines, Wini. *Young, White, and Miserable: Growing Up Female in the Fifties*. Chicago: University of Chicago Press, 1992.

Brokaw, Tom. *The Greatest Generation.* New York: Random House, 1998.

Chafe, William H., and Harvard Sitkoff, eds. *A History of Our Time: Readings on Postwar America.* New York: Oxford University Press, 1999.

Charters, Ann, ed. *The Portable Sixties Reader.* New York: Penguin Classics, 2003.

DeGroot, Gerard J. *The Sixties Unplugged: A Kaleidoscopic History of a Disorderly Decade*. Basingstoke, UK: Pan Macmillan, 2008.

Didion, Joan. *Slouching Towards Bethlehem: Essays.* New York: Farrar, Straus and Giroux, 1968.

Doyle, Michael William. "Staging the Revolution: Guerrilla Theater as a Countercultural Practice, 1965–1968." In Braunstein and Doyle, *Imagine Nation*, 71–98.

Ehrenreich, Barbara. *Fear of Falling: The Inner Life of the Middle Class.* New York: Pantheon, 1989.

Galbraith, John Kenneth. *The Affluent Society.* New York: New American Library, 1958.

Gitlin, Todd. *The Sixties: Years of Hope, Days of Rage*. New York: Bantam Books, 1987.

Grunenberg, Christoph, and Jonathan Harris, eds. *Summer of Love: Psychedelic Art, Social Crisis and Counterculture in the 1960s*. Liverpool: Liverpool University Press, 2005.

Harris, Jonathan. "Abstraction and Empathy: Psychedelic Distortion and the Meanings of the 1960s." In Grunenberg and Harris, *Summer of Love*, 9–18.

Hollinger, David, and Charles Capper, eds. *The American Intellectual Tradition*. vol. 2. 6th edition. New York: Oxford University Press, 2011.

Huxley, Aldous. *Doors of Perception*. London: Chatto and Windus, 1954.

Laing, R[onald] D[avid]. *The Politics of Experience and the Bird of Paradise*. London: Penguin, 1967.

Laing, Stuart. "Economy, Society and Culture in 1960s Britain: Contexts and Conditions for Psychedelic Art." In Grunenberg and Harris, *Summer of Love*, 19–34.

Leary, Timothy. "Turning on the World." In Charters, *Portable Sixties Reader*, 331–43.

Lemke-Santangelo, Gretchen. *Daughters of Aquarius: Women of the Sixties Counterculture*. Lawrence: University Press of Kansas, 2009.

Lloyd, Sharon A., and Susanne Sreedhar. "Hobbes's Moral and Political Philosophy." *The Stanford Encyclopedia of Philosophy*. Spring 2011 Edition. Edited by Edward N. Zalta. http://plato.stanford.edu /archives/spr2011/entries/hobbes-moral/.

Lydon, Michael. "The Rolling Stones—At Play in the Apocalypse." In Charters, *Portable Sixties Reader*, 306–16.

Matusow, Allen J. "Rise and Fall of a Counterculture." In Chafe and Sitkoff, *A History of Our Time*, 378–99.

McKay, George. "The Social and (Counter-) Cultural 1960s in the USA, Transatlantically." In Grunenberg and Harris, *Summer of Love*, 35–62.

Medeiros, Walter. "Mapping San Francisco 1965–1967: Roots and Florescence of the San Francisco Counterculture." In Grunenberg and Harris, *Summer of Love*, 303–48.

Michals Debra, "From 'Consciousness Expansion' to 'Consciousness Raising': Feminism and the Countercultural Politics of the Self." In Braunstein and Doyle, *Imagine Nation*, 41–68.

Miller, Timothy. *The Hippies and American Values.* Knoxville: University of Tennessee Press, 1991.

———. "The Sixties-Era Communes." In Braunstein and Doyle, *Imagine Nation*, 327–52.

Monteith, Sharon. *American Culture in the 1960s*. Edinburgh: Edinburgh University Press, 2008.

Murden, Jon. "Psychedelic Liverpool?" In Grunenberg and Harris, *Summer of Love*, 269–80.

O'Neill, William L. *Coming Apart: An Informal History of America in the 1960s.* New York: Random House, 1971.

Onkey, Lauren. "Voodoo Child: Jimi Hendrix and the Politics of Race in the Sixties." In Braunstein and Doyle, *Imagine Nation*, 189–214.

Rauscher, Frederick. "Kant's Social and Political Philosophy." *The Stanford Encyclopedia of Philosophy.* Summer 2012 Edition. Edited by Edward N. Zalta. http://plato.stanford.edu/archives/sum2012/entries/kant-social-political/.

Rossinow, Doug. "'The Revolution Is About Our Lives': The New Left's Counterculture." In Braunstein and Doyle, *Imagine Nation*, 99–124.

Roszak, Theodore. *The Making of a Counter Culture.* 1968. Reprint, Los Angeles: University of California Press, 1995.

Shildt, Axel, and Detlef Siegfried, eds. *Between Marx and Coca-Cola: Youth Cultures in Changing European Societies, 1960–1980.* New York: Berghahn Books, 2005.

Siegfried, Detlef. "'Don't Trust Anyone Older Than 30'? Voices of Conflict and Consensus between Generations in 1960s West Germany." *Journal of Contemporary History* 40, no. 4 (Oct. 2005): 727–44.

Sontag, Susan. "What's Happening in America" (1966). In Charters, *Portable Sixties Reader*, 119–23.

Stevens, Jay. "The Counterculture." In *The Social Fabric: American Life from the Civil War to the Present.* 6th ed. Vol. 2. Edited by John H. Cary, Julius Weinberg, and Thomas L. Hartshorne, 309–27. New York: HarperCollins, 1991.

Toffler, Alvin. *Future Shock.* New York: Random House, 1970.

Tomlinson, Sally. "Psychedelic Rock Posters, History, Ideas, and Art." In Charters, *Portable Sixties Reader*, 291–305.

Watson, Peter. *The Modern Mind: An Intellectual History of the 20th Century.* New York: HarperCollins, 2001.

Wolfe, Tom. *The Electric Kool-Aid Acid Test.* New York: Farrar, Straus and Giroux, 1968.

Young, Marilyn B. Foreword. In Braunstein and Doyle, *Imagine Nation*, 1–4.

"Youth: The Hippies." *Time*, 7 July 1967, 20–22.

1960s Documentary Film

Perceptions of the Vietnam War in the USA and in Germany

MICHAEL HOENISCH

"'It's the Revolution, girl—can't you feel it?'" With these exuberant words Frenesi greets her skeptical rescuer from a confrontational demonstration in 1960s San Francisco: a significant moment in Thomas Pynchon's fictional retrospective view of the American 1960s and 1970s.[1] Frenesi turns out to be one of the central figures of Pynchon's *Vineland* (1990), a highly contradictory representative of the upheavals of this period and also of one of its crucial aspects. She appears as the cameraperson of "24fps," a film collective that strains to record the public events initiated by the rebellious youth movements trying to shake up the establishment. Participation in these public confrontations included documenting them for a wider public, misinformed by the commercial media, and for history. The 'revolution' may not be televised on mainstream TV, but it must be documented by the participants themselves for an alternative public they hoped would emerge.[2] Pynchon's penetrating analysis of the forces whose conflict transformed the US in the 1960s and 1970s recognizes the affinity between the excitement of change and the documentary impulse. Those who saw themselves on the crest of worldwide historical change had no doubts that every moment of their struggle was relevant and needed to be documented. The experience of

1 Pynchon, *Vineland*, 117.
2 Scott-Heron, "Revolution Will Not Be Televised," 61.

"now" needed to be made permanent. To produce your own images strengthened your new identity as an activist and provided you with tools to challenge the establishment. The war in Vietnam emerged as one of the central battlegrounds of the wide-ranging social and cultural conflicts of the 1960s.

THE BATTLE OF IMAGES

The war divided the nation and produced competing perspectives on the problems looming in its wake. Images of the war and of the protest against it were available on American TV and movie screens, and they travelled around the world. American TV networks, generally mainstream, covered the events in Vietnam more and more as both the military involvement and the struggles about its justification intensified. The US government itself intervened in the battle of images. As the conflict escalated, the Department of Defense produced documentaries that tried to legitimize the war—for example, *Why Vietnam* in 1965 expected to continue the successful World War II series *Why We Fight,* while *Screaming Eagles in Vietnam* in 1967 was intended to glamorize the arrival of the 101st Airborne Division in Vietnam. This version of government propaganda completely ignored the rapid changes taking place during this period. Technical innovations in filmmaking, developed by the Direct Cinema filmmakers, and the self-confidence of the youth movements, which expected to create their own form of communication and influence the course of events, created a critical momentum that challenged TV reporting and the government. The perspectives of the TV networks, of course, had the widest reach in this battle of images, although their reception was often ambivalent. But alternative forms of documenting the war and the protest against it had a considerable and growing impact, especially among the young generation who faced conscription to fight in Vietnam. Some of these documentaries were broadcast by mainstream TV, like Peter Davis's criticism of government propaganda in his *The Selling of the Pentagon* (1971), which triggered considerable debates and put CBS under sufficient pressure to issue soon afterwards a kind of retraction, *The Rebuttal of the Selling of the Pentagon* (1971). Other documentaries received only limited support from mainstream media, like Emile de Antonio's *In the Year of the Pig* (1968), but reached relevant audiences more directly on college campuses and at protest meetings. In the context of the growing protest against the war, expressed across different perspectives, documentary film contributed to the delegitimization of American military activity in South East Asia.[3]

The end of the war was not the end of the conflicts about its meaning. In retrospect, the military perspective was summarized in 1979 by General Westmoreland, commander in Vietnam from 1964 to 1968 and Chief of Staff of the Army from 1968 to 1972. His extremely narrow-minded justification of the war follows the common cliché of the military victory at the front lost by weakness and betrayal at home—by incompetent politicians and subversives, "the vocal and emotional elements in our society who chose to resist actively national policy."[4] The thirteen-hour documentary by Peter Arnett and Michael MacLear, which was broadcast, not on the major networks, in 1982 under the title *The Ten Thousand Day War: Vietnam: 1945–1975,* claimed for itself a liberal perspective in the battle of images; as did the 1983 network response to Arnett's film, Richard Ellison's and Stanley Karnow's *Vietnam: A Television History.* The debate continued to address a wide audience in docudramas like Francis F. Coppola's *Apocalypse Now* (1979) or Oliver Stone's *Platoon* (1987) and *Born on the Fourth of July* (1989). One of the most challenging retrospective perspectives of the Vietnam conflict was created in Trinh T. Minh-ha's analytical and highly experimental film *Surname Viet Given Name Nam* (1989), which participated in the expansion of documentary aesthetics. The contradictions of this war still haunted Errol Morris's documentary about the life of Robert McNamara, *The Fog of War* (2003). The recent wars in Iraq and Afghanistan were frequently seen under the shadow of the war in Vietnam: as finally exorcizing the older defeat in South East Asia or as extending previous horrors and failures. Errol Morris's film about images of torture in Abu Ghraib, *Standard Operating Procedure* (2008), and the very different documentary by Junger and Hetherington, *Restropo* (2010), about one particular US Army outpost in Afghanistan, can be included in this continuing controversy.[5] *Human Terrain: War Becomes Academic* (2010) by James Der Derian, David Udris and Michael Udris investigates specific counterin-

3 Barnouw, *Documentary*, 262–88; Barsam, *Non-Fiction Film*, 314–16.
4 Westmoreland, "Vietnam in Perspective," 118.
5 Grajeda, "Winning and Losing," 1–23.

surgency methods the military had used in Vietnam and continued to develop for the wars in Iraq and Afghanistan, as well as the role of academic intellectuals in recent American wars.

The Vietnam War could be documented more easily than other wars. Before the practice of 'embedded journalism' was introduced—a lesson from that conflict—it was easy, with sufficient motivation and means, to travel to and in South Vietnam and try to publish one's information and experience: reporters for print or film media or working on their own, peace activists, participants in the war and others used these opportunities. The genesis of the book *Vietnam—Why? An American Citizen Looks at the War* (1968) demonstrates how easy it was to get access to the war zone. Its author, Flavio Bisignano, financed his journey to Vietnam with his own savings and used his experience as a former Merchant Marine to get free passage to Saigon on a merchant ship in 1967. As John Carlos Rowe describes it, Bisignano blended smoothly with the professional journalists and regularly took part in their routine activities. The credentials he acquired easily even let him participate in combat operations: "before returning to California, he obtained first-hand experience in search-and-destroy patrol, an airstrike on Vietcong jungle sanctuaries, and naval operations in the Gulf of Tonkin."[6] Like others, Bisignano tried to authenticate his report by focusing on his personal experience. Rowe's analysis of the literary and ideological concepts that structure Bisignano's narrative and other personal accounts of the Vietnam War questions the claim of eye-witness reports to a privileged, more authentic perspective. While these accounts benefited from the high status of personal experience as a criterion of truth in the 1960s and 1970s, and positioned themselves as corrective responses to the mass media narrative, they share basic ideological assumptions with the dominant media.

DOCUMENTARY FILM AND RESISTANCE TO THE WAR

Under pressure from government, justifications of the war and the 'normalization' of the conflict by the TV networks, the protest movement produced, on limited budgets, documentaries whose impact continued to grow

6 Rowe, "Eye-Witness," 148.

over time. The enthusiasm and moral commitment behind these documentary projects was an apparently unlimited reservoir from which all parts of the 'Movement' drew their energy. In fact, the civil rights movement for equal rights, primarily of African Americans, and the anti-war movement were closely intertwined. They shared the appeal to justice, the impatience with the status quo, the grass roots ideals and many forms of protest. Many who were apolitical but restless felt attracted to both. Michael Herr concludes his important book about the Vietnam War, *Dispatches* (1977), with a melancholic variant of this perception: "Out on the street I couldn't tell the Vietnam veterans from the rock and roll veterans. The Sixties had made so many casualties, its war and its music had run power off the same circuits for so long they didn't even have to fuse. . . . What I'd thought of as two obsessions were really only one, I don't know how to tell you how complicated that made my life."[7] Because African Americans provided a disproportionately large number of the soldiers, and victims, on the battlefields, they quickly perceived that injustice and racism at home were mirrored in South East Asia. The documentary film *No Vietnamese Ever Called Me a Nigger* (1968) announces already in its title this fusion of domestic and overseas experience and protest. During interviews along the protest march through Harlem on April 15, 1967, black bystanders and war resisters explain in various ways their understanding of how the global system works, in Vietnam and at home.

A radical perspective was represented in the documentaries which the Newsreel Collective produced about anti-war as well as civil rights protest. Starting in 1967, the Newsreel Collective assembled civil rights activists, New Left critics of 'the system' and anti-war radicals in a determined effort to develop documentary film as a weapon in the struggle for change. Newsreel filmmakers expected documentaries to function as a medium that would organize their followers and demonstrate to a wide and heterogeneous audience that they shared a common position in a global context and in history. The struggle for freedom and grassroots democracy in the streets of the US could be linked to the protest movements in other parts of the developed world and to revolutionary struggles in post-colonial countries. In this way, the various factions of the protest movement would be enabled to discover their bond of solidarity in a worldwide struggle for liberation.

7 Michael Herr, *Dispatches*, 258.

With world revolution as a subtext, local protest acquired strong legitimacy. Factional frictions would be more easily subsumed under the concept of a global movement. In this context, the conflict in Vietnam could be perceived as the front line of historical progress. Through identification with anti-colonial struggles, the consciousness of racial discrimination, developed in protests for black civil rights, could be extended to Asians. Older stigmatizing stereotypes of Asians could be reversed: the caricature images of Chinese laborers who built the railroads in parts of the US; of Philippine savages in the Spanish-American war; of Japanese killers in World War II, and of North Korean robot soldiers in the Korean War. In contrast, the Vietnamese could be perceived as model fighters for the noble cause of universal freedom. Michael Renov has analyzed this perspective of idealization in early Newsreel Collectives documentaries like *The People's War* (1969) and *Only the Beginning* (1971).[8] His arguments about ideological distortions in these early anti-war documentaries carry some weight, but neglect the historical and cultural context in which these films were produced. In addition, his psychological framework and implied ideal of ethnographic 'truth' are themselves based on unexamined ideological premises.

A more diverse representation of the Vietnam conflict is developed in Peter Davis's panorama of its impact on certain parts of American society, *Hearts and Minds* (1974). Its dramatizing construction of people and events enhanced its emotional appeal and popular success; in 1974 it received an Academy Award for Best Documentary Feature. But it has not been an unqualified success with all audiences and film critics. *Hearts and Minds* opens with idyllic scenes of a Vietnamese village, which might evoke Renov's criticism of idealization. But the film uses footage of Vietnam mainly to reveal the brutalities of the war. Search and destroy missions, torture, the use of Agent Orange and the effect of intensive bombing are shown and related to the suffering of the people; some of the victims are identified by their names and speak in their own voices. However, Davis's documentary casts a much wider net over the situation in the US. The range of voices he assembles includes critical intellectuals like Daniel Ellsberg and skeptical politicians like Senators William Fulbright and Robert Kennedy; advocates of the war like General Westmoreland and George Coker, the celebrated survivor of captivity in North Vietnam. But the greatest emphasis is given

8 Renov, "Imaging the Other," 255–68.

to a chorus of war critics, and especially to those young men who refused to be drafted or who turned against the war after their experience in Vietnam. Veterans against the war provide the film with a platform, where heroism and rejection of the war can be merged; where the moral criticism of the war is legitimized and the pro-war voices are marginalized. *Hearts and Minds* makes it clear that it condemns the war. However, the effort to unfold a pluralistic panorama of protest relies heavily on a Hollywood style of drama. As Richard Barsam points out, "No other film about Vietnam used so expansive a frame in its coverage, or was supported by such lavish Hollywood financing. A year after the war ended . . . official Hollywood could afford to discover its conscience and to take sides."[9] The ambivalent reactions to this important documentary are the result, one could argue, of an inherent contradiction: *Hearts and Minds* assembles strong images and verbal statements, which condemn the war; but it refuses to relate them to a coherent, more analytical perspective of this military excursion.

THE JOURNALIST AS OBSERVER/PARTICIPANT

More coherence is achieved, although at a price, by those documentary films and written texts which criticize the war on the basis of the 'superior truth' of subjective experience. The focused and factual attitude of journalists adds professionalism to this perspective of personal authenticity. David Bradbury's documentary *Front Line* (1979) about the film reporter Neil Davis constructs this perspective in characteristic ways. The rejection of the war relies mainly on a few occasional shots of Lyndon B. Johnson, as the representative of the ignorance and deceitfulness of politics, and their contrast with the main body of the film: battle scenes Davis mostly experienced himself. Davis reported on military conflicts in South East Asia for eleven years, until his death on the battlefield. His film reports were watched regularly by TV audiences in the US and worldwide. The film presents Davis in somewhat tropical scenery as he remembers his journalistic work and comments on the war scenes the film assembles, mostly recorded by him. Some footage is designated as not his own, but from archives; and some of the commentary is spoken not by him but by Richard Oxenburg. But Davis,

9 Barsam, *Non-Fiction Film*, 316.

the footage he took, and the comments he makes in the film's present tense constitute the perspective of this documentary.

Davis's concept of the truth about the Vietnam War is summarized in the title of the film. As shown in *Front Line,* Davis did his film work in combat situations alongside the South Vietnamese and Cambodian soldiers who did much of the close-up fighting. He even crossed over into liberated territory and recorded the villagers supporting the Vietcong. His insistence to work at "the real front line" is driven by a version of the journalistic ethic, which he expresses without any analysis in the demand that "the truth must be presented." His form of the truth is focused on the gory and practical details of killing and survival on the ground, and on the courage to face death. Images of helicopters, structurally important in many films about the Vietnam War, as in de Antonio's *In the Year of the Pig* and Francis Coppola's *Apocalypse Now,* have only peripheral roles in *Front Line*; in fact, the huge military machine is sidelined in favor of combat at close range. Although there are occasional brief references to the cynicism of the politicians and to the anti-war movement in the US, the focus on battle scenes is by no means used as a direct denunciation of the barbarism of war, although it could be understood like this by some audiences in specific contexts. War, for Davis, is an existential arena where individuals are tested and certain values are proven, courage most of all. In contrast to the numerous combat scenes, Davis's quiet and understated commentary and his non-ostentatious posture do much to moderate the emphasis on violence. Like the words of the protagonist in *Apocalypse Now*, which accompany the escalating brutalization of his 'mission', the scenes of Davis's spoken commentary demonstrate a contrasting world of reason and human dignity.

Courage, however, is not the only value emphasized in *Front Line*. Davis emphasizes the close comradeship he experiences by sharing the life of the foot soldiers. Reversing the negative racial stereotype of 'Asians,' Davis appreciates their humane qualities, although they remain invisible as individuals. The comradeship with the 'Asians' is contrasted implicitly with the distant cynicism of politicians in the US. In the course of the film a perspective is developed, which is common in war narratives: the contrast between the corruption of civilian life and the pure, existential experience of combat. An ideal of masculinity, softened by Davis as commentator, and a certain mystique of war emerge as essential parts of this perspective of the reporter as participant. When Davis keeps coming back to the phrase "death

Fig. 1: North Vietnamese tank at the gate of the presidential palace.

Screenshot from *Front Line* (David Bradbury, 1980).

is a lady," which he picks up from 'Asian' soldiers, a rare reference is introduced to a world outside male comradeship. Davis's own death in battle, referred to by the narrator, personalized the presence of death as a theme of the film. The female connotation implies a certain attractiveness, even seductiveness of dying in combat. The pure existential battle experience involves a pull towards dissolution of the self up to the point of death.

The reporter's perspective is vitalized by the awareness that the scenes he documents and distributes through the media may have some influence on various audiences and, in some instances, may become part of history. The nude young girl running away from bombardments, the execution of a prisoner on the street in front of the camera—both scenes included in *Front Line*—have become icons of the Vietnam War.

The final scenes, which document the conquest of Saigon by the Vietcong, show Davis at his best. Over images of hasty retreat, Davis remembers how he stayed behind to record the end (fig. 1). His cool and modest attitude, the implied awareness of the historical moment, and his sharp eye for the significant image, merge in a convincing demonstration of the reporter's perspective. Bradbury's film leaves on the periphery what other Vietnam documentaries try to focus on: the complex political situation in the US and in Vietnam as well as the cultural and historical dimensions of this conflict. However, within its circumscribed perspective, *Front Line*, while not free of contradictions, represents a significant effort to penetrate the "fog of war" that surrounded this US military excursion from the beginning, and to focus on the price of war: human life.

Documentary Film and Intellectual Intervention

Emile de Antonio's perspective on the Vietnam War differs radically from those documentaries which try to achieve authenticity through personal experience. *In the Year of the Pig* (1968), his Vietnam film, constructs a certain type of historical narrative based on philosophical principles. De Antonio did not visit Vietnam but invested considerable research in documenting the conflicting positions which, in his view, drive the historical process, and to develop his thesis about the nature of this conflict. De Antonio always opposed the dominant media, although he had some success within their networks; rather, he appealed to the critical public sphere which developed during the protest movement of this period. His documentaries were intended to provide 'the Movement' with a radical critique of the establishment. Beyond this immediate concern, *In the Year of the Pig* is an endeavor of enlightenment about the historical processes that obstruct or enable the struggle against oppression, in Vietnam as well as in the US. De Antonio's fusion of intellectual analysis and radical criticism of the status quo into a new form of documentary montage made his film effective in the context of protest and placed him in a prominent position in the history of American documentary film.

Emile de Antonio did not start out as a filmmaker; but the various resources he brought to it, including his competence as an art and cultural critic, led him easily to the genre of documentary. As the son of a wealthy Italian-American medical doctor—he named his production company, Turin, after the birthplace of his father—he acquired early on the social skills and contacts he relied on in his film work. At the same time he was drawn to radical groups as a student at Harvard in the late 1930s, and he learned to deal with different ways of life during his job as a longshoreman and in the army during World War II. After a period of studying and teaching philosophy, he drifted into the bohemian art scene of Greenwich Village, where he lived among young and upcoming artists like John Cage, Andy Warhol, Robert Rauschenberg and others. After viewing the film *Pull My Daisy* (1959), a representation of the Beat scene that included Allen Ginsberg and Jack Kerouac, de Antonio became convinced that film, in its anti-Hollywood form, was a medium in which he wanted to be involved. He turned himself into the distributor of *Pull My Daisy;* he got involved with the New American Cinema Group and the Film-Makers' Cooperative, where Jonas Mekas was active; and he eventually procured footage of the Army-McCarthy hearings of 1954, from which he produced, in a long process of experimentation, his first documentary film. *Point of Order* (1963) was a first step in the direction of a new form of documentary film, and it established de Antonio's position among filmmakers, as well as among left-liberal and radical critics of the witch-hunting methods of McCarthyism. With his film *In the Year of the Pig*, de Antonio intervened in one of the central issues of the protest movement and explored a wide range of new documentary methods.

In the Year of the Pig is the result of intensive research in libraries and film archives in many countries and of an equally intensive editing process. Taking a determined stand in heated debates about the on-going war in Vietnam, the film received mostly favorable reviews, became a commercial success, quickly turned into an attraction of anti-war protest, and increased de Antonio's status as an innovative documentary filmmaker. In 1970 it received an Oscar nomination as the best documentary feature. Its success was achieved in spite of the considerable demands it makes on the attention and intellectual resources of most audiences.

The opening sequence, which functions as a prologue, confronts the viewer with a highly abbreviated summary of de Antonio's method. Immediately, it calls attention to the artificiality of filmic construction. These images are isolated from their contexts and not connected by some kind of narrative or causative line, but separated by black spaces. There is no commentary to assist the viewer—something de Antonio always rejected as authoritarian. Neither is there the impression of a 'found story' represented 'objectively' as in Direct Cinema—an approach de Antonio often ridiculed. Still, these images are highly charged and challenge the viewer to decipher them and understand their relationship to each other. Some were already iconic images in circulation, as the one of the Buddhist monk on fire; their context is shown only later in the film. Others are superficially self-explanatory, as that of the American soldier on whose helmet the anti-war slogan is reversed: "make war not love." In the context of the film as a whole, this slogan condenses the destructiveness of the war in one image. Some of these images remain incomprehensible without external information, confronting the viewer with the limits of his understanding. The second of these images shows this inscription on an unidentified background: "As soon as I heard of American independence my heart was enlisted. 1776." Underneath appears the handwritten name "Joseph Angel." De Antonio has spoken about this image on various occasions. The inscription appears below the statue of Lafayette in Union Square in Manhattan, where de Antonio had a studio at the time. In Lafayette's engagement for American freedom and independence, de Antonio saw a historical parallel to his own engagement for the independence of another colonial country. In the name "Angel" he recognized a Puerto Rican graffito and a reference to the struggles for Puerto Rican independence.[10] Although the prologue positions the viewer in a state of incomplete understanding, its isolated images indicate a sketchy, abstract pattern of contrasts: past vs. present, US vs. Vietnam, critics of the war vs. its representatives, civilians vs. the military (fig. 2 and fig. 3). One unifying element is the sound underlying the prologue. At first barely noticeable or comprehensible, it rises to a crescendo of helicopter noise, which de Antonio had carefully composed for a hyper-realistic effect, the sound of an escalating war. The artificiality of documentary constructions is not demonstrated for its own sake but to raise the awareness of the audience of their position: in an unstable situation of not-knowing, of very limited knowledge and of guess-work, viewers are challenged to work out coherence and meaning through their own efforts. In a more accessible way than in the prologue, de Antonio, then, makes the viewer a collaborator, guided by the filmmaker, in the construction of the whole film.

10 Amman et al., "Ein schriftliches Interview mit Emile de Antonio," 377–78.

Fig. 2: Screenshot from the prologue of In the Year of the Pig *(Emile de Antonio, 1968).*

The film begins with footage of the colonial past of Vietnam. The alternating montage of marching troops and a coffee house scene demonstrates the combination of military power and everyday rule in Vietnam under French occupation. The 'natives' who pull the foreigners in rickshaws are turned away with an arrogant gesture, and the 'masters' relax in the café among themselves. Native subservience, the montage indicates, is enforced by the troops of the occupiers. These opening scenes demonstrate de Antonio's thesis that colonialism was at the root of the conflict; they also introduce the viewer to de Antonio's basic premise: "History is the theme of all my films."[11] In the *Year of the Pig* follows the Vietnam conflict from these early beginnings to the escalation of American military activity, including the bombing of North Vietnam, after the Tonkin Bay incident of 1964 and further to the controversial election of Thieu in 1967; in fact, the montage towards the end predicts the defeat of the US years later. However, *In the Year of the Pig* is not constructed as a straightforward linear historical narrative but in a complex pattern of conflictual images and voices. In contrast to other documentaries about Vietnam, like *Front Line* or even *Hearts and*

11 de Antonio, "Theme of All My Films," 21.

Fig. 3: Another screenshot from the prologue of In the Year of the Pig *(Emile de Antonio, 1968).*

Minds, *In the Year of the Pig* uses a wide range of pro- and anti-war figures and images to develop a long-range and dialectical historical perspective of this conflict. As some of the isolated images of the prologue indicate, and some of the speakers later emphasize, de Antonio's concept of history is based on the premise of liberation through conflict, from colonial rule and from oppression worldwide. From de Antonio's perspective, the American colonies in the past were part of the same movement of history towards liberty as the people of Vietnam, and their supporters in the US, in the present.

To put this concept of history on the screen, de Antonio developed a documentary method which he has called collage. Others have used the term mosaic. Bill Nichols, one of his best interpreters, points to "the strategy of contention."[12] For this purpose, *In the Year of the Pig* includes interviews with more than 50 individuals, footage from various archives and excerpts from American TV, American government films and other sources, the result of intensive research. From this material de Antonio constructs a complex pattern, in which many voices and images are in conflict with each other and no one can claim to represent the whole truth, but which ultimate-

12 Nichols, "Voice of Documentary," 57.

ly represents a meaningful concept. Within this pattern, various villains, heroes and in-between attitudes are represented. However, some figures stand out as particularly trustworthy: the "real authorities," as de Antonio called them.[13] Among them, Philip Devillers, Jean Lacouteur and others, but particularly Paul Mus and Daniel Berrigan, carry considerable weight throughout the film.

The "real authorities" do not appeal to the viewer by positions of power or status. In fact, Philip Devillers is identified only by his name, Paul Mus by his name, place and profession: "professor of Buddhism, Yale." Instead, their appeal is based on their intimate knowledge of the facts, their precise understanding of historical and cultural developments, and on their belief in the open mind of the viewer. When they explain details of Ho Chi Minh's life and of the history of Vietnam, they dissolve the clichés propagated by the mainstream media and unfold the historical dimension usually excluded. In contrast to the ignorant and brutal utterances of, for example, Generals Curtis LeMay and Mark Clark, they represent an informed and humane attitude. Gradually, the real authorities attract the viewer into a sphere of moral conviction and of reliance on what de Antonio clearly expected to be the most potent power in the conflicts of history: the ultimate power of reason.

While *In the Year of the Pig* positions the "real authorities" in contrast to the cynicism of politicians and generals, it also demonstrates the fragility of their appeal in relation to the brutal and dumb practice of war. Several sequences in the middle of the film contrast the futility of the 'search and destroy' missions of the US Army with the hollow phrases of Hubert Humphrey and General Westmoreland that are inserted; and they demonstrate the limits of the voices of reason, which tend to be drowned in the noise of war. Here, the still images in the prologue of the soldier almost completely covered by ammunition belts and of the soldier whose helmet carries the slogan "make war not love" are expanded in sequences of direct brutality. The helicopter sound of the prologue is merged here with images of combat scenes. While close-up fighting scenes were used in *Front Line* to demonstrate a specific journalistic ethos, *In the Year of the Pig* selects battle footage that confronts the viewer with the dehumanizing effect of war. The victims are mainly terrorized civilians. American soldiers are

13 de Antonio, "Radical Scavenging," 12.

shown as infected by the brutality of war when they look at the destruction of rice supplies and of forests simply as jobs to be done, or even enjoyed; or when, in one famous scene, the veneer of decorum is ripped away and commander George S. Patton, with a sudden weird smile on his face, praises his soldiers as "a bloody good bunch of killers." Two figures are placed in specific positions within the contest of images. One is Ho Chi Minh. Early in the film the story of his life is told by Jean Lacouture, and some of his philosophy is explained by Professor Mus. A scene with Ho and Mus's historical explanation of Vietnamese survival strength appears at the end. Mus's description of Ho Chi Minh emphasizes the blending of Marxist and Confucian thinking. When Mus, not yet identified, first introduces Ho, his voice is heard over images of Vietnamese landscapes. At this point, one might suspect the idealization of Vietnam which Renov criticizes in documentaries by the Newsreel Collective. However, in the context of Mus's explanation, Ho Chi Minh is made to represent the survival of Vietnam, at all times based on simple village life, ties to ancestors and growing food—the continuity of cultural and material life. De Antonio adds an anti-colonial and patriotic perspective when he inserts the comparison of Ho Chi Minh with George Washington in the words of Republican Senator Thruston B. Morton: "The thing that I think we felt right is that Ho Chi Minh, communist or no, is considered by the people of Vietnam, and I'm speaking now of the millions in South Vietnam, as a George Washington of his country."

The other person who is placed in a special position is Daniel Berrigan, priest and peace activist. Berrigan is shown speaking to the camera, with a calm and reasonable voice, about his experience in North Vietnam during a period of intensified American attacks: "There is nothing that has not been attacked." His conclusion about this massive military intervention is, first of all, that it is a failure: "the war is not working." The people of North Vietnam continue their lives facing the world's biggest machine of destruction. While Paul Mus focuses on the specific conditions in Vietnam, Berrigan draws general conclusions. The concentration of power, he argues, operates outside the real world of humans, which is continually produced by being imagined. In a world trying to humanize, the destructiveness of power is failing because it is anachronistic like "the dinosaur." In Berrigan's philosophical view, not only US military intervention is failing but a long historical period as a whole: "it means the end of the giant, it means the last days of superman."

De Antonio felt close enough to Berrigan's philosophical views to make a documentary with the Berrigan brothers and the Plowshare Eight about their peace activities, released in 1982 under the title *In the King of Prussia*. In de Antonio's wider perspective, the Vietnam War was a horrible but transitory period in a long-term and global historical process. *In the Year of the Pig* does not include scenes of the rising tide of protest in the US—and de Antonio had to defend this approach against some critics—because the film aims at a deeper and more permanent form of protest and criticism that looks beyond the military disaster in Vietnam. He confronts the commercial media, Hollywood in particular, and the commercialization of life in general. In a variation of Plato's cave image, de Antonio agrees with Plato that we do not see the real world but only its shadows, but with a difference: "the shadow on the wall is the dollar sign."[14] Like Berrigan, de Antonio acts on the assumption that the real world has to be first imagined and then produced, which he attempts in the complex aesthetic structure of his documentaries. Therefore, he moves against the dominant media, often by using against them what they discard, an approach he has called "radical scavenging." His documentary project is conceived as a continuous uphill battle against the immorality and deceit of various factions of the establishment. It is based on a tough struggle against the weight of the power elite and frequently achieves its aesthetic aim: the appearance of ease and effortless elegance dealing with gravity, which he associates with ballet dancing: "And as I've made each film, it's become almost a balletic motion, in that I could feel the resistance of the Establishment against what I was doing."[15] For de Antonio, the history of the Vietnam War is not something that can be found and then revealed to the viewer, but a process of conflict that has to be created in the filmmaker's mind and then constructed in the form of a documentary film. Although the final product is polemical, he describes his working method in terms of poetry: "The individual frames, the pieces of the film are like words in a poem: they're just like all the words lying in the dictionary. It's how they're put together and used

14 de Antonio, "Emile de Antonio Interviews Himself," 302.
15 de Antonio, "Radical Scavenging," 3–4.

which is finally what matters."[16] There is a strong impulse of utopian expectation in de Antonio's films. While they were produced, and used, as interventions in the current protest movement, their polemical perspective relies on an implicit view of a better world.

THE VIETNAM WAR IN RETROSPECT: A LESSON?

The clash of American perspectives on the Vietnam War did not, of course, end with military action or in the immediate post-war period. An interesting retrospective view of this crucial issue of 1960s and 1970s protest movements came out in late 2003, Errol Morris's documentary *The Fog of War*. It is based on Morris's 20 hours of interviews with Robert McNamara, Secretary of Defense under President John F. Kennedy and Lyndon B. Johnson from 1961 to 1968—his late deliberations about his long life. Although the *Fog of War* reaches from McNamara's youth to the present tense of the film, the period of seven years as manager of the Vietnam War is its center.

Errol Morris has developed a specific documentary style ever since he broke with Direct Cinema conventions in the late 1970s with his *Gates of Heaven* (1978) and with his very successful documentary intervention in a murder case with *The Thin Blue Line* (1988). Like these earlier films, *The Fog of War* is based on Morris' sharp perception of how individuals and social contexts interact and on his skillful interview technique. It also resembles them in its approach of drawing attention to its method. Morris explicates the interview situation, for example, when McNamara comments on it at the beginning, or when Morris' voice is heard asking questions or making comments. Tracing his life, not always chronologically, the film makes use of McNamara's reflections and soul searching to develop an elegantly designed structure of a prologue, 11 "lessons," and an epilogue. In McNamara's memories and Morris's visual comments on them, the film reflects and problematizes various significant aspects of American society in the twentieth century. In spite of the pedagogical connotation of the term 'lesson', these sections do not present anything like teaching material. Within an almost philosophical conceptual frame, they unfold the ambiguities and complexities of the situations McNamara tried to control.

16 Westerbeck, "Some Out-Takes," 140–43.

Under the title "Belief and seeing are both often wrong," lesson 7 starts with the problem of attacks on American warships in the Gulf of Tonkin in August 1964. President Johnson, who had his own doubts about whether these attacks had actually taken place, used them to get extended war powers from Congress and to begin bombing North Vietnam. De Antonio had been guided by his distrust of the establishment and his trust in the statements of American seamen to present this incident as pretense for a wider war. Morris focuses on McNamara's uncertainties at the time and his decision, in a situation of conflicting information, to trust the top military; only in retrospect can he accept the fact that in reality no attack had occurred. Morris comments on this situation by including voice recordings from that time that discuss whether any attacks took place: while Admiral Sharp expresses doubt, he is overruled by General Burchinal, who insists that the attack was a fact. In retrospect McNamara refers to the "mind set" at the time to explain his mistake, and Morris shows falling domino pieces over a map of Vietnam to explicate McNamara's reference to the domino theory. Morris's clever montage methods let the audience get a glimpse behind the veil of power. Unlike de Antonio's polemical stance, Morris's approach of correlating relevant, often contradictory, facts resembles rather the work of a detective, which he knew through personal experience. When McNamara speaks at the time of a "battle for the hearts and minds," the film comments on it with images of bombings. When President Johnson says in a recorded conversation that "we're losing," Morris follows up with a public speech in which McNamara claims that "we" have stopped losing the war.

Morris does not always comment on McNamara's actions at the time but leaves much to the audience. When McNamara, in retrospect, expresses his belief that the war was the result of misunderstandings, something he tried to address in a post-war visit to Vietnam, the film gives him space to develop his questionable arguments: that the US were wrongly perceived by the Vietnamese as new colonialists, and that the Vietnamese could have achieved everything they did without the high cost of war. In fact, Morris is more interested in documenting McNamara's contradictory perceptions, not in denouncing them. He views McNamara with respect and a sharp awareness of his ultimately tortured life. Philipp Glass's indeterminate music enhances the atmosphere of ambivalence that Morris achieves. The epilogue shows McNamara driving his car without a declared destination and commenting that he is "damned." By merging McNamara's life with its social and political contexts through highly intelligent montage, Morris's perspective lets McNamara emerge as a complex representative of one section of the American power elite at the time of the Vietnam War: its hubris as much as its honest self-doubts and its moral failure in a period of crisis.

Perceptions of the Vietnam War in Cold War Contexts

Public controversy about the Vietnam War in the US was, of course, not insulated from global conflicts between the two dominant political systems in the 1960s. The war emerged as a test of the legitimacy of US policy and American values in many parts of the world, and as a catalyst of documentary interventions in the struggle for people's 'hearts and minds'. As a focus of Cold War conflicts, Berlin offered very different opportunities for documentary filmmakers in the East and in the West. Documentaries produced only a few miles apart developed perspectives of the Vietnam War that shared a critical impetus. But the documentaries by the team 'Heynowski & Scheumann' in East Berlin and the young German filmmaker Harun Farocki in West Berlin differed radically in their methods and the targets of their criticism.

Walter Heynowski and Gerhard Scheumann were attracted to postwar Berlin and pursued their journalistic careers on this difficult terrain with great skill and success. The German film industry, concentrated in Berlin, had been destroyed even more thoroughly than most other industries in the course of the war. But film was considered by the Allies an important medium to reach, and possibly re-educate, the traumatized population. The Soviet Military Administration (SMA) initiated film screenings soon after they moved into Berlin, and film production began in the Soviet sector not much later. In 1946, SMA also founded the East German film company DEFA, which changed its legal status several times and produced a large number of fiction and documentary films until the end of the German Democratic Republic. DEFA stock is now available through the DEFA Foundation distributor TOBIAS in Berlin-Adlershof and through the DEFA Film Library of the University of Massachusetts in Amherst. Heynowski and Scheumann began to work with DEFA in 1965. After their great success *The Laughing Man* (1965) about a German mercenary soldier, they held a privileged position within DEFA. After 1969 they ran their own separate studio, "H & S," where they enjoyed excellent working conditions in many ways: technical equipment and support, financing, distribution and leeway to develop their documentary aesthetics, as long as they did not cross certain political red lines—which they eventually did. Their documentaries, more than 70 over 25 years, focused on three major areas: survivals of fascism in Germany, the struggles in Chile under Allende and Pinochet, and the war in Vietnam and Cambodia.[17]

Among the Vietnam documentaries of Studio "H & S," *Pilots in Pyjamas* (1968, 311 min.) stands out because of the size of the project. The film is based on many hours of surprisingly detailed interviews that Heynowski and Scheumann conducted with captured American pilots in Hanoi. *Am Wassergraben* (1978, 15:18 min.) uses those pictures of the My Lai massacre on March 16, 1968, which the US Army photographer Ronald Haeberle did not hand over to the military but published in the US; images of the village taken by Heynowski and Scheumann ten years later; and interviews with several survivors, in an effort to reconstruct the perspective of the victims. Their short documentary *Remington Cal. 12* (1973, 15 min.) is a particularly stringent realization of their aesthetic approach.

Remington Cal. 12 begins with references to hunting: shots at flying birds, short remarks by hunters about Remington projectiles used for hunting, and a detailed examination of one Remington cartridge. Caliber 12, not generally available for hunting, is shown to contain 20 tiny arrows, which fragment in human bodies—a killing method forbidden by the Geneva Convention. The effects of this cartridge on materials that range from hard to soft to organic are demonstrated in a setting of technical testing. Remington/Dupont as producer of guns and ammunition for hunting animals is briefly brought into the widening perspective. The film avoids polemical rhetoric and drains emotional connotations of its commentary in an attitude of technical inspection and sober reporting. But the perspective changes when the film shifts from a hunting to a military context. The bestselling song "Ballad of the Green Berets" accompanies brief scenes of American Special Forces preparing for action. Images of helicopters and a glimpse of a dark-haired prisoner provide a brief reference to Vietnam. The carefully constructed escalation of images of potential violence leads to a sequence

17 Steinmetz, "Heynowski & Scheumann," 365–79.

in which a Special Forces soldier handles his gun and praises the deadly effects on humans of this particular type of cartridge (fig. 4). The film does not include any battle scenes or even images of direct violence against people. In a sequence of economically placed short scenes, it develops an image-based associative line of argument: that killing in Vietnam is done as a form of animal hunt. The didactic conclusion is attached in the printed words of an army publication, which report that the US is testing new weapons in the war in Vietnam. The film avoids representation of actual events in Vietnam. Instead, it uses various image sources—from arranged and staged scenes, American film material, and some printed pages—to develop the careful visual construction of an argument: that the Vietnam War is a culmination of a culture of violence. In the wide range of documentaries critical of the Vietnam War, *Remington Cal. 12* is not unusual, except in one essential aspect. It implies the concept of an entire society which fuses war, the weapon industry and fighters into a system without an alternative.

A different form of radical documentary criticism of the Vietnam War emerged in the context of the Deutsche Film- und Fernsehakademie Berlin (dffb) and the student movement in West Berlin. The Berlin film academy, the first academic training institution in the Federal Republic of Germany, opened its doors in 1966 with expectations that it would provide an essential impetus for the recovery of German film after the destructions of the war. Escalating confrontations brought the student movement also into this institution. Students began to make films about the conservative cold war press, the killing by police of student Benno Ohnesorg, the shooting of student leader Rudi Dutschke, and about the war in Vietnam. They occupied the film academy and changed its name to Dziga Vertov Academy. In November 1968, 18 of the students were expelled, among them Harun Farocki. Decades and many films later, Farocki started teaching at the dffb and became a professor at the University of Vienna.

Farocki's film *Nicht löschbares Feuer* (*Inextinguishable Fire*, 1969) broke with several documentary conventions in ways that left significant traces in the history of the genre. In the US, Jill Godmilow responded to Farocki's film almost 30 years later with his own *What Farocki Taught Us* (1998).[18] *Nicht löschbares Feuer* deals with the use of napalm in Vietnam

18 Kahana, *Intelligence Work*, 341–47.

Fig. 4: Screenshot from Remington Cal. 12 *(Heynowski and Scheumann, 1973)*

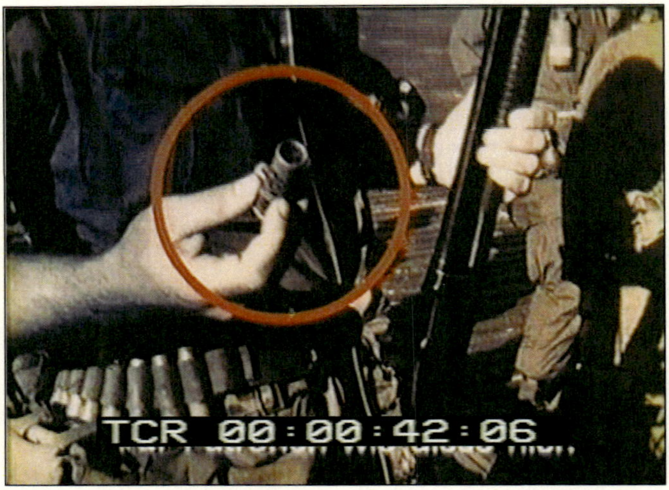

with rigorously anti-illusionary methods. The film emphasizes its non-realistic method and appeals to the intellect, to morality and, at the end, to the need for action. With minimal props, it creates something like a laboratory space and atmosphere, where people perform functions as non-actors and actions are staged as demonstrations of intellectual analysis. After reading, in a neutral voice, the report of napalm effects on one victim, Farocki demonstrates the limits of images trying to represent reality directly when he burns himself with a cigarette and explains how much hotter napalm is (fig. 5). The images of napalm effects, he argues, would close our eyes and stop our analysis. Opposing the heat of napalm with the coolness of his representation, Farocki proceeds to demonstrate, in a Brechtian form of 'estrangement', or anti-illusionary showing, the process of production whose end result is napalm. His analysis looks beyond the war in Vietnam and the use of napalm at the division of labor and the production for destruction and profit. Relying on the assumption that the logic of capitalistic production can be reversed, and made to serve human needs, the film leads up to an appeal to transform analysis into action: now.

Fig. 5: Screenshot from "Nicht löschbares Feuer" *(Harun Farocki, 1969).*

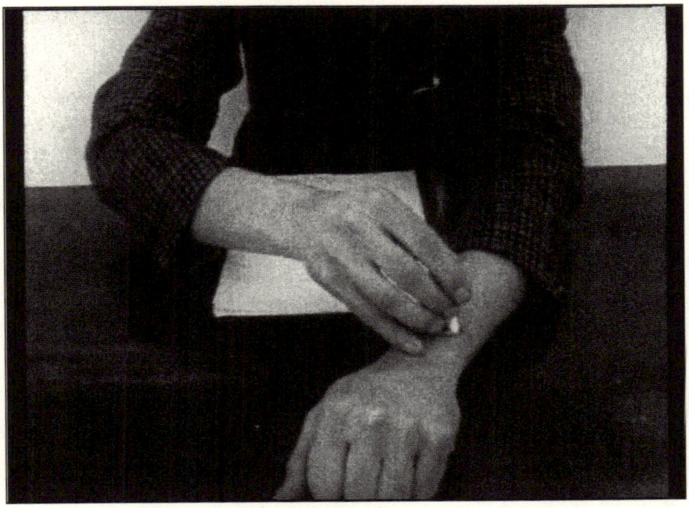

Farocki's subsequent films, more than 90so far, develop his method of analysis and didactic demonstration, but without the activism of this early film. In 1969, however, Farocki could see himself as one of many carried along by worldwide historical change. In Berlin, still occupied by the war-time Allies, the sectors in the West provided the space for a new alliance, where American and German youth movements interacted closely in the protest against the war in Vietnam. Beyond, but also on the fringes of existing institutions and political structures, a culture of transatlantic opposition to cold war mentalities and the Vietnam War emerged under they eyes of the Western Allies. At the Freie Universität, initiated and financially supported by the US as an alternative to the university in East Berlin, professors who had emigrated and returned taught a younger generation. Herbert Marcuse, by that time a professor in San Diego and a guest professor at the Freie Universität Berlin, spoke to big crowds in a series of lectures in 1967. American SDS and German SDS, the student organizations, developed close contacts.[19] The war in Vietnam provided a common focus for a wide

19 Klimke, *The Other Alliance*, 10–39.

spectrum of the countercultural impetus which shook up the 1960s. Representations by the dominant media lost their legitimacy for those who expected a better world, and producing their own images was an essential part of 1960s activism.

In the 1960s, images of the war in Vietnam were a daily presence in American homes, and they circulated around the globe. Those who resisted this military excursion had grown up with TV and understood the specific power of images, joined the struggle over their control and hoped to reach out with their own visual interventions to a different and wider, ultimately global public. The Vietnam War provided for a heterogeneous and widely dispersed countercultural movement an opportunity to fuse various local and international issues in a utopian desire for a better world. In Germany, the reaction against the involvement of an older generation in fascism and war was a strong motive in an anti-war stance, although not infrequently as an unacknowledged subtext—as in Farocki's documentary about napalm.[20] In the US, a tradition of idealistic hope for a 'new world' pervaded many forms of 1960s protest. De Antonio's critical analysis of the Vietnam War includes a patriotic subtext about a better America.[21] Todd Gitlin, president of SDS from June 1963 to June 1964, published his dissertation about the media perception of the American student movement in 1978 under the title "The Whole World Is Watching"—a distinct echo to the seventeenth-century Puritan belief that "the eyes of all people are upon us" and that a small group of the committed was, in fact, a historical avant-garde, whose actions needed to be recorded. Documentary critiques of the Vietnam War varied widely in their perception and their aesthetic realization, but shared, more or less, the hope that the images they produced were historical documents and would shape the course of events towards a better world without war.

FILMOGRAPHY

Apocalypse Now. Directed by Francis F. Coppola. *Apocalypse Now Redux*, extended version. München: Universum Film, 2009. DVD.

20 Kahana, *Intelligence Work*, 343.
21 Hoenisch, "History Is the Theme," 235–66.

The Fog of War. Directed by Errol Morris. Culver City, CA: Sony Pictures Classics, 2004. DVD.

Frontline. Directed by David Bradbury. Mullumbimby, Australia: Frontline Films, 1979. DVD.

Hearts and Minds: A Historic Visual Chronicle of the Vietnam War. Directed by Peter Davis. Produced by Touchstone-Audieff Production for BBS Productions. Orland Park, IL: MPI Home Video, 1991. VHS.

In the Year of the Pig. Directed by Emile de Antonio. Emile de Antonio: Films of a Radical Saint. Chatsworth, CA: Home Vision Entertainment, 2008. DVD.

Nicht Löschbares Feuer. Directed by Harun Farocki. Harun Farocki Filme 1967–2005. Berlin: Absolut MEDIEN, 2009. DVD.

Remington Cal.12. Directed by Walter Heynowski and Gerhard Scheumann. Berlin: Progress Film-Verleih, 1972.

Why Vietnam? Washington, DC: US Department of Defence, 1965.

Bibliography

Amman, Frank, Benjamin Gabel, Roy Grundmann, Kristin Vincke, and Reiner Walther. "Ein schriftliches Interview mit Emile de Antonio." In *Der amerikanische Dokumentarfilm der 60er Jahre*, edited by Mo Beyerle and Christine N. Brinckmann, 377–78. Frankfurt: Campus Verlag, 1991.

Barnouw, Erik. *Documentary: A History of the Non-Fiction Film*. New York: Oxford University Press, 1974.

Barsam, Richard M. *Non-Fiction Film: A Critical History*. Bloomington: Indiana University Press, 1992.

Capps, Walter H., ed. *The Vietnam Reader*. New York: Routledge, 1991.

de Antonio, Emile. "'History Is the Theme of All My Films': An Interview with Emile de Antonio." By Gary Crowdus and Dan Georgakas. *Cineaste* 12, no. 2 (1982): 20–28.

———. "*In the King of Prussia*: Emile de Antonio Interviews Himself (1982)." In *Emile de Antonio: A Reader*, edited by Douglas Kellner and Dan Streible, 301–308. Minneapolis: University of Minnesota Press, 2000.

———. "Radical Scavenging: An Interview with Emile de Antonio." By Bernard Weiner. *Film Quarterly* 25, no. 1 (Autumn 1971): 3–15.

Gitlin, Todd. "The Achievements of the War-Protest Movement." In Capps, *Vietnam Reader*, 157–67.

Grajeda, Tony. "The Winning and Losing of Hearts and Minds: Vietnam, Iraq, and the Claims of the War Documentary." *Jump Cut* 49 (Spring 2007): 1–23.

Herr, Michael. *Dispatches.* New York: Avon, 1978.

Hoenisch, Michael. "'History Is the Theme of All My Films': Geschichtskonstruktionen in Emile de Antonios *In the Year of the Pig* (1969) und Barbara Kopples *Harlan County, U.S.A.* (1976)." In *Die Repräsentation sozialer Konflikte im Dokumentarfilm der USA*, edited by Michael Hoenisch, 235–66. Trier: Wissenschaftlicher Verlag Trier, 1996.

Kahana, Jonathan. *Intelligence Work: The Politics of American Documentary.* New York: Columbia University Press, 2008.

Klimke, Martin. *The Other Alliance: Student Protest in West Germany and the United States in the Global Sixties.* Princeton: Princeton University Press, 2010.

Lewis, Randolph. *Emile de Antonio: Radical Filmmaker in Cold War America.* Madison: University of Wisconsin Press, 2000.

Nichols, Bill. "The Voice of Documentary." In *New Challenges for Documentary*, edited by Alan Rosenthal, 48–63. Berkeley: University of California Press, 1988.

Pynchon, Thomas. *Vineland.* New York: Penguin, 1991.

Renov, Michael. "Imaging the Other: Representations of Vietnam in Sixties Political Documentary." In *From Hanoi to Hollywood: The Vietnam War in American Film*, edited by Linda Dittmar and Gene Michaud, 255–68. New Brunswick: Rutgers University Press, 1990.

Rowe, John Carlos. "Eye-Witness: Documentary Styles in the American Representation of Vietnam." In *The Vietnam War and American Culture*, edited by John Carlos Rowe and Rick Berg, 148–74. New York: Columbia University Press, 1991.

Scott-Heron, Gil. "The Revolution Will Not Be Televised." In *The Norton Anthology of African American Literature*, edited by Henry Louis Gates and Nellie Y. McKay, 61–62. New York: Norton, 1997.

Steinmetz, Rüdiger. "Heynowski & Scheumann: The GDR's Leading Documentary Film Team." *Historical Journal of Film, Radio and Television* 24, no. 3 (2004): 365–79.

Westerbeck, Colin J., Jr. "Some Out-Takes from Radical Film Making: Emile de Antonio." *Sight and Sound* 39, no. 3 (1970): 140–43.

Westmoreland, William C. "Vietnam in Perspective." In Capps, *Vietnam Reader*, 116–24.

Zinn, Howard. "The Impossible Victory: Vietnam." Chap. 18 in *A People's History of the United States*. New York: Harper Perennial Modern Classics, 2005.

Fiction in the 1960s and the Notion of Change

American and European Concepts of Postmodernism

Tomasz Basiuk

The Crisis Today

The current fiscal and, in some places, political crisis, which includes insurgencies and massive demonstrations taking place in the US and in some European and Arab countries seems reminiscent of the social and political turmoil associated with the 1960s. With events connected to the civil rights movement, as well as the 1969 student riots in Paris and in Warsaw, the Prague Spring, and the Stonewall Inn riots in New York, that the same year, the decade has gone down in history as a time in which a demand for change was especially vivid. Popular culture has since canonized the 1960s in just this way. In the summer of 1969, the Woodstock Festival seemed like a happy marriage of popular culture and radical politics. Many popular culture texts heralded change, and subsequent representations of the era continued this tradition, for example Miloš Forman's 1979 film *Hair*, based on a 1968 musical. The tradition was not without its precedents, for example in the 1950s films *The Wild One* (1953) and *Rebel Without a Cause* (1955), which glorified a young, usually male and heterosexual person as bearer of a message about social change.[1] Retrospectively, the radical tone of some of these representations is partly belied by a naïveté that their op-

1 Rado and Ragni, *Hair*; Paxton, *The Wild One*; Stern, *Rebel Without a Cause*.

timistic zeal betrays. Their messages may also seem incongruous with present-day predicaments.

Despite the current unrest, a dose of skepticism about revolutionary action seems widespread today. This skepticism has resulted in a reevaluation of the 1960s in popular representations of that decade. To offer just one example, fascination with and skepticism about the decade seem evenly balanced in the TV series *Mad Men* (2007 – present).[2] The show focuses on male advertising executives, whose many faults include not just the characters' evident hunger for cash but their equally evident misogyny and homophobia as well as their self-indulgent smoking and drinking. Moreover, the characters' drive for economic success is presented as a positive trait, however ambivalent it may seem to us in the context of the financial crisis heralded by the Lehman Brothers' bankruptcy. Nonetheless, being profit-driven is intimately linked to the characters' creativity. Their business acumen and relentlessness are not new but their focus on the management of symbolic rather than commodity exchanges is. This new focus makes these characters and their work revolutionary. Working in the fledgling field of mass advertising, the characters of *Mad Men* are inventing a new branch of the industry by upgrading to a newly professional level what had so far seemed a relatively minor component of a market pursuit focused on manufacturing and on sales. The protagonists of *Mad Men* are effecting a change in the organization of social life through their capable, if calculating, manipulation of consumer behavior, which they hope to influence with communication techniques. Their work is sometimes almost poetic, especially in the etymological sense of creating new representations, even though retrospectively it must also appear as blatantly exploitative and perhaps destructive of some treasured traditions.

The series' representation of change is thus ambivalent: successful implementation of some changes may have had the negative consequences of promoting an unabashedly consumerist ethic and, simultaneously, perfecting techniques for turning the deliberation of public issues into aesthetically pleasing spectacles, orchestrated by PR specialists. Much is suggested by some characters' rooting for Richard Nixon and helping out in his 1960 presidential campaign (when Nixon lost to John F. Kennedy, who was apparently better prepared for the spectacle of the televised debate). The mak-

2 Weiner, *Mad Men*.

ers of *Mad Men* establish a connection between developments in social communication, including the growing role of Public Relations in political life, and a market economy driven by consumption that was spurred on by advertising. These developments confirm the reservations which the German cultural critic Walter Benjamin voiced in "The Work of Art in the Age of Mechanical Reproduction" (1936) about the spectacle of power and those articulated in the French Situationist Guy Debord's attack on what he described as the society of the spectacle in 1967.[3] But once again: the interesting aspect of this TV series is the way in which it portrays these developments (whose problematic consequences are common knowledge to us today) as revolutionary changes that required courage, cunning, and determination to put in place.

DEFINING POSTMODERNISM

Somewhat like the fairly complex and ambivalent representation of change in the series *Mad Men*, the intellectual and aesthetic practice of postmodernism in the 1960s offers a nuanced and, quite possibly, helpful way to grasp the concept of change as it applies to the present time. The relationships between novelty and tradition, change and continuity, originality and imitation have been at the center of interest to postmodernism, which was seen as a call for change, while it also questioned the idea that a radical breaking with the past was possible—not so much for conservative reasons but as a matter of intellectual rigor. Due to the relative longevity of postmodernism as an intellectual formation and as an analytical tool with which to discuss artworks and cultural practices and discourses, the articulation of its premises has evolved between the end of the 1960s and the early 1990s, by which time postmodernism seems to have exhausted itself as a consciously adopted intellectual position. Postmodernism's history in the 1960s may be thought of as that decade's *Nachträglichkeit*—a sort of Minerva's owl flying out at dusk. Although the idea of change as revolutionary, radical, and political seems a dominant motif of the era, postmodern-

3 Benjamin, "Work of Art in the Age of Mechanical Reproduction" in *Illuminations*; Debord, *Society of the Spectacle*.

ism offers an alternative perspective that may not so much contradict the epoch's longing for change as in some ways complicate it.

The term 'postmodernism' has a past which precedes its currency in American Studies and, more broadly, in literary and cultural studies. As early as the 1870s, the word postmodern was used with reference to French Impressionist painting, and in the 1930s the term *postmodernismo* became current in the context of Latin American poetry. In the United States, it had been used about architecture before it became a prominent term in literary criticism. Ihab Hassan began consistently to use the term to describe some contemporary fiction starting with his 1971 study *The Dismemberment of Orpheus: Toward a Postmodern Literature.*[4] Hassan was trying to pinpoint what he saw as an important shift in literary and intellectual paradigms that had been taking place for more than a decade, a development in which the 1960s seemed at the time to represent an apex. In a later essay "Toward a Concept of Postmodernism," included in his 1987 text *The Postmodern Turn*, he attempted to represent what he saw as a historical shift away from modernism with a table of paired-up terms describing specific ways in which modernism and postmodernism differed.[5] These pairs of terms, which may be seen as binary oppositions, include many that were borrowed from others. For example, Hassan juxtaposes "rhizome" (postmodernist) with "root (modernist)," taking both terms from Gilles Deleuze and Felix Guattari. With such pairs of oppositions, Hassan suggests that modernism is grounded in thought which presumes a center, while postmodernism operates in a decentered way, analogous to the rhizome, which is composed of many strands. Modernism is associated with depth and a hierarchical arrangement of categories, one in which some categories are subsumed under a more general one (as Hassan's word "hypotaxis" suggests).

On the other hand, postmodernism, described as paratactical, connotes surface play and a complex interrelatedness among elements. Thus, in postmodernism any particular surface effect is overdetermined, as it cannot be reduced to an underlying cause. The features of postmodernism which Hassan discusses at greatest length are indeterminacy and immanence; the latter term, opposed to transcendence, suggests that the meaning of any one

4 For example: "The modern age discovers the postmodern at its center." Hassan, *Dismemberment of Orpheus*, xviii. The words "postmodern" and "postmodernism" appear throughout.

5 Hassan, "Toward a Concept of Postmodernism," 84–96.

sign is not situated beyond the phenomenal but depends, in an indeterminate way, on the complex interplay of the perceptible signifiers. There is no meta-level containing an explanation of the world we know. There is just the world as it appears: "The world is everything that is the case," as Ludwig Wittgenstein famously put it, though in this case it might be more accurate to say: the appearance of the world is all that the case is.[6] To draw on Wittgenstein's late period, there is no meaning to be extracted from linguistic utterances other than that which is produced by what he called language games: these are semiotic practices whose internal rules arise from those practices themselves.[7]

The intellectual investment in defining postmodernism involves a certain debunking of rationality, especially the tradition of the Enlightenment. In the wake of World War II, Max Horkheimer and Theodor Adorno put in question the belief that human rationality guarantees either progress or ethical answerability. In *Dialectic of Enlightenment* (1944, 1947), they described widespread but unfounded trust in reason's ability to contain its own destructive ambitions as a slippery slope.[8] Three decades later, the French philosopher Jean-François Lyotard argued in *The Postmodern Condition* (1979) that the grand narratives about rationality, representing a heritage of the Enlightenment and legitimizing the quest for knowledge and with it universities as social institutions, had lost their credibility in the postwar decades.[9] Lyotard identified two now-debunked grand narratives about rationality. One was the narrative of speculation, which promised that knowledge would yield understanding and that there was a hidden layer of meaning to be grasped in the pursuit of knowledge. The other was the narrative of emancipation, which anticipated that knowledge would yield freedom from the constraints posed by the body and its ailments, by natural

6 Wittgenstein, *Tractatus Logico-Philosophicus*, proposition 1, 25.

7 Language games are not predetermined but immanent to practice: "But how many kinds of sentence are there? Say assertion, question, and command?—There are *countless* kinds: countless different kinds of use of what we call 'symbols', 'words', 'sentences'. And this multiplicity is not something fixed, given once for all; but new types of language, new language-games, as we may say, come into existence, and others become obsolete and get forgotten. (We can get a *rough picture* of this from the changes in mathematics)." Wittgenstein, *Philosophical Investigations*, proposition 23, page 11, emphases in the original.

8 "Myth is already enlightenment, and enlightenment reverts to mythology." Horkheimer and Adorno, *Dialectic of Enlightenment*, xviii.

9 Lyotard, *Postmodern Condition*, 37–41.

disasters, and by social injustice: that it would take us to a better tomorrow. These grand narratives answered the question *why* seek knowledge, but they have been superseded by what Lyotard calls input-output productivity: the question about *how* to achieve a specific goal. The *how* question is far more important nowadays than the *why* question, in which we seem to have lost interest.

Lyotard's immediate context for these reflections was the state of Western universities, which he believed had aligned themselves to this shift in thinking about knowledge due to pressures from the marketplace as well as from governments. But he also offers a philosophical explanation by focusing on certain intellectual developments. In particular, Lyotard finds in Wittgenstein's concept of language games an apt reflection of the debunking of the grand narratives about reason. Language games are always local and therefore do not guarantee a unifying theoretical perspective, which the narrative of speculation promised. And because knowledge is descriptive rather than prescriptive, the practical applicability of knowledge to the solving of real-life problems is always in question, as it was not in the narrative of emancipation.[10] Bereft of those justifications, we have turned to solving local problems without bothering with the big picture. The loss of the grand narrative of emancipation seems especially troubling from the viewpoint of change. The absence of the principle of emancipation does not mean that change will not occur but it does suggest that we cannot project what that change will be.

Some intellectuals embraced the debunking of grand narratives noted by Lyotard and affirmed the indeterminacy and immanence posited by Hassan. Jacques Derrida famously invoked the concept of "play" to talk about how signifiers interact in ways that are irreducible to any one paradigm, endlessly deferring the meaning which they seem to promise. Unlike the dyadic formula for the sign which consists of the material signifier and the conceptual signified, postulated by Ferdinand de Saussure, Derrida conceptualized the signifier as always shy of completion. He asserted that signifiers refer to one another rather than to their signified, displacing de Saussure's vertical relationship between the signifier and the signified with a

10 Lyotard made this argument in 1979, the year Margaret Thatcher became the British prime minister and one year before Ronald Reagan was elected US president. Today both politicians are seen as promoting neo-liberalism and dismantling the welfare state.

horizontal, rhizome-like interplay of signifiers.[11] This interplay, which carries the promise of a meaning but never quite delivers that meaning, is indeed overdetermined, or, as Hassan has put it, it is both indeterminate and immanent to the game itself. There is no outside, no meta-plane on which meaning may be said to reside, and neither is there any way in which to predict the outcome of the game. To describe the interplay of signs in very practical terms, the English critic Terry Eagleton invites us to think of looking up a word in a dictionary. As you do so, you do not find an actual concept but rather a definition composed of more words. The dictionary has a horizontal, rhizome-like structure in which signifiers refer the user to other signifiers by seeming to promise access to their referent: the signified. But this access is deferred, and all that is ever apparent is the play of difference between words.[12]

The logic of open-ended and indeterminate play has been the focus of possible political, as much as aesthetic, change in the work of Gilles Deleuze and Felix Guattari. They turned inside-out the psychoanalytic model, grounded in the idea of the unconscious mind driven by repressed desires, proposing instead that desire needs to be conceived not in terms of what is lacking but as a mechanism that is inherently productive.[13] In their reinterpretation, desire arises from the interplay of the senses and of affects, produced by our bodies, and of concepts, produced by the part of the body called the mind. This interplay continually churns out new meanings and is capable of achieving unprecedented and unforeseen results by combining material signifiers in new ways, not unlike in the artistic technique of assemblage.

Assessing Postmodernism as a Political Response

For some thinkers at least, such as for Derrida and for Deleuze and Guattari, there was a fair amount of optimism in the broad range of ideas describable as postmodernist. But other views on postmodernism have been

11 Derrida, "Structure, Sign, and Play," 278–91.
12 Eagleton, *Literary Theory*, 111.
13 Deleuze and Guattari, *Anti-Oedipus*, 1–9.

more reserved or outright pessimistic. In particular, the idea that getting rid of some foundational principles, including those that were a heritage of the Enlightenment, would be somehow liberating was attacked by conservative and by some progressive thinkers alike. Speaking from a self-defined progressive position, Jürgen Habermas argued that modernity was an incomplete project, prematurely abandoned in a way that was pointless and damaging.[14] To Habermas, the postmodernist refusal of a clear program for action constituted a refusal of the political, which betrayed an underlying investment in maintaining the status quo. Contrary to its revolutionary appearance, postmodernism was effectively conservative. Habermas' argument provoked a response from Lyotard, who came to postmodernism's defense by presenting it as the very stuff of change. In 1982, Lyotard published a brief paper called "Answering the Question: What is the Postmodern?" whose title alludes to Immanuel Kant's 1784 "What is Enlightenment?" (*Was ist Aufklärung?*), which postulates that Enlightenment is the age of humanity's reaching maturity.[15]

Lyotard's reply to Habermas is grounded in a critique of the notion of totality and a correlate elevation of difference. Lyotard holds that a political program which projects a *totality* of social life is far more problematic than the fragmented worldview of the postmodernists, which Habermas deems politically ineffectual. Lyotard makes this argument by calling on Kant's Third Critique, called *Critique of the Power of Judgment*, which distinguishes between the aesthetic of the beautiful and the aesthetic of the sublime (*die Schönheit / das Erhabene*) by explaining aesthetic experience as an interplay between the human faculties of reason and of the imagination, or presentation (*Darstellung*). The faculty of reason is responsible for coming up with a concept; the faculty of the imagination then tries to come up with an appropriate presentation of the concept. Kant notes that sometimes we can grasp a concept but do not have an adequate presentation of it. For example, we understand the geometric concept of the infinite line but we cannot draw one, or even imagine it in its entirety. A presentation marked by the dissonance between the faculties is given the name "sublime," while a presentation based on harmony between the faculties is "beautiful." Reiterating Kant's position that judgments of taste are based in common sense,

14 *Habermas*, "Modernity: An Incomplete Project," 3–15.

15 Lyotard, *Postmodern Condition*, 71–82.

Lyotard argues that the aesthetic of the beautiful is a matter of consensus. We perceive as beautiful such presentations of concepts as we are already familiar with. The aesthetic of the beautiful is thus a kind of lazy aesthetic. Lyotard argues that it is connected to realism: what comes to us easily and seems to be based in common sense seems real to us. The aesthetic of the beautiful is thus particularly conservative: it presents to us that which we already know well, confirming its reality. Referring to TV series as one of his examples, Lyotard speaks of the "around the house and in the backyard kind of realism," whose sociopolitical function it is to reassure the viewers that their lives are worth living. He then proceeds to subdivide the aesthetic of the sublime—in which the concept and its presentation do not coincide through consensus—into what he calls the mode of regret and the mode of assay. In the mode of regret, which is modernist, the presentation is available but the concept is evaporated. As Lyotard puts it, the solace of good form is offered but that form is emptied of content. Modernism is thus rather like an empty church. One can enjoy its architecture and the elaborate decorations, but there is no longer a presence to which these forms seem to be pointing. In the mode of assay, which is postmodernist, a concept that is as yet without its presentation is given an indirect expression through a form that is newly invented. The new form is not immediately readable but it attempts to justify itself in a performative way: showing what it is doing by doing it. The mode of assay—of trying out new forms—can be grasped as a kind of gesturing toward a concept that so far has not had its proper presentation.

The question here is how do we even comprehend such new forms, and how does the artist come up with them? To explain how a new presentation can explain itself, Lyotard calls on the paradoxical temporality of the future anterior (future in the past)—the temporality of something that "will have been done"—which is "performative" in the sense that it determines the conditions of its legibility.[16] In the mode of assay, a work is illegible until the moment when it manages to justify its own means of expression. The mode of assay may be called the properly poetic mode, etymologically

16 According to Derrida, the Declaration of Independence is performative in this sense because the words "We the people" came to denote the American nation only *after* the Declaration had been completed, as the Declaration was that which rhetorically gave rise to the new nation. Derrida, "Declarations of Independence," 7–15.

speaking, because it produces a completely new form. Lyotard contends: "A work can become modern only if it is first postmodern. Postmodernism thus understood is not modernism at its end but in its nascent state and this state is constant."[17] Postmodernism is thus defined in terms of a logical precession rather than as a historical epoch. One could speculate that whatever was postmodern may become modernist once the concept evaporates, and it may also become beautiful, and hence realistic, once it is familiar enough.

Far from being merely an abstract argument about aesthetic processes, Lyotard's definition of postmodernism is explicitly political. It was intended as a response to Habermas and seems to have anticipated other critiques of Habermas' unwittingly universalist position. For example, Seyla Benhabib's *Situating the Self* (1992) polemically engages Habermas on the grounds that he fails to understand the specific condition of the gendered, and the minority, subject. Lyotard's linking of the aesthetic and the political is also reminiscent of Jacques Rancière's more recent argument that aesthetics is intrinsically political, because it involves the sorting of everything into that which is perceptible and that which is not. Aesthetics is "distribution of the perceptible" (*partition du sensible*), and that distribution determines who is a political subject and who gets to be represented.[18] Rancière is in effect saying that access to the political sphere, defined as the most preliminary stage at which you either will or will not be heard as a political subject, may depend on your successful aesthetic self-presentation. And although he does not call on the sublime, Rancière's argument is akin to Lyotard's because both are interested in making perceptible something that was not. Moreover, they believe that such aesthetic work of making visible something that was invisible has important political consequences.

A deep distrust of postmodernism on political grounds is nonetheless found in major theorists of the postmodern. For Fredric Jameson, who works within the Marxist critical tradition, postmodernism is a politically relevant category because it allows for useful periodization, also in terms of modes of production.[19] The postmodern epoch is characterized by mass production of representations. The representations which proliferate in con-

17 Lyotard, *Postmodern Condition*, 79.

18 Rancière, *Le partage du sensible*, 9, *passim*.

19 Jameson, *Postmodernism*, 3–5.

temporary culture often draw on the past in a nostalgic manner. Nostalgia is an important category for Jameson, and one that has a special significance for popular culture. It is a relationship to the past that is imaginary because it erases any sense of a causal link between the past and the present. In nostalgia, the past becomes separated from the present, floating around in its own mythic time.[20] Jameson's nostalgia is similar to "frozen time" in Guy Debord's *Society of the Spectacle*, as both notions presume a perspective in which the past has no effects in the present. Debord looks at the museum as the institution which safely contains the past, making it available for our enjoyment rather than as a tool for making sense of the present. Daniel Mendelsohn makes use of a similar figure in a 2011 essay on *Mad Men* in *The New York Review of Books*, when he asserts that the series appeals to viewers who did not live through the 1960s, except perhaps as children.[21] Watching *Mad Men* offers them the fantasy of having been there, which may be especially appealing to people born in the era but incapable of remembering much about that decade (as would be the case for Mendelsohn). While the visual realism of *Mad Men* seems to encourage nostalgic enjoyment, its connection to the Madison Avenue of today arguably works the opposite effect by establishing a causal link between the 1960s and the present.

Jameson equates postmodernism with a late stage of capitalism, characteristic of economically developed countries. Late capitalism confounds Marx's distinction between the economic base and the ideological superstructure by making cultural production an important part of the economy. By superstructure Marx meant culture, education, religion, family, and many other social institutions whose ideological function was that they misrepresented the real economic relations determined by who controlled the means of production. The change in late capitalism is that once television and other forms of infotainment became big business, superstructure has become a major component of the base. One result of this development is what Jameson calls the disappearance of critical distance. Any critique of capitalism (presumably including Jameson's) is readily subsumed into the

20 One may be in danger of succumbing to the allure of nostalgia when talking about the sixties, for example. The present essay is an attempt to bulwark against this possibility.

21 Daniel Mendelsohn, "The Mad Men Account," *New York Review of Books*, February 24, 2011, 4–6.

base and returned to the market in the form of a product. This process is often described as co-optation. Jameson himself is at a loss about how to regain a position of critical distance, but the advantage he finds in the term postmodernism is that it allows him to define the contemporary epoch in terms of a particular mode of cultural production.

An aesthetic correlative in Jameson of the postmodern loss of critical distance is his well-known distinction between parody and pastiche: parody depends on a linguistic norm, and by parodying someone's speech or writing style, we emphasize the manner in which that style deviates from that norm by exaggerating the distance between them. In pastiche, the distance disappears because the norm itself is gone:

> Pastiche is, like parody, the imitation of a peculiar or unique, idiosyncratic style, the wearing of a linguistic mask, speech in a dead language. But it is a neutral practice of such mimicry, without any of parody's ulterior motives, amputated of the satiric impulse, devoid of laughter and of any conviction that alongside the abnormal tongue you have momentarily borrowed, some healthy linguistic normality still exists. Pastiche is thus blank parody.[22]

Defined this way, pastiche is a distinctly postmodernist trope that corresponds to the loss of critical distance.

THE QUESTION OF AUTHORIAL CONTROL

Robert Coover's short story "The Magic Poker" (1969) and Donald Barthelme's "I Bought a Little City" (1974) are self-conscious pastiches in Jameson's sense, as is Witold Gombrowicz's *Ferdydurke* (published in Polish in 1937), which Hassan mentions as one of postmodernism's founding texts. These works seem bound on preventing any position from which their playfulness could be given a particular meaning. Coover's narrator "wanders the island, inventing it" and repeatedly changes his or her mind about the story's events. In fact, there is little reason to believe that there is a single narrator. Coover relies heavily on intertextuality to create the mul-

22 Jameson, *Postmodernism*, 17.

tiple strands of his narrative but the way he alludes to other texts, such as fairy tales, does not help elucidate his meaning; rather, it leads to chaos.

Barthelme and Gombrowicz both exemplify a satirical intent in their work, but the satire is undermined by the absence of a position from which it is waged. Barthelme's story "I Bought a Little City" may be read as a critique of private property, but it can equally be read as a general critique of any reformist intentions. The fact that the narrator is both a capitalist and a reformist complicates the reading of the story as satire by making it rather difficult to know against whom the critical edge is turned. Gombrowicz presents a similar difficulty even though his satire is turned against some easily recognizable social phenomena of interwar Poland.[23] But, set as he is on debunking the falsehoods surrounding him, the novel's first-person narrator sees himself as equally fake as the next person. Everyone in the novel merely pretends to be what they are: whether teacher or school principal, or the modern-minded wife of an engineer, everyone is role-playing, and the protagonist's exposing of this situation in no way suggests that he has found a way out of this predicament, which affects him, too.

Gombrowicz implies that in order to be a rebel, you need to be recognized as one; however, in trying to achieve that recognition, you will likely end up conforming to other people's expectations of a rebel. This hopeless conundrum is just a particular instance of the way that everyone is enslaved by what Gombrowicz refers to as Form. Form is what endows our actions with meaning and simultaneously renders them inauthentic. Gombrowicz's response is to enact a loss of control over his own text by claiming that he does not know how to end his novel and by interrupting its narrative with interludes in the form of philosophical fables, preceded by mocking prefaces. These prefaces illustrate that the author succumbs to literary forms instead of masterfully wielding them. Gombrowicz's preface to "The Child Runs Deep in Filibert" reads in part: "I'm a captive to a Preface. . . . The law of symmetry requires it. . . . Even if I wanted to [omit it,] I can't." The

23 I might anecdotally add that a former schoolmate of Gombrowicz who was my neighbor assured me that the novel's satirical portrayal of a secondary school teacher making students repeat in unison that this or that author was great—as in: "Słowacki was a great poet, now repeat"— is a faithful rendition of an actual professor's pedagogical method. It is therefore delicious irony that Gombrowicz's *Ferdydurke* has been made mandatory reading at Polish schools.

author's apparent helplessness is reflected by the first-person narrator's grotesque mishaps.

By contrast to these examples, John Barth's "Night-Sea Journey" and "Lost in the Funhouse" (1968) are more directly parodist by virtue of relying on something like a linguistic norm. "Night-Sea Journey" reads like a pastiche composed of fragments of philosophical and theological discourses, drawing on Jungian, Existentialist, and Christian inspiration. However, once the reader grasps the mock allegorical character of the piece and its literary jest has become evident—the narrator is a spermatozoid—pieces of the jigsaw puzzle fall neatly into place. Likewise, the story "Lost in the Funhouse" offers an explanation for its self-reflexive form. This story allegorizes a teenager's shyness as metafictional commentary by suggesting that every word is painfully deliberated. Indeed, the entire cycle of stories collected in *Lost in the Funhouse* is readable as a kind of allegorization of the stages in one's life. "Frame Tale," which opens the cycle, reads: "Once upon a time there was a story that began: once upon a time there was a story that began . . ." and so on *ad infinitum*, in a loop which we are prompted to imagine as a Möbius strip (whose model can be made from a strip of paper half-twisted and having its ends connected to form a loop, as Barth directs us to do with "Frame Tale"). A Möbius strip has only one surface, though it appears to have two. While the geometrical properties of the Möbius strip correspond to the canon-like form of "Frame Tale," the combination of shape and of the endlessly repeated message suggest a DNA sequence.

The next story, "Night-Sea Journey," dramatizes the moment of conception, or fertilization, while "Lost in the Funhouse" illustrates the extreme self-consciousness of adolescence. Other stories may be read in a similar manner. Such allegoric composition stabilizes and partly neutralizes the experimental dimension of these fictions because we understand how to read them. These stories begin as what Roland Barthes calls *scriptible*, or writerly text, meaning that the reader is invited to co-invent the work in reading it. But they end up seeming more *lisible*, or readerly, meaning that we are expected to figure out a sense that has been encoded in the work from the beginning.[24] One could thus argue that Barth's stories are modernist to Gombrowicz's more postmodernist novel, despite their chronology

24 Barthes, *S/Z*, 4. The distinction forms part of Hassan's comparative table.

suggesting the reverse. There is, nonetheless, a similarity in the message they communicate. The narrator of "Night-Sea Journey" discovers that he is powerless in the face of the higher forces which manipulate and ultimately determine his journey and its destination. It dawns on him that all he has with which to oppose this powerful logic is his puny "negative resolve" which may not even have any impact on "that which I am about to become." This mock-heroic message is suggestive of Gombrowicz's sense that the most authentic gesture is to admit the loss of authorial control. In the end, Barth seems to hold on to his authorial control more tightly than Gombrowicz, and possibly his work suffers for it, appearing a little too clever.

Barth obsesses about escaping the inevitability of literary repetition in a way that Gombrowicz does not. Barth's position in the famous essay "The Literature of Exhaustion" (1967) is that everything has been tried before, which leaves little room for originality except by way of commenting on this condition. According to Barth, such metacommentary on the impossibility of original work is the postmodernist solution to the problem of originality.[25] A writer's originality was hardly a concern for Gombrowicz, who thought that everyone was caught in the embarrassing situation of imitating others and conforming to their expectations while pretending to be an autonomous individual. Gombrowicz was simply attempting an adequate representation of this deeply shaming mechanism. In his journal, however, he suggested that the contradiction between conformism and imitation on the one hand and posing as one's own man on the other was less prevalent in younger, less decadent cultures, such as that of Latin America, where he lived for many years.[26]

TRANS-AMERICAN AND TRANSATLANTIC LITERARY TRANSACTIONS

Gombrowicz found himself on a tour in Argentina at the outbreak of the Second World War and decided not to return to Europe. He had just turned thirty-five and had published *Ferdydurke* two years earlier. He settled down

25 Barth, *Friday Book*, 62–76.
26 Gombrowicz, *Diary*, 71–72.

in Buenos Aires, in the then run-down Retiro district. Working an office job and living very modestly, he wrote some of his most important work. Gombrowicz, who was probably homosexual most of his life, married upon his return to Europe in 1963, at the age of fifty-nine. [27] He died in France in 1969, leaving his literary estate to his wife Rita. Gombrowicz never returned to Poland, where his books were not in print, and where the Communist establishment saw him as incorrigibly bourgeois and decadent. He was also eyed with suspicion by the Polish diaspora, both in Argentina and in France, who saw him as disturbingly apolitical. Although he was introduced to Jorge Luis Borges, by Gombrowicz's own account their meeting was disappointing. He did become friends with some young Argentinian literati whose help he enlisted in translating *Ferdydurke* into Spanish.[28]

The first English translation of *Ferdydurke* by Eric Mosbacher was from the French, and was published in 1961 (a more recent translation from the Polish by Danuta Borchardt, with a foreword by Susan Sontag, appeared in 2000). Thus, Gombrowicz's debut novel became known to the American literary public in the beginning of the 1960s, propelled in part by a strong interest in writings from Latin America, where he still resided. Gombrowicz was read alongside Borges, and later Alejo Carpentier, Julio Cortàzar, and Gabriel García Márquez. His literary journey was thus somewhat similar to that of the group of writers whose primary textual space was the important literary review *Sur*, founded by Victoria Ocampo, a literary prodigy and daughter of an Argentian industrialist. For many years this privately funded journal served as a gateway between Latin American literatures and the North, meaning both North America and Europe. It published many translations into Spanish and promoted Latin American writers.

In terms of his North American reception, Gombrowicz rode the tide of a growing interest in Latin American letters, in which the crucial term for a while was magic realism, a mode of writing which combined exotic-seeming elements of the Latin American reality (such as the sudden appearance of tens of thousands of swarming butterflies in which a lovely girl

27 For anecdotal evidence of Gombrowicz's same-sex activity in Buenos Aires, see Arenas, *Before Night Falls*, 80–81.

28 This collective translation from the Polish, published in Buenos Aires in 1947, was directed by Virgilio Piñera and Humberto Rodriguez Tomeu in collaboration with Witold Gombrowicz.

dissolves in Márquez's *One Hundred Years of Solitude*) with playful inventiveness and a grotesque treatment of ordinary or serious themes. Although *Ferdydurke* does not literally form part of the magic realist movement for precise historical and geographic reasons, its playfulness and the grotesque, exoticized descriptions of life in rural Poland make it akin to works by some Latin American authors. The interest in magic realism is in evidence in John Barth. For example, in his 1979 essay "The Literature of Replenishment," Barth favorably compares Márquez to Borges, who was the idol of the earlier essay "The Literature of Exhaustion."[29] Ihab Hassan also discusses the influence of Latin American writers on postmodernist fiction in the US, and he mentions Gombrowicz as a forerunner of postmodernist literature.

SOME NORTH AMERICAN GREATS AND THE QUESTION OF REPRESENTATION

In the Anglo-American context, the American forerunners of postmodernism and the beginnings of postmodernism were variously identified. The English literary historian Tony Tanner points to *The Recognitions* (1955), the debut novel of William Gaddis, as America's first postmodern novel.[30] *The Recognitions* anticipates some themes that inform poststructuralist theory. Gaddis is interested in the idea of copies without originals, which corresponds to Jean Baudrillard's notion of the *simulacrum* as copy for which there is no original. Baudrillard's argument in *Simulacra and Simulations* (1994) contradicted Plato's theory that a copy was always inferior to the original.[31] Baudrillard's influential notion of the precession of simulacra includes, as the penultimate stage, the idea of a sign which hides the absence of any reality to which the sign seems to refer. In the final stage of the precession, which is the stage of the simulacrum proper, no relation is posited between the sign and any reality other than the sign itself. In *The Recognitions*, the theme of art forgeries includes the counterfeit practice of creating works that had never really been painted by the old masters and, in

29 Barth, *Friday Book*, 204–5.
30 Tanner, *City of Words*, 393–94.
31 Baudrillard, *Simulacra and Simulations*, 4–5.

one instance, the "discovery" of a work by a master painter whose own existence had been hypothetical.

Art is a point of departure for postmodern speculation also in Thomas Pynchon's 1963 debut novel *V.* In chapter seven, titled "She Hangs on the Western Wall," which tells the story of a character's disillusionment with a work of art, a collector is overcome with a desire to possess Botticelli's *Birth of Venus* which he arranges to have stolen from the Uffizi Gallery in Florence. The complicated plot, which involves cutting the painting from its frame and hiding it, rolled up, in a hollowed-out, potted tree, succeeds. However, once the work is in his hands, the collector feels disenchanted. Contemplating it, he sees merely paint laid on a canvas, and a ridiculous arrangement of figures: a nude woman standing in a seashell and trying to cover herself up, another female figure holding a cape and attempting to veil the first, and two floating male figures blowing air at the nude female. All of a sudden, the work makes very little sense. The narrative logic determining its meaning seems irrelevant, and the figurative representations become ludicrous. The merely material layer of the work is deeply dissatisfying once something like a grand narrative informing it and supplying a sense of depth has been lost. This subplot bears a striking similarity to Lyotard's thesis about grand narratives being without credibility today and seems to dramatize Lyotard's mode of regret: the solace of good form may be offered but the content is no longer to be found.

One of Pynchon's most recognized themes is conspiracy and the related notion of paranoia. Pynchon's second novel *The Crying of Lot 49* (1966) makes extensive use of both themes. Its heroine, Oedipa Maas, is put in charge of executing the will of her former lover, a real estate mogul. In attempting to penetrate the byzantine complexity of his holdings, she stumbles upon what seems to be an underground organization whose main goal is to break the government's postal monopoly with an alternative, secret system for sending messages. This alternative postal service uses stamps which differ in small details from the government-issued stamps and has specially marked waste bins used as mailboxes. Letters are delivered late at night in designated bars. However, Oedipa is ultimately unclear about her discovery of an alternative to her own boring world of suburbia. She thinks she may only be imagining this alternative, or may have been tricked into seeing those things, perhaps as a postmortem joke by her late lover, or maybe she has gone mad. Oedipa thus resembles the character Oedipus in

Sophocles's play, in that she is obligated to conduct an investigation but discovers, in the course of her detective work, that her own existence is at stake. Indicative of Pynchon's interest in mind-altering substances and the question of how and why they are controlled, a motif of LSD use runs through the novel. Crucially, it is never made clear whether LSD is connected to the underground world whose existence Oedipa suspects, or if it is a substance controlled and secretly distributed by the government in order to manipulate the general populace, as Oedipa's conversation with her shrink suggests.[32] Indeed, the strange post stamps that Oedipa's late lover was collecting may suggest that the underground postal service is in fact distributing LSD. But if that is the case, it is unclear who supplies the drug and why; moreover, a reverse reading is also possible: the regular US post stamps, which most users in the 1960s would lick in order to affix them to the envelopes, might be saturated with LSD, in which case using the underground postal service would be a way to avoid taking the drug. The reader has no way of resolving this dilemma, or even having it confirmed.

As critic John Johnston argues about *The Crying of Lot 49*, the novel portrays the logic of paranoia, of an obsessive suspicion of a conspiracy, on multiple plot levels, in order to question that very logic.[33] Johnston supplements this reading with a discussion of the political implications of what he describes as the "semiotic regime of paranoia," which determines the logic of interpretation by casting specific actors in roles such as the scapegoat or the culprit. Such paranoiac logic can be persuasive because it offers a satisfyingly coherent account. Johnston's analysis bears a striking similarity to the notion of the empty signifier developed in political theory by Ernesto Laclau, who assumes that discursive systems inevitably privilege certain signifiers over others (and hence are "paranoiac" in Johnston's sense).[34] However, Laclau insists that it is possible to keep such discursive systems from petrifying into one-sided, biased, and hence oppressive regimes by keeping their central signifiers "empty" and thus foreclose their meaning. For example, democracy is a privileged signifier in our world, but it is important to keep it content-less in the sense that its referent should not be defined once and for all. A useful distinction for discussing postmodernist

32 LSD was outlawed in 1966, the year that the novel was published.
33 Johnston, "Paranoia as Semiotic Regime," 47–78.
34 Laclau, *Emancipation(s)*, 36–46.

aesthetics in connection to the political has been suggested by Paul Maltby in *Dissident Postmodernists* (1991).[35] Maltby argues that Donald Barthelme, Robert Coover and Thomas Pynchon are more concerned with reality than some other postmodernist writers. These writers are producing fiction that is sign-reflexive rather than self-reflexive, or concerned with its own procedures. Sign-reflexive fiction is concerned with the ways in which signs are used to represent reality. Rather than examine their own procedures for some abstract intellectual enjoyment, these works examine how their own generic assumptions determine the resulting representations, and consequently they critique mimetic conventions. The intention behind these works is linked to their investment in explaining how we make representations of the world.

Such sign-reflexivity is readily apparent in novels by Gaddis and Pynchon, as well as in Gombrowicz. It is less evident in Coover or Barth, especially in their short fictions, which are exercises in form making rather than attempts to put forth critical representations of our concepts of the world. Maltby's category of sign-reflexivity, however tentatively defined, offers a perspective from which postmodernist fiction of the 1960s appears relevant to a broader historical and theoretical context instead of being reduced to mere playfulness and formal experimentation.

CONCLUSION

American literary postmodernism of the 1960s needs to be seen as participating in the international, and even intercontinental, circulation of ideas and of literary tendencies. Postmodernism risks being read reductively unless it is placed in a historicizing transatlantic context, as well as understood to cross the Americas. Geographically, the term "postmodernism," and the literary practices it denotes, have traveled back and forth between South and North America (mostly from South to North), as well as between the Americas and Europe. Historically, the decade of the 1960s represents a fulcrum for a discussion of postmodernism in American literature because of the great number of experimental works of fiction published then—both by US authors and in translation—and also because these works occasioned

35 Maltby, *Dissident Postmodernists*, 42, *passim*.

a sustained critical effort to define postmodernist aesthetics. However, a narrowing focus on the period's formal experimentation is insufficient to sustain interest in its literary achievements. At best, it risks succumbing to merely nostalgic enjoyment. To forestall this outcome, postmodernist fiction and its critical elaboration, for example by Hassan, should be studied alongside non-American writings which influenced American postmodernism and with a view to theoretical insights that the category "postmodernism" inspired.

Once the 1960s postmodernism is set in this broader context, it invites comparison with the demand for change prompted by the current economic crisis in Europe and in the US. Today's demand, which manifests itself primarily as popular protest, is undisciplined in so far as it lacks a specific political project. The forms it takes are primarily aesthetic, rather than argumentative. This is one reason why the 1960s literary discourse can illuminate the present crisis of representation. The postmodernist aesthetic was especially concerned with the possibility of a radical break from the past and of negating the prevalent way of doing things. Writers of the period voiced the desirability of such a break and of such negation even as they questioned their viability, noting that what seemed like change might be merely simulation. An analogously dialectical approach promoting change and also questioning its meaning seems characteristic of the present moment. No doubt this is so because today's political protesters have internalized some aspects of the postmodernist sensibility, and they intuitively understand how representation can be immediately assimilated to simulation. This does not mean they feel at home in a world in which this keeps happening. American postmodernists of the 1960s, their literary predecessors from other parts of the world, and critics applying a wide range of theoretical approaches to reflect on postmodernist aesthetics have struggled with remarkably similar problems.

BIBLIOGRAPHY

Arenas, Reinaldo. *Before Night Falls*. Translated by Dolores M. Koch. New York: Viking, 1993. Originally published as *Antes que anochezca* (Barcelona: Tusquets Editores, 1992).

Barth, John. *The Friday Book: Essays and Other Nonfiction.* New York: Putnam, 1984.

———. *Lost in the Funhouse: Fiction for Print, Tape, Live Voice.* Garden City, NY: Doubleday, 1968.

Barthelme, Donald. "I Bought a Little City." *New Yorker*, November 11, 1974, 42–44.

Barthes, Roland. *S/Z.* Translated by Richard Miller. Malden, MA: Blackwell, 1974. First published 1970 by Le Seuil in Paris.

Baudrillard, Jean. *Simulacra and Simulations* (*Simulacres et simulations*, 1981). Translated by Sheila Faria Glaser. Ann Arbor: University of Michigan Press, 1994.

Benjamin, Walter. *Illuminations*. Edited and translated by Hannah Arendt. London: Fontana, 1968.

Coover, Robert. *Pricksongs and Descants: Fictions.* New York: Dutton, 1969.

Debord, Guy. *Society of the Spectacle.* Translated by Fredy Perlman and John Supak. Detroit: Black and Red, 1977. Originally published as *Société du spectacle* (Paris: Editions Buchet-Chastel, 1967).

Deleuze, Gilles, and Felix Guattari. *Anti-Oedipus.* Translated by Robert Hurley, Mark Seem, and Helen R. Lane. New York: Viking Press, 1977.

Derrida, Jacques. "Declarations of Independence." *New Political Science* 7, no. 1 (Summer 1986): 7–15.

———. "Structure, Sign, and Play in the Discourse of the Human Sciences." In *Writing and Difference*, translated by Alan Bass, 278–93. Chicago: University of Chicago Press, 1978. Originally published as *Écriture et la différence* (Paris: Seuil, 1966).

Eagleton, Terry. *Literary Theory: An Introduction.* 1983. Minneapolis: University of Minnesota Press, 2008.

Gaddis, William. *The Recognitions*. New York: Harcourt, Brace, 1955.

Gombrowicz, Witold. *Diary*. Translated by Lillian Vallee. Evanston, IL: Northwestern University Press, 1988.

———. *Ferdydurke* (1937). Collective translation from Polish directed by Virgilio Piñera and Humberto Rodriguez Tomeu in collaboration with Witold Gombrowicz. Preface by Witold Gombrowicz and note by the translators. Buenos Aires: Argos, 1947.

———. *Ferdydurke* (1937). Translated from French by Eric Mosbacher. London: Macgibbon and Kee, 1961.

———. *Ferdydurke* (1937). Translated from Polish by Danuta Borchardt. With a foreword by Susan Sontag. New Haven: Yale University Press, 2000.

Habermas, Jürgen. "Modernity: An Incomplete Project." *New German Critique* 22 (Winter 1981): 3–15. Reprinted in Thomas Docherty, ed., *Postmodernism: A Reader*. New York: Harvester Wheatsheat, 1993, 98–109.

Hassan, Ihab. *The Dismemberment of Orpheus: Toward a Postmodern Literature*. New York: Oxford University Press, 1971.

———. "Toward a Concept of Postmodernism." In *The Postmodern Turn: Essays in Postmodern Theory and Culture*, 84–97. Columbus: Ohio State University Press, 1987.

Horkheimer, Max, and Theodor W. Adorno. *Dialectic of Enlightenment*. Translated by John Cumming. New York: Herder and Herder, 1972.

Jameson, Fredric. *Postmodernism, or, the Cultural Logic of Late Capitalism*. Durham: Duke University Press, 1991.

Johnston, John. "Paranoia as Semiotic Regime in *The Crying of Lot 49*." In *New Essays on* The Crying of Lot 49, edited by Patrick O'Donnell, 47–78. Cambridge: Cambridge University Press, 1991.

Laclau, Ernesto. *Emancipation(s)*. New York: Verso, 1996.

Lyotard, Jean-Francois. *The Postmodern Condition: A Report on Knowledge*. Translated by Geoff Bennington and Brian Massumi. With a foreword by Fredric Jameson. Minneapolis: University of Minnesota Press, 1984. See esp. "Answering the Question: What is Postmodern?" translated by Regis Durand, 71–82.

Maltby, Paul. *Dissident Postmodernists: Barthelme, Coover, Pynchon*. Philadelphia: University of Pennsylvania Press, 1991.

Paxton, John. *The Wild One*. Directed by László Benedek. USA: Stanley Kramer Productions, 1953. DVD.

Pynchon, Thomas. *The Crying of Lot 49*. Philadelphia: Lippincott, 1966.

———. *V: A Novel*. Philadelphia: Lippincott, 1963.

Rado, James, and Gerome Ragni. *Hair*. Directed by Miloš Forman. USA and West Germany: CIP Filmproduktion, 1979. DVD.

Rancière, Jacques. *Le partage du sensible: esthétique et politique*. Paris: La Fabrique, 2000.

Stern, Stewart. *Rebel Without a Cause*. Directed by Nicholas Ray. Burbank, CA: Warner Bros. Pictures, 1955. DVD.

Weiner, Matthew. *Mad Men*. USA: Weiner Bros., Silvercup Studios, Lionsgate Television, 2007–present. AMC TV channel.

Tanner, Tony. *City of Words: American Fiction 1950–1970.* New York: Harper and Row, 1971.

Wittgenstein, Ludwig. *Philosophical Investigations.* Translated by G. E. M. Anscombe. Oxford: Blackwell, 1953.

———. *Tractatus Logico-Philosophicus*. Translated by C. K. Ogden, with assistance from G. E. Moore, F. P. Ramsey, and Wittgenstein. With an introduction by Bertrand Russell. London: Routledge and Kegan Paul, 1922.

Information, Communication, Systems

Cybernetic Aesthetics in 1960s Cultures

CRISTINA IULI

> On the walls hang graceful, abstract designs that look like snail shells, plus computer variations on op designs by Jeffrey Steele and Bridget Riley. . . .
>
> From the ceiling hangs a huge mobile by Britain's Gordon Pask that responds electronically to lights flashed on it by visitors. . . . Taped sounds of computer-composed music fill the air, and computer-made poetry is on view. Some of it reads rather like Alice in Wonderland as rewritten by Charles Olson.
>
> "CYBERNETIC SERENDIPITY," *TIME*, OCTOBER 4, 1968

In his 1979 global bestseller, *La Condition Postmoderne*, French philosopher Jean François Lyotard identified in the convergence of linguistics and cybernetics a crucial nexus for the configuration of postmodernism. This perspective implicitly shed a new light on the interpretation of the 1960s not as a decade primarily defined by movements of protest, liberation and emancipation, but as the epochal threshold of an epistemological paradigm shift. Rooted in cybernetics and affecting the hard sciences and the humanities alike, such a shift entailed the decline of epistemologies based on the distinction between a subject of knowledge and an object to be known, and the parallel emergence of one based on the systemic relation between elements, information, function and communication. This new epistemology replaced a view of nature and society as "given" facts or entities existing in the world independently from our knowledge of them, with one in which both nature and society are inseparable from our ways of knowing and describing them. In the 1960s a cybernetic-derived understanding of nature and society as effects of information and communication started to circulate among the scientific and cultural élites and progressively extended across social zones to become generalized by the mid-1970s. Lyotard's seminal report on the status of knowledge in the late 1970s identified the information revolution as the crucial conceptual force governing the shift from a modern to a postmodern society. However, he did not discuss the set of cultural operations by means of which the new regime of signification that emerged as the discourse of cybernetics and information in the years around World War II gained currency and became progressively stabilized after the war. Indeed, by the mid-1950s the concepts of *information*, *communication*, and *systems* had grown common in the vocabulary of the hard sciences and were disseminated across social and aesthetic practices and discourses,[1] becoming, by the late 1970s, an epistemological dominant in the US and in Europe.[2]

This essay argues, first, that the epistemological revolution propelled by cybernetics in the 1940s and 1950s and its corollary redefinition of the concepts of information and communication prompted, from the early 1960s, a radical revision of art, literature, and aesthetics and a lasting transformation

1 According to art historian Jack Burnham, however, experiments and inquiries over the aesthetic potential of cybernetics took place, first, in Europe, while the US lagged behind by "five or ten years." Burnham, *Beyond Modern Sculpture*, 343, cited by Shanken, "Cybernetics and Art," 255.

2 The emergence of such regimes is one of the consequences of the massive program of techno-military-scientific investments that restructured the twentieth-century US scientific infrastructure in relation, first, to World War II and, second, to the Cold War competition for global political-scientific hegemony. On this and related issues, see Kay, *Who Wrote the Book*; Hayles, *How We Became Posthuman*; Clarke and Dalrymple Henderson, *From Energy to Information*; Heims, *Cybernetic Group*.

of their methodologies and conceptual apparati. Such a revision generated a shift in the concept of art and in the notion of the artwork from object to process, from static to performative, and from closed to open system. The understanding of a work of art as an open system was based on the concept of the feedback looping of information in meaning-systems cooperatively made by participants, objects, signs, and events.

Second, this essay claims that a shift parallel to the redefinition of the artwork in a systemic perspective also affected the reception of the artwork and the literary work. As a consequence, signification, reading practices, and textual interpretation were reconceived as a circular model of communication, where notions of information, medium, and user replaced notions of sender and receiver presupposed by linear, non-specialized theories of communication. These ideas, germinated within the cybernetic paradigm, had a crucial impact on the emergence of the notion of the "death of the author" and the "literature machine" formalized by structuralist poetics in the 1960s, thematized and explored in much experimental literature of the time, and expanded and developed in post-structuralist theories of meaning.

Third, this essay also suggests that the transformative impact of cybernetics on later reformulations of the Cartesian mind/body distinction as information/materiality (already implicit, for instance, in Marshall McLuhan's notion of the media as extensions of man) should be considered within the frame of non-essentialist claims about the relation between the body and subjectivities, so crucial to countercultural movements in the 1960s, from feminism to anti-racism, to anti-psychiatry. The non-essentialist edge of cybernetics is a further aspect of the progressive potential of cybernetic ideas, which, together with other aspects of this explanatory model, authorizes a reconsideration of the entire cybernetic paradigm that explains it away from the Cold War ideology and control paranoia and in relation to the broader epistemological shift that swept through the 1960s and 1970s.[3]

The cybernetic worldview promoted a systemic notion of meaning based on the ongoing interactions of human and nonhuman elements functionally connected in a communication circuit. This meant that the Cartesian epistemology based on the subject/object distinction, securing process-

3 See Galison, "The Ontology of the Enemy"; Aspray, "The Scientific Conceptualization of Information"; Beninger, *Control Revolution;* Turner, *From Counterculture to Cyberculture*; Clarke, *From Energy to Information.*

es of knowledge, was radically destabilized and reconfigured around the non-anthropocentric notions of input-output-communication-feedback loop-system. As a consequence, meaning-making processes and their descriptions were also reformulated, while cultural, social, and institutional practices as well as formal aesthetic innovations in the arts and in literature were modeled in relation to the cybernetic definitions of meaning and knowledge. For this reason, the fourth claim of this essay is that the cybernetic paradigm should be reassessed as a powerfully transformative conceptual paradigm which contributed to generating radical changes in how disciplinary subjects were studied and how knowledge was produced and disseminated within institutions of knowledge and in society at large. These practices were generally reoriented toward interdisciplinary approaches. The metaphorical potential of this paradigm shift was fully explored in experimental literature, art installations and performances, in radical architectures, critical pedagogies and in anthropology and family therapy. From this vantage point, a fresh look at some key fictional and theoretical literature from the 1960s in the US and in Europe will reveal the transnational and transatlantic dimension of the cybernetic paradigm and contribute to draft a more accurate map of the field of forces shaping the literary and cultural tensions of the decade.

On the North American scene, for instance, Thomas Pynchon's *The Crying of Lot 49*, William Burroughs's *Nova Trilogy* (1961; 1962; 1964), and Marshall McLuhan's *Understanding Media: The Extensions of Man* (1964) should be considered as frontal explorations of the potential of cybernetic ideas in creative processes. Similarly, some of the works of Italian writer Italo Calvino, particularly his short stories from the early 1960s, *Cosmicomiche* (1963–64; 1965) and *Ti con zero* (1967), as well as his essay "Cybernetics and Ghosts" (1967), should be seen in the larger context of the impact of cybernetic ideas on the study of mental processes in linguistic translation and visual perception. All these works continued the concerns of Italian linguist and philosopher of science Silvio Ceccato, founder and director of the Centro di Cibernetica dell'Università di Milano (1957).[4] Cec-

4 Ceccato elaborated an original theory of the observer that anticipates some crucial epistemological implications subtending the shift from first to second order cybernetics in the late 1970s. He also collaborated with avant-garde artists based in Milan and Rimini, who were then investigating the potential of cybernetic ideas for aesthetic purposes and interactive, kinetic art. Ceccato authored several

cato introduced in Italy the cybernetic ideas of Norbert Wiener and collaborated with avant-garde artists based in Milan and Rimini who were then investigating the potential of cybernetic ideas for aesthetic purposes and interactive, kinetic art.[5]

Finally, on the British cultural front, cultural critics have already retrieved the significance of Roy Ascott's installations, as well as his art education programs for the dissemination of cybernetic ideas within the context of a systems aesthetics.[6] Far less frequently discussed in relation to the development of a cultural poetics of the 1960s in Europe is the near mythical exhibition Cybernetic Serendipity, which opened in London in 1968 and looped back to the US, traveling to Washington, DC, and San Francisco between 1968 and 1970. Similarly neglected is the contribution of anti-architect Cedric Price's experimental architecture. Both cases testify to the intellectual and popular appeal that cybernetics ideas were gaining across the 1960s. This series of permutations, contaminations, and aesthetic recon-

scientific publications but also wrote a number of non-specialized essays that crossed the academic/general public divide (La Cibernetica per tutti, and La mente vista da un cibernetico, both published in 1970–72 but based on experimental work done from the late 1950s).

5 In particular, Ceccato's research directly influenced the work of "Gruppo V," the Rimini-based group led by Pino Parini, but the discursive shift of cybernetics fully entered the poetics of all the North Italian avant-garde groups working on Arte Cinetica: the Milan-based "Gruppo T," founded in 1959, with the manifesto Miriorama 1, by Giovanni Anceschi, Davide Boriani, Gianni Colombo, and Gabriele Devecchi; the Milan-based "Gruppo MID"; the Padua-based "Gruppo N," which existed until 1966. All these groups participated, in different years, in the international exhibition on computing and art "Nove Tendencije" held in Zagreb from 1961 to 1973, as documented by Margit Rosen in the recently published documentary history of the exhibition, *A Little-Known Story*. For a more detailed account of the Centro di Ricerche Cibernetiche, see Parini, "Fra arte cibernetica e didattica." A fifth group "Ti.Zero" funded in 1968 was based in Turin. For this and for the Italian kinetic, interactive, and cybernetic avant-garde, see Mari, Gruppo N, and Gruppo T, "Arte e libertà." An entire chapter should be delivered here on the nexus of cybernetics, industrial production, the beginning of a national industry of calculating machines and kinetic art in Italy, but it would be outside the scope of this essay. See, in particular, the catalogue of the exhibition Arte Programmata. (Negozio Olivetti, Milano 1962). Milano: Officina d'Arte Grafica Lucini, 1962, now reprinted in Meneguzzo, Morteo, and Saibene, *Programmare l'Arte*; for a detailed account of the kinetic art scene in 1960s Italy, see Granzotto and Margozzi, *Arte programmata e cinetica*, and Vergine, *L'arte Cinetica in Italia*.

6 See Ascott, *Telematic Embrace*. For a historical survey of systems aesthetics, see Shanken, "Reprogramming Systems Aesthetics."

figurations reveal that cybernetics did not only haunt the visual and literary imagination of the decade. Neither did it simply provide the visual arts, literature, architecture and critical practices with the most powerful metaphor of the times for addressing contemporaneity in the shape of the massive financial and techno-scientific reorganization Western societies were then currently undergoing. In fact, the circulation of cybernetic ideas in the 1960s ignited a lasting, crucial transformation of our definition of literature, art, and society and provided the epistemological foundations for the radical politics of the 1960s, as it subtly revolutionized the notions of meaning, act, communication, information, and event both in their socio-political and aesthetic-literary manifestations.[7] This development occurred in spite of the fact that the discourse of cybernetics cannot be fully disarticulated from fantasies of technical total control spurred by the unexpected success of Wiener's bestseller *Cybernetics, or Control and Communication in the Human and the Machine* (1948), whose title reinforced the association between cybernetics, control, and the techno-military infrastructural complex that Wiener partly wrote against.

CYBERNETICS AND ITS DISSEMINATION

As historians of science and cultural institutions have pointed out, interdisciplinary collaboration among scientists, promoted in the war years by research centers involved in the war effort, had fostered a cross-disciplinary methodological approach toward science and knowledge based on the concepts of communication, control and functional performance.[8] Immensely popularized by Wiener's 1948 book, *Cybernetics, or Control and Communication in the Animal and the Machine*, cybernetics, defined as the "sci-

7 On Wiener's anti-military stance and on the critical impact of cybernetics, see also Triclot, "Norbert Wiener's Politics."

8 In this connection we should mention—at the very least—Vannevar Bush's Office of Scientific Research and Development and, later, Norbert Wiener (MIT) and John Von Neumann (Princeton) interdisciplinary methodologies in the environment of the Macy's Conferences on Cybernetics (1946–1953). See also Mendelsohn, Roe Smith, and Weingart, *Science, Technology, and the Military*; Leslie, *Cold War and American Science*; Edwards, *Close World*; Heims, *Cybernetic Group*.

ence of control and communication in the animal and the machine,"[9] provided both the conceptual framework and a basic vocabulary for the convergence of two distinct notions of information and communication. The first, crossing several traditions of communication theory, kept the two terms separate, casting information as a quantity of semantic content that can be transferred from sender to receiver, and communication as the act that transfers—more or less successfully—that content through a specific medium external to both.[10] The second binds information and communication together in three ways: first, by highlighting the convergence of medium, information, and communication in the coding/decoding act functional to the transfer of informational content; second, by defining the message as "a discrete or continuous sequence of measurable events distributed in time,"[11] and third, by considering the organization of all the elements constitutive of such communicational circuit. Both models combine semantic and quantitative aspects of communication, and both had been used in rather general terms in physics, biology, and mathematical logic in the late nineteenth and early twentieth centuries. But it was only in World War II engineering and information science that they became more specific.[12] As a result of Wiener's cybernetic explanation, they converged to define a purposeful communicative environment (cybernetic system), in which information is fed into the system (as input), and system behavior (output) is functionally steered by built-in servomechanisms that re-inject information (as new input) back into the system (feedback), thus redirecting its next operation toward functional success.[13] As Heinz Von Foerster would later comment, "It is this circular organization which sets cybernetic systems

9 Wiener, *Cybernetics*.

10 See on the several disciplinary traditions of communication studies, see Hartley, *Communication, Cultural and Media Studies*.

11 Wiener, *Cybernetics*, 7.

12 Clarke, in "Communication," has discussed Roman Jackobson's model of communicative functions in relation to Claude Shannon's Diagram of a Communication System (1940). This is also dicussed in Kay, *Who Wrote the Book.*

13 The notions of behavior, message, information, control and feedback were elaborated by Wiener together with Arturo Rosenblueth and Julian Bigelow, and appeared as systemically connected as the incipient discourse of cybernetics outside the anti-war effort from which it originally arose in a 1943 paper "Behavior, Purpose, and Teleology." See Rosenblueth, Wiener, and Bigelow, "Behavior, Purpose, and Teleology."

apart from others that are not so organized."[14] Wiener's quantitative definition of information was to find scientific support by Claude Shannon, the Bell laboratories engineer who was also a frequent guest at the Macy's Conferences and who authored, with Warren Weaver, the immensely influential *Mathematical Theory of Communication* (1948). From the vantage point of acoustic engineering, Shannon and Weaver were adamantly clear about what information was. First of all, they declared, "Information in communication theory is used *in a special sense that must not be confused with meaning*. It refers to what you could say, not to what you do say."[15] Second, they gave a systemic, relational definition of information that helped generating interdisciplinary convergence at that conjuncture of intellectual history. Shannon and Wiener's systemic definition of information—that is, what you could say in a potentially infinite set of possibilities—overlapped with other systemic definitions of information emerging from other fields of knowledge, such as, for instance, structural linguistics, which similarly emphasized the grammatical and systemic value of language rather than its semantic aspects. As Shannon and Weaver put it, "the concept of information applies not to the individual message, but to the situation as a whole."[16] Thus, the two mathematicians at once cast the semantic value of communication as technically irrelevant, established the value of information in systemic terms, and shed a new light on Wiener's formulation of a message as "a discrete or continuous sequence of measurable events distributed in time."[17]

Once it was established that messages carried information, not meaning, that information was a quantitative and not a qualitative measure, and that its value was systemic and not individual, two consequences ensued. First, it became conceptually possible to redescribe any system—whether living or nonliving—in the universal language of information, because, from a functional point of view, living organisms and machines were conceived as operators that transfer information in similar ways. After Shannon had demonstrated that information could be measured logarithmically, it was clear that by computing the transfer of information in quantitative terms, the behavior of humans and machines could be computed, automated, and

14 von Foerster, "Opening Address."
15 Shannon and Weaver, *Mathematical Theory of Communication*, 100. My italics.
16 Ibid.
17 Wiener, *Cybernetics*, 7.

controlled, and that living and nonliving organisms could be reorganized—descriptively if not ontologically—within a unified theory of information.[18] It is this quantitative notion of information that allows us to better understand the qualifying clause in Wiener's original formulation of cybernetics as the science of control and communication "in the animal and the machine." Second, systemic understandings of information, communication, and meaning shareable, to a certain extent, among distinct disciplines provided the ground for a productive overlapping of linguistics, semiotics, mathematics, sound and communication engineering, neurophysiology, and genetics. It also accounted for a significant degree of conceptual convergence among the disciplines across the science/humanities divide around the concepts of code, information, feedback, system, and communication. These concepts clustered in a powerful constellation of tropes that organized the discourse of cybernetics as the discourse of Information, Communication, and Systems. But it was the new notion of information which provided a sort of meta-code for translating all forms of knowledge as informational quantity, or information, recoding all knowledge in the language of machine communication, the binary code. This conceptual convergence also fed the fantasy of a possible re-unification of all knowledge as controlled flux of information across disciplinary domains, from information systems to biological systems to cultural systems, leaving no material leftovers. Recent inquiries in media studies, history and philosophy of science and literary criticism have disclosed the significant disunity and heterogeneity of positions within the cybernetic paradigm.[19] And yet, the semantic and terminological convergence it fostered across disciplines accounts for both the proliferation of cross-disciplinary projects and for the metaphoric association of cybernetics with art, literature and aesthetics. Information, communication, and systems became crucial operators from the early 1960s.

This moment in the history of ideas explains Lyotard's insistence on cybernetics as the crucial epistemological paradigm for the redefinition of knowledge, aesthetics and complex systems as systems that exchange information (Lyotard). It also clarifies the shift from objectual to processual

18 As is well known, genetic offered the most powerful terrain on which fantasies of total convergence between living and nonliving systems were projected. See Kay, *Who Wrote the Book*, and Roof, *Poetics of DNA*.

19 See, for instance, Geoghegan, "From Information Theory."

(or post-objectual) understandings of aesthetic expressions so ubiquitous in the 1960s poetics, a shift several critics have seen as a defining condition for the emergence of postmodernism.

CYBERNETICS AND AESTHETICS: AT THE BEGINNING WAS POSTMODERNISM

In his long 1953 poem, "The Kingfishers," the American poet Charles Olson explicitly referenced the the shift in focus, from object to process, implied in cybernetic epistemology, and subjected the technical jargon of mathematics and Wiener's formulations to metaphoric suggestions:

> To be in different states without a change
> is not a possibility
>
> We can be precise. The factors are
> in the animal and/or the machine the factors are
> communication and/or control, both involve
> the message. And what is the message? The message is
> a discrete or continuous sequence of measurable events distributed in time[20]

The lines ventriloquize Wiener in order to exploit the tension between a formal and a semantic definition of message and to emphasize the potential of poetry as a generator of formal ambiguities. Poetry here softens the rigidity of the mathematical formulation by redistributing its terms across the poetic lines, subjecting each element of the citation to new syntactical and semantic pressure. This act of suspension, de-signification and re-signification generates ambiguities and irregularities within the poetic form, injecting instability in the hermeneutic process. The explicitly evoked cybernetic circuit is disrupted by means of ironic suspensions and inversions, which force the process of signification beyond the formal boundaries of the poem. Irony and inversions highlight the impossibility of pure self-reference and point instead to meaning as the impermanent emergence of a systemic relation between the formal organization of the poem and its ma-

20 Olson, *Selected Writings*, 170–71.

terial and immaterial outside, the former exemplified, for instance, by sounds, printed words, the reader as a concrete person, and the latter by grammar and syntax, or by the reader as a reservoir of mental processes and associations. Wiener's formulation is destabilized by the poetic form, closed by internal organization and semantically open to the outside and to the irreducible complexity of the world. Each word—different states, change, possibility, communication, control, message, events, time—becomes the generator of new poetic tension interminably activated and re-activated at each reading. The poem exploits the epistemological consequences of the relation between art and society conceived after the cybernetic paradigm and turns it into an element of its own form: information and behavior, message and meaning are the contingent events of ongoing processes of communication among interconnected systems.

This dialectics of closure and openness sheds light on one of the key formal consequences of the poetics of cybernetics: art is no longer conceived as the manifestation of the autonomous and self-sufficient object, but as a cybernetic system operating in/as a network of feedback loops in the cultural sphere and in society at large. The poetic and political implications of this renewed understanding of art, which shifts the burden of aesthetic attribution and evaluation from artifact to process, from object to performance, from author to cooperative communication, and from intention to indetermination, cannot be overestimated. Indeed, the interactivity between systems implied by the cybernetic view of art and society depends on cooperation and may potentially generate a more democratic approach to both the processes of composition, and the actualization of and fruition of the artistic event and to the fabrication of the social environment more generically.

The aesthetic and political implications of interactivity were clear to European avant-garde intellectuals and artists. In the early 1960s, for instance, the Italian novelist and literary critic Italo Calvino was exploring the relationship between scientific knowledge, mythology and storytelling. He investigated the potentialities of nonlinguistic codes (mathematical and biological codes, mainly) and nonanthropomorphic relations and concepts (such as distance; time; geometry) as propellers of the imagination and generators of semantic, rhetorical and figural disturbances that creatively disrupt the automatisms of myth and storytelling.[21] It was specifically in the essay "Cybernetics and Ghosts" published in 1968 but referring to a series of conferences he delivered in 1967 in different Italian cities, that Calvino discussed the hypothesis of a computer-generated literature and its aesthetic consequences.[22] Calvino's interest in the concept of a "writing machine" that the discourse of cybernetics opened to the imagination does not focus on its successful performances, but on its potential for generating chaos, disorder, and noise. And noise, in Shannon and Weaver's mathematical theory of communication, increases uncertainty, and information, provided that information be understood as "a measure of the freedom of choice in a system."[23] As Calvino puts it in the essay, "the true literature machine will be one that itself feels the need to produce disorder, as a reaction against its preceding production of order."[24] Calvino is not troubled by the dissolution of the authorial function in a computational network, but is committed to ask a question: what would replace the trope of originality that rhetoric and literary theory hadve traditionally assigned to the figure of the author? He is concerned with finding a conceptual device that could both substitute the myth of the author and be a vector of genuine alteration in language and in the imagination. He points to the void at the heart of the compositional process and to the aesthetic and rhetorical labor necessary to cover this void over with the figure of the genius—as in Romanticism—or under the function of consciousness. At the same time, Calvino denounces the failure of aesthetic as a philosophical discourse to address the void without always begging the further question. Authorship, in Calvino's view, is always already dissolved in writing:

> The so-called personality of the writer exists within the very act of writing: it is the product and the instrument of the writing process. A writing machine that has been fed an instruction appropriate to the case could also devise an exact and unmistakable "personality" of an author, or else it could be adjusted in such a way as to evolve

21 For a detailed accounts of this stage of elaboration and creativity in Calvino's career, see Belpoliti, *L'Occhio di Calvino*; Blazina, "Italo Calvino"; Bucciantini, *Italo Calvino*.

22 The full title in Italian is, "Cybernetics and Ghosts (Literature as a combinatorial practice)."

23 Shannon and Weaver, *Mathematical Theory*, 109.

24 Calvino, "Cybernetics and Ghosts," 11.

> or change "personality" with each work it composes. Writers, as they have always been up to now, are already writing machines; or at least they are when things are going well. What Romantic terminology called genius or talent or inspiration or intuition is nothing other than finding the right road empirically, following one's nose, taking short cuts, whereas the machine would follow a systematic and conscientious route while being extremely rapid and multiple at the same time.[25]

Anticipating a problem that only second-order cybernetics and systems theory would beginstart to address, what Calvino asked is actually asking here is: "Hhow do consciousness and communication relate? Is literature a fact of consciousness or one of communication?" Clearly, in his study, Calvino assumes the cultural, logical, and even technological nature of the "I" as an effect of discourse. And yet, he highlights the gap between the self-assertion of the "I" and its non-coincidence with itself, displacing onto the act of reading and onto "the eye of the reader" the decisive ground for the production of meaning. "Once we have dismantled and reassembled the process of literary composition," he writes, "the decisive moment of *literary life* will be that of reading."[26] In Calvino's cybernetic vision, reading does not only activate the potentialities of a given textual artifact, but also carries the circular logic of cybernetic systems that actualize meaning in the medium of language. That is why, in Calvino's view, machine-generated literature will continue to be "a place of privilege" within human consciousness, because it is "a way of exercising the potentialities contained in the system of signs belonging to all societies at all times. The work will continue to be born, to be judged, to be destroyed or constantly renewed on contact with the eye of the reader."[27] Reading, in thisway, is the cognitive function that connects and reconnects the literary work in each contingent actualization to the open and indeterminable reservoir of sensuous, incarnated meaning that coincides with the total possibilities of communication. It is the fundamental form of interaction integrating the literary work into society and to individual readers through a network of feedback loops connecting processes, objects, and systems of consciousness and communication.

25 Ibid., 13.

26 Ibid. My italics.

27 Ibid., 14.

We can now better understand Calvino's optimism toward the vanishing of the figure of the author, "that personage to whom we persist in attributing functions that do not belong to him."[28] He addresses the author as the "exhibitor of his own soul in the permanent Exhibition of Souls, . . . the exploiter of sensory and interpretive organs more receptive than the average. . . . That anachronistic personage, the bearer of messages, the director of consciences, the giver of lectures to cultural bodies."[29] Thus framed, the dispersion of the author does not only not appear as a tragic loss, but rather a positive asset, as it inaugurates a self-conscious paradigm shift in western aesthetics, opening its formulations to more undetermined cooperative practices among the elements of the cybernetic circuit.The British artist Roy Ascott theorized (and practiced) the relation between cybernetics and aesthetics along similar lines to Calvino's own inquiry.[30] As Edward Shanken has argued, Ascott noted in retrospect "that the 'recognition that art was located in an interactive system rather than residing in a material object . . . provid[ed] a discipline as central to an art of interactivity as anatomy and perspective had been to the renaissance vision.'"[31]

But what is an art of interactivity? In the apt formulation of Luis Arata, it is one that "favors multiple points of view that can coexist even if they appear mutually exclusive; it celebrates the creative value of play; it is a catalyst for emergence; and it tends to be ultimately pragmatic."[32] In other words, it is a mode of production, a perspective and a methodology for navigating the hyper-complex environment in which humans coexist with living and nonliving systems and heterogeneous materials and discourses in flows of communication. An art of interactivity can be described, with cybernetician Gordon Pask, as an art capable of generating "an aesthetically potent environment," which "encourages the hearer or viewer to explore it,

28 Ibid.

29 Ibid.

30 Shanken reports that Ascott claimed precedence as the artist responsible for first introducing cybernetic theory into art education and for having disseminated the concept of a cybernetic vision in the UK. See Shanken, "Cybernetics and Art," 259.

31 The letter is quoted in Shanken, "Cybernetics and Art." Usselmann, in "The Dilemma of Media Art," reports a letter written by Ascott to Ealins in which Ascott claims his pioneering role in disseminating cybernetic ideas in the UK art scene.

32 Arata, "Reflections on Interactivity," 219.

to learn about it, to form an hierarchy of concepts that refer to it; further, it guides his exploration: in a sense, it makes him participate in, or at any rate see himself reflected in, the environment."[33]

CYBERNETIC SERENDIPITIES

According to its curators, reviewers and cultural historians, the first comprehensive European exhibition entirely dedicated to the convergence of cybernetics and aesthetics, *Cybernetic Serendipity: The Computer and the Arts*, which opened in London at the Institute of Contemporary Arts on August 2, 1968, allowed viewers to experience what it meant to be in aesthetically potent environments. In the words of its curator, Jasia Reichardt, it was the first exhibition that attempted to demonstrate "all aspects of computer-aided creative activity: art, music, poetry, dance, sculpture, animation. The principal idea was to examine the role of cybernetics in contemporary arts."[34] The exhibition, an immense success attracting over 40,000 visitors across social classes and cultural zones, was organized around three main sections: the first dedicated to computer-generated and interactive graphics design, films, music and poetry; the second, to "cybernetic devices as works of art, cybernetic environments, remote control robots and painting machines"[35]; and the third, to machines demonstrating the use of robots, automation, and to the history of cybernetics. The exhibition included robots, poetry, music and painting machines, as well as all sorts of works emergent from the convergence of computation, chance, and interactivity. In this respect, the curator's emphasis on the organizational and epistemological aspects of the exhibition should be taken seriously. As she wrote, the exhibition "was an intellectual exercise that became a spectacular exhibition in the summer of 1968."[36]

---

33 Pask, "Colloquy of Mobiles," 34; Pask was present at the exhibition with his interactive installation "The Colloquy of Mobiles" (see figure 1). See also Pask, "A comment, a case history and a plan."

34 Reichardt, Press release.

35 Reichardt, Cybernetic Serendipity, 6. For a retrospective assessment of that moment of cultural history, see also Reichardt, "In the Beginning." On the institutional history of the exhibition, see Usselmann, "The Dilemma of Media Art"; MacGregor, "Cybernetic Serendipity Revisited."

36 Reichardt, Press release.

Figure 1: Gordon Pask, Colloquy of Mobiles. *A version of the installation presented at Cybernetic Serendipity.*

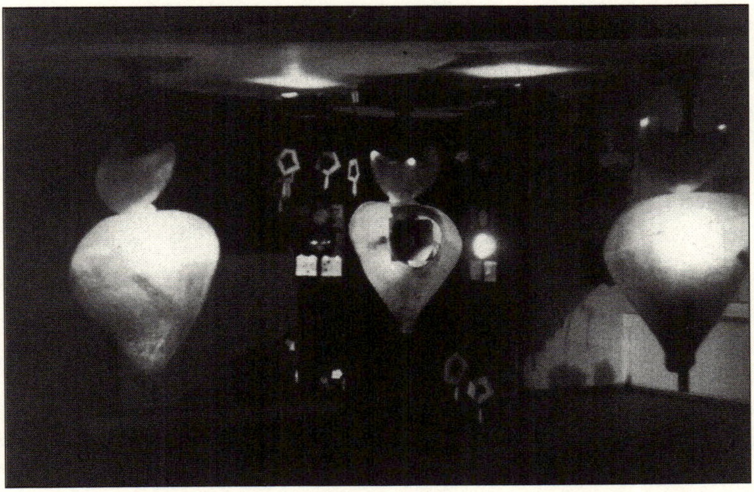

Gordon Pask Archive at the Department of Contemporary History, University of Vienna

The list of contributing artists remains impressive today, and reveals that Gordon Pask may have been one of the lynchpins connecting cybernetics across the Atlantic (fig. 1). In any case, by 1968 the intellectual appeal of cybernetics had ramified across several disciplinary domains, and across cultural practices and cultural formations.[37] The list of contributors included Gordon Pask, Bruce Lacey, Wen Ying Tsai, James Seawright, Nam June Paik, Jean Tinguely, John Cage, Lowell Nesbitt, Eugenio Carmi, Nanni Balestrini, Bryon Gysin and many others. As the first great display of systems aesthetics, the exhibition was particularly keen to document and expose the engagement of computer-generated events with the material and infrastructural conditions of their occurrence. Similarly, the intense preoccupation

37 Further discussion of the aesthetic elaboration of Gordon Pask's cybernetics exceeds the purposes of this essay. However, it develops issues so far discussed, as can be inferred by a close reading of his essay "A Comment, a Case History and a Plan" in which he details the installation "A Colloquy of Mobiles." On Pask, see also Fernandez, "Aesthetically Potent Environments." See also Haque, "The Architectural Relevance of Gordon Pask."

with audience interactivity and involvement shed light on the epistemological and creative potential of cybernetics and on the radically democratic impulse inscribed in its systemic understanding of art as the manifestation and realization of a communicative circuit. Significantly, by transforming experience into information, the material, embodied quality of phenomenal experience did not vanish, but was reorganized, re-synthetized, and resignified in the communication continuum connecting users, equipment, and cultural conditions. In a 1968 essay published in *Artforum*, art historian Jack Burnham claimed that "A systems viewpoint is focused on the creation of stable, on-going relationships between organic and non-organic systems."[38] As Mitchell Whitelaw observes in a retrospective review of Cyberentic Serendipity in light of Burnham's incipient insights into systems art, "What emerges is a sense of a moment in history when artists, working with and without high technology, were engaged in a post-representational, post-object practice concerned with provoking an awareness of the real as an extensive, relational, dynamic network of processes."[39]

A similar concern for and interest inthe aesthetic potential of participatory social practices served to foreground several examples of avant-garde art in the 1960s: Cedric Price's planning for The Fun Palace (1964) and Potteries Thinkbelt (1967), which were projects for complex, interactive systems in which light, low-impact, highly adaptable and inexpensive building materials could be used to assemble, disassemble and reassemble space in relation to the needs, desires, and preferences of users, in a sort of real-life building block game.

Initiated in 1962 as a collaborative project between Architect Cedric Price and avant-garde, agit-prop theater director, Joan Littlewood, the Fun Palace project displayed the principles of constructivist epistemology and exemplified the performative quality of avant-garde theater. By collapsing the boundaries between performer, performance and audience, and by physically embodying transformation as a structural principle, the Fun Palace became paradigmatic of a constellation of concepts of space, place and art thoroughly dependent on the cybernetic definition of communication and its related concepts: feedback loop, information, function, process.[40] In his

38 Quoted in Whitelaw, 1. For an assessment of the evolution of cybernetic into digital aesthetics, see Gere, "New Media Art."

39 Whitelaw, 2.

40 Littlewood, "A Laboratory of Fun."

reconstruction of the Fun Palace project, Stanley Mathews writes that the collaboration with Littlewood worked as a frame for Price's revolutionary ideas. Littlewood wanted to create a theater of pure performativity, a space of "cultural bricolage" where people could experience directly the intense transformative power of drama as actors. Together, the two intellectuals developed the plan of the Fun Palace as a site of permanent education for the East London working classes and as "an interactive environment, a new kind of architecture capable of altering its form to accommodate the changing needs of the users."[41] Gordon Pask participated in the planning, the most ambitious aim of which was to create an improvisational architecture capable of "learning, anticipating, and adapting to the constantly evolving program. An array of sensors and inputs would provide real-time feedback on use and occupancy to computers which would allocate and alter spaces and resources according to projected needs."[42] After much planning and bureaucratic defeat, the project failed: in 1975 Price declared the Fun Palace project obsolete, but its legacy was reinvested by Price in the InterAction Center in Kentish Town (1976). The lasting influence of the Fun Palace is disseminated across late twentieth-century and contemporary architecture, testifying—I would argue—to the cultural and aesthetic success of the cybernetic paradigm and to the socially transformative impact of avant-garde ideas it contributed to nurturing.[43]

POTENT AESTHETIC ENVIRONMENTS AND THE COOPERATIVE PRODUCTION OF MEANING

That an entire zone of Cybernetic Serendipity was dedicated to proto-digital poetics and textual composition should be no surprise. Among the items on display in that section of the exhibition was Nanni Balestrini's "Tape Mark I," the first Italian example of experimental, computer-generated, combinatorial poetry, exhibited in Edwin Morgan's translation, and a detailed re-

41 Mathews, *From Agit Prop.*

42 Mathews, *From Agit Prop.* See also Mathews, "Fun Palace"; Lobsinger, "Cedric Price"; Lobsinger, "Cybernetic Theory"; Wilken, "Calculated Uncertainty."

43 Mathews, *From Agit Prop.* For an explanation and a comment on Cedric Price's groundbreaking ideas on the relation between social, technical, and aesthetic environments, and innovative architectural concepts, see Mathews, "Cedric Price."

production of its compositional flowchart. The poem is composed out of material from three citations from three separate texts: Michihiko Hachiya's *Hiroshima Diary*, Paul Goldwin's *The Mystery of the Elevator*, and Lao Tzu's *Tao Te Ching*. It was first performed on an IBM 7070 computing machine at the Electronic Center of the Lombard Provinces Savings Bank in Milan, in October 1961.[44] Series of sentence segments were assembled according to basic syntactical rules to connect into regular, four-beat lines, and the lines into regular stanzas. The sequences were then translated into an algorithm and fed into the machine (fig. 2).

The great variational potential of the machine, the selective operations of the poet, and the capacity of readers to impose order or project meaning on random combinations of words exemplify—in spite of and beyond Balestrini and Italo Calvino's many divergences on issues of aesthetics and literature—Calvino's claims about literature as the privileged manifestation of the coupling of communication and consciousness, and of reading as "a way of exercising the potentialities contained in the system of signs belonging to all societies at all times."[45]

In the early 1960s, avant-garde literature and arts were starting to self-consciously process the mutation of the relation between texts and readers/users by employing metafictional devices to signal interruptions, divergences, textual meanderings, and all sorts of interference in the narrative and in the reading process. The excess of data, information, and signs derived from the proliferation of technology for the recording, storing and sorting out of information operated as an ongoing source of interference in the communication system, and of disturbance in the reading process. This new configuration of the media system forced the novel to refashion itself into what Steven Connor sees as a template for the re-synchronization and

44 Balestrini, "Tape Mark I." A small, exemplary selection of poems was published in *Almanacco Letterario Bompiani 1962*, and ignited an intense discussion about the end of art, machine-poetry, the death of the author, etc. The 1962 issue, published in November 1961 and focused on the aesthetic and linguistic potential of computers, displayed a cover illustrated by Bruno Munari and several illustrations by members of Gruppo T. On May 15, 1962, Munari, who was then working for Olivetti whom also displayed installations in the celebrated cybernetic exhibition, "Arte Programmata" at the Olivetti Store in Milan Sergio Morando, ed., *Almanacco letterario Bompiani: 1962. Le applicazioni dei calcolatori alle scienze morali e alla letteratura*. (Milano: V. Bompiani & C., 1962).

45 Calvino, "Cybernetics and Ghosts," 14.

actualization of cognitive, communicative, and technical possibilities activated in the act of reading.[46]

Thomas Pynchon and Donald Barthelme recorded early the cybernetic moment and delivered a literature of interaction that assumed the transformation of reading practices within multiple communication circuits. Pynchon's short story "Entropy" (1960), for instance, traces the sentimental failure of a relationship as a communicative block and represents it as the

Figure 2: Nanni Balestrini, Algorithm for Tape Mark I

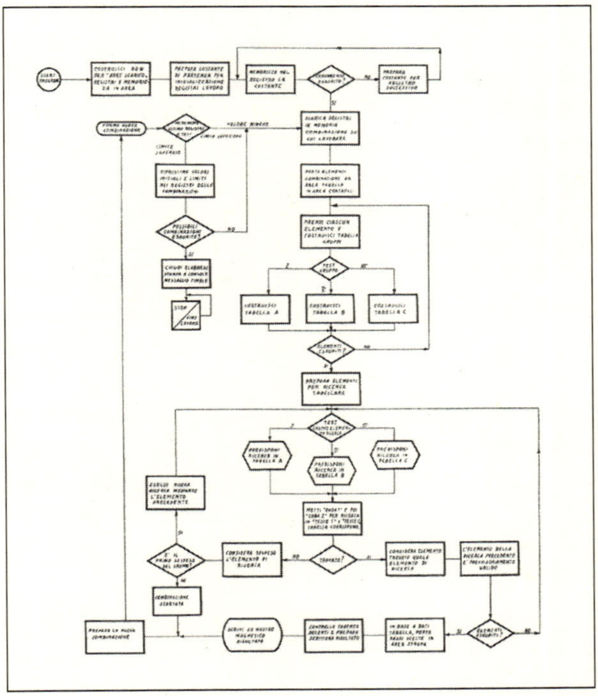

Nanni Balestrini, Algorithm for Tape Mark I, on display in the exhibition Cybernetic Serendipity. This reproduction is from Almanacco Letterario Bompiani 1962, Valentino Bompiani, Milano, 1962, 146. Courtesy of Nanni Balestrini.

46 Connor, "Postmodernism and Literature," 77–78.

disorganization of an entropic system comparable to a closed cybernetic circuit. In his first novel, *The Crying of Lot 49* (1966), the trope of entropy, a crucial concept in Shannon's Mathematical Theory of Communication and in Second Order cybernetics, provides the ground for questioning theories of communication, meaning production and actualization, and technologies of memory. The novel's protagonist, Oedipa Maas, is to recover her defunct ex-husband Pierce Inverarity's stamp collection. Because of its obscure iconography, the collection works as a reservoir of historical and geographical exoticism left behind Inverarity's "own annihilation." It dramatizes the relation between meaning and memory as a tension between disorder and order in a sequence of metaphoric permutations around the figures of meaning as specter and signs as spectacle. In the stamp collection, meaning is suggested as a possibility that requires the decoupling of sign from referent in order to allow Oedipa to track new patterns of visual consumption. As implied by the temporal and spatial exoticism foregrounding the "spectacular" windows of the stamps, the stamp collection is not different in kind from the serial production of Hollywood historical melodramas, or from a freeway view of San Narciso. In all cases, Oedipa is haunted by the intuition that all the figures she encounters might hold some retrievable pattern, some incorporated desire to communicate. But what message, if any, she cannot grasp, as she clearly states in her vista over San Narciso:

> The ordered swirl of houses and streets, from this angle, sprang at her now with the same, unexpected, astonishing clarity as the circuit card had. Though she knew less about radios than about Southern Californians, there were to both outward patterns a hieroglyphic sense of concealed meaning, of an intent to communicate. There'd seem no limit to what the printed circuit could have told her.[47]

In the metaphor of the hieroglyphic, the materiality of inscription and the abstraction of coding are collapsed and recast in a spatial figuration of outside and inside that, at first sight, seems to suggest that meaning is the result of a process of decoding, of bringing to the surface of things the hidden significance they encapsulate. However, what becomes clearer in the course of the narrative is that the problem of meaning Oedipa Maas has to face is not so much one of resolving equations among signs. She is not called on to

47 Pynchon, *Crying of Lot 49*, 14.

discover the meaning of inscriptions, how they are all equally meaningful and how they circulate and create order by pointing out to the outside, to a reference that exists already out there. On the contrary, she is to produce order and generate meaning by shattering inscriptions, signs, and words and by reorganizing their mutual relation. Indeed, she has to deconstruct the apparent unity between meaning/sign symbolized by inscriptions and reactivate the semantic potentialities repressed by their code.

Above and beyond the signs saturating the communicative space in which the protagonist moves, there seems to linger some "unexpected" possibility that threatens to disrupt the visible (or predictable) configuration of signs and patterns and to open the way to a new trail of meaningful associations. Such a possibility can be triggered only, in Oedipa's vocabulary, by a "revelation"; it is a pure virtuality always on the verge of happening, but never with certainty. At least so much is suggested, for example, in Oedipa's struggle to decode the Tristero system by way of an accumulation of revelations, but also, in earlier moments of the narrative, by her observation of the finale of the "Baby Igor" movie, when Oedipa describes the surprise of the unlikely ending as "one of those Hollywood distortions in probability."[48] This distortion would not terminate the "uproar from the TV set. She could imagine no end to it."[49] Instead, it would temporarily interrupt TV-generated noise by inserting a noise of a different order in the noisy randomness of media communication. It is only in this way that Oedipa can imagine possibilities for unprecedented, if contingent, articulations of new "patterns" in the signifying chain.

The semantic overlapping between linguistic and control science, or information, also encouraged a rethinking of the relation between technology, consciousness and knowledge as the contingent effect of the ongoing process of exchange of information between machine and living organism; or, to put it differently, as the ever changing result of communication between the central nervous system and the media. In his groundbreaking *Understanding Media: The Extension of Man* (1964), Marshall McLuhan offered a view of the media as an extension of human consciousness beyond the physiological limits of the body, conceptualizing them as an electric extension of the central nervous system. As he put it, "The personal and social

48 Ibid., 28.
49 Ibid., 24.

consequences of any medium—that is, of any extension of ourselves—result from the new scale that is introduced into our affairs by each extension of ourselves, or by any new technology."[50] This perspective allowed for the reintegration of every element caught in mental and communication processes (physiological, material, abstract, symbolic, affective) in a single circuit of signification stemming from flows of data. At the same time, it also emphasized the immanent, systemic, and technological substratum of human mental processes and linguistic practices, thus downplaying the explanatory force of anthropocentric theories of consciousness and subjectivity.

The writer who best incorporates Marshall McLuhan's theories about the extension and externalization of consciousness as a technological organization of data is perhaps William Burroughs, whose work foregrounded both the language of information and communication theory and the development of an anti-aesthetics of reception. By casting noise as proper to communication, irreducible to meaning, and unresolved by the signal to noise ratio of information theory, Burroughs's poetics of the 1960s—especially his so-called cut-up trilogy, *The Soft Machine* (1961), *The Ticket That Exploded* (1962), and *Nova Express* (1964)—shows the relation of noise to communication and meaning akin to the discourse of information, which conceptualizes it as the emergence of "order out of noise". But it is especially his famous definition of language as a virus feeding on human life to replicate itself that can be best understood as an embodiment and an aesthetic manifestation of the continuity between flows of information and the materiality of the body implied in McLuhan's own definition of the electric body. For, in Burroughs's view, the carriers of viral attacks are not specific kinds of code, such as the alphabetic code or human language, but coding itself as a sheer possibility—as information. It is coding as the potential for communication that extends beyond language to all communicative supports, gets manifested as the control of information and as the manipulation of codes, is maximized by the mass media, and becomes coextensive with human consciousness. In Burroughs's world, if coding is viral, communication is totalitarian because it imposes its own forms and patterns of control on human consciousness, which is literally "spoken" by language. The only way out of this entropic condition is to develop strategies of defamiliarization that make the parasitical nature of language visible by

50 McLuhan, *Understanding Media*, 16.

producing noticeable counter-signals, disturbances, noise. Noise, through its presence and absence, produces intermittence of the signal that disturbs linearity and generates uncertainty and oscillation, thus creating the conditions for the emergence of new hermeneutic possibilities.

By resisting rhetorical conventions, grammar, and syntax, it becomes possible to conceive of the liberation of individuals from the tyranny of pre-established meanings and to imagine a poetics of decomposition that does not aim at recreating new, well-ordered objects or well-organized, linear narratives. On the contrary, this poetics leaves around visual and sonic left-overs, statics, word-objects, all viral material that cannot be recontained in conventional narrative objects, but can only be reused by receptors or readers. Cut-ups and fold-ins are the key recombinant strategies devised by Burroughs to generate a guerrilla warfare aimed at maximizing semantic disturbances, noise, statics in the system. Noise interrupts a sedimented or unidirectional system of relations by disrupting the position of elements within a cybernetic circuit and by recursively generating negative feedback. Noise in the novels is produced by the breaking down of the grammatical, syntactical, rhetorical, and semantic elements of communication with other elements of communication.

As we have seen in the other instances of cybernetic aesthetics discussed so far, the adoption of a systemic understanding of communication implies that meaning always emerges as an effect of the feedback-looping of information among the elements of the cybernetic circuit. Thus, the role of the user, the viewer, or the reader, becomes crucial to the activation of processes of signification, because it works as the mediator between aesthetic systems and the open environment in which they are situated. This observation allows us to conclude by reconnecting writers as dissimilar as Calvino and Burroughs on the terrain of the mediation between what Calvino called "the eye of the reader" and "an expanding universe." Although their poetics are immensely different, with Calvino's universe expanding into the totality of all signs of all time, and Burroughs's universe contracting into the radical decomposition of language as noise, both authors insist on the value of the unfamiliar, the mechanical, the nonhuman element of the cybernetic circuit as a means to training perception in order to open many unexpected venues of awareness, and to keep open the "eye of the reader" toward the potentially of an expanding universe.

BIBLIOGRAPHY

Arata, Luis O. "Reflections on Interactivity." In *Rethinking Media Change: The Aesthetics of Transition*, edited by David Thorburn and Henry Jenkis, 217–25. Cambridge, MA: MIT Press, 2003.

Ascott, Roy. *Telematic Embrace: Visionary Theories of Art, Technology, and Consciousness*. Edited by Edward A. Shanken. Berkeley: University of California Press, 2003.

Aspray, William. "The Scientific Conceptualization of Information: A Survey." *Annals of the History of Computing* 7, no. 2 (1985): 117–40.

Balestrini, Nanni. "Tape Mark I." In Reichardt, *Cybernetic Serendipity*, 55.

Barthelme, Donald. "Report." In *Unspeakable Practices, Unnatural Acts*, 49–58. New York: Pocket Books, 1976. First published 1968.

Belpoliti, Marco. *L'Occhio di Calvino*. Torino: Einaudi, 1996.

Beninger, James R. *The Control Revolution: Technological and Economic Origins of the Information Society*. Cambridge, MA: Harvard University Press, 1983.

Blazina, Sergio. "Italo Calvino, un linguaggio tra scienza e mito." *Chroniques italiennes* 75/76 (2005): 59–75.

Brand, Stewart. *From Counterculture to Cyberculture: The Whole Earth Network Catalogue and the Rise of Digital Utopianism*. Chicago: University of Chicago Press, 2006.

Brown, Paul, Charlie Gere, Nicholas Lambert, and Catherine Mason, eds. *White Heat Cold Logic: British Computer Art; 1960–1980*. Cambridge, MA: MIT Press, 2009.

Bucciantini, Massimo. *Italo Calvino e la Scienza: Gli alfabeti del mondo*. Roma: Donzelli, 2007.

Burnham, Jack. *Beyond Modern Sculpture: The Effects of Science and Technology on the Sculpture of this Century*. New York: George Braziller, 1968.

Burroughs, William. *Nova Express*. New York: Grove Press, 1964.

———. *The Soft Machine*. New York: Grove Press, 1967. First published 1961 by Olympia Press in Paris.

———. *The Ticket That Exploded*. New York: Grove Press, 1964. First published 1961 by Olympia Press in Paris.

Calvino, Italo. "Cybernetics and Ghosts." In *The Literature Machine*, translated by Patrick Creagh, 3–27. London: Pan/Secker & Warburg, 1987. Originally published as "Cibernetica e fantasmi" (1967) in *Una pietra sopra* (Torino: Einaudi, 1980).

Clarke, Bruce. "Communication." In *Critical Terms for Media Studies*, edited by W. J. T. Mitchell and Mark B. N. Hansen, 131–44. Chicago: University of Chicago Press, 2010.

Clarke, Bruce, and Linda Dalrymple Henderson, eds. *From Energy to Information: Representation in Science, Technology, Art and Literature*. Stanford: Stanford University Press, 2002.

Connor, Steven. "Postmodernism and Literature." In *Cambridge Companion to Postmodernism*, edited by Steven Connor, 62–82. Cambridge: Cambridge University Press, 2007.

Edwards, Paul. *The Close World: Computers and the Politics of Discourse in Cold War America*. Cambridge, MA: MIT Press, 1996.

Fernandez, Maria. "Aesthetically Potent Environments: How Gordon Pask Detourned Instrumental Cybernetics." In Brown et al., *White Heat Cold Logic*, 53–70.

Galison, Peter. "The Ontology of the Enemy: Norbert Wiener and the Cybernetic Vision." *Critical Inquiry* 21, no. 1 (1994): 228–65.

Geoghegan, Bernard Dionysius. "From Information Theory to French Theory: Jackobson, Lévi-Strauss, and the Cybernetic Apparatus." *Critical Inquiry* 38, no. 1 (Autumn 2011): 96–126.

Gere, Charlie. "New Media Art and the Gallery in the Digital Age." Tate Papers, Autumn 2004, 1–12. http://www.tate.org.uk/research/tateresearch/tatepapers/04autumn/gere.htm.

Granzotto, Giovanni, and Mariastella Margozzi. *Arte programmata e cinetica: da Munari a Biasi a Colombo e*. Rome: Il cigno Galileo Galilei, 2012.

Haque, Usman. "The Architectural Relevance of Gordon Pask." *Architectural Design* 77, no. 4 (July/August 2007): 54–61. http://www.haque.co.uk/papers/architectural_relevance_of_gordon_pask.pdf.

Hartley, John. *Communication, Cultural and Media Studies: The Key Concepts*. 3rd ed. London: Routledge, 2002.

Hayles, N. Katherine. *How We Became Posthuman: Virtual Bodies in Cybernetics, Literature, and Informatics*. Chicago: University of Chicago Press, 1999.

Heims, Steve J. *The Cybernetic Group: Constructing a Social Science for Postwar America*. Cambridge, MA: MIT Press, 1991.

Jameson, Fredric. *Postmodernism, or the Cultural Logic of Late Capitalism*. Durham: Duke University Press, 1991.

Kay, Lily E. *Who Wrote the Book of Life? A History of the Genetic Code*. Stanford: Stanford University Press, 2000.

Leslie, Stuart W. *The Cold War and American Science: The Military-Industrial-Academic Complex at MIT and Stanford*. New York: Columbia University Press, 1993.

Littlewood, Joan. "A Laboratory of Fun." *New Scientist*, May 14, 1964.

Lobsinger, Mary Lou. "Cedric Price: An Architecture of Performance." *Daidalos* 74 (2000): 22–29.

———. "Cybernetic Theory and the Architecture of Performance: Cedric Price's Fun Palace." In *Anxious Modernisms: Experimentation in Postwar Architectural Culture*, edited by Sarah Williams Goldhagen and Réjean Legault, 119–39. Montreal: Canadian Centre for Architecture; Cambridge, MA: MIT Press, 2000.

Lyotard, Jean François. *The Postmodern Condition: A Report on Knowledge*. Translated by Brian Massumi. Minneapolis: University of Minnesota Press, 1984.

MacGregor, Brent. "Cybernetic Serendipity Revisited." In Brown et al., *White Heat Cold Logic*, 83–93.

Mari, Enzo, Gruppo N, and Gruppo T. "Arte e libertà: Impegno ideologica nelle correnti artistiche contemporanee." *Il verri* 12 (1963): 133–35.

Mathews, Stanley. "Cedric Price and the Architecture of Complexity." A+DS Architecture and Design Scotland. http://www.ads.org.uk/access/features/stanley-mathews-cedric-price-and-the-architecture-of-complexity.

———. *From Agit Prop to Free Space: The Architecture of Cedric Price*. London: Black Dog, 2007.

———. "The Fun Palace as Virtual Architecture: Cedric Price and the Practices of Indeterminacy." *Journal of Architectural Education* 59, no. 3 (2006): 39–48.

McLuhan, Marshall. *Understanding Media: The Extensions of Man*. New York: McGraw Hill, 1964.

Mendelsohn, Everett, Merritt Roe Smith, and Peter Weingart, eds. *Science, Technology, and the Military*. Vols. 1–2. Dordrecht: Kluwer Academic Publishers, 1988.

Meneguzzo, Marco, Enrico Morteo, and Alberto Saibene, eds. *Programmare l'arte: Olivetti e le neovanguardie cinetiche*. Exhibition Catalogue. Truccazzano, Milano: John & Levi, 2012.

Morando, Sergio, ed. *Almanacco letterario Bompiani*: 1962. Milano: V. Bompiani, 1962.

Olson, Charles. *Selected Writings*. Edited by by Robert Creeley. New York: New Directions, 1967.

Parini, Pino. "Fra arte cibernetica e didattica." *Metasound*. Platform of the music label Radical Matters. http://www.radicalmatters.com/metasound/pdf/Fra_arte_e_ciberneticai_1_2Dic.2007.pdf.

Pask, Gordon. "The Colloquy of Mobiles." In Reichardt, *Cybernetic Serendipity*, 34–35.

———. "A Comment, a Case History and a Plan." In *Cybernetics, Art and Ideas*, edited by Jasia Reichardt, 76–99. London: Studio Vista, 1971. The Pangaro Archive of Gordon Pask. http://pangaro.com/pask/index.html.

Pynchon, Thomas. *The Crying of Lot 49*. Philadelphia: Lippincott, 1966.

———. *Slow Learner: Early Stories*. New York: Little, Brown / Back Bay Books, 1985.

Reichardt, Jasia. "In the Beginning." In Brown et al., *White Heat Cold Logic*, 71–81.

———, ed. *Cybernetic Serendipity: The Computer and the Arts*. ICA London, August 2 – October 20, 1968. London: Studio International, 1968.

———. Press release for the exhibition Cybernetic Serendipity: The Computer and the Arts, ICA London, Aug. 2 – Oct. 20, 1968. http://www.medienkunstnetz.de/exhibitions/serendipity/.

Rey, Yveline, and Bernard Prieur, eds. *Systemes, ethiques: Perspectives en therapie familiale*. Paris: ESF Editeur, 1991.

Roof, Judith. *The Poetics of DNA*. Minneapolis: University of Minnesota Press, 2008.

Rosen, Margit, ed. *A Little-Known Story about a Movement, a Magazine, and the Computer's Arrival in Art: New Tendencies and Bit International; 1961–1973*. In collaboration with Peter Weibel, Darko Fritz, and

Marija Gattin. Karlsruhe: ZKM Center for Art and Media, 2011. Distributed by MIT Press.

Rosenblueth, Arturo, Norbert Wiener, and Julian Bigelow. "Behavior, Purpose, and Teleology." *Philosophy of Science* 10, no. 1 (1943): 18–24.

Schubert, Howard, and Mark Wigley. "Il Fun Palace di Cedric Price." *Domus* 866 (January 2004): 14–24.

Shanken, Edward A. "Cybernetics and Art: Cultural Convergence in the 1960s." In *From Energy to Information: Representation in Science, Technology, Art and Literature*, edited by Bruce Clarke and Linda Dalrymple Henderson, 255–77. Stanford: Stanford University Press, 2002.

———. "Reprogramming Systems Aesthetics: A Strategic Historiography." Proceedings of the Digital Arts and Cultures Conference, 2009. *After Media: Embodiment and Context*. University of California, Irvine: Digital Arts and Culture 2009. http://escholarship.org/uc/item/6bv363d4.

Shannon, Claude E., and Warren Weaver. *The Mathematical Theory of Communication*. Urbana: University of Illinois Press, 1949.

Triclot, Mathieu. "Norbert Wiener's Politics and the History of Cybernetics." In *The Global and the Local: The History of Science and the Cultural Integration of Europe*, Proceedings of the 2nd ICESHS, Cracow, Poland (September 6–9, 2006), edited by M. Kokowski, 763–66. Launched in December 23, 2007. http://www.2iceshs.cyfronet.pl/proceedings.html.

Turner, Fred. *From Counterculture to Cyberculture: Stewart Brand, the Whole Earth Network Catalogue, and the Rise of Digital Utopianism*. Chicago: University of Chicago Press, 2006.

Usselmann, Rainer. "The Dilemma of Media Art: Cybernetic Serendipity at the ICA London." Rainer Usselmann. *Text and Images* (blog). http://www.rainerusselmann.net/.

Vergine, Lea. *L'arte Cinetica in Italia*. Roma: Galleria Nazionale d'Arte Moderna, 1973.

von Bertalanffy, Ludwig. *General Systems Theory: Foundations, Development, Applications*. New York: George Braziller, 1968.

von Foerster, Heinz. "Opening Address." *International Conference, Systems and Family Therapy: Ethics, Epistemology, New Methods* (Paris, France, October 4th, 1990). In Rey and Prieur, *Systemes, ethiques*, 41–54.

Whitelaw, Mitchell. "1968/1998: Rethinking a Systems Aesthetic." *ANAT Newsletter* 33 (June 1998). http://creative.canberra.edu.au/mitchell/papers/RethinkingSystemsAesthetic.pdf.

Wiener, Norbert. *Cybernetics; or, Control and Communication in the Animal and the Machine*. 2nd ed. Cambridge, MA: MIT Press, 1961.

Wilken, Rowan. "Calculated Uncertainty: Computers, Chance Encounters and 'Community' in the Work of Cedric Price." *Transformations* 14 (March 2007). http://www.transformationsjournal.org/journal/issue_14/article_04.shtml.

Frost's Negotiations with Khrushchev

National Health, Poetics, and the Fate of West Berlin

GRZEGORZ KOSC

The collective Cold War imagination did not take long to single out Robert Frost's "Mending Wall"—his old poem of 1914—as best expressing postwar diplomatic strife.[1] Not considered nearly as important in earlier decades, the poem suddenly became, as Steven Axelrod has argued, a "necessary" poem without which no postwar anthology of American poetry seemed conceivable. Popularly read as an eloquent expression of several Cold War sentiments such as the desire to contain communism or the yearning to withdraw into a snug rural-looking suburban spaces, it perfectly "organized," asserts Axelrod, "public ambivalences about the world starkly divided by an iron curtain."[2] To the ears of many, the poem also sounded a class-conscious high-minded scorn for Khrushchev's wall, scorn that nourished a sense of separateness from and superiority to the Soviets. Didn't the Communists—so the reasoning went—fit Frost's description of the brutish neighbor, the "moving-in-darkness" and "old-stone savage armed"? Though Frost warned against easy readings of the poem and explained that it locked together a nationalist and a "one-worlder" in an irresolvable tension, "Mending Wall" spoke to Americans as an unequivocally "wall-

1 *The Worcester Sunday Telegram*, for instance, argued that in "Mending Wall" Frost was nothing less than "referring" to the Berlin Wall. See "People," *Worcester Sunday Telegram* (Worcester, MA), September 9, 1962, in Robert Frost Collection, 1887–2008, 12:11.

2 Axelrod, "Frost and the Cold War."

tearing" poem, expressing the universalist ideology of brotherhood of mankind that the West arrogated to itself in its public-image war against the Communist block. It became part of a cunning strategy that effectively positioned the West's antagonists as gracelessly and pettily jealous of their territory.

Yielding to such liberal readings, "Mending Wall" seemed to sculptor Leo Cherne a perfect choice for his design of a monument he was planning to build in West Berlin for the second anniversary of the construction of the Berlin Wall in 1963. The planned monument, which was to rise against the western face of the Wall, was to be inscribed with an excerpt from Frost's poem, in both English and German, and was intended to announce that the people of goodwill—implicitly, Westerners—wanted the wall taken down (fig. 1). Without consulting Frost first, Cherne even began making arrangements for the poet to meet Willy Brandt to discuss this anti-wall campaign.

Characteristically, when he was finally informed of the various arrangements made for him, the poet flatly refused and extricated himself from Cherne's elaborate plans. In an ironic and obviously patronizing letter, Frost told the sculptor to go ahead with the project if he must, but he made it clear that he had no wish to be involved in this folly. Frost also suggested that he had been misunderstood–he couldn't see how one could easily get rid of walls—and wrote, obliquely, that braving walls is not good for one's health:

> But you mustn't ask me at my age to storm the barricades for the fun of laughing the whole thing off with the Russians. I suppose I should have to gather myself together and brave it if this were an order from the top to do something really dangerous for my country. This is at once dangerous to health but not dangerous enough to anything else.[3]

The letter effectively discouraged the sculptor and ultimately prevented him from pursuing his project any further. (Eventually Cherne organized a different commemorative event, without the poet's contribution whatsoever.[4])

3 Frost's response to Leo Cherne is attached to the sculptor's letter to the poet of Nov. 29, 1961, folder 41, box 2, Robert Frost Collection, 1866–1996 (originally Frost 906129 [8] 321).

4 Cf. Smith, *Rescuing the World*, 52.

Figure 1: Leo Cherne's design of the Berlin Wall monument with an excerpt from "Mending Wall" in German and English

Robert Frost Collection, 1866–1996, Frost MS-1178, box 2, folder 41 (new catalogue). Rauner Library, Dartmouth College, Hanover. Courtesy of Dartmouth College Library.

More importantly, the letter testifies to the great complications in Frost's attitude to the Cold War and points to a huge discrepancy between the Cold-War politically expedient readings of his poetry and Frost's own complex understanding of it, even in this new postwar context.

The letter serves as a revealing introduction to this essay's major objective—an interpretation of a meeting Frost had with Nikita Khrushchev about the future of West Berlin. The meeting took place in Gagra, Abkhazia, on September 7, 1962, culminating the poet's ten-day visit to the Soviet

Union. I explore the main subjects of this conversation—the details of which are known from two independent first-hand accounts by Frost's companions F. D. Reeves and Frederick B. Adams—in the light of Frost's lifelong preoccupations with such themes as the nature and scope of human knowledge, the appropriate borderlines of lasting and thriving nations, US-Russian relations, and the question of loyalty. Echoing the chasm between Frost's intended meaning in the poem "Mending Wall" and its Cold War appropriations, I will show that the poet envisioned for himself a role far more complicated than any of those into which Cold War America had tried to mold him. Useful as it may have been for the Kennedy administration to keep Frost in Washington, DC, sending him on a diplomatic mission sponsored by the State Department involved considerable political risk. Frost demonstrated a truly "poetic" or soulful approach to diplomacy by investing the meeting with deep conflicting desires, which he felt were also at work in the process of poetic composition. More universally, the essay will suggest that the poet's imaginative response to the Iron Curtain richly illustrates how the dividing line "from Stettin to Trieste" provoked in both ideological blocs, well into the 1960s, strong desires for the Other, the unthinkable, and a vantage point from which they could look back on themselves and comprehend their own historicity.

Though today few would take seriously the idea of a summit between a poet and the leader of a superpower, and even fewer would accept such a summit in the midst of Cold War, Frost himself thought it absolutely natural. Never did it occur to him that, as a poet, he might be out of his depth in international diplomacy. He always claimed a special role for poets in the political world, and his meeting with Khrushchev must have struck him as wholly appropriate. Frost was once asked whether he concurred with Percy B. Shelley that poets were "unacknowledged legislators of the world," attuned to the harmonies towards which all creation strove and towards which human history was heading, albeit slowly. He responded with an emphatic No.[5] Poets, he believed, are not attuned in any special way to some inherent order of the universe, for there may not be one. He argued that such pursuits belonged to the preoccupations of philosophers, making them ill-suited for the position of political power. "I'm no Platonist," Frost explained, "to agree with Plato that the philosopher should be king. Neither

5 Cook, *Living Voice*, 65–66.

do I agree with him that the poet should be suppressed. The poet would make a better king than the philosopher."[6] Precisely the difference of poetry from philosophy makes the former, in Frost's view, akin to politics and makes poets better suited for the job of political leadership and international diplomacy than philosophers will ever be. Frost believed that statesmanship and poetry had much in common, because neither strained to acquire the knowledge of a wider truth. If philosophy, he thought, was the love of truth, poetry, more modestly and similarly to politics, showed more interest in creating habitable and sufficiently safe and enduring environments. In short, writing poetry has much to do with shaping state borders. In Frost's view, the occupation of poets corresponds to that of politicians and statesmen insofar as they all, state leaders and poets alike, create habitable human realms. Poetry, too, consists, in the main, of wall-building; if it sometimes also involves wall-tearing, that is only because the poet intends to move the wall elsewhere, to push it outward thus enlarging the realm of intelligibility.[7] When confronting Khrushchev, Frost saw both of them as involved in more or less the same business, partners in the same trade.

GOOD AND BAD MAPS

Frost's "negotiations" with the Premier stemmed from the poet's complex views on a whole series of political maps that haunted him and played the role of important correlates for his sense of the beautiful and the ugly. Frost occasionally talked of the aesthetic aspects of the geographical outlines of nations or city states (outlines he confusingly called "maps"), always suggesting that they rehearsed the same tensions as poems by asserting realms of intelligibility and meaning against the expanse of meaningless nature. He would call some of the maps "good" and others of them "bad," both epithets having clearly poetic implications. A country with "good" borders is, in this way, like a good poem, a provisory "stay against confusion" balanc-

6 Frost, *Collected Prose*, 192–93.

7 For Frost's insistence that poets should play the same role in Washington as politicians, see *Collected Prose*, 342, 193; cf. Thompson and Winnick, *Later Years*, 272. The poet liked to entertain his audiences by telling them, as if in confidence, that his real purpose was to set up a Secretary of Poetry or of the Arts in the Cabinet. See Frost, *Collected Prose*, 193; Frost, "Playful Talk," 183.

ing its meaning-making with the recognition of its limitations. Good borders, too, mark out a habitable realm guaranteeing safety and internal order but are not airtight, providing the citizens with openings into a wider world and offering them insights into the relative provisionality of their realm. Frost believed that the West, and the US within it, should be marked out as good poems, realms of intelligibility and stable meaning that nevertheless would not preclude awareness of the wider world or the conditionality of that meaning. Inasmuch as West Berlin was the opening onto the Other, it was, for the West, a place of danger and opportunity.

With the island of West Berlin set deep in East German territory, the outlines of the West resonated in the poet's imagination with ancient territorial formations and geography-conditioned cultures and styles of expression. To begin with, Frost saw the city—linked as it was to the West by a motorway and designated air corridors—with the map of ancient Athens in mind. Ancient Athens was a small city-state closely walled in except for one opening onto a narrow corridor between the famous Long Walls leading to the port in Piraeus and the sea. As a result, Athenians were rather confident of their native worldview but not completely isolated or ignorant of the wider world. The opening of Athens to foreign lands through a single port and the narrow, long corridor connecting the city with the docks promoted wider experiences which, even if incongruous with local values and prejudices, had to be regularly accommodated. Occasionally Frost recalled with great fondness the moment he saw the map of Plato's city-state for the first time. He liked to point out that he instinctively sensed in its outlines an important poetic lesson: "I don't know what I could do with it [the map of Athens] . . . but something I know I . . . was in. . . . I remember the look of that map . . . and what I had to do with it with nothing on it except the looks."[8] For Frost, the "look" of Athens illustrated the sensual and epistemological boundaries of a "good" poem.

Significantly, in Frost's mind, the maps of ancient Athens and of the West with its opening in West Berlin contrasted with two other maps—those of less worldly ancient Greek provinces. Athenian borders, for instance, were significantly less closed than the outlines of Laconia (Sparta). Like Athens, Laconia had a port, at Gythium, but the province was sur-

8 Robert Frost's lecture, Athens College, March 23, 1962, Guide to the Collection of Robert Frost Lectures of Edward C. Lathem, 1941–1962, box 2.

rounded not only by walls but also by chains of mountains, the Parnon and the Taygetus. This mountain-hedged plain was thoroughly internalized by Spartans, who were less curious about the outside world than Athenians, possibly in proportion to the degree to which the Laconic mountains outgrew Athenian walls.

Most isolated, however, was Boeotia. The Boeotian plain, large and sprawling, was surrounded by mountains with only a few passes. "Access to the sea was there, to the east or southwest to the Corinthian Gulf," writes one classical historian, but the plain itself was fertile enough to stifle any curiosity whatsoever. "There was not much to tempt a Boeotian to lift his eyes above the surrounding hills and mountains to the sea."[9] Hence the province's notoriety for its inhabitants' widespread dull-wittedness.[10]

Now, if the link between the geography of a people and their open-mindedness seems so natural, so should Frost's tendency to associate the outlines of states with poetry. He saw the map of Athens relevant to his art because the relative openness or closure of political realms, as illustrated on maps, often dictate analogous qualities in the language and poetry practiced within those realms. Each community develops a language that to a great extent reflects the integrity of its territory and the nature of its borders. For instance, the geography of Athens produced the so-called Attic style of oratory, functional and restrained, quite concise, with few redundant descriptions or folly in expression, but with considerable "fresh noticing of details." The recognition of detail and variety in the Attic style was moderated by the sense of wholeness and by the need for generalization and abstraction. Athenians' verbal expression bore witness to their disinterested experience of the wider world through their port.

The functional conciseness and closure characteristic of the Attic style reach a certain extreme in the verbal expression developed in Laconia by Spartans, whose view was consistently enclosed by high mountain ranges. Accordingly, Laconic language appeared almost dumb, a little crude, to the more worldly Athenians. But the truly uncurious style was the Boeotian. If the Boeotian map is ugly by being too closed, Boeotian phrases too were blind to experience, thoughtlessly repeated and caricaturely proverbial. On the continuum of maps and equivalent styles of verbal expression, as we

9 Boardman and Hammond, *Cambridge Ancient History*, 289.
10 For a related discussion, see Davis, "Laconic Response."

move from Athens to Boeotia, the language becomes more schematic, dogmatic, generalized and blind to experience. What Frost was "in" in poetry was striking a golden mean between, on the one hand, conciseness and functionality and, on the other, disinterested curiosity. Frost called it a tension between Platonic "justice," that is, minding one's own business and magnanimity or the largeness of spirit.

The significance of West Berlin in Frost's imagination, of the city planted deep in the territory of the West's ideological enemy, the Soviet bloc, becomes clear when we see its map against the ancient city-states their verbal styles. Other, more contemporary maps also shaped the poet's understanding of the Berlin case. Frost valued highly the map of Ireland (which was on his mind most forcefully during his June 1957 visit[11]). He thought the country's outlines "beautiful" and "poetic" precisely for the same reason that prevented Athenians from becoming too parochial; that is, he admired the patch of Northern Ireland saving Eire from becoming too snug in its Catholicism.[12] The Irish Republic had become autonomous ten years earlier, in 1948, and throughout the 1950s the poet saw, to his satisfaction, various tensions between Eire government and the Unionists.

In the same way, the poet appreciated and thought beautiful the blurry-edged map of the Jewish state within Palestine. Frost often called himself an "old Balfourite," evoking the figure of Arthur James Balfour, whom he called "the fellow who in a way created Israel—and gave it more than it could keep."[13] Of course, Frost is alluding to the Balfour Declaration by the British foreign secretary who set the rules of the British support for the establishment of the Jewish nation. Given that the declaration explicitly said that "nothing shall be done which may prejudice the civil and religious rights of existing non-Jewish communities in Palestine,"[14] Balfour gave Jews more than they "could keep," that is, more than they could take for granted and complacently think of as their own forever. The British statesman gave them a state for the integration of which they would have to work, and he made sure their efforts were to be perennially frustrated by the protected presence of the Arabs. The Israelis were given so much, in terms

11 Meyers, *Robert Frost*, 307

12 Robert Frost Collection 1887–2008, Tape 140. Quinn, "Frost and Ireland."

13 "Old Poet," 101.

14 "Balfour Declaration," *Encyclopedia Britannica* 2008, Encyclopedia Britannica Online, 15 Nov. 2008, http://search.eb.com/eb/article-9011963.

of protecting the freedom of all the people involved, including the Palestinians, that their home would perennially have to be negotiated and never taken for granted.

Balfour founded Israel on the recognition of the full rights of all the people living in Palestine, something that potentially could bring the undoing of the Jewish nation. In 1960 Frost saw the Israelis engaged in an effort to accommodate the Palestinian minority. "But Israel has taken care of waifs—of the body and of the intellect," he wrote, probably referring to the new country's social programs extended to the Arab minority as well.[15] The poet's praise for Balfour's gift was limitless: the statesman even gave them opportunity to become something more than a stable Jewish nation. He made them look like a good poem—a nation dynamically asserting its beliefs and recognizing its limits.[16] He expected the Israelis would want to repeat the certainties of their home culture but those certainties would now have to be repeatedly confronted with, and would have to allow for, the Arab presence. Frost sensed in such language a source for the poetry of the highest order.

The "capitalist island" of West Berlin evoked all of the above maps of difficult beauty. The Western "outpost of freedom" was something of the port Piraeus opening the Athenian worldview to everything incongruous with the Athenian creed. Checkpoint Charlie, where the West exposed itself to communism, brought to mind Ireland's susceptibility to Protestant loyalism along the borders of Ulster; it constituted the West's soft spot like Israel's underbelly, dangerously vulnerable and stretching today along the borderlines of the Gaza Strip and the West Bank. Nothing less than this open-

15 "Old Poet," 101. For a more critical view of Israel's social policies toward the Palestinian minority after the war, see Lustick, *Arabs in the Jewish State.*

16 Frost was angered that the walls between Israel and the Palestinian territories were becoming impenetrable and unmovable: "Stones and stones, and walls and walls, and barbed wire, wire, wire. The shame of it! That barbed wire was invented in America! Wherever I look I see that fence!" See "Old Poet," 98; cf. Smythe, *Robert Frost Speaking*, 148. In his view, Israel would err if they sought too great a security to the point of effectively insulating themselves from all outside world: "Israel is a going concern—something the world must recognize. But one Hebrew told me, 'We've never had security since the age of Solomon.' I told him, 'You're doing fine without it!'" See "Old Poet," 106. He believed that like a good poem, the Jewish state should be engaged in maintaining its worldview against encroaching experience, but should also keep acknowledging alterity by allowing that of the Palestinians.

ness and the related openness of the verbal expression of Westerners was at stake in the Gagra negotiations with unsuspecting Khrushchev.

But through West Berlin, the West also courted, dangerously, another extreme, a version of ugliness that Frost feared more than a nation's or a poem's closure. The capitalist territory a hundred miles inside the body of the communist bloc threatened to open the West to communism with the result that the West might be infected beyond healing. The fear was that the city might take in too much of the variety of life and as a result become disoriented. Frost sometimes suggests that, to avoid such shapelessness, he is even ready to accept Laconic and Boeotian styles and poems—poems that are relatively narrow-minded and analogous to a map with no ports. Certainly inferior to the Attic realm, Laconia and Boeotia are the lesser evil to a shapelessness to be avoided at all costs. Tracing the line of the growing openness of a nation from the ancient archetypes of Boeotia, through Laconia and Athens, Frost's readers arrive at the most dangerous mindset at the other end of the continuum—too great alertness to what he liked to call "too much," too full recognition of all life without holding to one's own narrower but viable beliefs. The open and shapeless realm found expression in a style called "Asiatic," which was scorned by Horace, Cicero and Quintilian, and which Frost himself found abhorrent.[17]

Frost feared that West Berlin would be a place where "too much" would pry the West open. The city could become the origin of his culture's ugly and excessive openness. In the long run the opening at Berlin could make America and the West culturally incoherent:

> There is nothing like a good map. And the evidence of that is that we've got a good map—from the Atlantic to the Pacific—laid out neat, however we got it, by hook or by crook, I don't say; it's a great map. And Berlin is the worst map the world ever saw. See, bad maps make bad troubles. Maps do it—that's all—maps do it.[18]

By the same token, the outlines of the US had been "good" and beautiful until America acquired military bases in the Pacific, that is to say, as long

17 Cicero, *Ideal Orator*, 23–32; Quintilian, Institute XII 10.12–14; Frost, "Playful Talk," 187.

18 Cook, *Living Voice*, 194.

as the nation had an integrated shape with clear outlines.[19] By the 1950s the poet became worried by the frayed edges and fragments of America's western border. In his view, the US projecting its power on the Pacific gaped wide open like Pound's cantos. In 1960, Frost wrote: "It took me a long, long time to get over the idea that the Pacific Ocean was going to be more important in our history than the Atlantic. If I ever got over it."[20] Characteristically, the fragmentation of America's Western border and the country's expansion into a flurry of little islands all over the Pacific—processes which took place during his lifetime—were traumatic for Frost who believed that a neatly-bordered country is the requisite condition for a healthy self. Frost feared similar formlessness on the West's eastern border.

For all its promise, West Berlin posed a serious threat to the West by making it vulnerable. It was, Frost even said once, "a big mistake, like the Danzig Corridor. Here we are with Communist territory all around us. That should never have been. That is why Khrushchev can rant and threaten us."[21] In the postwar territorial settlement, the poet sensed the ghost of the map of the pre-World War II Germany and of East Prussia separated from the main body by the Danzig corridor. To Frost, both arrangements looked like the self that shows itself exposed in a poem consisting of incoherent fragments, a worldview capitulating to experience, and giving in to incongruous details. The poet seems to have felt confirmed in his views on the nature of all human-made forms, whether nations, poems or artifacts. Frost apparently saw the German efforts to re-incorporate East Prussia and become one people—territorially coherent and drawing strength from that coherence over the heads of the Polish majority in the Western Prussia—as analogous to writing poetry. More generally, the desire to connect East Prussia with the Reich illustrated any epistemological effort to round off one's realm and make it snug, immune to too much of experience in excess of an integrated worldview. According to Frost's analogy, the Polish Corri-

19 The poet absorbed the view of American democracy as largely territorial from his father. William Prescott Frost, Jr. was convinced that the US had become too vast for it to remain one nation. He believed that America would ultimately split up into six or seven regional independent nations. Frost recalled that when he was a boy, his father once spread out a map of North America and drew out the approximate boundaries of his hypothetical future nations. See also Stanlis, *Frost as a Philosopher*, 100, 230, 268, 430, 433.

20 Frost, *Collected Prose*, 220.

21 Smythe, *Robert Frost Speaks*, 147.

dor constituted the "prose" or the "dirt" intrusion, and was designed to prevent the German mind from becoming perfectly circular and self-referential—that is, overly poetic. In the aftermath of the war, the geographical outlines of the capitalist West and the communist East again spurred Frost to aesthetic distinctions. Two ideologically coherent collective bodies became locked territorially and torn between the conflicting desires of, on the one hand, purging themselves of the "other" body and, on the other, uniting with the antagonist (what Frost was tempted to call "love"). If the war started with the Danzig Corridor, it ended with the cyst of West Berlin. Europeans made a historical loop and returned to a map that was again, arguably, ugly. In short, Frost came to the negotiating table with this complex vision of West Berlin as a point of openness for both ideological bodies. He saw the city's uncertain status as both an opportunity and a danger for the West and the East, the two blocs precipitously balanced between beauty and ugliness. West Berlin offered an occasion for both societies to confront each other and negotiate their different spheres in a way that, to Frost's mind if not to Khrushchev's, seemed most poetic. Intuitively and imaginatively, he sought to reenact the ambivalence of West Berlin through a series of gestures that may be construed as the rehearsals of the West's expansive aggression and its vulnerability.

FROST AS TOM WHIPPLE

The only surviving photograph of this historical visit on September 7, 1962 shows Frost, strangely, seated on his bed and receiving Khrushchev. It is a peculiar picture showing a remarkable reversal of roles and probably a glaring violation of the Kremlin's diplomatic etiquette; the poet, instead of being given an audience with the leader of the Soviet Union, is granting one to the Premier. How could that have happened? When the time came to go see Khrushchev, Frost announced that he did not feel well. When everybody thought the meeting would never materialize, Khrushchev, informed of the poet's ailment, ignored the dignities of his office and visited him in his hotel. The photograph shows Frost in his pajamas on his sickbed receiv-

Figure 2: Frost with Nikita Khrushchev, Gagra, Abkhazia, September 7, 1962

Robert Frost Collection, 1866–1996, Frost MS-1178 [29]: 31. Rauner Library, Dartmouth College, Hanover. Used with the permission of the Estate of Robert Lee Frost. Courtesy of Dartmouth College Library.

ing the statesman. "I sat up on the edge of the bed and went at it," the poet later told the reporters (fig. 2).[22]

To suggest that he was faking illness would be to risk charges of cheap sensationalism and—most importantly—to ignore the man's growing frailty. After all, the visit took place three months before Frost was hospitalized and less than five months before he died. I would rather see the poet's illness as the catalyst for a turn of events that perfectly capped off Frost's scheme, which consisted of making the Premier meet—against all local rules—"an ordinary American citizen."

In the months surrounding the visit, Frost often observed that in Russia the more democratized relations of the communist state coexisted with the remnants of her monarchical past. Leningrad, for instance, struck him as "still a royal city" with a "lingering royalism" remarkably different from

22 "Frost Gives Picture of Soviet Premier As Big and Unafraid," *New York Times*, September 9, 1962.

the atmosphere of Moscow, which was more of "a people's city."[23] He felt the Soviet Premier's kingly air and was awed by the man's power of nothing less than royal magnitude. "We won't call them [Soviet leaders] kings any more," he chuckled at a press conference after his return home to the US, but suggested that, after cameras and microphones were turned off, that he certainly would call them such.[24] At other conferences he was less discreet: he called Khrushchev "a mighty monarch,"[25] and teased everybody that he was ready to call the Soviet Union "democracy . . . by courtesy."[26] To the poet's mind, making Khrushchev meet an "ordinary American citizen" like himself was a momentous move, revolutionizing ancient power relations in Russia that were largely untouched by the Bolshevik revolution and were now enjoyed by the Communist elites. The huge recognition the Premier granted the poet by visiting him, sick, in his hotel room—that is, by visiting "somebody from the street," as Frost liked to say of himself in this context—only heightened the meeting's significance as Kremlin's capitulation to American-style egalitarianism.

Such interpretation is corroborated by several public talks he gave at the time. Back then, Frost was drawn to—if not obsessed by—a true story of Tom Whipple he read in a book for children by Walter D. Edmonds, a writer of historical novels and his friend.[27] Tom Whipple was a "Yankee lad" who in 1837 sailed to Russia, where he insisted on meeting the Czar, Nicholas II, because at home he believed he could, if he wanted to, meet President Andrew Jackson. The boy persisted, despite being reminded by many

23 "Muscovites Hear Reading by Frost; The Topic: A Wall," *New York Times*, September 6, 1962. See also "U.S. Poet Twits Russians with 'Why a Wall?'" *Chicago Tribune*, September 1, 1962, n.p. Robert Frost Collection 1887–2008, 12:11.

24 "Muscovites Hear Reading by Frost."

25 Max Lerner, "Frost Flavor," *New York Post*, September 11, 1962.

26 "Poet Frost Finds Nikita Not Afraid of a Fight," *Chicago-Sun-Times*, September 9, 1962, 4 (Robert Frost Collection 1887–2008, 12:11).

27 In the days of America's wartime alliance with Russia, the story was widely promoted. It was first recorded by Maria Child and retold by several writers. Frost knew it from Walter D. Edmonds's *Tom Whipple*. For Frost's different renditions of the story preceding his visit to the USSR, see, to name only a few, his reading at Yale, New Haven, May 19, 1961, Tape 140, Subseries E: Recordings (Tapes), Robert Frost Collection, 1887–2008; lecture, Dartmouth College, May 23, 1961 (14–15) and reading of April 11, 1961 at American Academy of Arts and Letters (14), both from Guide to the Collection of Robert Frost Lectures of Edward C. Lathem, 1941–1962, box 2.

Russians that their Czar was obviously not accessible to his subjects or any foreigners of the same lowly stature: "You know, Whipple, the Emperor's a pretty hard man to get to see." In the story many people try to explain to the boy the difference between an empire and a democratic country:

> Tom thought it over, but he shook his head. He said he couldn't see it that way. He could see it might apply to a Russian farmer, in a manner of speaking; but he was a United States citizen. Martin Van Buren, now, he could see the Emperor, couldn't he? Mr. Dallas [the American diplomatic minister] nodded his head; that was true. Then why couldn't Tom Whipple?[28]

By making Khrushchev take time to meet an average American like himself, Frost created a precedent incongruous with Russian political culture; he had the Soviet leader follow an American principle. Afterwards, at home, he told journalists he did not know whether he had the right to expect to influence Khrushchev's decision on the Berlin wall but that he was satisfied by "[coming] off the street as a tramp poet and [making] to the mighty monarch . . . one little request."[29] The nature of the request aside, Frost reenacted the story of Tom Whipple showing that "a boy in America was in those days . . . equal to Czar," and the Czar for a while, out of fancy or curiosity, played by those foreign and more crucially anti-monarchical rules. Only a year before he himself received a royal treatment from Khrushchev, Frost told his students that the Czar hosted the boy as if he was dealing with the head of the state. The Emperor called "a cavalcade of horses and sent him [Tom Whipple] up to see Moscow."[30]

Not only did Frost use the meeting on West Berlin to "invade" Russia with American egalitarianism, but also the Soviet "Czar" showed unusual magnanimity and careless openness to an alien political tradition. The poet never tired of repeating Walter Edmonds's story before and after his visit to the Soviet Union, how the Emperor accepted with no reservations the boy's gift, an acorn he picked up in Mount Vernon, where George Washington lived and died. "This nut's right off one of his [Washington's] personal

28 Edmonds, *Tom Whipple*, 44.

29 Seymour Topping, "Frost Gives Picture of Soviet Premier as Big and Unafraid," *New York Times*, September 8, 1962.

30 Robert Frost's lecture, Dartmouth College, May 23, 1961, 15, Guide to the Collection of Robert Frost Lectures of Edward C. Lathem, 1941–1962, box 2.

trees," Tom told Nicholas II. "I thought you'd appreciate it, being as it comes from the home of the greatest man of the U. S. A., greater even than Old Hickory."[31] As the story goes, the monarch certainly appreciated the gesture and planted the acorn in his garden. Frost was delighted that Khrushchev demonstrated a similar "compassion," "magnanimity," or "the largeness of soul" that allowed Frost to plant in the Soviet Union an American democratic principle. The poet sowed seeds of American-style egalitarianism by establishing the precedent that the First Secretary of the Communist Party was accessible to anyone.

HORSE-TRADING WITH KHRUSHCHEV

But the Gagra summit had other important themes which resonated with the collective desires invested in the divided German capital—themes which, in Frost's view, were also at work in poetic composition. One of the most difficult to explain is Frost's proposal that Khrushchev recklessly swap territories with the United States the way people used to trade horses in the olden days to try their luck and get a thrill out of life.

After the poet had returned to Moscow, he told journalists gathered in the hotel lobby that his conversation with Khrushchev reenacted the old story of a tramp poet asking the monarch magnanimously to promise he would do something for him before knowing first what it will be. He suggested to the Soviet Premier that they accept each other's proposal for the swapping of territories without knowing beforehand the terms of the deal. "I asked him," the poet announced, "if there was something of ours that he wants, and something of his that we wanted, then we could swap."[32] Though afterwards Frost sometimes denied he got that far,[33] the two first-

31 Edmonds, *Tom Whipple*, 54.

32 Topping, "Robert Frost Finds Khrushchev," 1; cf. "Poet Frost Calls Host Khrushchev 'a Ruffian, Not Afraid of a Fight,'" *Los Angeles Times*, September 9, 1962, F1. In a letter to Lawrance Thompson, Frost made plans for the visit: "I'd like a chance to ask the great Kruschev [sic] to grant me one request and then ask him a hard one." See Thompson and Winnick, *Later Years*, 310. On another occasion, he said he was going to discuss with Khrushchev "cultural exchanges": "Oughta get together and swap a little." Mertins, *Life and Talks-Walking*, 417.

33 Thompson and Winnick, *Later Years*, 322.

hand witnesses of the meeting, F. D. Reeve and Frederick Adams, confirm Frost's original story, adding that the poet specifically used the term "horse-swapping" for it.[34] Thompson and Winnick's biography of the writer is precise, then, to almost the word when it states that Frost "propose[d] a kind of horse-trade with the United States. . . . He was sure the United States would accept the terms of any proposal he made."[35]

Needless to say, anything resembling "horse-swapping" has been unheard of in diplomacy, because the term signifies blind and unpremeditated exchange. And yet it is precisely what Frost seems to have contemplated and proposed in Gagra. He meant something similar to the "coat swapping" his idol James Guild, an itinerant artist of early America, describes in his journal:

> While on my road I saw an [sic] young man on a head and my coat was almost wore out. I hollows out to him, say friend how will you swap coats, I want to trad [sic] a little today? Take off your coat and through it to me and Ill through you mine before wee see them. This done, I caught the coat and through him the dollar and says good by sir. I made 3 or 4 dollars in this bargain.[36]

An avid reader of American local-color humorists, Frost may also have had in mind a very specific story by Augustus Baldwin Longstreet "The Horse-Swap," in which two men engage in expert horse trading eventually to walk away from the deal feeling outsmarted by each other, for both their newly-swapped horses had major flaws artfully hidden.

While at first sight, Frost's offer seems too goofy to deserve serious consideration, upon closer analysis the proposal should at least be recognized as dovetailing with several of Frost's central concerns, such as the danger of excessive appetite or the counterproductive nature of gift giving. Paradoxically, with those concerns in mind, the most generous offer on Frost's part seems to reflect cunning Cold War gaming. By agreeing beforehand to grant Khrushchev whatever the Premier asked for, the poet fantasized he might see his old beliefs confirmed—that avariciousness is deadly and that giving is at bottom taking away. He indulged in the fancy that

34 Cf. Reeve, *Robert Frost in Russia*, 124; Adams, *To Russia with Frost*, 38.

35 Ibid., 321

36 Guild, "James Guild," 260. For Frost's interest in Guild, see Nash, "Poet and the Pirate," 320–21.

Khrushchev might be too greedy for territorial gain and if the Premier had the USSR take too large a mouthful, the communist bloc might choke on it.

For what it is worth, the poet probably absorbed the popular imaging of Khrushchev at the time as embodying, with his breadth and girth, the territorial voraciousness of the Soviet Union. Cartoons of the late 1950s and early 1960s typically evoked the Premier's appetites as a metaphor for the USSR's aggressive expansionism. One published in August 1961, shows Khrushchev closing in on the entire globe and lying that his tough position on Berlin was a symptom of this craving, "Es geht ja gar nicht um Berlin" (fig. 3). Still another, entitled "Another Toothache for Khrushchev," shows West Berlin as Khrushchev's one bite too far.[37] Given this unreasonably generous offer—that the US would yield to the Soviets whatever they ask for—Russia may have suicidally overextended herself. She may have ended up like Rome in Frost's favorite account by Edward Gibbon; or like the poet's dog Winnie, which "got her face and mouth full of porcupine quills and died under the choloroform [the Frosts] had to give her for the really terrible operation of getting them out."[38]

In other words, offering a horse-swap was Frost's way of checking how much of a good statesman, perhaps even a poet, Khrushchev was. The poet wondered whether the Premier would demonstrate wisdom when taking in new territory; whether he would adopt the kind of attitude poets—at least the best of them, he reasoned—show when they provisorily domesticate nature through their meaning-making forms. Frost wanted to see if the Soviet leader was as wise as poets when showing care not to take in too much of life and nature, in fear that their art will capitulate to such pressure. Frost seems to have hoped that Khrushchev intuitively understood that shaping a nation was very similar to writing poetry, and if one wanted to be good at it, one had to be guided by caution. Poetry, Frost said, was "caution with which to be brave."[39]

37 John Collins, "Another Toothache for Khrushchev," McCord Museum of Canadian History, online exhibition *Where to Draw the Line: Editorial Cartoons in Quebec, 1950–2000*, http://www.musee-mccord.qc.ca/en/collection/artifacts/M965.199.5042/.

38 Gibbon ranked fourth on Frost's 1958 list of his most favorite books. Frost, *Collected Prose*, 199. For the poet's story of his dog, see his *Selected Letters*, 398.

39 Frost, *Notebooks*, 49.

Figure 3: Fritz Behrendt, "Es geht ja gar nicht um Berlin!" [This has nothing to do with Berlin]

August 1961 „Es geht ja gar nicht um Berlin!"

Reprinted from *Trotzalledem, Eine Auswahl von 100 politischen Karikaturen* (Rotterdam: Nijgh & van Ditmar, [s.d.]). Used with the permission of Renate Behrendt.

In other words, in Frost's view, West Berlin, South Korea, and South Vietnam were all for the taking. The best statesmen, however, should think twice before reaching for any of these territories, because any such territorial gain would be hard to integrate into a political and cultural entity that would survive and last. Paradoxically, to Frost's mind, a truly aggressive move in these negotiations—horse-swapping-style—would be less a rapacious demand for more territory and more a cold-headed resolve to refrain from expansion and, rather, to induce the other party to take in more land. By now it should be clear that Frost's proposal was less wacky than it seems at first sight. In fact, the proposed blind swapping of territories along the Cold War front could become, if undertaken by two equally savvy politicians, a truly nuanced contest of restraint. Wary of simple expansion, both parties would rather seek to make their maps more integrated, and therefore aesthetically shapelier—if not as closed as Boeotia.

What one needs for horse swapping then is "horse sense." In one notebook entry Frost explains that "horse sense" is not any special cunning or shrewdness: "Horses have no special sense more than a cow or chicken. Horse sense means the sense a man has in trading and handling horses."[40] Rather, it is a practical sense or good judgment that will save a farmer when he becomes "over elated" at a deceptively good opportunity. It is an instinct that will prevent him from adopting, too readily, a too large animal that, in the long run, may become nothing but a liability. What seems a great gain at first may turn out impossible to accommodate, or to integrate into the farm's workings or household economy. In another notebook the poet mentions, for instance, a farmer who "opened his mouth a hundred dollars too soon on a lot of cows."[41] The man bought a herd of cows too cheaply and before he knew, his assets, depleted by the cost of fodder and vet bills, were in a shambles. Other notebook entries on horse trade also show "horse sense"; they sound like warnings against buying a horse that may become a white elephant: "Never buy a critter that you cant [*sic*] easily turn."[42] Of course, one major horse that Frost, this instinctive classicist, had in mind was the most gigantic horse in all history, the Trojan horse. The Trojans have come down in history as too eager to allow within their walls a horse's likeness which they thought was a gift but which turned out to be a catastrophic liability. In Frost's notebooks one finds scattered expressions of caution mindful of the Trojans' fatal mistake: "You mean to say he wants two hundred dollars for that old warhorse?"[43]

To Frost's mind, Germany—as well as all of postwar Europe—posed a danger to both the United States and the Soviet Union, each of which would be well-advised to keep the Old World outside their gates. For a nation to outgrow what they are capable of at their historical time may be as dangerous as "engorging a donkey." It may cause the "dilation" of one's bodily structures: "Witness the many who in the attempt have suffered a dilation from which the tissues and the muscles of the mind have never been able to

40 Ibid., 485.
41 Ibid., 17.
42 Ibid., 17.
43 Ibid., 639.

recover natural shape. . . . And they gape in agony."[44] Qualifications for poetry writing as well as statesmanship consist—to paraphrase one of Frost's notebook entries—of being "fastidious" at the mouth, if quite capacious at the innards.[45]

Frost identified this special quality, which he looked for in Khrushchev, in certain animals that he deemed particularly beautiful, models for both poems and nations. When offering his poet friend Robert Francis advice regarding the desirable attitude toward experience, the old poet counseled the "moderate attachment" of hummingbirds. "You've got to learn to hover," he told Francis. The self's ideal relation to experience—and that applies to all the self's manifestations, including nations and poems—is that of a hummingbird sipping nectar from a flower through a hair-thin tube-like beak. The bird incorporates outside matter in an uninterrupted but carefully regulated flow, is satisfied with one flower at a time for a long time, and knows better than to try to drink rapaciously from all flowers in the area. Frost's figure of the hummingbird strongly resembles the map of Athens and the city's controlled and limited involvement with the wider world through the corridor, which on a map literally looked like a bird's beak. Frost looked for the same analogies in the West's moderate openness to communism through West Berlin. He also understood a hummingbird's mode of life to be the very opposite of that represented by the Soviet Union and the US at their most voracious. In "A Prayer to Spring" he writes of hummingbirds as shapes of unparalleled beauty:

> And make us happy in the darting bird
> That suddenly above the bees is heard,
> The meteor that thrusts in with needle bill,
> And off a blossom in mid air stands still.[46]

Puritanly built and, arguably, self-disciplined, satisfied with a modest intake of nectar, the bird serves as a model for an ideal poem as well as an ideal state. Whether the West with West Berlin would become such an ideal—not too widely open, not too tightly closed—remained to be seen.

44 Frost, *Collected Prose*, 115.
45 Frost, *Notebooks*, 525.
46 Frost, *Collected Poems*, 21.

MAGNANIMITY AND THE LIMITS OF LOYALTY

The two sentiments discussed—the somewhat aggressive democratization of the USSR, Tom-Whipple style, and the testing of Khrushchev's art of cautious statesmanship—were complicated by one more element directly opposite in its nature. It was Frost's full and reckless responsiveness to the host country, his "magnanimity" as great as that evinced by Khrushchev when the politician descended from the pedestal of Soviet Premiership to visit the poet in his hotel room. This sentiment requires a very cautious wording not to misrepresent or too simplistically put into question Frost's obvious patriotism.

Difficult to reconcile with Frost's other sentiments, this radical openness to the Soviet point of view was much in keeping with the poet's lifelong appreciation of "magnanimity," which, he believed, had to balance with Socratic "justice" or "minding one's own business." He insisted that people should place certain limits on their loyalty to their worlds—whether their family, their region or their country—and should be careful not to miss the moment when "an attachment should be left for an attraction." This alertness to whatever his trip to Russia might bring—he said he had the disloyalty of "a mathematician or a landscape gardener"[47]—is manifest in Frost's frequent insistence that he did not go there merely to represent America's interests. He liked to think of his visit—though officially sponsored by the State Department and fully blessed by President John F. Kennedy—as off-limits and adventurous, if not semilegal. "I wasn't sent by the Government I was invited there[.] I wasn't sent by the Government to Russia[;] I wasn't an emissary at all I was invited and it was approved of accepted but I was asked by Russia."[48] Inasmuch as he was there at the invitation of the USSR, he felt he had been given license to be as recklessly receptive to Communism's alterity as poets must be to experience if they want to fashion a good poem.

Indeed, he was charmed by the USSR in general, by most of the Russians he met, and by Nikita Khrushchev in particular. The poet's alertness to his Russian experience found its culmination in the conversation with

47 Frost, *Selected Letters*, 294.

48 Robert Frost's lecture, Ford Hall Forum, December 2, 1962, Guide to the Collection of Robert Frost Lectures of Edward C. Lathem, 1941–1962, box 2.

Khrushchev and the famous quipping about Kennedy's liberalism, which was often figured as bodily softness and a lack of spunk. The poet reportedly chuckled at the Premier's joke about the West being very much like Tolstoy, who confessed to Gorky that he was "too old and too weak and too infirm to do it but still having the desire." Khrushchev's idea, of course, was more general about the West's passivity as regards its old defunct economic system, but it was also in its essence a jab at President Kennedy's ineffectiveness as the Executive and his unmanliness. Though eventually the poet politely deflected the joke by allowing "that [tardiness] might be true of the two of them [Khrushchev and Frost] but that the United States was too young to worry about that yet," he also—disastrously for his relationship with the President—brought the joke home. As soon as he got off the plane in New York City on September 9, he told journalists that Khrushchev felt the US was "too liberal to fight." The poet could not have said this at a worse moment; he struck a blow precisely in the months when Kennedy was finding it difficult to maintain the image of a politician with a manly resolution.[49] As is widely known today, the President felt this was an unforgivable indiscretion on Frost's part, amounting to a final breach of trust between them, and he never forgave the statement.[50]

That day, in Gagra, Frost left other traces of his "magnanimity" toward Russia that made him compromise his loyalty to his home country. For instance, he gave Khrushchev a copy of his poetry collection *In the Clearing* (1962) inscribed "To Premier Khrushchev / from his rival in friendship / Robert Frost / Gagra / Sept 7, 1962." [51] To be sure, *In the Clearing* had arrived fresh off the press, and it was natural for Frost to offer it as a souvenir. However, given the volume's content and the special occasion, one wonders about the gift's appropriateness. With poems such as "Our Doom to Bloom," "A-Wishing Well," and "America Is Hard to See," the volume expresses enough of weary resentment toward the US—enough of the temptation to annul or put behind the whole legacy of the West, which

49 For more on this discourse about Kennedy lacking manly resolve, especially in his confrontations with Khrushchev, see, for instance, Dallek's account, in *JFK*, of the mood in the aftermath of the Vienna summit in the summer of 1961, and then a year later when he was to respond to the Soviet buildup in Cuba, 415–17, 535–40.

50 Monteiro, "Liberal Imagination," 153.

51 Adams, *To Russia with Frost*, 17–18.

Frost repeatedly describes as a vapid and barren stretch of wasteland—to make the book seem a very injudicious gift to this leader of the West's Cold War belligerent. Finally, the telegraph Frost sent, before flying back home, to his secretary and lover Kathleen Morrison, also suggests that he felt the entire visit involved a serious transgression on his part: "BACK FROM CRIMEA, ALL CRIMES ACCOMPLISHED."[52]

While it is unclear how far Frost went in Gagra—actually four hundred kilometers east of Crimea—in suspending or complicating his allegiance to the US and even less clear how far he imagined he did, in an unpublished 1948 draft of "Speaking of Loyalty," he went far enough to shock many of his contemporaries given the opportunity:

> There is such a thing as having to break with an attachment and go with an attraction. I may be so attracted to Russian that I may want to go there and live for a while I may want to live there for life. I may want to help the Russian [illegible] come here in America even as it is in Russia.[53]

The passage is remarkable for its apparent disloyalty to his home country and to his present self, and it shows the poet awakened to the potentialities of the future. The text unfolds toward a greater embrace of the Russian cause, much like a poem dynamically evolving, opening up to experience and ever disloyal to its initial or current premises. Though not a poem by any standards, the passage shows Frost occasionally inclined to lose his bearings on the page and yield to unruly sentiments as they make themselves felt in writing. This self-abandonment to a given situation is in his view an important element, if necessarily balanced by an opposing self-

52 Thompson, *Later Years*, 323.

53 Frost, *Notebooks*, 323. After the Bolshevik Revolution, he entertained the notion that the Communist Russia might turn out to be holding a key to humanity's future. Frost's thinking about loyalty is far too complicated to discuss in this essay, but back in 1917 it seemed that his loyalty to humanity as such could override his loyalty to his home country. As early as August 15, 1917, he wrote to Nathan Haskell Dole (1852–1935), asking him for lessons in "socialistic" Russian so that he would know how to address "porters, waiters, chambermaids, bootblacks, and barbers": "So I can go ahead and engage passage for Russia (I advise myself to go the long way round by the Pacific Ocean and Siberia, would you?)". His teasing remark that Communism is further west and that Americans may be *manifestly destined* to get there is revealing. See Frost's letter, Aug. 15, 1917, box 22, Thompson-Frost Collection.

possession, of not only poetic composition but also both an individual and collective approach to political and historical change.

To sum up, embodying as he did various desires of the containment myth—such as isolation, seclusion, and conquest by superior reasonableness—Frost was used for propaganda purposes by the Kennedy administration and by the wider cultural entourage of the Camelot court. And yet the poet had his own vision of his role in the Cold War, one that dramatically manifested itself during his visit to the Soviet Union. He approached the meeting with Khrushchev and the problem of West Berlin in the way artists write poems by marking out, afresh, an experiential and intellectual territory. Like writers "colonizing" their surrounding with their forms, he tried to conquer the Soviet Union by planting a truly egalitarian principle in the heart of Russia. In addition, however, Frost yielded to the USSR and to Khrushchev and came close to betraying his people (or was radically loyal to what he thought was his people's mission), very much in the way poets betray their worldviews when they become "attracted" to the possibilities appearing on the page.

More generally, the Frost-Khrushchev summit shows that West Berlin was a site of emotional investments for many people on both sides of the ideological divide. The barrier running across the German city, uncrossable for societies on both sides, reenacted the drama of a self, asserting itself against the universe but unable to become entirely snug in its world. Such a self is haunted by the Other, stirred to the mixed desires of conquest and submission. To Frost's mind, the relative openness of both blocs in Berlin could potentially reflect the ideal shape of a poem, a healthy self, and finally a lasting and enduring state. For the sake of the future, the poet felt, all three model entities should not only hold to their beliefs but also respond to and learn from fresh experience.

BIBLIOGRAPHY

Adams, Frederick B., Jr. *To Russia with Frost.* Boston: Club of Odd Volumes, 1963.

Axelrod, Steven. "Frost and the Cold War." Conference paper, 21st Annual Conference of American Literature Association, San Francisco, May 29, 2010.

Boardman, John, and N. G. L. Hammond. *Cambridge Ancient History*. Vol. 3. *The Expansion of the Greek World, Eighth to Sixth Centuries B.C.* Cambridge: Cambridge University Press, 1982.

Cicero. *On the Ideal Orator* (*De Oratore*). New York: Oxford University Press, 2001.

Cook, Reginald Lansing. *Robert Frost: A Living Voice.* Amherst: University of Massachusetts Press, 1974.

Davis, Matthew. "The Laconic Response: Spartan and Athenian Mindsets in Robert Frost's 'Mending Wall.'" *Literary Imagination* 7, no. 3 (2005): 289–305.

Edmonds, Walter D. *Tom Whipple.* Illustrated by Paul Lantz. New York: Dodd, Mead, 1944.

Frost, Robert. *Collected Poems, Prose, and Plays.* Edited by Richard Poirier and Mark Richardson. New York: Library of America, 1995.

———. *Collected Prose.* Edited by Mark Richardson. Cambridge, MA: Harvard University Press, 2007.

———. *Notebooks.* Edited by Robert Faggen. Cambridge, MA: Harvard University Press, 2009.

———. "Playful Talk." *American Academy of Arts and Letters and the National Institute of Arts and Letters: Proceedings* 12 (1962): 180–89.

———. *Selected Letters.* Edited by Lawrance Thompson. New York: Holt, Rinehart, and Winston, 1964.

Guide to the Collection of Robert Frost Lectures of Edward C. Lathem, 1941–1962. Manuscript MS–1012. Rauner Library. Dartmouth College, Hanover.

Guild, James. "James Guild, from Tunbridge, Vermont, to London, England: The Journal of James Guild, Peddler, Tinker, Schoolmaster, Portrait Painter from 1818 to 1824." Edited by Arthur Wallace Peach. *Proceedings of the Vermont Historical Society* 5 (September 1937): 249–314.

Lustick, Ian. *Arabs in the Jewish State: Israel's Control of a National Minority.* Modern Middle East Series. Austin: University of Texas Press, 1980.

Mertins, Louis. *Robert Frost: Life and Talks-Walking.* Norman: University of Oklahoma Press, 1965.

Meyers, Jeffrey. *Robert Frost: A Biography.* Boston: Houghton Mifflin, 1996.

Monteiro, George. "Robert Frost's Liberal Imagination." In *Roads Not Taken: Rereading Robert Frost*, edited by Earl J. Wilcox and Jonathan N. Barron, 153–75. Columbia: University of Missouri Press, 2000.

Nash, Ray. "The Poet and the Pirate." *New Colophon* 2, no. 8 (February 1950): 311–21.

"Old Poet in a New Land." *Coronet* 50 (September 1961): 97–111.

Quinn, Gerard. "Robert Frost and Ireland." *Recorder* 13, no. 1 (Spring 2000): 136–37.

Reeve, F. D. *Robert Frost in Russia.* Brookline, MA: Zephyr Press, 2001. First published 1964 by Atlantic-Little, Brown.

Robert Frost Collection, 1866–1996. Frost MS-1178. Rauner Library, Dartmouth College, Hanover.

Robert Frost Collection, 1887–2008. Amherst College Archives and Special Collections. Amherst College.

Smith, Andrew F. *Rescuing the World: The Life and Times of Leo Cherne.* Albany: State University of New York Press, 2002.

Smythe, Daniel. *Robert Frost Speaks.* New York: Twayne, 1964.

Stanlis, Peter J. *Robert Frost: The Poet as Philosopher.* Wilmington, DE: ISI Books, 2007.

Thompson-Frost Collection, no. 10044-a. University of Virginia, Charlottesville.

Thompson, Lawrance, and R. H. Winnick. *Robert Frost: The Later Years.* New York: Holt, Rinehart and Winston, 1976.

A Tale of Three Bridges

Pont Saint-Michel, Paris, 1961; Trefechan Bridge, Aberystwyth, Wales, 1963; Edmund Pettus Bridge, Selma, Alabama, 1965

SHARON MONTEITH

The mobilization of different publics to protest national or local laws, policies, and events is a key feature of democratic life, and it was especially so in the 1960s. This essay examines three demonstrations of civil disobedience that took place in the first half of the decade. Each group campaigned nonviolently for a different cause but all demanded recognition of an ethnic minority group's rights whether in France, Wales, or the US South. It explores the extent to which these protests have become a focus of public commemoration and considers the role of politicians and the media in the act of remembrance, with a demonstration's meaning enhanced in one case, and marginalized or suppressed in the others. The bridge acts as an arc of history and cultural memory, drawing the separate episodes together in a shared perception of social justice. An overworked metaphor, it will hopefully be enlivened in this transnational and transatlantic context through the axiom that memory activist and filmmaker Medhi Lallaoui expressed as the need for all citizens to be "on equal memorial terms with others."[1] This is

1 With Agnès Denis, Lallaoui made a film about the Paris protest, *Le silence du fleuve*: *17 octobre 1961* (1991), and is quoted in House and McMaster (298). House and McMaster's study is a thorough and careful account that recognizes

the kind of ethical turn that would unite the moral with the memorial in public discourse. But this discussion is mindful of the improbability of such unity when ethnic membership and territorial definitions of national remembrance are at stake and community memories contested, measured, and ranked in national contexts.

The bridge is not only an anchor for the discussion but also a site of solidarity for protestors and a conceptual apparatus that carries an ethical burden; governments have inherited responsibilities for the violence that took place during two of the demonstrations, and for the recognition of all. Constitutional and republican conceptions of identity are grounded in the continuities that disenfranchised protestors attempt to rupture, and W. James Booth warns how slippery a national sense of accountability can be: "Most fundamentally, because we are not one with the perpetrators, because we do not share with them a political identity, we are not accountable for their injustices."[2] Racial injustices have been successfully folded into a national narrative of resolution and redemption in the US; accountability for such injustices remains caught up in controversy in France; and, as something of a control in this experiment, the campaign for Welsh nationalism is ongoing in the UK; and, of course, the mass media will always ensure that some events are prized, just as they obscure or forget others.

In 2015 it will be 50 years since civil rights protestors crossed the Edmund Pettus Bridge over the Alabama River, connecting Selma to Montgomery via Highway 80. The demonstration of March 7, 1965, when marchers were attacked by state troopers with clubs and tear gas, was filmed by television cameras and broadcast around the nation and across the Atlantic. That broadcast and two subsequent marches—one aborted on March 9, and the other successful on March 24 when some 25,000 people arrived in Montgomery having walked 54 miles in five days—led to the bridge being described as the "Bridge of Freedom." That image has been continually reinforced, not only by politicians and the media but by the protestors themselves, as when veteran Selma activist Amelia Platts Boynton titled her memoir *The Bridge Across Jordan* (1979), contributing to Selma's place in movement mythology by fixing the Edmund Pettus Bridge in

the political tensions that have prevented full commemoration on both sides of the French-Algerian divide.

2 Booth, "Communities of Memory," 250.

a long history of African American struggle located in religion and faith. SNCC Chairman then, and US Congressman now, John Lewis (D-GA), has been crucial in ensuring that the bridge remains a fixture in movement history, most recently in the memoir *Across That Bridge* (2012). Lewis was leading the march when he suffered a fractured skull; he was the seventh patient treated at Selma's Good Samaritan Hospital of 55 people admitted on the afternoon of "Bloody Sunday."[3] Lewis received the Presidential Medal of Freedom in 2011, and his testimony underlines the event's significance in a long arc of racial justice in which he includes the election of President Obama, the Occupy Movement, and the Arab Spring, and that is made to recall the French Revolution and the activism of Mahatma Gandhi, as well as "other social transformations down through the ages [that] came to pass because people decided they deserved to live under a higher conception of reality."[4]

The symbolic role that the Edmund Pettus Bridge has accrued is understood in stark contrast to an event that was largely hidden from history and only quietly acknowledged on its fiftieth anniversary in 2011: the shooting and drowning of Algerian protestors by Paris police during a peaceful demonstration on October 17, 1961. The story sticks like a fishbone in the throat, as historian of public memory Edward T. Linenthal describes those indigestible stories that each nation has but does not want to tell.[5] A delayed form of metropolitan memorialization began in the 1990s, and in 1999 the tragic and brutal murder of between 100 and 300 Algerians was tacitly acknowledged by Prime Minister Lionel Jospin.[6] Then, in 2001, Bertrand Delanoë, the socialist, and North African-born mayor of Paris, placed a memorial plaque on the bridge at Saint-Michel, as a formal

3 Good Samaritan Hospital Emergency Room log, March 7, 1965, reproduced in Bond and Lewis, 570–72.

4 Lewis, *Across That Bridge*, 174.

5 Linenthal, "Epilogue," 213.

6 The number of dead is not precise because it is not definitely known. See, for example, Brunet, and House and McMasters who indicate that killings were taking place at the hands of murder squads and who cite a social worker in the *bidonville* slums in 1961 who alleged that "among those who were recovered from the Seine were blokes who had been arrested elsewhere than on the demonstrations because the police knew they were FLN. The police took advantage of the opportunity to liquidate them" (135). In the documentary *Drowning by Bullets* (1992), an officer who would not involve himself expresses deep regret over what happened.

acknowledgement that a "bloody repression of the peaceful demonstration" had taken place there (‹‹à la mémoire de nombreux Algériens tués lors de la sanglante répression de la manifestation pacifique du 17 octobre 1961››). The protests in Paris and in Selma, Alabama, may be read alongside a peaceful protest that took place in Aberystwyth in 1963. On 2 February, student members of Cymdeithas yr Iaith Gymraeg (the Welsh Language Society), protesting for equal status for Welsh with English, conducted a sit-in on Trefechan Bridge. Its fiftieth anniversary in 2013 was celebrated with a political rally and a reconstruction of the protest, followed by the performance of a play, but limited attention was paid to the protest outside of Welsh nationalist circles. The demonstration in Wales helps us to think about why three non-violent protests on three different bridges should be assiduously remembered or persistently forgotten.

It is the differences between them that illuminate a common strategy in which an actual bridge begins as a protest site and thereafter potentially functions as a memory site. In French historian Pierre Nora's formulation, memory sites are material, symbolic, and/or functional. He argues that public memory is a form of heritage that "relies entirely on the materiality of the trace, the immediacy of the recording, the visibility of the image" and acknowledges the role of media memories in forging collective memories, asserting that "ours is an intensely retinal and powerfully televisual memory."[7] If the protest on the Edmund Pettus Bridge has become symbolic of racial change, a range of different media were crucial in making that happen. The media's role also helps us to understand why a demonstration of Welsh nationalism could have been overlooked as a national story, and how the colonial French context contributed to the erasure of the horrific murders that took place in Paris in 1961. The writer James Baldwin once warned that, "To overhaul a history or to attempt to redeem it . . . is not at all the same thing as the descent one must make in order to excavate a history. To be forced to excavate a history is also to repudiate the concept of history, and the vocabulary in which history is written . . ."[8] This essay therefore examines some of the excavations one must make in order to comprehend the comparative significance of three very different protests in 1960s transatlantic cultural history and it acknowledges that memory work

7 Nora, "Between Memory and History," 13, 17.
8 Baldwin, *Above My Head*, 480–81.

is often hard work performed in different "vocabularies"; it demands that attention be paid to facts and realities that are not easily or openly faced when the link between nation-state and cultural memory is so politicized.

PARIS 1961 AND PONT SAINT-MICHEL

In 1961 a shocking event took place in one of the most celebrated capital cities in the world. Why then, did the shooting and drowning of nonviolent protestors by Paris police during a peaceful demonstration on October 17, 1961 not receive international opprobrium? French Algerians and Algerian migrants organized a peaceful protest to oppose a curfew to which only they were subject and which was rigorously enforced from 8:30 p.m. each night, its rationale to prevent the FLN (Algeria's National Liberation Front) from collecting funds in the evenings. The Pont Saint-Michel in Paris is made representative here because it was only one of a number of bridges where Algerian demonstrators met their deaths. The extent of the violent repression undertaken by French police was suppressed, and only in recent decades has this demonstration been mobilized by political groups or found place in historical studies. The Paris protest in particular makes manifest the complexities of remembering and forgetting, inclusion and exclusion in the context of France's war with the pro-independence FLN.

The bodies of the dead could not be committed to the ground for a timely Muslim burial, a further insult to the Algerian community, and the risk in the years that followed was that the Algerian dead would exist only in what Nora has described as a "moment" of history, "torn away from the movement of history, then returned; no longer quite life, not yet, like shells on the shore when the sea of living memory has receded."[9] This romantic metaphor both evokes the effect and conceals the trauma. If *lieux de mémoire* are not made available to "block the work of forgetting, to establish a state of things, to immortalize death, to materialize the immaterial"[10], the risk is that victims of atrocities of which subsequent governments are ashamed will be lost to public memory as well as lost to history. Like the anonymous Arab in Camus's *L'Étranger* (1942), who lies not only dead but outside of

9 Nora, "Between Memory and History," 12.
10 Ibid., 19.

history in that novel, this event epitomizes the problem of the erasure of the dead and, whether unclaimed from the river Seine after October 17 or "lost" to families following deportation on October 19, their families too were typically rendered silent. As Roy Rosenzweig and David Thelan summarize in *The Presence of the Past* (1998), "The world seldom believes the horror stories of history until they are documented in the mass media."[11] Journalists were not completely silent at the time. Indeed, *l'Humanité's* cover story of 17 October 1961 was accompanied by a photograph of graffiti reading ‹‹ici on noie les algeriens›› (Here is where Algerians are being drowned), and journalist René Dazy witnessed the demonstration on Pont Saint-Michel: "They marched in good order, the leaders at the front, with an inexpressible dignity."[12] But police records of the night of October 17 were not made available until 1999 when the Archives de la Prefecture opened the files. Over the course of the night, it is recorded that some 11,538 people were arrested but that police prefect Maurice Papon's report listed only three people dead, despite eye-witness testimony that police were hauling demonstrators over the city's bridges into the Seine.[13] Limiting media coverage was a key factor in closing down the story, with most newspapers expected to accept the explanation that Paris police had successfully contained an incident that could otherwise have escalated and that police officers had defended themselves against marauding protestors (fig. 1).

The significance of the protest is missing from most studies of social movements and occluded from studies of the era, excepting those that focus specifically on Paris.[14] For example, secrecy around the violence of the police response allowed cross-cultural commentators, such as Arthur Marwick in his comparative study of cultural revolutions, *The Sixties* (1998), to assume that despite discrimination against Algerians in France, "there was no real analogue of the American race issue."[15] It is also hard to imagine that students who rallied in May 1968 and organized a general strike to protest police brutality could have known about the events of 1961; had they

11 Rosenzweig and Thelan, *Presence of the Past*, 98.

12 The cover image is reproduced at http://3.bp.blogspot.com/_Zl30kmKdHQM/SttIW9vCG4I/AAAAAAAACWo/c5obLfl7wf8/s1600/UneHuma.jpg. Yasmina Adi made a documentary film with that title in 2011; Dazy in *Vérité-Liberté* 13 (November 1961) quoted in House and McMaster, 120.

13 See Cole; House and McMaster.

14 See Ross.

15 Marwick, *Sixties*, 547.

Figure 1: Algerians emerge from a Paris subway station with their hands on their heads after being arrested in Paris, Oct. 17, 1961.

Courtesy of the Press Association

known, they could have harnessed them to their cause. In the early 1960s hostility to imperialism was gaining momentum as a worldwide force with African independence struggles, students in the US civil rights movement reading Frantz Fanon and adapting his philosophy of strategic violence to cultures of resistance, and French youth protesting against conscription to fight in France's war against Algeria.

Maurice Papon had been a prefect in Algeria before he was made Paris police commissioner in 1958. Only when events conspired to bring Papon into the media spotlight for a different reason, did the extent of police repression on October 17, 1961 make banner headlines. In 1981 evidence emerged that during the Nazi occupation and Vichy regime, Papon had participated in the deportation of some 1690 Jews to Auschwitz. He was finally sentenced to ten years in prison in 1998. Jean-Luc Einaudi, whose *La Batallie de Paris 17 octobre 1961* had been published in 1991, then alleged that Papon's actions in 1961 also constituted a crime against humanity and, in turn, Papon accused Einaudi of libel for stating that he had ordered "a massacre." Einaudi was granted the legal right to call the murders a massacre but controversy persists among both politicians and historians as to the number of deaths verified and the politics of activist groups in recovering what happened.[16] Such groups are crucial in building cultural memory of the event, though. A group of French Algerians, for example, initiated a March for Equality and Against Racism in 1983 and their spokesperson, Farïd Aichoune, declared in a statement that collapsed time, "It was yesterday in the middle of Paris; it was our mothers and fathers who were being killed: but for the oldest among us, it was us too."[17]

Different groups, including government bodies and professional historians, manage cultural memory in the national imaginary. When countries formalize the link between memory and nation by establishing a national cultural policy, the remit is to promote national heritage but also to protect it by ensuring certain government controls over the production and communication of a culture's memory. Novelist and intellectual André Malraux was appointed France's first Minister of Culture in 1959 and served until 1969, resigning when President Charles de Gaulle left office. The shameful event that occurred in 1961 could not be easily enfolded into a narrative of a heroic French resistance with which both de Gaulle and Malraux were associated—even though it could be argued that Algerian nationalist strategies were modeled on the French Resistance in World War II. De Gaulle even awarded Papon the Legion of Honor in 1961, though the prefect would be stripped of the award in 1999.

Historians act as custodians of the past in the way that Pierre Nora understood when he conceptualized *les lieux de mémoire* as national sites of memory, rallying many of the nation's professional historians to spend ten years and seven volumes mapping France's memory sites. Nora's overreaching thesis was imbued with the determination to preserve consensually France's key memorial sites. France's war with Algeria is not included in

---

16 See, for example, Jim House, "Leaving Silence Behind."
17 House and McMaster, *Paris 1961*, 293.

the seven volumes translated into English as "Realms of Memory," and, therefore, neither are the events in Paris in 1961, or, indeed, a detailed evocation of cultural memories around Algeria's gaining independence from colonial France in 1962. That a memory project of such note and importance should ignore Algeria is striking when the nation's relationship goes back to the French invasion of Algeria in 1830. In this context, Nora's memory project is best read alongside David Assouline's three-volume study of immigrants in France, *Un siècle d'immigrations en France* (1996–1997), that traces that relationship. Historical studies impose narratives on the past to make it legible, and while historians interpret memories as sources, they are often skeptical of what may be emotional or aggrieved. Nevertheless, historians like Einaudi, House and McMaster, Cole, and others who have painstakingly reconstructed the demonstration and its context have had to engage submerged micro-historical participant accounts. In his 1950 study of collective memory, Maurice Halbwachs distinguished between autobiographical and historical memory, the former framed by different group identities and the idea of community, the latter forged in particular cultural moments and national contexts. As studies of the 1961 protest allow, the memories of different publics are more far more complex and contradictory than a nation's public history.

History is perspectival and counter perspectives disturb what may be couched as a dominant official, national, and colonial perspective on events. In *Language, Counter-Memory, Practice* (1977), historian and philosopher Michel Foucault investigates the kind of a historiography that "disturbs what was previously considered immobile."[18] We see this in action when we consider the ways in which public knowledge of the events in Paris in 1961 was mired in doubt. While the French government embarked on a damage limitation exercise, the Selma bridge crossing has been mobilized very successfully as a national celebration of democracy in action. Although African Americans were beaten and tear-gassed, through multiple anniversaries and politicians' strategic allusions to Selma, the annual bridge crossing is the largest commemorative event to harness the nation's political culture to the activism of a "minority" group. Its success is brought into relief by the Welsh demonstration.

18 Foucault, *Language*, 160.

ABERYSTWYTH 1963 AND PONT TREFECHAN

The demonstration that took place on February 2, 1963 was organized by students at the universities of Aberystwyth and Bangor. The Trefechan Bridge over the River Rheidol was chosen as a functional site for a protest to rally locals to the campaign to make Welsh an official language but only with the benefit of time and an emphasis on heritage has it been more properly understood as what it was: part of a much wider project to preserve Welsh as a national language. It has now been described as "one of the most important protests in modern Welsh history," by the National Library of Wales[19], with Pont Trefechan "one of the key historic events that help to structure the Welsh nation-building project" according to the only detailed study of the event published in 2008 by Rhys Jones and Carwyn Fowler.[20]

In 1962 during his BBC Welsh Annual Lecture, Saunders Lewis, former president of Plaid Cymru, Wales's national party, had declared, "Restoring the Welsh language in Wales is nothing less than a revolution. It is only through revolutionary means that we can succeed."[21] Protecting Welsh from the hegemony of English already had a long history going back to the Middle Ages, but Lewis's declaration of 1962 inaugurated a new incarnation of the movement for change in the form of the Welsh Language Society. Protestors who rallied as a result of his speech were inspired by "spiritual leaders," in the figures of Mahatma Gandhi and Martin Luther King Jr., and by acts of civil disobedience like the sit-ins that began in 1960 in Greensboro, North Carolina. One Welsh historian has described the demonstrators' decision to stage a sit-in as "a technique popular with protestors across the world from North Carolina to Warsaw."[22] The Welsh students began by marching with placards but did not gain the attention they craved. Consequently, some 40 of them chose to stop traffic moving in or out of

19 "I was there!" 20 March, 2008 at http://www.llgc.org.uk/index.php?id=1514&no_cache=1&tx_ttnews%5Btt_news%5D=995&cHash=d78545199ea44475493a7fa6a5932db2.

20 Jones and Fowler, 84.

21 Quoted in *Tynged yr Iaith*: The Welsh Language Society, Broadcasting in Welsh, The Welsh Language Act at http://www.llgc.org.uk/ymgyrchu/Iaith/TyngedIaith/index-e.htm.

22 Dylan Phillips, *Trwy Ddulliau Chwyldro: Hanes Cymdeithas yr Iaith, 1962–92* (Llandysul: Gomer, 1998), 236, cited in Jones and Fowler, 78–9.

Aberystwyth by blocking the bridge with their bodies. Traffic was halted but, disappointingly for the demonstrators, no-one was arrested. Had they been, they could have protested the fact that they were unable to exercise a basic human right to use their national language in official life. Police procedures and legal processes, including trials, were conducted in English with Welsh having no official status. The students hoped to assure themselves of the kind of publicity Lewis had provoked by refusing to submit to those processes.

If the Welsh sit-in is a control in this essay's discussion, it is because the protest did not realize its potential at the time. Only now that memory of the event has been reactivated, has its meaning been reconfigured, as in 2008 when cultural geographers Jones and Fowler published *Placing the Nation: Aberystwyth and the Reproduction of Welsh Nationalism* and lifted the demonstration out of its silo of "local" interest to receive detailed exploration as a component of Welsh nationalism. Also in 2008 the National Library of Wales initiated a website forum to seek out veterans of the Trefechan bridge protest, creating an online form of museology. The Library situated the protest in a series of campaigns launched in the 1960s, including those for radio and television services to be delivered in Welsh that were realized in 1977 and 1982 respectively. The demonstration is attributed with more meaning in retrospect, once inserted into a timeline as the beginning of the Welsh Language Society's policy of civil disobedience. It led to the 1967 Welsh Language Act, albeit weakened by the recommendation rather than requirement that Welsh be accepted as valid in law. In 1963 the students located the struggle for linguistic identity against the erosion of culture and the British government's failure to care enough about losing Welsh—and they made it a civil rights issue with the bridge a site of non-violent direct action.

Times have changed. In 2008 Jones and Fowler went so far as to assert that, "there is no finer example of the tangled politics of place and how it intermeshes with the broader politics of the nation that the protest on Trefechan Bridge."[23] The Welsh Minister for Heritage announced in February 2011 that a new Welsh Language Measure would involve a Welsh Language Commissioner whose remit would extend that of the Welsh Language Board established in 1993. In March 2011, following a referendum

23 Jones and Fowler, 84.

on the law-making powers of the Welsh Assembly, the language question was again firmly on the agenda. Now that it has been rolled into the idea of democracy-in-action, this demonstration may receive further recognition. Changing methodologies for preserving cultural memories are reflected in the growth of new media and the cyber-grid of media networks now so salient in storytelling. Methods of recovery research are developing with online platforms proving an effective way to pursue memory studies by amassing oral histories in the form of participant accounts, as the National Library of Wales is doing. Definitions of the archival are shifting in the digital age and providing internet access to photographs of the protest is one way to bring the event to public attention. At the time the event did receive limited coverage in major national papers (*The Observer*, *Times*, and *Guardian*) and longer and illustrated reports in *Cymro*, *The Western Mail*, and the *Daily Post* but there is little in the images to spark the imagination.

Figure 2: Protest gyntaf Cymdeithas yr Iaith, Pont Trefechan (Geoff Charles)

Courtesy of the National Library of Wales

Even though the students positioned themselves as part of a wider transnational student movement while picketing, that symbolism was not picked up, and placards and slogans are barely visible in the shots on the bridge. If the demonstration stopped traffic and the photograph stops time, both needed to evoke the moment using stronger symbolism (fig. 2).

In protest movements iconography is crucial, as in the starkly symbolic visual imagery of black protestors set upon by white officials in Selma as recorded by photojournalists like John Karales in a strikingly evocative photograph of marchers holding the US flag against the backdrop of a stormy sky published in *Look* magazine. Or in the aerial shot below (fig. 3).

On the fiftieth anniversary of the Trefechan Bridge protest in February 2013, new digital technologies and social media networks were vital for creating audiences for the staging and promoting of a rally and a play. The protest was recreated only days after a census revealed that now even fewer communities in Wales use the language as their first. Today's activists promoted the sit-in protestors as "founders" of a movement and the play titled *Y Bont* (The Bridge), staged by Theatr Cymru and performed on the streets of Aberystwyth, emphasized that. The play was a community performance, co-written by a bilingual Welsh author, Catrin Dafydd, writer Ceri Elen, author and Welsh language activist, Angharad Tomos, with Theatr Cymru director Arwel Gruffydd. Based on interviews with protestors, the 2013 cast included some 60 students of four Welsh universities.[24] Reenactment is a ritual that proves most effective in shaping communal memory because, as Paul Connerton observes, it is explicit in reference to "prototypical" persons or events, "whether these are understood to have a historical or mythological existence."[25] In that sense, reenactors may be learning a lesson from Selma.

24 See "500 in Pont Trefechan rally, 50 years on," February 2, 2013 at http://cymdeithas.org/node/3954; Polly March, "Production to mark 50 years since Pont Trefechan protest," January 26, 2013, BBC Wales Blog at http://www.bbc.co.uk/blogs/wales/posts/production-to-mark-50-years-since-pont-trefechan-protest.

25 Connerton, *How Societies Remember*, 61. A forthcoming television documentary about the event also promotes the protest on the grounds of its contemporary relevance as well as its importance to history.

Figure 3: Civil rights marchers cross the Alabama river on the Edmund Pettus Bridge at Selma, March 21, 1965 (anon.).

Courtesy of the Press Association

MEDIA-MADE SELMA

That the television media filmed the confrontation in March 1965 distinguishes the tale of this protest from the others. Built in 1940, the bridge had been named for Edmund Winston Pettus, the last Confederate general to hold a seat in the US Senate; its name carried forward the ideology that was adapted as massive resistance to racial integration, balking at federal intervention in the region. The bridge's original meaning would change irrevocably in 1965, as former SNCC organizer Charles Cobb summarized in 2008: "What happened as a result of that decision [to march] has fixed the bridge in most minds today in a manner that its designers and earlier Chambers of Commerce could not have imagined."[26] As one journalist asserted, it has come to symbolize "a moment in history when an old order fell . . . the new have leaped the bounds of Dixie and sounded throughout the nation."[27]

Commemoration of the Selma-to-Montgomery March was underlined in 1992 when a museum was established close to the bridge, and the voting rights protests that took place there are memorialized each year in a "Bridge Crossing Jubilee" honoring symbolic figures with Freedom Flame awards.[28] There are a number of reasons why this particular local struggle for voting rights should symbolize a cataclysmic social shift. Even though the Civil Rights Act had been passed in 1964, reference in that Act to the right to vote was limited to federal elections so discriminatory rules remained in force for local elections. The protest made it clear that another Congressional Act was necessary and President Johnson signed the Voting Rights Act into law in August 1965. Yoking an event to the passing of legislation fixes its importance in the nation's history. Selma was more than 80% black in 1965 but only 275 black people were registered to vote alongside 9,800 whites. The fact that by the end of the decade Selma had elected black representatives to office in both town and county elections made sure that this Black Belt town would be remembered as a beacon of change[29] and that 1965 would be referenced as "a pivotal turning point (in a positive sense) for the relationship between government and culture" as forged

26 Cobb, *Road to Freedom*, 229.

27 Rex Thomas, "Selma Marked End of an Era in Deep South," *Northwest Arkansas Times*, March 16, 1975, 7A.

28 The five-day celebration of civil rights activism typically attracts over 25,000 people, and has included politicians such as Presidents Clinton and Obama, Secretary of State Hillary Clinton, Rev. Jesse Jackson, Congressman John Lewis, Martin Luther King, Jr.'s family, Rev. Al Sharpton, and celebrity-activists including Harry Belafonte and Dick Gregory. Sponsors include the National Voting Rights Museum and Institute, the Southern Christian Leadership Conference, and American Airlines.

29 For example, Karen M. McDearman, "Black Belt," *The New Encyclopedia of Southern Culture: Geography* ed. Richard Pillsbury (Chapel Hill: University of North Carolina, 2006), 158.

through legislation.[30] The image of Selma as a template for the black franchise would not be lost on politicians. Its symbolism was underlined by the presence of Dr. Martin Luther King, Jr. and although the grassroots struggle was waged by the Selma Improvement Association and SNCC, largely without help from King or the SCLC, the march was the first struggle in which King involved himself after being awarded the Nobel Peace Prize.[31] Therefore, for some it would become "Dr. Martin Luther King's historic Selma-to-Montgomery March" and attached to his memory, especially as a result of the speech he made at the end of the march, "How Long? Not Long!"[32] Divergent readings of the event, and clashes of strategy between organizations, feature in histories of the event, as does the virulent anti-movement response to the campaign.

If both sides of the civil rights showdown agreed on a single thing, though, it was that the clash between police and protestors on the Edmund Pettus Bridge was one of the most striking visual images of confrontation recorded by the media. Selma mayor Joseph Smitherman actively opposed the demonstration but would observe that civil rights organizations had "picked Selma just like a movie producer would pick a set."[33] "Bloody Sunday," as the March 7 demonstration came to be known, was itself a powerful sound bite, and civil rights organizers were keenly aware that Sheriff Jim Clark fit the mold of arch villain and would perform for the media in ways that would throw positive light on the black freedom struggle. Clark's penchant for wearing a military helmet was probably designed to echo General Patton but SNCC's Bernard Lafayette saw the irony of a sheriff modeled on the image of the savior-hero, observing that Clark was

30 Kammen, *In the Past Lane*, 77. The VRA brought tremendous progress in black voter registration not only in Alabama, but all over the South. Within five years the number of black voters had doubled throughout the South and in Mississippi it has risen from 6 to 67%. Also the number of black elected politicians in the South climbed from 72 in 1965 to 711 in 1970.

31 A number of historians, from August Meier to Adam Fairclough, have also argued for reading King in the light of the bridge metaphor that textures this essay, with the SCLC acting as a bridge between the militant and conservative wings of the movement—that is to say, between SNCC and CORE on the one hand and the NAACP and National Urban League on the other, connecting the "Big Five" civil rights organizations of the 1960s.

32 For example, Christopher Wren, "Turning Point for the Church," *Look* 29 (May 18, 1965): 31.

33 Smitherman interviewed in the *Eyes on the Prize* episode "Bridge of Freedom."

"trying to play John Wayne in a movie where the Duke was a white segregationist sworn to uphold the good America and the black protestors were the bad guys trying to tear it down."[34] Cameramen and photo-journalists turned to Clark as a caricature of a southern sheriff because, in advance of the march, he had confronted Reverend C. T. Vivian at a voting rights demonstration, hitting Vivian in the face and threatening to damage television news equipment. The encounter was screened for a shocked public[35] and national and international spectators caught a glimpse of the quotidian brutality black citizens faced. When, at 9:30 p.m., the ABC network cut from a broadcast of the film *Judgment at Nuremberg* (1961) to fifteen minutes of footage of Clark's officers joining with state troopers to bludgeon peaceful marchers, it was clear how the scene would play in collective memory. Mayor Smitherman admitted to the makers of television series *Eyes on the Prize*, "I did not understand how big [the Selma story] was until I saw it on television." After seeing the bloodshed on television, a furious President Johnson tasked his attorney general Nicholas Katzenbach to write the most robust voting rights act he could. He pushed the Voting Rights Act through a reluctant Congress two days later. The bridge crossing commemorates the ultimate trigger for that legislation, creating the impetus to tell the story again each year.

The bridge crossing is a local and predominantly African American ritual but it is also steeped in national nostalgia. President Clinton's second inauguration in 1997 took place on Martin Luther King Day and in his speech he recalled King and Selma both when he promised that America would build a bridge towards the twenty-first century, "a bridge wide enough and strong enough for every American to cross over to a blessed land of new promise." Clinton was the first standing President to march across the Edmund Pettus Bridge on the 35th anniversary.[36] When Barack Obama announced his candidacy for Democratic nominee for President, he was invited to speak at the annual commemoration and he took a symbolic

34 Lafayette quoted in Halberstam, *Children*, 490.

35 See Graham and Monteith, "Introduction," for the role of the media in Selma and more generally in civil rights contexts.

36 William Jefferson Clinton, "Second Inaugural Address, January 20, 1997," *American History: From Revolution to Reconstruction and Beyond*, http://www.let.rug.nl/usa/presidents/william-jefferson-clinton/second-inaugural-address-1997.php

walk over the bridge on Sunday March 4, 2007, honoring those who marched in 1965: "I am here because somebody marched. I'm here because you all sacrificed for me. I stand on the shoulders of giants."[37] In this way Obama paid tribute to the movement and inserted himself in its timeline. In March 2008 Democratic nominees Hillary Clinton and Obama were scheduled to give near simultaneous speeches at two different Selma churches just a block apart on commemoration day. The news media reporting their presence at the anniversary of the march was crucial to their campaigns. Later, when Obama's speeches were billed as "The Road to the White House," that road, it was implied, could not be traveled unless it included crossing the bridge at Selma.

Since 2007, Obama has paid his respects each year at the bridge crossing. Indeed, prior to his inauguration in January 2009, after a short march across the bridge, a prayer of thanks was said. Obama's Presidency could therefore be described by the London *Times* as "Promised Land at last for the children of Bloody Sunday."[38] Obama secured a romantic as well as a political foothold in a civil rights success story, largely exorcised of militancy in the popular imagination. Selma was the real launch of his presidential campaign insofar as in that place he began to stake out his position on race, using the Selma movement to signal his debt to, and his distance from, the Moses generation of civil rights activists for the African American franchise. As a member of the Joshua generation growing up in the post-civil rights moment, Obama not only walked across the bridge but he pushed wheelchair-bound Reverend Fred Shuttlesworth, a notable veteran of the movement. When in his 2007 speech Obama hailed those of the Moses generation who died before they could "cross over the river to see the Promised Land," a long tradition of civil rights struggle was evoked, as it would be in *The Bridge*, David Remnick's 2010 biography of America's first black President. The inside cover of Remnick's study features an iconic photograph of John Lewis and Hosea Williams of the SCLC facing down

37 For Senator Obama's Selma speech, see "Obama's Selma speech. Text as delivered," *Voices*, *Chicago Sun-Times*, March 5, 2007, http://voices.suntimes.com/early-and-often/sweet/obamas-selma-speech-text-as-de/. For the video recording, see C-Span, March 23, 2008, http://www.c-spanvideo.org/ program/204519-1

38 James Bone, "Promised Land At Last for the Children of Bloody Sunday," *Times*, January 21, 2009.

Fig. 4: Sen. Barack Obama pushes the wheelchair of civil rights leader Fred Shuttlesworth who is greeting former president Bill Clinton in Selma, Ala., Sunday, March 4, 2007.

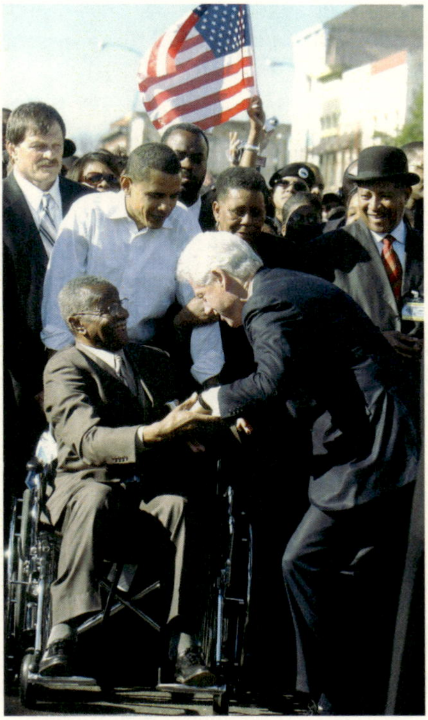

Courtesy of the Press Association

troopers and the last in a series of epigraphs is Lewis's statement that "Barack Obama is what comes at the end of that bridge in Selma" (fig. 4).

Angela Da Silva, who founded the National Black Tourism Network in 1996, observed in 2002 that, "Everyone wants to march across the Edmund Pettus Bridge…and everyone wants to do it singing 'We Shall Overcome' at the top of their lungs."[39] The reenactment of the Selma-to-Montgomery March passes through Dallas county and into Lowndes county, infamous as "bloody Lowndes" in the civil rights era.[40] Also in 2002, Robert L. Woodson, Sr., President of the National Centre for Neighborhood Enterprises, decried what he called "the civil rights poverty-political complex" for its failure to prevent poor people living in squalor in Lowndes, without sewers or septic tanks, their children studying in school buildings with only coal-fired furnaces for heating.[41] Despite President Clinton's attempt to underline Selma's national symbolism as the new millennium dawned, veterans who had marched every year were also beginning to worry. One man told a journalist, "Older folks keep marching but the younger people aren't getting into it."[42] Whether Selma was successfully popularized by civil rights tourism or sanitized to ineffectuality in failing to provide a platform for local civil rights initiatives in the 2000s, Obama proved crucial in reviving national interest in the bridge crossing ritual that some feared would die in the twenty-first century.

MEMORY AND CULTURAL FORMS

In the US the national revival of popular interest in the civil rights movement may be traced back to the Public Broadcasting System's airing of the six-hour, six-part documentary series *Eyes on the Prize* between January 22 and February 26, 1987. Produced by Henry Hampton's Boston-based Blackside, Inc., the documentary told the stories of key moments of the movement through archival footage and contemporaneous interviews and continues to inform popular understanding of US racial history. In Selma, though, as John Lewis has observed, even children "know better than any historian the details of what happened on March 7.... They've heard the story so many times, from parents and grandparents, from neighbors and

39 Quoted in Tim Funk, "Black History Comes Alive in Southern Cities," *Daily Helmsman* (5 February 2002), 11.

40 See, for example, Jeffries.

41 William Raspberry, "Civil Rights Failure," *Washington Post*, March 18, 2002.

42 Floyd Tolbert quoted in Samira Jafari, "Marchers Want Youth to Follow in Footsteps," *Herald-Sun*, Durham, North Carolina, March 6, 2005, A10.

friends—from the people who were there."[43] Cultural memory is dependent on stories, and in the 1960s, the civil rights movement had been the inspiration for a plethora of representations across cultural forms including fiction, popular film, painting, and photography, though many have been forgotten. *The Stone Face* (1963) is a transnational civil rights novel by African American journalist and writer William Gardner Smith that culminates in the 1961 Paris massacre as witnessed by its journalist protagonist:

> Simeon saw old men clubbed after they had fallen to the ground, sometimes by five or six policemen at a time, their bodies beaten after the men were dead. In scenes of terrible sadism, Simeon saw pregnant women clubbed in the abdomen, infants snatched from their mothers and hurled to the ground. Along the Seine, police lifted unconscious Algerians from the ground and tossed them into the river.[44]

Rushing to the rescue of a woman and child, Simeon is beaten by police, arrested and held with "literally thousands of Algerians" (204) in a sports stadium. While Simeon is released because he is a "foreigner" rather than an Algerian "other," throughout the novel he is twinned with Ahmed, a student radicalized by the cause and the "brother" whose world has intersected with his own, who is murdered on a Paris street during the demonstration. Simeon's experience of trying to understand the liberal acceptance he enjoys, in contrast to the violence and disdain shown Ahmed, presages his return home because, he has come to understand, "America's Algerians were back there" (210). The "stone face" of the title initially refers only to America's white supremacists but by the end of the narrative it includes "the face of the French cop…the face of the Nazi torturer at Buchenwald and Dachau, the face of the hysterical mob at Little Rock, the face of the Afrikaner bigot and the Portuguese butcher in Angola, and yes, the black faces of Lumumba's murderers" (205–6). Smith punctures the Parisian "fantasy world" (175) in which Simeon finds little racism and much acceptance but in which he has continually grappled with his responsibility to the civil rights movement. Once the Algerian demonstration takes possession of the city's streets, this man who lost an eye in a childhood battle with racist boys can

43 Lewis, *Walking with the Wind*, 323.
44 Smith, *Stone Face*, 201.

no longer turn a blind eye to the long arc of transatlantic civil rights struggle, or to the battle he must fight at home.

Smith's novel was unusual in the 1960s and it was not published in France. What happened suffered institutional neglect and much of its meaning has had to be reconstituted by memory work, oral histories passed down as a community's heritage, and fictions of memory that attempt to correct or change readers' perceptions of what has been denied and repressed. In "Public Memory and Its Discontents" (1994), Geoffrey Hartman argues that literature "counteracts in the one hand the impersonality and instability of public memory and on the other the determinism and fundamentalism of a collective memory based on identity politics."[45] Arts can be compensatory, exposing a past atrocity, as Smith does in *The Stone Face*, or exploring it as subsequent generations have done when bringing this event to the fore, a reminder of the importance of what Marianne Hirsch in her study of the children of Holocaust survivors calls "postmemory" as a means to describe "those who grow up dominated by narratives that preceded their birth, whose own belated stories are evacuated by the stories of the previous generation shaped by traumatic events that can neither be understood nor recreated."[46]

Leïla Sebbar's novella *La Seine était rouge* (The Seine was red) is one of a clutch of fictions that imagine October 17, 1961 across different genres to include crime and detective fiction.[47] Published in 1999, it was written by an author whose heritage bridges France and Algeria: Sebbar is the daughter of an Algerian father and a French mother spending her childhood in Algeria and adulthood in France. *La Seine était rouge* is a self-consciously multi-voiced, cross-generational memory text that explores the ties between generations and the memories which separate them. Its modernist structuring emphasizes the difficulty of coming to a consensual understanding of what happened, or of agreeing on the event's meaning across the generations, with each character's voice contained in separate sections. Maurice Halbwachs described ties between generations as a "passé vecu,"

45 Hartmann, *Geoffrey Hartman Reader*, 422.

46 Hirsch, *Family Frames*, 7.

47 For example, Georges Mattei, *La Guerres des gusses* (1982); Didier Daeninckx's *Meurtres pour mémoire* (1984); Nacer Kettane, *Le sourire de Brahim* (1985); Mehdi Lallaoui, *Les beurs de Seine* (1986), all of which are acknowledged by Sebbar.

or "living deposit," and Sebbar explores the ways in which imagination also forges such links.[48] This quiet novel wears its historical research lightly but is powerful in its exploration of controversial issues such as survivors' guilt and strategic forgetting, as when a barman in Bonne Nouvelle speaks up for the first time 35 years later:

> None of us provoked anything. I'm a witness to that, no one . . . they were hitting Arabs while insulting them. . . . [The police] thought their co-workers had been wounded; that's what the radio wanted them to believe. Lies. . . . I didn't see any wounded cops either in the street or on the sidewalk. I saw my compatriots, several bodies stretched out in front of the Gymnase and the Rex. Algerians had bullet wounds, not just injuries from the beatings. And the folks looking down from an apartment building were taking picture . . . journalists were there too. . . . There were hats, scarves, shoes scattered on the concrete.[49]

Sebbar's novel is dedicated to the dead, and to others who tried to keep the event in view, but she explores in most detail the struggle of young people striving to understand their parents' silence on the issue, whether due to grief, humiliation, shame, the fear of not being believed, or rage. Louis is the son of a French mother who marches with Algerian friends and is arrested with them in 1961; Amel is French Algerian and her family demonstrates; Omer's father is deported from France on October 19 after the demonstration. Seeing her mother's testimony on film, Amel is overcome by the fact that neither she (only nine years old when taken to the demonstration) nor her grandmother bequeathed memories to her in a more personal way. They seek to protect her from an aspect of her inheritance that brings them only pain, and Susan Sontag once posited that too much remembering makes us bitter because to make peace with the past, or to reconcile ourselves to it, "it is necessary for memory to be faulty and limited."[50] But Sebbar posits that Amel's foremothers' protection of her is a failure to understand that a bridge already exists between their experience and hers, and that Amel can make their experience meaningful through her own life. In this way, Sebbar enacts what David Lowenthal describes in the

48 Halbwachs, *On Collective Memory*, 140.
49 Sebbar, *La Seine était rouge*, 78–9.
50 Sontag, *Regarding the Pain*, 103.

evocatively titled *Possessed of the Past* (1996), that "heritage no less than history is essential to knowing and acting."[51]

Amel and Omer map the events of October 17. They follow the route Louis takes in his film about the massacre, each following the other toward the possibility of amassing truths about an event that occurred before any of them was born but which they each believe should be inscribed on the cityscape. They visit monuments of national history and in the form of political graffiti, couched in the precise official language of monumentalism, they give notice of the events of October 1961. On the quai at Saint-Michel, Amel and Omer write in red letters:

> ON THIS SPOT ALGERIANS FELL
> FOR THE INDEPENDENCE OF ALGERIA
> OCTOBER 17, 1961.[52]

While this indicates a partial understanding of the demonstration, it forms a palimpsest on the city as a memory site because the words are inserted next to the plaque on the Saint-Michel fountain that honors members of the French Resistance. In this way, the characters force a new grid of understanding that disturbs republican forms of memory and ground their community memories in a civic framework. *La Seine était rouge* is a memory text in the way historian Bernard Bailyn describes memory, as "expressed in signs and signals, symbols, images and mnemonic clues of all sorts… it is ultimately emotional, not intellectual… a living and immediate if vicarious experience."[53] Bailyn allows that memory sites "lie all about us" but, as Sebbar reveals through her characters, they can remain unseen if the state "forgets" even what happens in the plain sight of its citizens. In this way, Sebbar's fiction imagines counter memorials that would alter the city's self-memorialization— in the way that the actual plaque on Pont Saint-Michel has done since 2001—but the fact that Amel and Omer use graffiti, and that their do-it-yourself-style historical record is necessarily incomplete, shows that the trauma they seek to represent does not "fit" comfortably into public commemoration. In *The Ethics of Memory* (2002), Avishai Margalit con-

51 Lowenthal, *Possessed of the Past*, xi.
52 Sebbar, 93.
53 Bailyn, "Slave Trade," 250–51.

tends that moral witnesses must testify what they witnessed with their own eyes, not provide testimony based on what they heard or discovered.[54] However, limiting the role of "witness" to witness-participants risks ignoring the roles that subsequent generations, and, indeed, the political fictions they write, can play in bringing a suppressed event to wider public consciousness.

CONCLUSION

Selma was inscribed in the social symbolic with speed and ease. It was difficult to contradict images emblazoned on public television. National media easily trumped counter-narratives of the Selma to Montgomery March promoted by Sheriff Jim Clark and others in the form of locally published propaganda, barely acknowledged then and largely ignored even by scholars now. President Johnson's public statement and the passing of legislation by Congress ensured Selma could be celebrated as a national success story; it could be narrated not only as a triumph for the civil rights movement but also as a federal victory against southern segregationist politicians holding out for states' rights. In this rhetoric, local and regional intransigence was overcome and President Johnson would borrow the discourse of the movement, declaring "We Shall Overcome" when he strengthened the 1964 Civil Rights Act with the Voting Rights Act. In 2001 Reverend James Webb, a local leader in Selma in 1965, declared that if the Edmund Pettus Bridge served a particular purpose, it was to "remind us never to slip into complacency."[55] It is not surprising that different publics seek noble and dignified forms of commemoration—a monument, a statue, a building named after an event, a museum—so that "we" do not fall into complacency or atrophy. Selma may have symbolized injustice but now it symbolizes the moral right and the agency of those African Americans who marched past their opponents into modernity to ensure full voting rights.

The events in Paris on October 17 entered mass consciousness only because of different—to borrow a phrase from Mark Osier—"social move-

54 Margalit, *Ethics of Memory*, 163–68.

55 Rev. James Webb quoted in Anita Weier, "A Bridge to Remember," The Madison, Wisconsin *Capital Times*, June 8, 2001 at cap.times.com.

ments for factual recovery,"[56] including those to open police archives initiated by Einaudi. Organizations such as *Au nom de la mémoire* (In Memory's Name) and *Mouvement contre le racisme et pour l'amitié entre les peoples* (Movement Against Racism and for Friendship between Peoples) are still campaigning for memories of the event to be shared, and individual memory activists, like Einaudi, have fought to persuade the French government to acknowledge—at least symbolically—that a state crime was perpetrated and to erect a national and collective memorial. So far they have failed. In the French context, local and federal have operated differently with responsibility strategically devolved to local officials. Local councils in the Paris suburbs and outlying areas, especially those that are socialist or broadly left wing, have renamed streets October 17, or dedicated plaques and organized memorial events. The possibility of leveraging a full acknowledgment after Prime Minister Jospin admitted some state responsibility was sidestepped by restricting memorialization to the city of Paris rather than aligning it with France, the government, or the war. In his study of imagined national communities, Benedict Anderson posited that "No more arresting emblems of the modern culture of nationalism exist than cenotaphs and tombs of unknown soldiers."[57] When there are no names to inscribe or bodies to bury, there is no need to specify the nationality of the deceased; it is already understood. While the plaque erected in Paris in 2001 does state "To the memory of the Algerians, victims of the bloody repression of a peaceful demonstration," at present, French Algerian citizens are commemorated only as "Algerian" others. A national memorial to those who died would act as a reminder that France was their home.

The act of excavating historical events is often motivated by the counter-memories Foucault defines and, particularly, by the need to have one's presence acknowledged, as in the "I was there" slogans peppering the walls of the Selma museum, or the question "Were you there?" posed by the National Library of Wales to prompt people to share their memories of the Trefechan Bridge protest. In France, there is a continuing danger in only remembering the demonstrators on October 17, 1961 as victims, with what they were demonstrating against ignored. While Premier Nicolas Sarcozy did not commemorate the anniversary on 17 October 2012, a communica-

56 Osiel, *Mass Atrocity*, 270.
57 Anderson, *Imagined Communities*, 17.

tion from the office of the Prime Minister François Hollande stated ‹‹La République reconnaît avec lucidité ces faits à propos de la sanglante répression de la manifestation d'Algériens à Paris le 17 octobre 1961. Cinquante et un ans après cette tragédie, je rends hommage á la mémoire des victims›› (The French Republic clearly recognizes the fact that in Paris on October 17, 1961 Algerian demonstrators were killed in a bloody crackdown. Fifty-one years after this tragedy, I pay tribute to the memory of the victims).[58] It is hoped that what happened on the city's bridges may soon be memorialized in the national imaginary, if only according to the compromised ideal that Albert Camus's described in "Neither Victims nor Executioners" (1946): "not for a world in which murder no longer exists (we are not so crazy as that!) but rather one is which murder is not legitimate."[59]

BIBLIOGRAPHY

Anderson, Benedict. *Imagined Communities: Reflections on the Origin and Spread of Nationalism*. London: Verso, 1991.

Bailyn, Bernard. "Considering the Slave Trade: History and Memory." *William & Mary Quarterly* 58, no. 1 (2001): 245–52.

Baldwin, James. *Just Above My Head*. New York: Dell, 1990. First published 1979 by Dial.

Bond, Julian, and Andrew Lewis, eds. *Gonna Sit at the Welcome Table*. New York: Cengage, 2000.

Booth, James W. "Communities of Memory: On Identity, Memory, and Debt." *American Political Science Review* 93, no. 2 (June 1999): 249–63.

Boynton, Amelia Platts. *The Bridge Across Jordan*. New York: Carlton Press, 1979.

Brunet, Jean-Paul. "Police Violence in Paris, October 1961: Historical Sources, Methods, and Conclusions." *Historical Journal* 51, no. 1 (2008): 195–204.

Camus, Albert. *L'Étranger*. Paris: Gallimard, 1971. First published 1942.

58 ‹‹Hollande reconnaît la répression du 17 octobre 1961, critiques à droite›› *Le Monde*, October 17, 2012, http://www.lemonde.fr/societe/article/2012/10/17/francois-hollande-reconnait-la-sanglante-repression-du-17-octobre-1961 _1776918_3224.html.

59 Camus, "Neither Victims nor Executioners," 28.

———. "Neither Victims nor Executioners." In *Seeds of Liberation*, edited by Paul Goodman, 24–31. New York: Braziller, 1964.

Cobb, Charles E., Jr. *On the Road to Freedom: A Guided Tour of the Civil Rights Trail.* Chapel Hill: Algonquin, 2008.

Cole, Joshua. "Entering History: The Memory of Police Violence in Paris, October 1961." In *Algeria and France, 1800–2000: Identity, Memory, Nostalgia*, edited By Patricia M. E. Lorcin, 117–34. Syracuse: Syracuse University Press, 2006.

Connerton, Paul. *How Societies Remember*. Cambridge: Cambridge University Press, 1989.

Drowning by Bullets. Produced and directed by Philip Brooks and Alan Hayling. Brooklyn, NY: First Run/Icarus Films, ca. 1992. 52 min.

Edgerton, Gary R., and Peter C. Rollins. *Television Histories: Shaping Collective Memory in the Media Age*. Lexington: University Press of Kentucky, 2001.

Einaudi, Jean-Luc, and Maurice Rajsfus. *Les Silences de la police: 16 juillet 1942, 17 octobre 1961.* Paris: L'Esprit Frappeur, 2001.

Fager, Charles E. *Selma 1965: The March That Changed the South*. New York: Scribner, 1974.

Foucault, Michel. *Language, Counter-Memory, Practice: Selected Essays and Interviews*. Edited by Donald E. Bourchard. Ithaca, NY: Cornell University Press, 1977.

Gaddis, John Lewis. *The Landscape of History: How Historians Map the Past*. Oxford: Oxford University Press, 2002.

Graham, Allison, and Sharon Monteith. "Introduction." In *The New Encyclopedia of Southern Culture: Media,* edited by Allison Graham and Sharon Monteith, 1–30. Chapel Hill: University of North Carolina Press, 2011.

Halberstam, David. *The Children*. New York: Ballantine, 1998.

Halbwachs, Maurice. *On Collective Memory*. Chicago: University of Chicago, 1992.

Hartman, Geoffrey, and Daniel T. O'Hara, eds. *The Geoffrey Hartman Reader*. New York: Fordham University Press, 2004.

Hirsch, Marianne. *Family Frames: Photography, Narrative, and Postmemory*. Cambridge, MA: Harvard University Press, 1997.

House, Jim. "Leaving Silence Behind? Algerians and the Memories of Repression by French Security Forces in Paris in 1961." In *Memories of*

Mass Repression: Narrating Life Stories in the Aftermath of Atrocity, edited by Nanci Adler, Selma Leydesdorff, Mary Chamberlain, Leyla Neyzi, 137–56. New Brunswick, NJ: Transaction, 2009.

House, Jim, and Neil McMaster. *Paris 1961: Algerians, State Terror, and Memory*. Oxford: Oxford University Press, 2006.

Jeffries, Hasan Kwame. *Bloody Lowndes: Civil Rights and Black Power in Alabama's Black Belt*. New York: New York University Press, 2009.

Jones, Rhys, and Carwyn Fowler. *Placing the Nation: Aberystwyth and the Reproduction of Welsh Nationalism*. Cardiff: University of Wales Press, 2008.

Kammen, Michael. *In the Past Lane: Historical Perspectives on American Culture*. New York: Oxford University Press, 1997.

Lewis, John, with Brenda Jones. *Across That Bridge: Life Lessons and a Vision for Change*. New York: HarperCollins, 2012.

Lewis, John, with Michael D'Orso. *Walking with the Wind: A Memoir of the Movement*. New York: Simon and Schuster, 1998.

Linenthal, Edward T. "Epilogue: Reflections." In *Slavery and Public History: The Tough Stuff of American Memory*, edited by James Oliver Horton and Lois E. Horton, 213–25. New York: New Press, 2006.

Lowenthal, David. *Possessed by the Past: The Heritage Crusade and the Spoils of History*. New York: Free Press, 1996.

Margalit, Avishai. *The Ethics of Memory*. Cambridge, MA: Harvard University Press, 2002.

Marwick, Arthur. *The Sixties: Cultural Revolution in Britain, France, Italy, and the United States, c.1958–c.1974*. Oxford: Oxford University Press, 1998.

Monteith, Sharon. *American Culture in the 1960s*. Edinburgh: Edinburgh University Press, 2008.

Nora, Pierre. "Between Memory and History: Les Lieuex de Mémoire." Translated by Marc Roudebush. *Representations* 26 (Spring 1989): 7–25.

Osiel, Mark. *Mass Atrocity, Collective Memory, and the Law*. New Brunswick, NJ: Transaction, 1997.

Remnick, David. *The Bridge: The Life and Rise of Barack Obama*. New York: Random House, 2010.

Rosenzweig, Roy, and David Thelan. *The Presence of the Past: Popular Uses of History in American Life*. New York: University of Columbia Press, 1998.

Ross, Kristin. *May '68 and Its Afterlives*. Chicago: University of Chicago Press, 2002.

Sebbar, Leïla. *The Seine Was Red: Paris, October 1961.* Translated by Mildred Mortimer. Bloomington: Indiana University Press, 2008. Originally published as *La Seine était rouge: Paris, octobre 1961* (Paris: Thierry Magnier, 1999).

Smith, William Gardner. *The Stone Face.* New York: Farrar, Straus, 1963.

Sontag, Susan. *Regarding the Pain of Others.* London: Hamish Hamilton, 2003.

Contributors

Tomasz Basiuk received his doctoral degree from the University of Warsaw in 1997. His research interests include contemporary American fiction and life writing, critical theory, and queer studies. He has written on early Thomas Pynchon and on postmodernism generally, from the 1960s to the present, as well as the gay movement, including the Stonewall Inn riots of 1969. He published a monograph on William Gaddis, *Wielki Gaddis. Realista postmodernistyczny* (2003), and co-edited three volumes of papers on queer studies (*Odmiany odmieńca / A queer mixture* [2002], *Parametry pożądania* [2006], and *Out Here: Local and International Perspectives in Queer Studies* [2006]), as well as a collection of essays in American Studies titled *The American Uses of History: Essays on Public Memory* (2011). He also edited a "Gender and Sexuality," special issue of *Dialogue and Universalism* 20, no. 5–6 (2010), and serves on the editorial board of *InterAlia*, a queer studies e-journal (www.interalia.org.pl). In 2004–2005, he was Fulbright Senior Visiting Scholar at the CUNY Graduate Center. Basiuk was a director of the University of Warsaw American Studies Center from 2005 till 2012.

Duccio Basosi is FIRB researcher in History of International Relations at the Ca' Foscari University of Venice, where he also teaches at the Ca' Foscari Harvard Summer School. He specializes in international relations from the 1960s to the 1990s, with a focus on transatlantic relations, US foreign policy, European integration, and international political economy. He is the author of various articles and two monographs, *Il governo del dollaro* (2006) and *Finanza e Petrolio* (2012).

Andrea Carosso teaches American Studies at the University of Torino, where he is also director of the Masters Program in American Studies. His latest book is *Cold War Narratives: American Culture in the 1950s* (2012). He has also published book-length studies on American modernism and postmodern fiction—*T. S. Eliot e i miti del moderno. Prassi, teoria e ideologia negli scritti critici e filosofici* (1995) and *Invito alla lettura di Vladimir Nabokov* (1999). He has edited or co-edited books on critical and cultural theory and US urban culture (*Decostruzione e/è America. Un reader critico* [1994]; *Real Cities: Urban Spaces and Representations of Canada and the United States* [2006]; *Urban Cultures of/in the United States* [2010]; *Translating America: The Circulation of Narratives, Commodities, and Ideas Between Italy, Europe, and the United States* [2011]).

Russell Duncan came of age in the 1960s, turning eighteen years old in 1969 during the height of the Vietnam War and the end of the civil rights movement. For eight years he flew reconnaissance missions as a Captain in the United States Air Force. He currently holds the position of Professor of History in the Institute for English, Germanic and Romance Studies at the University of Copenhagen, Denmark, where he directs the Contemporary America Project in the Center for Transnational American Studies. Duncan has university degrees in Political Science (B.S.), Sociology (M.S.), and History (M.S. and Ph.D.). He teaches courses including: Vietnam War in History and Film; America in the World Since 1960; The Sixties in America; The Civil Rights Movement 1954–1968; US Politics and Government; American Intellectual History; Theories of International Relations; Globalization and World Order; American Culture; Interpreting America Through Art; and Hellfire Nation: America and Religion. He is the author or editor of more than a dozen books, including *Contemporary America* (2013), which he co-authored with Joseph Goddard; *Transnational America: Contours of Modern US Culture* (2004) and *Trading Cultures: Nationalism and Globalization in American Studies* (2002), both of which he co-edited with Clara Juncker, as well as *First Person Past: American Biographies* (1999). From 2006 to 2011, he held teaching and research positions and lectured at two dozen universities in Mainland China, Hong Kong, and Macau.

Michael Hoenisch is professor of American literature and culture at the John F. Kennedy-Institute for North American Studies of the Free University of Berlin, and currently Erasmus Coordinator. He publishes on American literature, documentary film, and Caribbean culture. For example, "Frederick Wiseman's Film *High School:* Institutionenkritik und Spontaneitätsideal," in *Der Amerikanische Dokumentarfilm der 60er Jahre*, ed. M. Beyerle and Ch. N. Brinckmann (1991); "'History Is the Theme of All My Films': Geschichtskonstruktionen in Emile de Antonios *In the Year of the Pig* (1969) und Barbara Kopples *Harlan County, U.S.A.* (1976)," in *Die Repräsentation sozialer Konflikte im Dokumentarfilm der USA*, ed. Michael Hoenisch (1996); "*E Pluribus Unum?* Ethnicity and Migrant Cultures in the U.S.A.," in *Amerikanismus/Americanism/Weill:Die Suche nach kultureller Identität in der Moderne*, ed. H. Danusser and H. Gottschewski (2003); "Erna Brodber: Postcolonial Constructions of 'the People,'" in *Anglo-American Awareness: Arpeggios in Aesthetics,* ed. G. Hermann-Brennecke and Wolf Kindermann (2005); "Postwar Reconstruction and the Representation of the Law: Documentary Film About the Nuremberg Trial," in *15th and 16th Russian-American Seminars* (2007); "Bilder neuer Kriege: Human Terrain" (forthcoming). He teaches courses on American literature and culture, Caribbean Studies, and documentary film, and lectures at European and American universities.

Cristina Iuli is an assistant professor of American literature at Università del Piemonte Orientale, Vercelli in Italy. She specializes in twentieth-century and contemporary American literature, theory, and science, and in the theories and aesthetics of modernity. So far, her most important publications have been the following monographs: *Effetti Teorici* (2002), *Giusto il tempo di esplodere:* Miss Lonelyhearts, *il romanzo pop di Nathanael West* (2004), and *Spell It Modern: Modernity and the Question of Literature* (2009). She has worked on late modernist aesthetics and the ideology of the human from a perspective influenced by current theories of social and living systems. Currently she is completing a book-length study of late modernism and posthumanism, as well as a critical reader on contemporary cultural theory. Iuli has been working on theories of meaning, focusing on cybernetics and its impact on the 1960s and contemporary culture, addressing the convergence of aesthetics, science, and literature in postmodernism in—among others—"Playing with Codes: Steve Tomasula's *Vas, an Opera in Flatland,*" in *Writing Technologies* 3 (2010); "The Public-Private Language of Science: Gregory Bateson's Metalogues," in *Public and Private in*

American History: Family, Subjectivity, and Public Life in the Twentieth Century, ed. Baritono et al. (Torino: Otto Editore, 2005); "Transcoding Science for Literature: Richard Powers's *The Gold Bug Variations*," in *Translating America: Importing, Translating, Misrepresenting, Mythicizing, Communicating America; Proceedings of the XX Aisna Conference,* ed. Marina Camboni, Andrea Carosso, and Sonia Di Loreto (Torino: Otto, 2010); and the forthcoming "Joseph McElroy's *Plus*, a Novel of Wonder." She has written chapters on American modernism and postmodernism for *Storia della Letteratura Americana dal 1850 al 2011*, edited by Sara Antonelli (2013), and edited "The Seventies, Now!" a special issue of *Enthymema* 7 (2012) (http://riviste.unimi.it./index/php/enthy-mema/index).

Clara Juncker (PhD. Tulane University, 1986) is Associate Professor of American Literature and Culture at the University of Southern Denmark. She is past president of the Danish Association for American Studies and the Nordic Association for American Studies and served on the Board of the European Association for American Studies. She has published widely in the United States and in Europe in the fields of Gender Studies, American Literature, African American Studies, Southern Literature, Cultural Studies, and Literary Theory. Her books include *Black Roses: Afro-American Women Writers* (1985), *Through Random Doors We Wandered: Women Writing the South* (2002), *Trading Cultures: Nationalism and Globalization in American Studies* (2002, ed. with Russell Duncan), *Transnational America: Contours of Modern U.S. Culture* (2004, ed. with Russell Duncan) and *Circling Marilyn: Text Body Performance* (2010). She has lectured at universities throughout Europe and the United States and at many universities in Japan, Korea, China, and Hong Kong. She remains fond of the sixties and was the youngest member of a women's conscience-raising group at the end of the decade, her love of lipstick notwithstanding.

Grzegorz Kosc is assistant professor of American studies at the University of Warsaw and the University of Lodz in Poland. He is the author of *Robert Lowell: Uncomfortable Epigone of the Grands Maîtres* (2005) and has co-edited, with Krzysztof Majer, *Tools of Their Tools: Communications Technologies and American Cultural Practice* (2009). Most of his research has focused on the 1960s. He has published on such 1960s figures as Kenneth Burke, Adrian C. Louis, and W. C. Williams, as well as on the Cold War in photography portraiture. He has contributed to *The Encyclopedia of the Sixties: A Decade of Culture and Counterculture,* ed. James S. Baugess and Abbe A. DeBolt (2011). His most recent book, *Robert Frost's Political Body: The Poetic Form and Embodied Power*, is forthcoming from Camden House (Rochester, NY). Kosc is currently working on a project involving Robert Lowell's prose.

Mark Meigs has held the position of Professor of American Cultural History and American Studies at the U.F.R. Études Anglophone at the University of Paris-Diderot since 2001. He is a member of the Bureau of the Laboratoire de Recherche sur les Cultures Anglophones. His major publications have dealt with the cultural implications of war, especially World War I (e.g., *Optimism at Armaggedon: Voices of American Participants in the First World War* [1997]). His next project will be expanding his work on World War I to include the significance of American war dead throughout the twentieth century. He also works on the history of American Cultural Institutions. He is writing a book on the cultural/historical geography of Philadelphia. He has worked as a consultant and been invited to speak at a number of museums. He holds degrees from Stanford University and the University of California at Berkeley.

Sharon Monteith is Professor of American Studies at the University of Nottingham. She researches the US South in cultural history and the 1960s, notably the civil rights movement. Her books include *Advancing Sisterhood? Interracial Friendships in Southern Fiction* (University of Georgia Press, 2000), *American Culture in the 1960s* (Edinburgh University Press, 2008), and *Film Histories*, which she co-authored with Grainge and Jancovich (EUP/Toronto 2006). She co-edited, with Peter Ling, *Gender and the Civil Rights Movement* (Garland, 1999/ Rutgers, 2004), with Suzanne Jones, *South To a New Place: Region, Literature, Culture* (LSU, 2002), and, with Allison Graham, the Media volume of *The New Encyclopedia of Southern Culture* (2011). She has contributed to collections including *Media, Culture, and the Modern African Freedom Struggle* (2002), *Emmett Till in Historical and Literary Imagination* (2008), *Poverty and Progress in the US South* (2007), the *Blackwell Companion to Southern Culture* (2007), and *American Cinema and the Southern Imaginary* (2011). She is completing a book about the civil rights movement called *SNCC's Stories: Narra-*

tive Culture and the Southern Freedom Struggle and most recently edited *The Cambridge Companion to the Literature of the American South* (2013).

Britta Waldschmidt-Nelson is deputy director of the German Historical Institute in Washington, DC. Her main research areas are African American Studies, Transatlantic Relations, Gender, and American Religious History. She is also particularly interested in the social and cultural history of the 1960s and was the main coordinator of an EU Intensive Program entitled "Coming Together or Coming Apart? Europe and the United States in the 1960s" in September 2011. Among her book publications are *From Protest to Politics: Schwarze Frauen in der Bürgerrechtsbewegung und im Kongress der Vereinigten Staaten* (1998), *Europe and America: Cultures in Translation* (2006), *Gegenspieler: Martin Luther King & Malcolm X* (2000, reprinted 2010), *Christian Science im Lande Luthers: Eine amerikanische Religionsgemeinschaft in Deutschland, 1894–2009* (2009), and *Dreams and Nightmares: Martin Luther King, Jr., Malcolm X, and the Struggle for Black Equality in America* (2011). Waldschmidt-Nelson is currently on leave from the University of Munich where she has taught American History since 1994. She has been a visiting scholar and guest lecturer at European and American Universities and is a member of the advisory board of the German Association of American Studies.

Index